Happy in Berlin?

Happy in Berlin?

English Writers in the City, The 1920s and Beyond

Happy in Berlin?

Englische Autor*innen der 1920er und 30er Jahre

Edited by | Herausgegeben von
Stefano Evangelista & Gesa Stedman

WALLSTEIN VERLAG

In cooperation with | In Zusammenarbeit mit

Literaturhaus Berlin

Content
Inhalt

Anna-Marie Humbert, Janika Gelinek, Sonja Longolius — 7
Fasanenstraße 23. A Preface
Fasanenstraße 23. Ein Vorwort

Stefano Evangelista, Gesa Stedman — 15
Happy in Berlin?
Happy in Berlin?

Stefano Evangelista — 53
Writing Decadent Berlin
Literarische Erkundungen der Berliner Dekadenz

Heike Bauer — 75
The Institute of Sexual Science and Sexual Subcultures in 1920s Berlin
Das Institut für Sexualwissenschaft und sexuelle Subkulturen im Berlin der 1920er Jahre

Gesa Stedman — 95
English Women Writers in Berlin:
From the Cage of Diplomacy to the Gestapo Prison
Englische Schriftstellerinnen in Berlin:
Vom Käfig der Diplomatie bis zum Gestapo-Gefängnis

Laura Marcus — 121
"Never be anchorage / never be safety / only be the kino."
Weimar Berlin Cinema and British Connections
»Never be anchorage / never be safety / only be the kino.«
Das Kino im Berlin der Weimarer Republik und seine Verbindungen zu Großbritannien

Annabel Williams
Touring Political Berlin: War, Revolution, and Fascism
Eine Tour durch das politische Berlin: Krieg, Revolution und Faschismus

Sandra Mayer
Chronicler and Eulogist of the "Gang": Stephen Spender Writing the Berlin Myth
Chronist und Laudator der »Gruppe«: Stephen Spender schreibt den Berliner Mythos

Sofia Permiakova
From the 1920s to the 2020s: The Myth of Weimar Berlin in Contemporary British Art, Music, and Literature
Von 1920 bis 2020: Der Mythos Berlin in der britischen Kunst, Musik und Literatur der Gegenwart

Patricia Duncker
AFTERWORD – Richtung Deutschland!
NACHWORT – Richtung Deutschland!

Select Further Reading
Ausgewählte weiterführende Literatur

Picture Credits
Bildnachweis

Acknowledgements
Danksagungen

Fasanenstraße 23. A Preface
Fasanenstraße 23. Ein Vorwort

"I am a camera with its shutter open, quite passive, recording, not thinking." This is Christopher Isherwood in the autumn of 1930 in his "Berlin Diary". In the spring of the previous year, Isherwood had travelled to Berlin in the footsteps of W. H. Auden, who had written that the city was "a bugger's daydream".[1] To begin with, Isherwood lived with Magnus Hirschfeld's oldest sister, then for a short time in the working-class district of Kreuzberg, and for the last two and a half years, until his departure in 1933, at Nollendorfstraße 17, in the gay and lesbian quarter of Schöneberg. Today there is a plaque commemorating his time in Berlin and the novels *Mr Norris Changes Trains* (1935) and *Goodbye to Berlin* (1939) which were written during this time.

When Isherwood said "I am a camera with its shutter open, quite passive, recording, not thinking"—it was to describe his mode of perceiving Berlin. Like a camera capturing the action: this is how one can imagine the villa at Fasanenstraße 23, at the corner of Kurfürstendamm, roughly two kilometers from Isherwood's flat in Schöneberg. The building that today houses the

»I am a camera with its shutter open, quite passive, recording, not thinking«, schrieb Christopher Isherwood im Herbst 1930 in sein Berliner Tagebuch (»A Berlin Diary«). Im Frühjahr des Vorjahres war er W. H. Auden nach Berlin gefolgt, der in einem Brief geschrieben hatte, die Stadt sei »der Traum eines jeden Schwulen«.[1] Zunächst wohnte Isherwood bei der ältesten Schwester von Magnus Hirschfeld, dann kurzzeitig im Arbeiterbezirk Kreuzberg und zog für die letzten zweieinhalb Jahre bis 1933 ins Schwulen- und Lesbenviertel Schöneberg, genauer: in die Nollendorfstraße 17, wo heute eine Gedenktafel an seine Berliner Jahre und die davon zeugenden Romane *Mr. Norris steigt um* (1935) und *Leb wohl, Berlin* (1939) erinnert.

»Ich bin eine Kamera mit offenem Objektiv, ziemlich passiv, aufzeichnend, nicht denkend«, so beschreibt Isherwood sein Berliner Wahrnehmungsprogramm. Wie eine Kamera, die das Geschehen festhält: So könnte man sich auch die nur rund zwei Kilometer von Isherwoods Schöneberger Wohnung entfernte Villa in der Fasanenstraße 23, Ecke Kurfürstendamm, vorstellen, die heute das Literaturhaus Berlin beherbergt, aber schon seit 1890 Zeugin der Wandlungen dieser Stadt ist. Man stelle sich also ihre Fassade als Kameragehäuse, ihre hohen Altbaufenster als Objektive vor. Passiv, aufzeich-

Literaturhaus Berlin has been a witness to the transformations of the city from as early as 1890. Imagine the façade as the camera case and its tall old windows as the lens. Passive, recording, not thinking. Who and what would it have recorded in the 1920s and 1930s? Who strolled past and peeped through the gate into the beautiful garden and its fountain, admiring its ancient trees?

Was it Christopher Isherwood himself? Or even, as we would like to imagine, was it Virginia Woolf who sauntered down Fasanenstraße in her week-long visit to Berlin at the end of January 1929? Woolf might have asked herself how writers in Berlin live, where, and under what sort of conditions they work, in order to write her world-famous essay *A Room of One's Own* (September 1929). Woolf travelled together with her husband, sister, and assorted friends in order to visit her lover, the author Vita Sackville-West. Together they followed the classic Berlin tourist programme of extravagant dinners in select restaurants, museum tours, visits to the opera, and, of course, a trip to the indoor wave pool in Lunapark. In the restaurant of the radio tower, which had opened only a few years earlier, the two writers celebrated their last evening together in the city with a panoramic view over the western parts of Berlin.[2]

Or, let us imagine, a few years later, Samuel Beckett, on his travels through Germany, getting out of the train in Berlin in December 1936 and wandering through the city on foot during the next few weeks: "With this sensitive gaze he scans the sur-

nend, nicht denkend. Wen und was hätte sie in den 1920er und 1930er Jahren aufgezeichnet? Wer ist an ihr vorbeigeschlendert, hat sich durchs Tor in den wunderschönen Garten mit Brunnen gewagt und seinen schon damals alten Baumbestand bewundert?

War es Christopher Isherwood selbst oder, wie wir uns gerne vorstellen mögen, gar Virginia Woolf, die bei ihrem einwöchigen Berlin-Besuch Ende Januar 1929 durch die Fasanenstraße schlenderte und sich möglicherweise gefragt hat, wie Berliner Schriftsteller*innen leben und wo sie unter welchen Bedingungen arbeiten, um dann ihren weltberühmten Essay *A Room of One's Own* (September 1929) zu schreiben? Jedenfalls reiste sie mit Ehemann und Schwester samt Anhang an, um ihre Geliebte, die Schriftstellerin Vita Sackville-West, zu besuchen und gemeinsam mit dieser das klassische Berliner Touristenprogramm zu bestreiten: ausschweifende Diners in ausgewählten Restaurants, Touren durch die Museen, Opernbesuche und natürlich auch eine Fahrt zum Wellenbad im Lunapark. Im Restaurant auf dem erst wenige Jahre zuvor eröffneten Funkturm feiern die beiden Schriftstellerinnen ihren letzten gemeinsamen Abend mit Blick über den Berliner Westen.[2]

Oder stellen wir uns, ein paar Jahre später, Samuel Beckett auf seiner Deutschlandreise vor, der im Dezember 1936 in Berlin aus dem Zug steigt und die Stadt in den nächsten Wochen meist zu Fuß durchquert: »Mit diesem sensiblen Blick tastet er die Oberfläche der Stadt ab und kommentiert ihre Architektur so geschmackssicher und selbstbewusst, wie er auch über Kunst spricht«.[3] Denkbar also, dass er von seiner Pension in der Budapester Straße auch durch die Fasanenstraße kam und an der Villa mit der Nummer 23 vorbeilief, nicht schlendernd, nein, denn

face of the city and comments about the architecture as tastefully and confidently as he talks about art".³ It is therefore conceivable that Beckett left his lodgings in Budapester Straße, walked along Fasanenstraße, and past the villa at number 23—not strolling, no, because Beckett was not a *flâneur*, but rather a brisk walker who conquered Berlin at high speed, with a certain sense of performance pressure, and keeping precise accounts.

From 1918 the entire plot of land in the Fasanenstraße 23 belonged to the Wertheim department store chain, who rented it out to the student exchange organisation *Alexander von Humboldt-Stiftung* between 1927 and December 1930. This foundation looked after international guests, such as the future Germanist and Hölderlin expert Pierre Bertaux. It is therefore very likely that Beckett, Isherwood, or Woolf would have stopped by the villa near Ku'Damm on their wanderings through Berlin, or even that they would have taken part in one of the literary evenings which regularly took place from 1927 in the Humboldt-Villa, as the building was called far into the 1930s. Did the Russian and the English literary worlds cross here, in today's *Literaturhaus*? Did the villa house gatherings that included future world-famous literati? It is certainly possible to imagine.

We have records of the legendary evenings of the adventurous Russian youth club *Na Cherdake* (English: In the attic), which literally took place under the roof of the Humboldt-Villa, even though Woolf, Beckett, and Isherwood came too late for this. Vladimir

Beckett war kein Flaneur, eher ein Durchschreiter, der mit hohem Tempo, genauer Buchführung und einem gewissen Leistungsdruck im Nacken Berlin eroberte.

Seit 1918 gehörte das gesamte Grundstück in der Fasanenstraße 23 dem Warenhauskonzern Wertheim, der es von 1927 bis Dezember 1930 an die Alexander von Humboldt-Stiftung vermietete, die hier als studentische Austauschorganisation ausländische Gäste betreute, wie zum Beispiel den späteren Germanisten und Hölderlin-Exegeten Pierre Bertaux. Sehr wahrscheinlich also, dass Beckett, Isherwood oder Woolf bei ihren Wanderungen durch Berlin auch an der Villa in der Nähe des Ku'Damms Halt machten, oder gar an einem der literarischen Abende teilnahmen, die seit 1927 regelmäßig in der sogenannten Humboldtvilla, wie sie noch bis weit in die 1930er Jahre hinein genannt wurde, stattfanden. Haben sich hier die russische und die englischsprachige Literaturwelt überschnitten? Gab es möglicherweise gar Zusammenkünfte einiger dieser später weltberühmten Literat*innen in der Fasanenstraße 23, dem heutigen Literaturhaus? Es könnte so gewesen sein.

Die legendären Club-Abende des experimentierfreudigen russischen Jugendclubs *Na Tscherdakje* (dt. »Auf dem Dachboden«), die sprichwörtlich unter dem Dach der Humboldtvilla stattfanden, sind jedenfalls belegt, auch wenn Woolf, Beckett und Isherwood hierfür zu spät gekommen wären: Am 13. November 1927 trug hier Vladimir Nabokov, der 1922 nach seinem Studium am Trinity College der University of Cambridge zur Familie nach Berlin zurückgekehrt war, unter dem Pseudonym V. Sirin Gedichte vor. Ohnehin war die Möglichkeit russische Musik, Literatur und insbesondere Filme zu konsumieren für viele englische Künstler*innen der

Nabokov, who had returned to his family in Berlin in 1922 after his studies at Trinity College Cambridge, came to recite poetry here on 13 November 1927, under the pseudonym of V. Sirin. Besides, for many English artists and writers in the 1920s, Soviet music, literature, and especially film were reason enough to travel to Berlin, as in London much Soviet art was only available in censored form. But back to Fasanenstraße 23: right into the middle of the 1930s, the publisher, novelist, and essayist Victor Otto Stomps organised public lecture evenings with his publishing house *Rabenpresse* in the Humboldt-Villa.[4] Maybe our English-speaking protagonists took part in book launches and lectures, especially since Isherwood, as well as W.H. Auden, spoke enough German to be able to join in.

In any event, Fasanenstraße 23 has long inscribed itself into the history of this city and has become an important part of its literary map. Alongside the Humboldt-Universität zu Berlin and the Bodleian Library in Oxford, it is therefore a particularly fitting stage from which to tell the story of the English-speaking authors who, after the First World War and well into the period of National Socialism, came to this city in order to partake of its diverse culture and of the sexual openness of the Weimar Republic. This is the story that we examine in the exhibition and in this accompanying book.

As inspiring as Berlin was to these writers from a literary standpoint, the tolerant and open climate of the city was also personally liberating. Christopher Isherwood came to terms with his homosexuality in

1920er Jahre Grund genug, einmal nach Berlin zu reisen, da in London sowjetische Kunst größtenteils nur in zensierter Form zugänglich war. Doch zurück zur Fasanenstraße 23: Noch bis Mitte der 1930er Jahre veranstaltete der Verleger, Romancier und Essayist Victor Otto Stomps Vortragsabende seines Verlags Rabenpresse in der Humboldtvilla.[4] Vielleicht haben unsere englischsprachigen Protagonist*innen hier Buchvorstellungen und Vorträgen gelauscht; zumal Isherwood, ebenso wie sein Freund W.H. Auden, recht gut Deutsch sprach.

Die Fasanenstraße 23 hat sich jedenfalls längst in die Geschichte dieser Stadt eingeschrieben, ist wichtiger Teil ihres literarischen Stadtplans geworden. Und so bietet sie sich neben der Humboldt-Universität zu Berlin (HU) und der Bodleian Library der Oxford University auch wunderbar als eine der drei Bühnen an, um die Geschichte der englischsprachigen Autor*innen, die nach dem Ersten Weltkrieg und bis in den Nationalsozialismus hinein in die Stadt kamen und sich an der vielfältigen Kulturszene und der sexuellen Offenherzigkeit der Weimarer Republik beteiligten, neu in einer Ausstellung und dem hier vorliegenden Begleitband zu erzählen.

So inspirierend wie Berlin auf diese Schriftsteller*innen gewirkt hat, so persönlich befreiend war auch das liberale und aufgeschlossene Klima vor Ort. Christopher Isherwood fand in seinem Schöneberger Kiez und im Umfeld von Magnus Hirschfelds im Jahr 1919 gegründetem Institut für Sexualwissenschaft endlich Anerkennung seiner Homosexualität; Virginia Woolf verbrachte hier eine aufregende, ja geradezu nervenaufreibende Woche mit ihrer Liebe Vita Sackville-West, wie ihre Tagebücher und Briefe bezeugen; und Samuel Beckett rannte seine wissbegierigen Marathons durch die

his Schöneberg neighbourhood and within the circle of Magnus Hirschfeld, who founded the Institute of Sexual Science in 1919. Virginia Woolf spent an exciting and undeniably nerve-wracking week with her lover Vita Sackville-West, as her diary and letters testify. Samuel Beckett, in his thirst for knowledge, ran a marathon through the Berlin museums and city quarters. In the exhibition, we attempt to approach such emancipatory moments through the perspective of a wide-angle lens ("shutter open!"), by reconstructing some of the important meeting places of those vibrant times. Think, for example, of the Romanische Café or Hirschfeld's Institute of Sexual Science, which were key spaces of intellectual exchange and networking during this time. The focus on these Berlin locations throws open a broad panorama of the very different ideas, hopes, but also fears of the many well-known and lesser-known protagonists of the 1920s and 1930s. The fact that the exhibition will be shown in a place that contributed significantly to the literary life of the time has a very special appeal.

We also want to build a bridge to the present: in many ways, the expatriates from the past are a mirror of the English-speaking authors who have come to Berlin in recent decades, increasingly so due to the confusion caused by Brexit, and who will still try to find ways to come. Around one hundred years later, Berlin has once again become a place of longing, successfully enticing artists from all over the world with its liberal and comparatively affordable at-

Berliner Museen und Quartiere. Wir möchten uns emanzipativen Momenten wie diesen mit der Kameraperspektive des Weitwinkels nähern (»shutter open!«), indem wir Ihnen in unserer Ausstellung verschiedene Begegnungsorte jener schillernden Zeit vorstellen. Zu denken ist hier beispielsweise an das berühmte Romanische Café oder auch an Hirschfelds Institut für Sexualwissenschaft, die zentrale Austausch- und Vernetzungsorte des intellektuellen Lebens waren. Mit der Fokussierung auf diese Berliner Schauplätze eröffnet sich ein breites Panorama an ganz unterschiedlichen Ideen, Hoffnungen, aber auch Befürchtungen der vielen namhaften sowie heute weniger bekannten Protagonist*innen der Berliner 1920er und 1930er Jahre. Dass die Ausstellung dabei selbst an einem Ort zu sehen ist, der nicht unwesentlich zum literarischen Leben dieser Zeit beigetragen hat, entfaltet hierbei einen ganz besonderen Reiz.

Und auch einen Bogen in unsere Gegenwart möchten wir schlagen: Die Expats von damals spiegeln in gewisser Weise die englischsprachigen Autor*innen wider, die im vergangenen Jahrzehnt und verstärkt durch die Verwirrungen des Brexits in die Stadt gekommen sind und womöglich noch kommen werden. Rund hundert Jahre später avanciert Berlin erneut zum Sehnsuchtsort, der mit seinen liberalen und im Vergleich noch bezahlbaren Reizen erfolgreich um Künstler*innen aus aller Welt wirbt. Auch dieser Gegenwartswirklichkeit tragen Begleitband und Ausstellung in Form einer begleitenden Veranstaltungsreihe mit zeitgenössischen englischsprachigen Autor*innen im Literaturhaus Berlin Rechnung. Was sehen wir, wenn wir die heutige Stadt durch ihre Augen, durch ihr »offenes Objektiv« sehen? Gerade in dieser Umbruchszeit, die Großbritannien und Europa auseinanderzu-

tractions. This contemporary reality is also taken into account in the volume as well as in the exhibition, as part of which the *Literaturhaus Berlin* will host a series of events with contemporary English-speaking authors. What do we see if we look through the eyes of today's city, through its "open lens"? In this time of upheaval, which threatens to drive Britain and Europe apart, it is more necessary than ever to look at our shared past, mutual inspiration, and closely interwoven present if we want to continue strengthening and expanding German-British ties despite Brexit.

This desire to remain connected also lies behind the newly established collaboration between the Berlin universities and Oxford. Founded in 2017, the Oxford-Berlin Partnership comprises the respective homes of the two curators and editors of this important project: Gesa Stedman, Professor of British Literature and Culture at the Centre for British Studies, Humboldt-Universität zu Berlin, and Stefano Evangelista, Associate Professor of English, Oxford University and Fellow of Trinity College. Gesa Stedman and Stefano Evangelista came to us in 2018 to introduce this project on English-speaking authors in 1920s Berlin and to discuss the idea of realising it at the *Literaturhaus Berlin*, together with two other locations: the Humboldt-Universität and the Weston Library of the Bodleian Library in Oxford. We wish to thank them for this wonderful opportunity for scholarly-literary collaboration. We would also like to thank the Arts and Humanities Research Council, the John Fell

treiben droht, ist der Blick auf die gemeinsame Vergangenheit, die gegenseitige Inspiration und die eng miteinander verwobene Gegenwart unbedingt notwendig, um die deutsch-britischen Verbindungen trotz des Brexits weiter zu stärken und auszubauen.

Davon zeugt auch die 2017 gegründete Oxford-Berlin Wissenschaftskooperation, an der auch die Humboldt-Universität zu Berlin und die Oxford University beteiligt sind, an denen die beiden Kurator*innen und Herausgeber*innen dieses wichtigen Projekts lehren: die Professorin für Britische Kultur und Literatur am Großbritannien-Zentrum, Gesa Stedman, und der Associate Professor of English an der Oxford University und Fellow des Trinity College, Stefano Evangelista. Sie waren es, die 2018 auf uns zukamen, um das Ausstellungsvorhaben englischer Autor*innen in Berlin der 1920er Jahre vorzustellen und am Literaturhaus Berlin sowie an den beiden anderen Standorten, der Humboldt-Universität und der Weston Library der Bodleian Library in Oxford, zu realisieren. Wir danken ihnen für diese wunderbare Gelegenheit der wissenschaftlich-literarischen Zusammenarbeit. Und wir bedanken uns sehr herzlich beim Arts and Humanities Research Council, dem John Fell Fund (Oxford University), dem Freundeskreis des Literaturhauses, dem Großbritannien-Zentrum der HU, der Humboldt Universitäts-Gesellschaft, der Initiative Oxford in Berlin, dem International Office der HU, der Stiftung Preußische Seehandlung sowie dem Oxford Research Centre in the Humanities (TORCH) für ihre großzügige Unterstützung.

Ihnen, liebe Leser*innen, wünschen wir viel Freude mit unserer Ausstellung, diesem Begleitband und

Fund (Oxford University), the Friends of the *Literaturhaus*, the Centre for British Studies, Humboldt-Universitäts-Gesellschaft, Oxford in Berlin, the International Office at the Humboldt-Universität zu Berlin, the Stiftung Preussische Seehandlung, and The Oxford Research Centre in the Humanities (TORCH) for their generous support.

We hope that you, dear readers, will enjoy our exhibition, this accompanying volume, and the events series. And, most importantly, always stay "Happy in Berlin", as much as possible!

Anna-Marie Humbert, Janika Gelinek,
and Sonja Longolius

der Veranstaltungsreihe. Und bleiben Sie unbedingt und so gut es eben geht: »Happy in Berlin«!

Ihre Anna-Marie Humbert, Janika Gelinek
und Sonja Longolius

Notes

1 Quoted by Julius H. Schoeps: "Where love is mostly hugger mugger." Christopher Isherwood, Magnus Hirschfeld und das Berlin am Vorabend der Katastrophe, in: Magnus Hirschfeld, ed. by Elke-Vera Kotowski and Julius H. Schoeps, Berlin 2004, p. 344.
2 Cf. Anne Olivier Bell (ed.): The Diary of Virgina Woolf. Volume Three: 1925–1930, London 1977, here pp. 215–279; Nigel Nicolson, and Joanne Trautmann (eds): A Reflection of the Other Person: Letters of Virginia Woolf, Volume Four: 1929–1931, London 1978.
3 Gaby Hartel: "Ein großer Fußgänger". Samuel Beckett ist viel gewandert – auch in Berlin, in: Obergeschoss still closed. Samuel Beckett in Berlin 1936/37, Exhibition Literaturhaus Berlin, ed. by Lutz Dittrich, Carola Veit, Ernest Wichner, Texts from the Literaturhaus Berlin, Edition 16, Berlin 2006, pp. 13–27, here p. 19.
4 Cf. Literaturhaus Berlin (ed.): Fasanenstraße 23, 3rd, extended edition, Berlin 2014, pp. 21–29.

Anmerkungen

1 Zitiert nach: Julius H. Schoeps: »Where love is mostly hugger mugger.« Christopher Isherwood, Magnus Hirschfeld und das Berlin am Vorabend der Katastrophe, in: Magnus Hirschfeld, hg. von Elke-Vera Kotowski und Julius H. Schoeps, Berlin 2004, S. 344.
2 Vgl. Anne Olivier Bell (Hrsg.): The Diary of Virgina Woolf. Volume Three: 1925–1930. London 1977, S. 215–279; Nigel Nicolson, Joanne Trautmann (Hrsg.): A Reflection of the Other Person: Letters of Virginia Woolf, Volume Four: 1929–1931, London 1978.
3 Gaby Hartel: »Ein großer Fußgänger«. Samuel Beckett ist viel gewandert – auch in Berlin, in: Obergeschoss still closed. Samuel Beckett in Berlin 1936/37. Ausstellung Literaturhaus Berlin, hg. von Lutz Dittrich, Carola Veit und Ernest Wichner, Texte aus dem Literaturhaus Berlin, Bd. 16, Berlin 2006, S. 13–27, hier S. 19.
4 Vgl. Literaturhaus Berlin (Hrsg.): Fasanenstraße 23, dritte, erweiterte Auflage, Berlin 2014, S. 21–29.

Stefano Evangelista, Gesa Stedman

Happy in Berlin?
Happy in Berlin?

How to be happy in Berlin? A 1929 English guide to the German capital promised readers a recipe. This included mixing with local artists and reading foreign papers in a café or two; watching a film in one of the ubiquitous cinemas; admiring the artificial lights and windows displays of the commercial districts; enjoying some wholesome and, even, unwholesome entertainment in the city's famed pleasure quarters; and perhaps finishing the day with some night-time gasometer viewing, taking in the uncanny beauty of the futuristic city that was behind Fritz Lang's *Metropolis* (1927).

If guidebooks provide good historical records of cultural expectations, then *How to be Happy in Berlin* shows us that Berlin had become much more than a tourist destination to people from Britain. Berlin had never had a role to speak of in the time-honoured institution of the Continental grand tour. Neither charming nor fashionable enough by nineteenth-century standards, the city had only been deemed worthy of its own English Baedeker in 1903. Yet, by the end of the 1920s, dry Baedekers

Wie wird man in Berlin glücklich? Im Jahr 1929 versprach ein englischer Reiseführer mit dem Titel »How to be Happy in Berlin« seinen Leser*innen ein Rezept. Zu den Zutaten gehörten Kontakte mit Berliner Künstler*innen, die Lektüre ausländischer Zeitungen in ein oder zwei Cafés, ein Besuch in einem der zahlreichen Kinos, die Besichtigung der beleuchteten Fassaden und Schaufenster in den Einkaufsvierteln und der Genuss einer Portion bekömmlicher und möglicherweise auch nicht ganz so bekömmlicher Unterhaltung in den berühmten Vergnügungsvierteln der Stadt. Den Abschluss hätte eine nächtliche Besichtigung der Gasometer bilden können, um einen Blick auf die gespenstische Schönheit der Stadt der Zukunft zu erhaschen, wie sie Fritz Lang in *Metropolis* (1927) portraitierte.

Wenn es stimmt, dass sich kulturelle Erwartungen der Vergangenheit gut in Reiseführern nachvollziehen lassen, dann belegt *How to be Happy in Berlin*, dass Berlin für Reisende aus Großbritannien weitaus mehr als nur ein simples Reiseziel geworden war. In der altehrwürdigen Institution der Grand Tour durch Kontinentaleuropa spielte Berlin bis dahin keine nennenswerte Rolle. Gemessen an den Standards des 19. Jahrhunderts verfügte die Stadt weder über den entsprechenden Reiz, noch über die nötige Eleganz. Erst im Jahr 1903 wurde Berlin mit einer eigenen

[Fig. 1: The futuristic city: photograph of the model for Fritz Lang's *Metropolis*, 1927]

[Abb. 1: Die futuristische Stadt: Fotografie des Models für Fritz Langs *Metropolis*, 1927]

were clearly no longer able to satisfy the growing curiosity of English travellers who wanted to feel themselves part of the fabric of the buzzing, living city. John Chancellor, the cosmopolitan author of *How to be Happy in Berlin* (whose real name was Ernest Charles de Balzac Willett), had lived in Paris for several years. But he believed that Ber-

Ausgabe des Baedeker gewürdigt. Doch am Ende der 1920er Jahre reichte ein trockener Baedeker bei weitem nicht mehr aus, um das wachsende Interesse englischer Reisender zu befriedigen, die in das pulsierende Leben der Stadt eintauchen wollten. John Chancellor, der kosmopolitische Autor von *How to be Happy in Berlin* (der mit richtigem Namen Ernest Charles de Balzac Willett hieß), hatte mehrere Jahre

lin easily trumped the aristocratic French capital in terms of vibrancy and potential: "She is the coming metropolis of Europe. Unless some disaster overtakes her, she cannot but achieve that destiny. Not only is she young in spirit, she is young in body. Compared to London and Paris, she was made yesterday."[1]

To find happiness in Berlin: this is a desire that motivated many English writers to board trains and boats, and make the long journey across the Channel and through Europe, even before political disaster, to adapt Chancellor's prophetic words, overtook the city and the whole of Germany in the 1930s, in the shape of Nazi dictatorship. Chancellor was himself a minor writer who specialised in crime fiction. By coincidence, 1929, the year his alternative guide was published, also saw the first arrival of Christopher Isherwood, who was to immortalise the hedonism of the last days of the Weimar Republic. In Berlin, Isherwood found personal happiness, in the form of homosexual love, but he also found the artistic material that was to make him famous as a writer. Other writers were disappointed. In 1905, E. M. Forster, on a short stop-over en route to his posting as a tutor to the von Arnim family in Nassenheide in Pomerania, complained of the city being "dirty, ugly, mean, full of unhappy soldiers",[2] a complaint taken up by successive writers. In the 1910s, the poet Rupert Brooke found the city alienating. And, in the very year of publication of *How to be Happy in Berlin*, Vita Sackville-West

in Paris gelebt. Trotzdem war er der Ansicht, dass Berlin die vornehme französische Hauptstadt an Lebendigkeit und Potenzial bei weitem übertraf: »Die Stadt ist die aufstrebende Metropole Europas. Solange keine Katastrophe über sie hereinbricht, steht dieser Bestimmung nichts mehr im Weg. Sie ist nicht nur geistig, sondern auch körperlich jung. Im Vergleich zu London und Paris ist sie quicklebendig«.[1]

Das Glück in Berlin finden: Von dieser Sehnsucht ließen sich etliche englische Schriftsteller*innen treiben, als sie in Zügen und auf Schiffen die lange Reise über den Kanal und durch Europa antraten; noch bevor die politische Katastrophe, um bei Chancellors prophetischer Formulierung zu bleiben, in den 1930er Jahren mit der Nazi-Diktatur über die Stadt und ganz Deutschland hereinbrach. Als Schriftsteller war Chancellor eher unbedeutend und hatte sich auf Kriminalliteratur spezialisiert. Zufälligerweise kam 1929, im Jahr der Veröffentlichung seines alternativen Reiseführers, auch Christopher Isherwood zum ersten Mal nach Berlin. Er war es, der den Hedonismus der letzten Tage der Weimarer Republik unsterblich machte. In Berlin fand Isherwood sein persönliches Glück in homosexuellen Liebesbeziehungen. Doch er fand auch den literarischen Stoff, der ihm zu seinem Ruhm als Schriftsteller verhalf. Andere Schriftsteller*innen waren enttäuscht von Berlin. Im Jahr 1905 beklagte sich E. M. Forster, der die Stadt auf dem Weg zu einer Anstellung als Lehrer bei der Familie von Arnim in Nassenheide in Pommern kurz besucht hatte, die Stadt sei »schmutzig, hässlich, mittelmäßig und voller unglücklicher Soldaten«.[2] Ähnliche Klagen kamen später auch von anderen Schriftsteller*innen. In den 1910er Jahren empfand der Dichter Rupert Brooke die Stadt als befremdlich. Ebenfalls im Jahr der Veröffentlichung von *How to be Happy in Berlin* klang Vita Sackville-West

sounded distinctly unhappy and keen to escape when she compared Berlin to a "coffin" writing to her lover Virginia Woolf.[3]

Hence the question mark in our title. What did it mean for English writers to look for happiness in Berlin? What did they seek and where did they find it in the city? How were their works shaped by their experiences in Berlin, and how did they, in turn, shape the city's image for future readers and visitors? Isherwood's iconic Berlin has been extensively enjoyed by readers and viewers, and just as extensively scrutinised by critics and biographers. The very prominence of *his* Berlin, however, has drowned out the voices of many other English writers who visited the city during its international boom in the early twentieth century. In fact, Isherwood and his close friends, W.H. Auden and Stephen Spender, who 'discovered' Berlin together around 1930, were part of a longer history of English literary encounters with the city. The long list includes familiar and less familiar names, ranging from the decadent poet Arthur Symons to the aristocratic diarist Evelyn Blücher, from the pacifist H.G. Wells to the Nazi-leaning Wyndham Lewis, from Rupert Brooke and T.E. Hulme to Virginia and Leonard Woolf, from psychoanalytic pioneer Alix Strachey to film enthusiasts Bryher and Kenneth Macpherson. Berlin left an important mark on all these writers. Many, but by no means all of these, visited the city in the roaring or, as they are called in German, 'golden' 1920s.

As we enter the centenary of the 1920s, it seems timely to look back on this complex and fascinating period in order to rediscover it and reassess it critically. This volume, and the related exhibitions in the Literaturhaus-Berlin, Humboldt-Universität, and the Bodleian Library, invite us to revisit Berlin through the eyes of English writers, focusing on a series of encounters that took place from the turn of the twentieth century to the onset of Nazism. To study what Berlin was for English writers in this period is not to tell one single story, as they came to the city for different reasons and reacted to it in sometimes profoundly different ways. As we shall see, Berlin incited both love and hatred, attraction and revulsion. It fascinated both left-wing and right-wing observers. What their responses have in common, though, is that they show that Berlin exposed English writers to new ideas, ways of life, and art forms, generating curiosity and strong emotions, and creating personal and professional connections that often had long-lasting consequences for their lives.

Der Beginn der 2020er scheint ein guter Zeitpunkt für einen Rückblick auf die abwechslungsreiche und faszinierende Epoche der 1920er Jahre, ihre Wiederentdeckung und ihre kritische Neubewertung. Dieser Katalog und die dazugehörigen Ausstellungen im Literaturhaus Berlin, an der Humboldt-Universität und in der Bodleian Library sind eine Einladung, Berlin noch einmal neu aus dem Blickwinkel englischer Schriftsteller*innen zu betrachten. Im Mittelpunkt stehen dabei mehrere literarische Begegnungen mit der Stadt, die sich zwischen der Wende zum 20. Jahrhundert und der Machtübernahme der Nationalsozialisten 1933 ereigneten. Eine Antwort auf die Frage, was Berlin englischen Schriftsteller*innen in dieser Zeit bedeutete, lässt sich nicht in einer einzigen Geschichte zusammenfassen. Denn sie kamen aus unterschiedlichen Gründen in die Stadt und haben zum Teil vollkommen unterschiedlich auf Berlin reagiert. Ganz offenbar stieß Berlin auf Liebe wie auf Abneigung, wirkte anziehend wie auch abstoßend. Links- wie rechtsgerichtete Beobachter*innen zeigten sich beeindruckt von der Stadt. Eines haben ihre Reaktionen allerdings gemein. Sie zeigen, dass englische Schriftsteller*innen in Berlin mit neuen Ideen, Lebensentwürfen und Kunstformen in Kontakt kamen, die Neugier und starke Emotionen in ihnen weckten. Zudem konnten sie persönliche und berufliche Bindungen eingehen, die ihr weiteres Leben in zahlreichen Fällen maßgeblich beeinflussten.

Berlin through English Eyes

In the early years of the twentieth century, Berlin underwent a series of rapid, radical transformations. At the close of the previous century, the old Prussian capital had become a 'Weltstadt' or world city, with

Berlin aus englischer Perspektive

Die ersten Jahre des 20. Jahrhunderts waren in Berlin von einer Phase rascher und einschneidender Veränderungen geprägt. Zum Ende des vorangehenden Jahrhunderts war die ehemalige preußische

massive industrial expansion and an influx of people from the countryside, matched by extensive urban development. With the creation of Greater Berlin in 1920, the city incorporated the sprawling suburbs and outlying villages to become, by some estimates, the third largest city in the world after New York and London with nearly 4 million inhabitants. The city suffered from hardship during and after the First World War, leading to hunger and strikes, severe homelessness, sickness, malnutrition, inflation, and revolutionary chaos. With the advent of the Dawes Plan in the early 1920s, inflation was stopped and Berlin began to pick itself up again before conditions deteriorated once more during the Great Depression.

The massive political and social tensions of these years inevitably shaped foreign impressions of the city. English accounts written before the First World War tended to emphasise Prussian militarism and bureaucracy, often with an openly patriotic intent. Berlin was typically associated with a lack of sophistication and social restrictions, in explicit or implicit contrast with a British love of individual freedom. The anti-German propaganda that dominated the British media before and during the war left a scar that proved hard to heal. At the end of the 1920s, John Chancellor still felt that he should disabuse English people of the idea that "every man, woman and child in the German Empire is thirsting for English blood".[4] Yet, at the same time, Germany's status as the former

Hauptstadt zur »Weltstadt« geworden. Der gewaltigen industriellen Expansion und dem Zustrom der Landbevölkerung wollte man mit umfangreichen Stadtentwicklungsmaßnahmen begegnen. Bei der Gründung von Groß-Berlin im Jahr 1920 wurden auch die weitläufigen Außenbezirke und Dörfer in Randlage in das Stadtgebiet überführt. Berlin war nun, so manche Einschätzungen, mit nahezu 4 Millionen Einwohner*innen nach New York und London die drittgrößte Stadt der Welt. Während und nach dem Ersten Weltkrieg herrschte großes Elend. Hungersnöte und Streiks, eine dramatische Zunahme der Obdachlosigkeit, die Ausbreitung von Krankheiten, Mangelernährung, Inflation und revolutionäres Chaos waren die Folge. Mit der Einführung des Dawes-Plans wurde die Inflation gestoppt. Berlin konnte sich noch einmal erholen, bevor sich die Bedingungen mit der Weltwirtschaftskrise erneut verschlechterten.

Unweigerlich prägten die massiven politischen und sozialen Spannungen dieser Jahre das Image Berlins im Ausland. Zahlreiche Engländer*innen verwiesen in ihren Berichten aus der Zeit vor dem Ersten Weltkrieg gern auf den preußischen Militarismus und die preußische Bürokratie, oft auch um den eigenen Patriotismus zu betonen. Als typisch für Berlin galt ein Mangel an Kultiviertheit und gesellschaftlichen Konventionen, denen man explizit oder implizit den Freiheitsdrang der Brit*innen entgegensetzte. Die antideutsche Propaganda, die während und nach dem Krieg die britischen Medien beherrschte, hinterließ eine Wunde, die nur schwer verheilte. Am Ende der 1920er Jahre fühlte sich John Chancellor noch immer bemüßigt, Engländer*innen von dem Irrtum zu befreien, dass es alle Männer, Frauen und Kinder im Deutschen Reich nach englischem Blut dürstete.[4] Gleichzeitig war es gerade der Status Deutschlands

enemy of Britain is precisely what piqued the curiosity of a rebellious post-war generation, epitomised by writers and intellectuals such as Alix Strachey, Elizabeth Wiskemann, W.H. Auden, Christopher Isherwood, and Stephen Spender, who were keen to make a fresh start. Choosing Berlin, these writers rejected Paris as the obvious foreign destination for artistically inclined Britons. Moreover, the very instability of the political situation in Germany had created an atmosphere of renewal and a carefree attitude to life that were profoundly different from Britain: there, winning the war had promoted a sense of conservative complacency, which meant that many of the customs and habits of the Victorians survived basically unchallenged. While Britain struggled to hang on to its past, Weimar Germany, and Berlin in particular, looked more boldly towards the future.

It is hardly surprising, therefore, that a ubiquitous element of visitors' fascination was the city's harsh and sometimes discontinuous modernity, which was the product of its demographic and political transformations. Visitors from Britain were struck by the sheer size and the fast pace or 'tempo' of the city, with its endless traffic and hectic social life. "Even in bad times," remarked Elizabeth Wiskemann, "Berlin had great attraction for the young. It had and has the most exhilarating physical climate I have ever known in Europe—one needed two hours' less sleep a night by comparison with London."[5]

als ehemaliger Feind Großbritanniens, der die Neugier einer rebellischen Nachkriegsgeneration weckte. Für diese Generation standen Schriftsteller*innen und Intellektuelle wie Alix Strachey, Elizabeth Wiskemann, W.H. Auden, Christopher Isherwood und Stephen Spender, die sich nach einem Neuanfang sehnten. Mit ihrer Entscheidung für Berlin kehrten die Autor*innen Paris als naheliegendem ausländischen Ziel für künstlerisch veranlagte Engländer*innen den Rücken. Außerdem trug gerade die instabile politische Lage in Deutschland zu der Atmosphäre der Erneuerung und zu dem unbeschwerten Lebensgefühl bei, die den spürbaren Unterschied zu Großbritannien ausmachten: Dort hatte der Kriegsgewinn eine Art konservative Selbstzufriedenheit befördert, die dazu führte, dass viele der viktorianischen Sitten und Gebräuche nahezu unverändert beibehalten wurden. Während Großbritannien energisch an seiner Vergangenheit festhielt, schritten das Deutschland der Weimarer Jahre und insbesondere Berlin immer weiter in Richtung Zukunft voran.

Es überrascht daher kaum, dass sich viele Besucher*innen immer wieder für die harte und manchmal brüchige Moderne der Stadt begeistern konnten, die ein Ergebnis des demografischen und politischen Wandels war. Besucher*innen aus Großbritannien zeigten sich fasziniert von der schieren Größe und der Rastlosigkeit oder dem »Tempo« der Stadt mit ihrem endlosen Verkehr und ihrer gesellschaftlichen Hektik. »Doch auch in schlechten Zeiten übte Berlin eine grosse Anziehungskraft auf die jungen Leute aus«, bemerkte Elizabeth Wiskemann. »Es konnte sich rühmen, das beschwingendste Klima aller mir bekannten europäischen Städte zu besitzen; man brauchte dort zwei Stunden weniger Schlaf als in London.«[5]

Places
The Radio Tower

Berlin's status as *the* up-and-coming modern city was embodied in the newly-built radio tower in western Charlottenburg, on Kaiserdamm. An iconic Weimar and contemporary Berlin photographic motif, the radio tower epitomised new technology, chic night-life, tourism, and, with its architectural nod at the Eiffel Tower in Paris, it claimed cosmopolitanism and an equal footing for Berlin in comparison to other, much older European capitals. The tower was opened in 1926 to coincide with the third great German radio exhibition ("Große Funkausstellung", an institution which continues to this day). It was a construction by the well-known architect Heinrich Straumer who was also known for building houses in the English country-house style in Berlin Dahlem and Frohnau, affluent western parts of the city. The radio tower sported a restaurant a third of the way up, to be reached by an ultra-modern lift, and features in numerous paintings, postcards, and photographs of the time. The radio tower's observation deck is 126 metres above ground and allows a sweeping view across the western parts of the city and the surrounding countryside. The construction weighs 600 tons. Although it was used for radio transmission only for a short period of time, its status as a tourist hotspot never changed. Britons visited it as part of the 'modern' round of sights to see in Berlin and John Chancellor included it in every tour he suggests in his guidebook *How to be Happy in Berlin*. Not the least of the visitors were writers and lovers Vita Sackville-West and Virginia Woolf, who spent a memorable evening in the restaurant 55 metres above ground exchanging views on their relationship: "It was SUPPRESSED RANDINESS. So there—You remember your admissions as the searchlight went round and round?", as Sackville-West wrote to Woolf on 6 February 1929.[a]

Orte
Der Funkturm

Der neugebaute Funkturm am Kaiserdamm im westlichen Teil Charlottenburgs war ein Symbol für den Status Berlins als moderne aufstrebende Stadt. Als Fotomotiv verfügt er im Berlin der Weimarer Republik und auch heute noch über Kultcharakter. Er stand für technologische Neuerungen, mondänes Nachtleben, Tourismus und sollte Berlin mit seiner architektonischen Anspielung auf den Pariser Eiffelturm als Weltstadt auf einen Rang mit anderen europäischen Hauptstädten mit einer längeren Geschichte erheben. Der Funkturm wurde 1926 anlässlich der dritten Großen Funkausstellung in Deutschland (die auch heute noch veranstaltet wird) eröffnet. Das Gebäude stammt von dem bekannten Architekten Heinrich Straumer, der auch für seine Wohnhäuser im englischen Landhausstil in Berlin-Dahlem und in Frohnau im wohlhabenden Westteil der Stadt bekannt war. Im Funkturm befand sich auf einem Drittel der Höhe ein Restaurant, das mit einem hochmodernen Aufzug erreicht werden konnte und auf zahlreichen Gemälden, Postkarten und Fotografien aus dieser Zeit zu sehen ist. Die Aussichtsplattform des Funkturms liegt in 126 Metern Höhe und bietet einen weiten Blick über den Westteil der Stadt und die umliegende Landschaft. Das Gebäude wiegt 600 Tonnen. Zwar wurde der Turm nur für kurze Zeit für Rundfunkübertragungen genutzt, doch seinen Status als Sehenswürdigkeit hat er niemals eingebüßt. Von britischen Berlin-Besucher*innen wurde er als Teil der »modernen« Besichtigungsrunde angesteuert. In John Chancellors »How to be Happy in Berlin« ist er in allen Touren als Sehenswürdigkeit aufgeführt. Nicht zuletzt besuchten auch die Schriftstellerinnen Vita Sackville-West und Virginia Woolf als Liebespaar den Turm und verbrachten im Restaurant in 55 Metern Höhe einen unvergesslichen Abend mit Gesprächen über ihre Beziehung: »Es war UNTERDRÜCKTE GEILHEIT: Da hast Du's – Du erinnerst dich an deine Eingeständnisse, als das Suchlicht immer rundherum ging?« schrieb Sackville-West am 6. Februar 1929 an Woolf.[a]

[Fig. 2: The radio tower, photograph by Martin Höhlig, 1928]

[Abb. 2: Der Funkturm, Fotografie von Martin Höhlig, 1928]

Berlin confronted visitors with an ugly, industrial modernity epitomised in gasometers and state-of-the art architecture such as the radio tower.

At the same time, its enormous palais, museums, operas, and windswept boulevards spoke of Prussian grandeur, intercut by the many railway lines which are a recurrent feature of both literary accounts and contemporary German films. The image of the railway lines captures the sense of fast-paced movement, both individual and collective. More broadly, the image of Berlin as a space of transit mirrors the transitional, almost liminal experience of English visitors, who mostly did not stay longer than a few months.

Thanks to the favourable exchange rate that followed Germany's defeat in the First World War, members of the well-to-do English middle classes were able to treat themselves to the best Berlin had to offer at the Hotel Excelsior, the Adlon, and expensive restaurants in the West. The situation normalised to a certain extent over the course of the 1920s, but Berlin still remained much more affordable than London or Paris. It followed that the vast majority of English writers spent their time in the affluent West of the city: in Grunewald, Charlottenburg, Schöneberg, and Tiergarten. With the exception of Auden, Isherwood, and Spender, the working-class reality of most Berliners largely escaped them. If they did venture into poorer areas such as Kreuzberg, Neukölln, or Prenzlauer Berg, this occurred during chaperoned visits. Some-

In Berlin wurden Besucher*innen mit einer hässlichen, industriellen Moderne konfrontiert, die in Gasometern und zeitgemäßer Architektur wie dem Funkturm ihren Ausdruck fand.

Gleichzeitig war in den eindrucksvollen Palästen, Museen, Opernhäusern und auf den breiten, zugigen Prachtstraßen noch der Glanz des alten Preußen zu spüren. Sie wurden von zahlreichen Bahnlinien durchkreuzt, die in literarischen Schilderungen und deutschen Filmen aus dieser Zeit ein wiederkehrendes Motiv sind. Das Bild der Bahntrassen fängt die Rastlosigkeit des einzelnen Menschen und der Gesellschaft ein. Im weiteren Sinne steht das Image, das Berlin als Transitraum hatte, für die zeitlich begrenzten Erfahrungen und vielleicht sogar für die Grenzerfahrungen englischer Besucher*innen, die sich in der Regel nicht länger als ein paar Monate in der Stadt aufhielten.

Nach der deutschen Niederlage im Ersten Weltkrieg war der Wechselkurs besonders vorteilhaft. Angehörige der wohlhabenden englischen Mittelklasse konnten sich daher das Beste leisten, das Berlin mit Hotels wie dem Excelsior oder dem Adlon und den luxuriösen Restaurants im Westen zu bieten hatte. Im Verlauf der 1920er Jahre normalisierte sich die Situation zwar ein wenig, doch das Leben in Berlin war noch immer deutlich erschwinglicher als in London oder Paris. Die überwiegende Mehrheit der englischen Schriftsteller*innen hielt sich daher im wohlhabenden Westteil der Stadt, in Grunewald, Charlottenburg, Schöneberg und Tiergarten, auf. Mit Ausnahme von Auden, Isherwood und Spender hatten sie keinerlei Vorstellung vom Alltagsleben der Berliner Arbeiterklasse. Und sollten sie sich doch einmal in ärmere Bezirke wie Kreuzberg, Neukölln oder Prenzlauer Berg begeben, dann nahmen sie in der Regel an organisierten, beaufsichtig-

times, of course, the masses appeared on the doorsteps of the rich: this was Countess Blücher's experience when, during the November revolution in 1918, she observed the crowds marching down Unter den Linden from her palais on Pariser Platz.

English writers created their own city geography, depending on the length and purpose of their sojourn. Some were keen to take in what Curt Moreck, in his alternative guide to the city, memorably called its "milestones of boredom", that is, the official tourist sights.[6] However, far more attractive were the Café des Westens and, later, the Romanische Café, where they could mix with the city's artistic crowd, read foreign papers, and absorb the atmosphere of Expressionism and Dada.

The spectacular new cinemas that sprang up in the 1920s on Kurfürstendamm, Nollendorfplatz, and Potsdamer Platz were also a strong draw. As for the night, there were the gender-bending pleasures of cabarets, known for their transvestite shows, and the bewildering number of gay and lesbian venues such as the Dorian Gray on Bülowstraße, which ran separate nights for men and women; or there was the rougher action of gay dives such as the Cosy Corner on Zossener Straße. Many men simply preferred to pick up rent boys, again for comparatively modest sums, in the notorious 'Passage'.

When we try to reconstruct what early twentieth-century Berlin looked like from the perspective of English writers, it is therefore important to pay attention to how

ten Besuchen teil. Manchmal drangen die Massen jedoch auch in die reichen Bezirke vor: Davon berichtete Fürstin Blücher, die während der Novemberrevolution 1918 von ihrem Palast am Pariser Platz die Massen Unter den Linden entlangmarschieren sah.

Englische Schriftsteller*innen eroberten sich die Stadt nach ihren eigenen Bedürfnissen, je nach Dauer und Anlass ihres Besuchs. Einige waren auf der Suche nach dem, was Curt Moreck in seinem alternativen Stadtführer als »Meilensteine der Langeweile« bezeichnete, womit er die offiziellen Sehenswürdigkeiten meinte.[6] Weitaus attraktiver waren das Café des Westens und später das Romanische Café, wo sie sich unter die Künstlerkreise der Stadt mischen, ausländische Zeitungen lesen und die expressionistische und dadaistische Stimmung in sich aufnehmen konnten.

Die eindrucksvollen Filmtheater, die in den 1920er Jahren am Kurfürstendamm, am Nollendorfplatz und am Potsdamer Platz aus dem Boden schossen, übten ebenfalls eine große Anziehungskraft aus. In den Nächten wurden in den für ihre Transvestiten-Shows bekannten Kabaretts die Geschlechtergrenzen ausgelotet. Zudem gab es eine beeindruckende Zahl von Schwulen- und Lesbenbars wie das Dorian Gray an der Bülowstraße, das wechselnde Abendprogramme für Männer und Frauen anbot. Wer es etwas rauer wollte, ging in Schwulenlokale wie das Cosy Corner an der Zossener Straße. Etliche Männer zogen es vor, sich in der stadtbekannten »Passage« gegen geringes Entgelt einen Stricherjungen zu organisieren.

Bei dem Versuch, das Berlin des frühen 20. Jahrhunderts aus dem Blickwinkel englischer Schriftsteller*innen zu rekonstruieren, darf auf keinen Fall die Rolle bestimmter Orte als Hotspots der

Places
Romanisches Café

When the Café des Westens closed in 1915, it was the Romanische Café, opposite the Kaiser-Wilhelm-Gedächtniskirche, which was to become Berlin's most important creative hub. Although it was neither particularly comfortable nor the food much good, artists, journalists, politicians, writers, theatre directors, intellectuals, psychoanalysts, and cosmopolitans from all over the world flocked here to talk, write, meet colleagues, hope for a new commission, or simply to be seen at the Café. It had different rooms for different purposes: those who already had a reputation met in the so-called "swimmer's pool" whereas passers-by had to content themselves with the so-called "non-swimmer's pool". The Romanische Café features in many images and texts from the early twentieth century, not least by English authors who proudly give accounts of meeting there their German counterparts and other Britons. It also appears in several modern novels and films set during the Weimar Republic, where it becomes a symbol of nostalgia for that vanished world.

Orte
Romanisches Café

Als das Café des Westens 1915 schloss, entwickelte sich das Romanische Café gegenüber der Kaiser-Wilhelm-Gedächtniskirche zum Treffpunkt der kreativen Hauptstadtelite. Obwohl es weder besonders gemütlich war, noch gutes Essen servierte, strömten Künstler*innen, Journalist*innen, Politiker*innen, Schriftsteller*innen, Theaterdirektor*innen, Intellektuelle, Psychoanalytiker*innen und Kosmopolit*innen aus aller Welt an diesen Ort, um zu diskutieren, zu schreiben, Kolleg*innen zu treffen, auf einen neuen Auftrag zu hoffen oder einfach nur im Café gesehen zu werden. Es gab dort verschiedene Räume für verschiedene Anlässe: Die Arrivierten trafen sich im so genannten »Schwimmerbecken«, die Laufkundschaft musste sich mit dem so genannten »Nichtschwimmerbecken« zufriedengeben. Es war derart berühmt, dass es auf zahlreichen Bildern und in vielen Texten erscheint, nicht zuletzt von englischen Autor*innen, die voller Stolz über ihre Treffen mit deutschen Berufskolleg*innen, aber auch mit anderen Landsleuten berichten. Das Romanische Café als nostalgisches Symbol einer vergangenen Welt taucht auch in mehreren Gegenwartsromanen und -filmen auf, deren Handlung in der Weimarer Republik spielt.

certain locations functioned as hotspots in the literary topography of the city. It is here that writers physically converged through their social circles. These spaces became open windows onto the city and, at the same time, symbolic of its different faces. It was in Berlin that the sociologist Georg Simmel identified the figure of the stranger as typifying the social relations of

literarischen Topografie Berlins außer Acht gelassen werden. An diesen Orten trafen die verschiedenen gesellschaftlichen Kreise der Schriftsteller*innen aufeinander. Sie boten einen Blick auf die Stadt und waren gleichzeitig ein Symbol für die vielen Gesichter Berlins. Hier verortete der Soziologe Georg Simmel seine Figur des Fremden als typische Erscheinung der sozialen Beziehungen einer modernen Großstadt.[7] Mit ihrer Mischung aus Nähe und Distanz, Zu-

[Fig. 3: A view of the Romanische Café, unknown photographer, 1928]

[Abb. 3: Blick in das Romanische Café, unbekannter Fotograf, 1928]

the modern metropolis.⁷ With their mixture of proximity and distance, belonging and non-belonging, English writers in Berlin were the quintessential strangers in Simmel's terms. Their condition as temporary—sometimes passing—visitors confers on their observations an original and still valuable form of authority on the city that complements the 'native' perspective of

gehörigkeit und Nichtzugehörigkeit waren englische Schriftsteller*innen in Berlin nach Simmels Definition der Inbegriff des Fremden. Durch ihren Status als vorübergehende – manchmal auch nur auf der Durchreise befindliche – Besucher*innen zeugen ihre Beobachtungen von einem originären und noch heute wertvollen Sachverstand über das Leben in der Stadt, der als Ergänzung zu den »einheimischen« Perspektiven großer deutscher Chronist*innen dieser Zeit wie

Places
Cosy Corner

This shabby gay bar was located in the Hallesches Tor district of Kreuzberg, at Zossener Straße 7. Isherwood fictionalised the Cosy Corner in *Goodbye to Berlin* (1939), where a working-class boy named Otto takes the autobiographical protagonist to "a cellar *Lokal*" called the Alexander Casino, described as "lit by red Chinese lanterns" and furnished with "big shabby settees which looked like the seats of English third-class railway-carriages".[b] Many years later, in *Christopher and His Kind* (1976), Isherwood imaginatively revisited the Cosy Corner as the place of his sexual initiation. The bar became symbolic of the complete rejection of bourgeois propriety that Berlin made possible for young Englishmen of his class and generation. Sordid in a thoroughly unassuming kind of way, the Cosy Corner was authentically decadent, as opposed to the commercialised venues that catered for tourists and curious straight clients in wealthier parts of town. In the Cosy Corner foreign visitors mixed with working-class boys who offered sexual favours for money. The English poet and editor John Lehmann left a less romanticised account of the goings-on that took place in the bar's toilets in his erotic memoirs, *In the Purely Pagan Sense* (1976).

Orte
Cosy Corner

Diese heruntergekommene Schwulenbar befand sich am Halleschen Tor in Kreuzberg in der Zossener Straße 7. Isherwood hat das Cosy Corner zu einem Schauplatz seines Romans *Leb wohl, Berlin* (1939) gemacht, in dem ein Arbeiterjunge namens Otto dem autobiografischen Protagonisten ein »Kellerlokal namens Alexander-Kasino« zeigt, das »von roten Lampions erhellt« wurde und in dem »große abgewetzte Sofas [standen], die den Sitzen in englischen Eisenbahnwagen dritter Klasse ähnelten«.[b] Viele Jahre später kehrte Isherwood in *Christopher und die Seinen* (1976) in seiner Fantasie zurück in das Cosy Corner und damit an den Ort, an dem er seine ersten sexuellen Erfahrungen gemacht hatte. Die Bar wurde zum Symbol einer völligen Abkehr von den Regeln des bürgerlichen Anstands, die Berlin jungen Engländern seiner Klasse und Generation ermöglichte. Mit seiner unprätentiösen Schäbigkeit war das Cosy Corner der wahre Ort der Dekadenz, ganz im Gegensatz zu den kommerziellen Veranstaltungsorten, die in den wohlhabenderen Stadtvierteln Tourist*innen und schaulustige heterosexuelle Gäste anlockten. Im Cosy Corner mischten sich ausländische Besucher unter Arbeiterjungen, die ihnen sexuelle Gefälligkeiten gegen Geld anboten. Die erotischen Memoiren *In the Purely Pagan Sense* (1976) des englischen Dichters und Verlegers John Lehmann enthalten weniger romantisierte Schilderungen des Treibens in den Toilettenräumen der Bar.

the great German chroniclers of this age such as Walter Benjamin, Franz Hessel, Siegfried Kracauer, Gabriele Tergit, and Kurt Tucholsky.

From Bloomsbury to Berlin, and Back

An especially important and lasting contribution was made by writers associated with the Bloomsbury group, which took its name after the area of central London where many of them were based. Politically liberal and sexually liberated, snobbish, gossipy, and paradoxically insular in a worldly kind of way, this literary coterie was a real powerhouse in Britain. The Berlin-Bloomsbury connection started before the First World War, with visits by E.M. Forster and Rupert Brooke. It was cemented by Alix Strachey's extended stay in 1924–25, when she was translating Freud and being analysed at the Berlin Psychoanalytical Institute, and later by Harold Nicolson's appointment as *chargé d'affaires* at the British Embassy. Nicolson was married to the aristocratic writer Vita Sackville-West who, at the time, was having an affair with Virginia Woolf. During his time there, the embassy served as a social hub for literary figures who visited the well-connected Nicolsons.

Nicolson, who was a writer in his own right, was fascinated by Berlin, and attempted to capture its distinctive charm in a short prose piece that appeared in Alfred Flechtheim's journal *Der Querschnitt*,

Walter Benjamin, Franz Hessel, Siegfried Kracauer, Gabriele Tergit und Kurt Tucholsky dienen kann.

Von Bloomsbury nach Berlin und zurück

Ein besonders wichtiger und anhaltender Beitrag kam von Schriftsteller*innen, die mit der Bloomsbury Group in Verbindung standen. Diese Gruppe hatte sich nach dem Stadtteil im Zentrum Londons benannt, in dem die Mehrzahl ihrer Mitglieder wohnte. Die Angehörigen dieses in Großbritannien ausgesprochen einflussreichen literarischen Zirkels waren politisch liberal und pflegten einen offenen Umgang mit Sexualität. Darüber hinaus neigten sie zum Snobismus, hatten einen Hang zum Tratschen und legten eine eigenartige, aber keineswegs weltfremde Borniertheit an den Tag. Die Verbindung zwischen Berlin und Bloomsbury hatte ihren Ursprung vor dem Ersten Weltkrieg, als E.M. Forster und Rupert Brooke der Stadt ihren Besuch abstatteten. Gefestigt wurde sie durch Alix Stracheys ausgedehnten Aufenthalt in den Jahren 1924 und 1925. Damals übersetzte sie Freud und unterzog sich einer Analyse am Berliner Psychoanalytischen Institut. Einen weiteren Anteil hatte die Ernennung von Harold Nicolson zum *Chargé d'Affaires* an der Britischen Botschaft. Nicolson war mit der adligen Schriftstellerin Vita Sackville-West verheiratet, die zu dieser Zeit eine Beziehung mit Virginia Woolf unterhielt. Während seiner Zeit in Berlin diente die Botschaft als gesellschaftlicher Treffpunkt für Literat*innen, die dem großen Freundes- und Bekanntenkreis der Nicolsons angehörten und dem Ehepaar ihre Aufwartung machten.

in 1929, the same year that Chancellor's guidebook was published. Nicolson singled out "movement" and "frankness" as the most characteristic traits of the city, and described it coming into its own at night, when the electric lights are out and people talk and smoke into the small hours.[8] Nicolson's contribution to *Der Querschnitt*, however interesting in itself, is important in highlighting two significant phenomena. The first is the cross-pollination between diplomacy and literary culture, amplified by the media's interest in fashionable society. The second is that the presence of English writers in Berlin fed into the cosmopolitan culture of Weimar Germany, which was highly receptive to foreign ideas. *Der Querschnitt*, for instance, published several English and American writers including D. H. Lawrence, Gertrude Stein, and Virginia Woolf—some of them in the original English.

The same year as Nicolson's contribution to *Der Querschnitt*, the Berlin-based magazine *Neue Rundschau* published a translation of Vita Sackville-West's 1924 short fiction *Seducers in Ecuador*, triggering a string of German translations and a popularity among German audiences that may appear surprising from an English point of view.[9]

Psychoanalysis was a key point of attraction for Bloomsbury intellectuals, who were aware that, next to Vienna and Budapest, Berlin was fast becoming one of the prime international centres of psychoanalysis. Modernist writers such as H.D.

Nicolson war selbst Schriftsteller und voller Begeisterung für Berlin. Den besonderen Charme der Stadt versuchte er in einem kurzen Prosastück einzufangen, das wie Chancellors Reiseführer im Jahr 1929 in Alfred Flechtheims Zeitschrift *Der Querschnitt* erschien. Darin stellte er »Bewegung« und »Offenherzigkeit« als besonders typische Eigenschaften der Stadt heraus. Er beschrieb, wie die Stadt zu nächtlicher Stunde, wenn die elektrischen Lichter erloschen und die Menschen bis in die frühen Morgenstunden rauchten und diskutierten, ihr wahres Gesicht zum Vorschein brachte.[8] Nicolsons hob in seinem als solches bereits interessanten Beitrag für den *Querschnitt* zudem zwei wichtige Umstände hervor. Erstens, dass sich die Diplomatie und literarische Kreise gegenseitig befruchteten, eine Tatsache, die sich durch das Medieninteresse an der feinen Gesellschaft zusätzlich verstärkte. Und zweitens, dass auch die englischen Schriftsteller*innen in der Stadt ihren Beitrag zu einer weltoffenen Kultur im Deutschland der Weimarer Jahre leisteten, das sehr empfänglich für äußere Einflüsse war. *Der Querschnitt* veröffentlichte beispielsweise mehrere Texte englischer und amerikanischer Schriftsteller*innen wie D.H. Lawrence, Gertrude Stein und Virginia Woolf – in einigen Fällen sogar im englischen Original.

Im Erscheinungsjahr von Nicolsons Beitrag in *Der Querschnitt* brachte das Berliner Magazin *Neue Rundschau* eine Übersetzung von Vita Sackville-Wests Kurzgeschichte *Seducers in Ecuador* (*Verführer in Ecuador*) aus dem Jahr 1924 heraus. Die Veröffentlichung zog eine Reihe deutscher Übersetzungen nach sich. Außerdem erfreute sie sich beim deutschen Publikum einer Beliebtheit, die aus englischer Sicht vermutlich ein wenig befremdlich anmutet.[9]

Die Psychoanalyse übte eine ungemeine Anziehungskraft auf die intellektuellen Bloomsburys aus.

[Fig. 4: Portrait of Virginia Woolf by Maurice Beck, published in *Der Querschnitt* 1930]

[Abb. 4: Porträt von Virginia Woolf von Maurice Beck, 1930 in *Der Querschnitt* veröffentlicht]

and her lover Bryher came to be analysed by prominent analysts such as Hanns Sachs and Karl Abraham. Abraham had founded the Berlin Psychoanalytical Institute in 1920 as a space of training analysis, intellectual debate, and networking among a cosmopolitan group of analysands and analysts. For English writers interested in psychoanalysis, Berlin became a place to find themselves, to liberate themselves from strict English sexual mores, but also to apprehend the experimental artistic applications of psychoanalytic theories. Alix Strachey vividly captures the heady mix of theory debates, analysis, and long partying

Sie hatten erkannt, dass sich Berlin neben Wien und Budapest mit großer Geschwindigkeit zu einem der angesehensten internationalen Zentren der Psychoanalyse entwickelte. Autorinnen der Moderne wie H.D. und ihre Geliebte Bryher kamen für Sitzungen bei den berühmten Psychoanalytikern Hanns Sachs und Karl Abraham in die Stadt. Abraham hatte das Berliner Psychoanalytische Institut 1920 als Ort für die Durchführung von Lehranalysen, den intellektuellen Austausch und die Vernetzung einer kosmopolitischen Gruppe von Analysand*innen und Analyst*innen gegründet. Aus Sicht englischer Autor*innen mit einem Interesse für Psychoanalyse war Berlin nun der Ort, an dem sie zu sich selbst finden und sich von der strengen englischen Sexual-

nights in her letters to her husband James. Here her experiences of Berlin's social life are couched in psychoanalytical terms, as Alix ironically describes the goings-on at a ball in terms of "Mother-Imago", "Sister-transference", and "injured Narcissism".[10] Apart from the many writers who left accounts of the lively psychoanalytical scene, numerous Britons were trained in Berlin to become analysts in their own right in Britain.

The Berlin Myth

To readers of English literature, the writer who is most closely associated with Berlin is of course Christopher Isherwood. Isherwood lived in Berlin, on and off, in the politically volatile period between 1929 and 1933. As an extension of the Bloomsbury-Berlin connection, back in Britain, his famous novels, *Mr Norris Changes Trains* (1935) and *Goodbye to Berlin* (1939), were first published by the Woolfs' Hogarth Press. Isherwood's Berlin writings drew heavily on his autobiographical experiences by fictionalising real people, including the author himself, and striving to portray an accurate topography of the city. At the same time, they mythicised the fragile, cosmopolitan,

liberal world of the Weimar Republic that had, by then, already disappeared, crushed under the foot of the Nazi regime. In a symbolic act, Isherwood claimed to have burnt the diaries he kept in Berlin, thereby destroying an historical record that could have undermined the carefully crafted wholeness of his fictional world. Moreover, after the war, he only went back to the city once, in 1952, having been commissioned to write an article for *The Observer*.

Popular though Isherwood's books have always been, it is largely thanks to their adaptations that they reached the global audience they enjoy today. In 1951, the American playwright John van Druten turned the Sally Bowles episode from *Goodbye to Berlin* into a play entitled *I am a Camera*, performed to large audiences on both sides of the Atlantic and later made into a film with set designs by the German artist George Grosz, famous for his Dada-inspired depictions and caricatures of 1920s Berlin.

The achievement of *I am a Camera* however pales in comparison to the enormous commercial success of Bob Fosse's 1972 musical film *Cabaret*. With Liza Minnelli's striking performance as Sally Bowles and its eight Oscars, *Cabaret* sealed Isherwood's global reputation as chronicler of the city, keeping his Berlin myth alive for a different generation.

Audiences that approach Isherwood through these adaptations certainly get to experience the luscious decadence of Weimar Berlin, visually and through the

Mythos der fragilen, kosmopolitischen und liberalen Welt der Weimarer Republik, die zu diesem Zeitpunkt bereits durch die Herrschaft der Nationalsozialisten ausgelöscht worden war. In einem symbolischen Akt hatte Isherwood nach eigenen Angaben seine Berliner Tagebücher verbrannt. Darüber hinaus besuchte er die Stadt nach dem Krieg im Jahr 1952 nur noch ein einziges Mal, um im Auftrag des *Observers* einen Artikel über Berlin zu schreiben.

Isherwoods Bücher erfreuten sich stets großer Beliebtheit. Doch den ungeheuren internationalen Ruhm, der ihnen inzwischen zuteil geworden ist, verdanken sie vor allem ihren Verfilmungen. Der amerikanische Drehbuchautor John van Druten entwickelte 1952 aus dem Kapitel über Sally Bowles in *Leb' wohl, Berlin* ein Theaterstück mit dem Titel *I am a Camera* (»Ich bin eine Kamera«), das beiderseits des Atlantiks ein großes Publikum fand. Auf Grundlage des Drehbuchs wurde später ein Film mit Kulissen des deutschen Künstlers George Grosz gedreht, der für seine vom Dadaismus inspirierten Darstellungen und Karikaturen aus dem Berlin der 1920er Jahre berühmt ist.

Allerdings war *I am a Camera* deutlich weniger erfolgreich als Bob Fosses Musicalfilm *Cabaret* aus dem Jahr 1972, der zum Kassenschlager wurde. Mit Liza Minnellis eindrucksvoller Darstellung der Sally Bowles und acht Oscars besiegelte *Cabaret* Isherwoods internationalen Ruf als Chronist der Stadt. Der Film sorgte dafür, dass der Mythos Berlins auch für eine neue Generation am Leben gehalten wurde.

Ein Publikum, das sich Isherwood über diese Verfilmungen nähert, erhält ohne Zweifel einen visuellen und musikalischen Eindruck von den dekadenten Ausschweifungen im Berlin der Weimarer Republik. Allerdings gehen andere Aspekte seiner Werke dabei verloren, beispielsweise die ausführlichen Schilderungen der Lebensrealitäten in der

[Fig. 5: George Grosz, Study for *I am a Camera*, watercolour and ink on paper, c.1952]

[Abb. 5: George Grosz, Studie für *I am a Camera*, Aquarell und Tinte auf Papier, ca. 1952]

medium of music. But they miss other important aspects of his writings, such as the effort to depict working-class Berlin, something that no other English writer attempted to the same extent. In Berlin, Isherwood exploited his status as a foreigner to become more socially mobile than he was in Britain. While his job as an English tutor took him into the houses of the rich, he gained access to the working-class world through the lovers he picked up in seedy gay joints such as the Cosy Corner, where young Berliners earned money as sex workers, often targeting foreign customers. Isherwood even lived for a time with the family of one of his lovers in a rundown tenement block on Simeonstraße, in a particularly poor part of Kreuzberg.

His first-hand experiences of urban squalor are captured in a story called "The Novaks", which speaks frankly and powerfully about poverty and ill health. It is telling that, before becoming a chapter in *Goodbye to Berlin*, "The Novaks" was published independently in the English magazine *New Writing*, edited by Isherwood's friend and fellow Berlin visitor John Lehmann, which had an openly antifascist agenda. Here, Isherwood's Berlin story appeared alongside translations from French, Russian, and Chinese literature, as well as a piece by the German Jewish writer Anna Seghers, who was already in exile in Paris.

It is also important to remember that Isherwood did not experience Berlin on his own, but as part of a group of up-and-coming young English writers that also com-

Berliner Arbeiterklasse, der sich kein anderer englischer Schriftsteller derart detailliert gewidmet hat. In Berlin machte sich Isherwood seinen Status als Ausländer zunutze und legte im Vergleich zu seinem Leben in Großbritannien eine deutlich höhere soziale Mobilität an den Tag. Durch seine Arbeit als Englischlehrer erhielt er zum einen Zugang zu den Häusern der Reichen. Zum anderen verschafften ihm seine wechselnden Liebschaften einen Einblick in die Welt der Arbeiterklasse. Die Männer lernte er in schäbigen Schwulenbars wie dem Cosy Corner kennen, wo junge Berliner ihrer meist ausländischen Kundschaft sexuelle Dienstleistungen gegen Geld anboten. Isherwood wohnte sogar eine Zeit lang bei der Familie eines seiner Geliebten in einer heruntergekommenen Mietskaserne in der Simeonstraße, die in einem besonders armen Teil Kreuzbergs lag.

Seine eigenen Erfahrungen mit dem Elend in der Stadt hat er in einer Geschichte mit dem Titel »Die Nowaks« festgehalten, in der er unverblümt und eindrücklich über Armut und Krankheit schreibt. Es ist bezeichnend, dass Isherwood »Die Nowaks«, die später zu einem Kapitel von *Leb' wohl, Berlin* wurden, zunächst als eigenständige Erzählung im englischen Magazin *New Writing* veröffentlichte, das eine klare antifaschistische Haltung vertrat. Herausgeber dieses Magazins war sein englischer Freund John Lehmann, der ihn ebenfalls in Berlin besucht hatte. Die Ausgabe enthielt neben Isherwoods Berliner Geschichte auch Übersetzungen französischer, russischer und chinesischer Literatur sowie einen Text der deutschjüdischen Schriftstellerin Anna Seghers, die zu dieser Zeit bereits im Pariser Exil lebte.

Darüber hinaus darf nicht vergessen werden, dass Isherwood Berlin nicht auf eigene Faust erkundete, sondern als Mitglied einer Gruppe aufstrebender junger Schriftsteller aus England, der auch

[Fig. 6: Cover of the *Radio Times* featuring Christopher Isherwood and Liza Minnelli, 20 April 1974]

[Abb. 6: Titelbild der Zeitschrift *Radio Times*, mit Christopher Isherwood und Liza Minnelli, 20. April 1974]

prised W. H. Auden and Stephen Spender. These writers developed in different directions but they all came from a similar background, which was one of privilege and respectability. In Berlin they tried to escape what they found suffocating about their upbringing and their native country. Isherwood put it succinctly years later: "One of my chief motives for wanting to visit Berlin was that an elderly relative had warned me against it, saying that it was the vilest place since Sodom".[11] Berlin was where one disobeyed one's elders. It was the antidote to Little England, with its smugness, security, and propriety. It was a stepping stone into an unknown wider world. The reference to Sodom aptly captures both the homosexual thrill and the city's readiness to appear in mythical terms, reflected also in Moreck's comparison with the labyrinth of ancient

W. H. Auden und Stephen Spender angehörten. Auch wenn diese Autoren völlig unterschiedliche Laufbahnen einschlugen, hatten sie alle doch einen ähnlich privilegierten und angesehenen Hintergrund. In Berlin wollten sie der beklemmenden Atmosphäre ihrer Kindheit und Jugend und ihrer Heimat entfliehen. Isherwood schrieb Jahre später in einem lakonischen Kommentar: »Einer der Hauptgründe meines Berlin-Besuchs war der Kommentar eines älteren Verwandten, der mich vor der Stadt gewarnt hatte. Seiner Meinung nach war sie einer der widerwärtigsten Orte seit Sodom.«[11] Berlin war der Ort, an dem man nicht auf die Älteren hörte. Die Stadt war das Gegenmittel zum spießigen, sicheren und anständigen Klein-England. Sie war das Sprungbrett in eine unbekannte größere Welt. Der Hinweis auf Sodom deutet sowohl auf die homosexuellen Reize als auch auf die Tauglichkeit der Stadt zur Mythenbildung hin, die auch Moreck mit seinem Vergleich mit dem Labyrinth im antiken Knossos und

Knossos, as well as the clichéd analogies with Babylon.[12]

Isherwood's, Auden's, and Spender's reactions to Berlin extend across a network of poems, fictions, letters, and autobiographical writings, where the city becomes attached to a personal and artistic mythology. Their paths through the city, their gazes, their erotic lives, even, frequently cross one another, drawing complex patterns of literary collaboration, emotional bond, and personal resentment. Their friendships were complicated: Auden, who was the first of this group to discover Berlin, was Isherwood's on-and-off lover for decades; and Isherwood and Spender, while they remained close all their lives, also came into conflicts more than once, as Isherwood suspected Spender of trying to "steal" Berlin material from him. While Isherwood's reputation peaked with the Berlin novels, Auden went on to become one of the most important English poets of the twentieth century. Spender is remembered more as a memoirist than as a poet, maybe due to his tendency to portray himself as naïve and inferior to the other two writers.

A famous photograph taken by Spender with his camera self-timer on the island of Rügen captures another fact about these writers that was extremely important in their attitude to Berlin: they were all extremely young. They faced the city with a mixture of lust for life and remarkable self-confidence. The Berlin myth created by these three writers—most strongly by Isherwood—has been so powerful because

mit seinen klischeehaften Anspielungen auf Babylon beschreibt.[12]

Wie Isherwood, Auden und Spender Berlin wahrgenommen haben, lässt sich in einer Fülle von Gedichten, Romanen, Briefen und autobiografischen Schriften nachlesen, in denen sie die Stadt zum Objekt ihrer persönlichen und künstlerischen Mythenbildung machten. Oft kreuzen sich ihre Wege und ihre Blicke in der Stadt, und auch erotisch sind sie miteinander verbandelt. Auf diese Weise entstehen komplexe Muster einer literarischen Zusammenarbeit, emotionalen Bindung und persönlichen Abneigung. Ihr freundschaftliches Verhältnis war komplex: Auden, der als Erster der Gruppe Berlin für sich entdeckte, war jahrzehntelang Isherwoods On-Off-Geliebter. Isherwood und Spender pflegten zwar ihr Leben lang ein enges Verhältnis, doch es kam auch mehr als einmal zu Konflikten, wenn Isherwood Spender unterstellte, dass er ihm Material aus seiner Zeit in Berlin stehlen wollte. Während Isherwoods Ruhm mit den Berlin-Romanen seinen Höhepunkt erreichte, wurde Auden zum wichtigsten englischen Dichter des 20. Jahrhunderts. Spender ist dagegen eher als Verfasser von Memoiren denn als Dichter in Erinnerung geblieben, womöglich weil er dazu neigte, sich immer wieder als naiv und den anderen beiden Schriftstellern unterlegen darzustellen.

Spender hat auf der Insel Rügen mit dem Selbstauslöser seiner Kamera ein berühmtes Foto geschossen. Darauf ist eine weitere Eigenschaft der Schriftsteller festgehalten, die ihren Blick auf Berlin maßgeblich beeinflusste: Alle drei waren ausgesprochen jung. Sie begegneten der Stadt mit einer Mischung aus Lebenslust und bemerkenswertem Selbstvertrauen. Der Berliner Mythos, den diese drei Schriftsteller – allen voran Isherwood – begründeten, war deshalb so prägend, weil er sich auf ein vorgefertigtes Narrativ

Places
Simeonstraße

This typical working-class street of old Berlin is located in the district of Kreuzberg. In 1930, Isherwood lived for a period at Simeonstraße 4, with the family of his teenage lover Walter Wolff. He wrote about this experience in *Goodbye to Berlin*, where the family are renamed Nowak and the address is moved to nearby Wassertorstraße. These changes aside, his descriptions realistically capture the harsh domestic life of working-class families in the city, where rapid population growth had caused a severe shortage of space. In Berlin's large tenement blocks, revealingly known as *Mietskasernen* or rent barracks, wealthier families typically occupied apartments in the front, while poorer tenants were crammed in less spacious—often downright insalubrious—accommodations in the many inner courtyards. Inner courtyards are a distinctive and now much beloved feature of Berlin's urban landscape. Already in the 1920s, writers such as Franz Hessel painted romantic images of the colourful shabbiness typical of inner courtyards. There is no doubt that Isherwood also romanticised working-class life, just as he eroticised the working-class male body in ways that will strike some readers today as problematic. Nonetheless, his curiosity for Berlin working-class culture, which he shared with Auden, is one of the most original aspects of his works. Some English writers reacted with disdain to urban poverty in Berlin. Most of them never even ventured into poor districts such as Kreuzberg.

Orte
Simeonstraße

Diese für ein Arbeiterviertel des alten Berlins typische Straße befand sich im Bezirk Kreuzberg. Im Jahr 1930 lebte Isherwood für einige Zeit in der Simeonstraße 4 bei der Familie seines Geliebten Walter Wolff. Von seinen damaligen Erlebnissen berichtete er in *Leb wohl, Berlin*. In diesem Roman heißt die Familie Nowak und wohnt an der nahe gelegenen Wassertorstraße. Abgesehen von diesen Unterschieden stellen seine Beschreibungen die harten Lebensrealitäten von Arbeiterfamilien in einer Stadt dar, in der das rasante Bevölkerungswachstum eine dramatische Verknappung des Wohnraums zur Folge hatte. In den großen Berliner Wohnblöcken, die bezeichnenderweise auch Mietskasernen genannt wurden, konnten sich wohlhabendere Familien Wohnungen im Vorderhaus leisten, während sich ärmere Mieter*innen – zum Teil unter höchst ungesunden Verhältnissen – in den weniger geräumigen Wohnungen der unzähligen Hinterhöfe drängten. Diese Innenhöfe sind ein typisches und heutzutage ausgesprochen beliebtes Merkmal der Berliner Stadtlandschaft. Schon in den 1920er Jahren zeichneten Schriftsteller wie Franz Hessel ein romantisches Bild von der farbenreichen Schäbigkeit, die in diesen Hinterhöfen zu finden ist. Auch Isherwood hat das Leben der Arbeiterklasse ohne Zweifel romantisiert, so wie er auch die Körper der Arbeiterjungen in einer Weise erotisiert hat, die einige Leser*innen heute als problematisch empfinden könnten. Nichtsdestotrotz macht sein Interesse für die Kultur der Berliner Arbeiterklasse, welches er mit Auden teilte, den besonderen Reiz seiner Werke aus. Etliche englische Schriftsteller*innen äußerten sich abfällig über die städtische Armut in Berlin und wagten in vielen Fällen nicht einmal den Schritt in arme Stadtbezirke wie Kreuzberg.

[Fig. 7: People queuing to swap firewood for potato peelings—
a favourite trade on Simeonstraße,
photograph by Carl Weinrother, 1930s]

[Abb. 7: Tausch von Feuerholz gegen Kartoffelschalen –
ein beliebtes Geschäft, Simeonstraße,
Fotografie von Carl Weinrother, 1930er Jahre]

it can be grafted onto a ready-made narrative of innocence and experience. From the 1950s onwards, the myth was stoked by the writers themselves, especially Isherwood and Spender, who repeatedly re-examined their Berlin years from different vantage points. At the same time, it has been amplified by popular culture and biography, which have repackaged it for successive generations of captive audiences. In approaching the Berlin myth, it is important to be aware of what went into its construction and of its evolving history, but also

von Unschuld und Erfahrung stützt. Seit den 1950er Jahren pflegten die Schriftsteller selbst diesen Mythos. Insbesondere Isherwood und Spender beschäftigten sich immer wieder aus unterschiedlichen Blickwinkeln mit ihren Berliner Jahren. Gleichzeitig wurde der Mythos durch die Populärkultur und biografische Werke weiter genährt und für das gefesselte Publikum aufeinander folgender Generationen neu in Szene gesetzt. Wenn man sich mit dem Berliner Mythos beschäftigt, muss man berücksichtigen, wie er konstruiert und immer neu erzählt wurde, aber auch diejenigen Aspekte beleuchten, die er nicht umfasst. Der Hedonismus der Weimarer Republik stellt

[Fig. 8: W. H. Auden, Stephen Spender, and Christopher Isherwood at Sellin on the island of Rügen, photograph by Stephen Spender, 1931]

[Abb. 8: W. H. Auden, Stephen Spender und Christopher Isherwood in Sellin auf Rügen, Fotografie von Stephen Spender, 1931]

of what it obscures. The hedonism of the Weimar Republic, for instance, looks very different from the point of view of the many homosexual men who entered the city's sex industry as exploited workers, rather than consumers.[13]

Gendered Perceptions

Part of the Berlin myth is the city's reputation for sexual tolerance and gender emancipation. In her published diary of post-First World War Berlin, the aristocratic salonnière Lady Helen d'Abernon

sich beispielsweise ganz anders dar, wenn man ihn aus der Perspektive jener zahlreichen homosexuellen Männer betrachtet, die nicht Konsumenten, sondern als Ausgebeutete Teil der Sexindustrie Berlins waren.[13]

Geschlechtsspezifische Perspektiven

Zum Berliner Mythos gehört auch, dass der Stadt ein Ruf als Ort der sexuellen Toleranz und der Emanzipation der Geschlechter vorauseilte. In ihrem in Buchform veröffentlichten Tagebuch aus ihrer Ber-

recounts being transfixed by the sight of a male prostitute dressed in female attire and wearing a military belt and scabbard round his waist. Many English writers' records contain encounters with what we would now call non-normative gender displays, from Arthur Symons's tour of the city's cabarets in the early 1890s to the many accounts of late Weimar nightlife. Such queer figures are somehow emblematic of the city: they express the spirit of defiant self-invention that marked Berlin's brand of modernity.

D'Abernon's illicit glimpses of the city's colourful sex life bespeak English women's desire to move freely in Berlin—something that became increasingly possible during the Weimar Republic. Mirroring to a certain extent new possibilities for women in Germany in general, the spaces English women could encounter in early twentieth-century Berlin, and the activities they could engage in, became more diverse. From chaperoned visits to soup kitchens or prisoner of war camps, these spaces evolved to tourist attractions, museums, book shops, parks, amusement arcades, balls, dances, clubs, bars, and, finally, political rallies. Women participated in all the activities that were available to men, from psychoanalysis to fancy-dress balls, from discussions in writers' cafés to bathing in the indoor swimming pool open to both sexes. In her memoirs, Elizabeth Wiskemann makes a striking comparison of her experiences of left-wing politics, as a woman, in London and Berlin: while, in

liner Zeit nach dem Ersten Weltkrieg berichtet die aristokratische Salonnière Lady Helen d'Abernon, wie sie der Anblick eines Strichers in Frauenkleidung und mit einem Militärgürtel mit Schwerthalter um die Hüften verwunderte und fesselte. Viele englische Schriftsteller*innen schilderten Begegnungen mit Menschen, deren Erscheinung wir heute als nicht der gängigen Norm entsprechenden Ausdruck der Geschlechtlichkeit bezeichnen würden: von Arthur Symons Erkundungen durch die Kabaretts der Stadt in den frühen 1890er Jahren bis hin zu den zahlreichen Berichten über das Nachtleben in der Endphase der Weimarer Republik. Die darin beschriebenen queeren Figuren stehen in gewisser Weise symbolhaft für die Stadt: Sie bringen den Geist der trotzigen Selbstinszenierung als Berliner Markenzeichen der Moderne zum Ausdruck.

D'Abernons unerlaubte Einblicke in das abwechslungsreiche Berliner Sexualleben zeugen vom Wunsch englischer Frauen, sich frei in Berlin bewegen zu können. In der Weimarer Republik gab es mit der Zeit immer mehr solcher Freiräume. Die Orte, die englische Frauen zu Beginn des 20. Jahrhunderts in Berlin besuchen und die Aktivitäten, an denen sie teilhaben konnten, spiegeln in gewissem Maße auch die neuen Möglichkeiten wider, die sich in dieser Zeit generell für Frauen in Deutschland boten. Die Gelegenheiten, die sich englischen Autor*innen boten, reichten von organisierten Besuchen in Suppenküchen oder Kriegsgefangenenlagern bis hin zum Besuch von Sehenswürdigkeiten, Museen, Buchläden, Parks, Vergnügungsparks, Bällen, Tanzveranstaltungen, Clubs, Bars oder sogar politischen Kundgebungen. Frauen nahmen an allen Aktivitäten teil, die auch Männern offenstanden, von Analysesitzungen bis zu Kostümbällen, von Gesprächsrunden in Autorencafés bis zu Ausflügen in Hallenbäder für beide Geschlechter.

the 1920s, she "had lived on the edge of the Bloomsbury world at home and was familiar with the preaching of all kinds of free love", it was only in Berlin that she truly became acquainted with revolutionary communism.[14]

As regards sexual politics, accounts of Berlin's opportunities for lesbian encounters can be found in Vita Sackville-West's letters to Virginia Woolf and even in Alix Strachey, who teased her husband with stories of lesbian courtship and plans to pay a visit to the Dorian Gray.[15]

It is important to remember that, as in Britain, homosexuality was still illegal in Germany at this point. Nonetheless in Berlin female and male homosexuality were publicly discussed and tolerated in ways that would have been unimaginable in Britain—indeed, almost anywhere else in the world. Homosexual relations were of course hardly condemned or hidden in emancipated Bloomsbury, but this was strictly behind closed doors. The country was still in the long shadow of the Oscar Wilde trials of 1895. E.M. Forster wrote his gay novel *Maurice* in the early 1910s but did not dare publish it all his life. And in 1928, Radclyffe Hall's lesbian novel *The Well of Loneliness* was charged with obscenity and banned, intensifying the taboo around this topic. *Maurice* and *The Well of Loneliness* are not pornographic books by any stretch of the imagination. What British society deemed unacceptable was that they gave readers ways of imagining self-fulfilment as homosexual

Elizabeth Wiskemann zieht in ihren Memoiren einen eindrucksvollen Vergleich zwischen ihren Erfahrungen als Frau in der linken politischen Szene in London und in Berlin: Zu Beginn der 1920er Jahre hatte sie »zu Hause am Rande der Bloomsbury-Welt gelebt und war es deshalb gewohnt, predigen zu hören, etwa freie Liebe aller Art«. Dem revolutionären Kommunismus war sie dagegen erst in Berlin wirklich begegnet.[14]

Was die Sexualpolitik anbelangt, finden sich Berichte über die Berliner Möglichkeiten für lesbische Begegnungen in den Briefen von Vita Sackville-West an Virginia Woolf und bei Alix Strachey, die ihren Ehemann mit Berichten über das lesbische Balzverhalten und ihren geplanten Besuch im Dorian Gray neckte.[15]

Es darf nicht vergessen werden, dass in Deutschland, wie auch in Großbritannien, Homosexualität zu dieser Zeit noch unter Strafe stand. Nichtsdestotrotz wurde weibliche und männliche Homosexualität in Berlin offen thematisiert und in einer Weise toleriert, die in Großbritannien – und im Grunde an fast jedem anderen Ort der Welt – undenkbar gewesen wäre. Im emanzipierten Bloomsbury wurden homosexuelle Beziehungen natürlich weder hart bestraft noch versteckt, allerdings wurden sie ausschließlich hinter verschlossenen Türen ausgelebt. Das Gerichtsverfahren gegen Oscar Wilde im Jahr 1895 warf noch immer seine Schatten über das Land. E.M. Forster schrieb seinen Roman *Maurice*, in dem er das Schwulsein thematisierte, bereits zu Beginn der 1910er Jahre, entschied sich jedoch aus Angst vor Repressalien zu Lebzeiten gegen eine Veröffentlichung. Und Radclyffe Halls lesbischer Roman *Quell der Einsamkeit* (»The Well of Loneliness«) wurde 1928 als obszön eingestuft und verboten, wodurch sich dieses Thema noch einmal mehr zum Tabu entwickelte. *Maurice* und *Quell der Einsamkeit* lassen sich beim besten Willen nicht als pornografische Literatur bezeichnen. Aus Sicht der britischen

men or women. In Berlin, by contrast, Magnus Hirschfeld's Institute of Sexual Science provided an international hub for queer activism and the free discussion of all manners of non-normative sexual identities.

Specialised homosexual periodicals already started appearing towards the end of the nineteenth century, including the pioneering journal of "masculine culture" *Der Eigene*, the *Jahrbuch für sexuelle Zwischenstufen*, linked to Hirschfeld, and the lesbian *Die Freundin*. Apart from providing useful information for gay people, the homosexual press aided the development of a literature about homosexuality. Indeed, one of the most prominent writers in the city's queer scene was the British-born John Henry Mackay, whose work brings together homosexual emancipation ideology and utopian anarchism. Born in Britain of Scottish-German parentage but transplanted to Germany at a very young age, Mackay formally counted as British until he took up German citizenship in 1905. His most famous work is the 1926 novel *Der Puppenjunge*, set in the underworld of Berlin rent-boys familiar to Auden and Isherwood. The iconic film *Anders als die Andern* (1919), starring Hirschfeld and his partner, Karl Giese, shows how interest in homosexuality also crossed into the vibrant world of Weimar cinema.

In this context, it is easy to grasp the anticipation with which English homosexual writers approached Berlin in the early twentieth century. Here was a place where

Gesellschaft waren diese Bücher inakzeptabel, weil sie Leser*innen eine Vorstellung davon vermittelten, wie ein selbsterfülltes Leben als Mann oder Frau mit homosexuellen Neigungen möglich sein konnte. In Berlin dagegen bot Magnus Hirschfelds Institut für Sexualwissenschaft einen internationalen Treffpunkt für queere Aktivist*innen und offene Gespräche über sexuelle Identitäten, die nicht der gängigen Norm entsprachen.

Bereits zum Ende des neunzehnten Jahrhunderts erschienen Zeitschriften für Homosexuelle, darunter das erste »Blatt für männliche Kultur« *Der Eigene*, das *Jahrbuch für sexuelle Zwischenstufen* unter Leitung von Hirschfeld und die lesbische Zeitschrift *Die Freundin*. Die homosexuelle Presse lieferte nützliche Informationen für Schwule und Lesben und trug außerdem zur Verbreitung von Literatur zum Thema Homosexualität bei. Zu den bekanntesten Schriftstellern der homosexuellen Szene Berlins gehörte der gebürtige Brite John Henry Mackay, der in seinen Werken homosexuelle Emanzipationsideologien und anarchistische Utopien miteinander verband. Mackay wurde in Großbritannien in einem deutsch-schottischen Elternhaus geboren, kam jedoch schon als kleines Kind nach Deutschland. Er galt offiziell als Brite, bevor er 1905 die deutsche Staatsbürgerschaft annahm. Sein bekanntestes Werk ist der Roman *Der Puppenjunge* von 1926, der in der Unterwelt der Berliner Stricher angesiedelt ist, mit der Auden und Isherwood ebenfalls vertraut waren. Der Kultfilm *Anders als die Andern* (1919), in dem auch Hirschfeld und sein Partner Karl Giese auftreten, ist ein Beleg dafür, dass das Interesse am Thema Homosexualität auch die pulsierende Welt des Weimarer Kinos erreicht hatte.

Vor diesem Hintergrund lässt sich gut nachvollziehen, welche Erwartungen englische homosexuelle

Places
The Institute of Sexual Science

Housed in an imposing building at the edge of the Tiergarten, the Institute was the symbol of the open attitude to sexuality for which Berlin became internationally renowned. As such, it was an object of curiosity for foreign visitors, not least from Britain, where queer culture was still compelled to exist entirely underground. The Institute was dominated by the figure of the homosexual rights campaigner Magnus Hirschfeld. Despite its name, science was only one part of the daily activities of the Institute, which also provided support to the public, and doubled up as a social hub of Berlin's queer life. Isherwood lived next door to the Institute, in an apartment owned by Hirschfeld's sister, for nearly a year in 1929–30. He immersed himself in the Institute's social networks, through which he came in contact with the French writer André Gide and the actor Conrad Veidt. Important though the Institute was for him, Isherwood made no mention of it in the Berlin novels, no doubt fearing that this topic would be too much for British readers or that it would make his sexual identity too public. Many years later, he looked back on the Institute with ambivalence in *Christopher and His Kind* (1976), describing it as "uncanny" and speaking of his fear of being turned into a specimen in its museum of sex. Both Magnus Hirschfeld and the Institute were considered important points of contact for liberal-minded foreign visitors, even if they themselves were not necessarily lesbian or gay, and are mentioned in passing in numerous accounts.

Orte
Institut für Sexualwissenschaft

Das Institut befand sich in einem imposanten Gebäude am Rande des Tiergartens und galt als Symbol für den offenen Umgang mit Sexualität, durch den sich Berlin weltweit einen Namen machte. Als solches übte es eine große Anziehungskraft auf ausländische Besucher*innen aus. Sie kamen nicht nur aus Großbritannien, wo die queere Kultur zu dieser Zeit ausschließlich im Untergrund stattfinden musste. Die zentrale Figur des Instituts war der Wissenschaftler und Aktivist für die Rechte Homosexueller Magnus Hirschfeld. Ungeachtet des Institutsnamens machte die wissenschaftliche Arbeit nur einen Teil der täglichen Abläufe aus. Das Institut bot auch Beratungen für die Bevölkerung an und erfüllte zugleich die Funktion als soziale Treffpunkt des queeren Lebens in der Stadt. Christopher Isherwood lebte von 1929 bis 1930 fast ein Jahr in einer Wohnung von Hirschfelds Schwester in direkter Nachbarschaft zum Institut. Er nahm am sozialen Leben des Hauses teil und kam auf diese Weise auch mit André Gide und dem Schauspieler Conrad Veidt in Kontakt. In seinen Berlin-Romanen hat Isherwood das Institut nicht erwähnt, obwohl es eine wichtige Rolle in seinem Leben spielte. Vermutlich befürchtete er, dass seine britischen Leser*innen von diesem Thema überfordert sein könnten oder er seine sexuelle Identität auf diese Weise zu sehr der Öffentlichkeit preisgeben würde. Viele Jahre später blickte er in *Christopher und die Seinen* (»Christopher and His Kind«, 1976) zwiespältig auf seine Zeit am Institut zurück, die er als »unheimlich« bezeichnete. Er schrieb außerdem von seiner Sorge, selbst zu einem Ausstellungsexemplar des Institutsmuseums zu werden. Sowohl Magnus Hirschfeld als auch das Institut galten als wichtige Anlaufpunkte für weltoffene Besucher*innen aus dem Ausland, die nicht zwangsläufig lesbisch oder schwul waren. In zahlreichen Aufzeichnungen werden sie beiläufig erwähnt.

[Fig. 9: Drawing of the Institute of Sexual Science, in Perles-Titus, *préparation scientifique d'hormone sexuelle. Hormones de rajeunissement d'après la prescription du Dr Magnus Hirschfeld et sous le contrôle médical constant de l'Institut pour la science sexuelle*, Berlin, c. 1930]

[Abb. 9: Zeichnung des Instituts für Sexualwissenschaft aus Perles-Titus, *préparation scientifique d'hormone sexuelle. Hormones de rajeunissement d'après la prescription du Dr Magnus Hirschfeld et sous le contrôle médical constant de l'Institut pour la science sexuelle*, Berlin, ca. 1930]

not only could one enjoy the notoriously permissive nightlife, but also do away with much subterfuge and euphemism. This feeling of sexual liberation can be seen in some of the poetry that Auden wrote around his time in Berlin, especially in a series of poems written in somewhat bumpy German. For both Auden and Isherwood, the German language became charged with a special sexual thrill, as though it stimulated the erotic imagination in ways that were not possible for English. Isherwood's case, however, shows that the Berlin brand of sexual freedom could also be alien and challenging to a young writer coming from Britain. Isherwood lived for several months in a building attached to the Institute of Sexual Science and used the social network of the Institute to get to know Berlin's gay culture. There is no doubt that the knowledge of himself and others that he acquired there had both im-

Schriftsteller*innen mit einem Berlin-Aufenthalt zu Beginn des 20. Jahrhunderts verknüpften. Hier konnten sie nicht nur das berüchtigte freizügige Nachtleben genießen, sondern auch weitgehend auf die üblichen Ausflüchte und Winkelzüge verzichten. Dieses Gefühl der sexuellen Befreiung lässt sich in einigen Gedichten nachvollziehen, die Auden während seiner Zeit in Berlin schrieb. Darunter ist vor allem eine in einem etwas holperigen Deutsch verfasste Reihe von Gedichten. Sowohl für Auden als auch für Isherwood ging von der deutschen Sprache eine besondere sexuelle Faszination aus, als könne das Deutsche die erotische Vorstellungskraft in einer Weise stimulieren, die dem Englischen nicht zu eigen war. Isherwoods Fall ist allerdings ein Beleg dafür, dass das Berliner Markenzeichen der sexuellen Freizügigkeit einen jungen Schriftsteller auch befremden und überfordern konnte. Isherwood lebte mehrere Monate lang in einem Nebengebäude des Instituts für Sexualwissenschaft und machte sich mit Hilfe des sozialen Netzwerks am Institut mit der Berliner Schwulenkultur vertraut. Die Erfahrungen, die er

[Fig. 10: Magnus Hirschfeld and Karl Giese in Richard Oswald's film *Anders als die Andern*, 1919]

[Abb. 10: Magnus Hirschfeld und Karl Giese in Richard Oswalds Film *Anders als die Andern*, 1919]

mediate and long-term consequences on his work. But, looking back on Hirschfeld in the autobiographical *Christopher and His Kind* (1976), he was deeply ambivalent about the German sexual reformer's scientific approach to sexuality. It is also worth pointing out that neither Hirschfeld's sexual science nor any of Isherwood's homosexual experiences made it into his Berlin novels, which played by the rules of public decorum of the English 1930s. The famous revelation that "Berlin meant Boys" came much later, and must be understood as part of an ongoing process of refashioning

dort über sich selbst und über andere sammelte, haben sich ohne Zweifel unmittelbar und auch langfristig auf sein künstlerisches Schaffen ausgewirkt. Allerdings äußerte er sich rückblickend in seinem autobiografischen Werk *Christopher und die Seinen* (»Christopher and His Kind«, 1976) skeptisch über den wissenschaftlichen Ansatz des Sexualreformers im Bereich der Sexualforschung. Interessant ist auch, dass weder über Hirschfelds sexualwissenschaftliche Thesen noch über Isherwoods homosexuelle Erfahrungen etwas in den Berliner Romanen zu lesen ist, die sich an den Regeln des bürgerlichen Anstands der 1930er Jahre orientierten. Die berühmte Offenbarung, dass »Berlin gleichbedeutend mit ›Jungs‹«

of the Berlin myth that was brought about by the decriminalisation of homosexuality in Britain (1967) and the rise of gay rights movements on both sides of the Atlantic.[16] This wave of frank writing about homosexuality also included John Lehmann's 1976 autobiography *In the Purely Pagan Sense*, which contains an account of the author's "education" in Berlin's *lokals* with Isherwood as guide.[17]

Cultures in Dialogue

Retracing the steps of English writers in Berlin enables us to uncover a lasting dialogue between cultures, characterised by a cosmopolitan opening. Returning to Britain or, as in the cases of Auden and Isherwood, moving across the Atlantic, writers brought with them new ideas and new types of knowledge, acting as overt or unconscious cultural mediators, both in a material and in a symbolic sense. Their ability to delve into German culture partly depended on their knowledge of the German language, which can sometimes be difficult to assess retrospectively. Linguistic difficulties notwithstanding, in the early part of the century English accounts frequently mentioned productions by Max Reinhardt and German versions of Shakespeare, showing that Berlin was widely regarded as a centre of innovative theatre. In the 1920s, the interest shifted towards cinema, with the rise to international prominence of the Universum Film AG, or Ufa, which turned Berlin into

war, kam erst viel später und offenbar im Zuge einer kontinuierlichen Umgestaltung des Berliner Mythos, der mit der Entkriminalisierung der Homosexualität in Großbritannien (1967) und dem Aufkommen der Schwulenrechtsbewegung beiderseits des Atlantiks einherging.[16] In diese Sammlung freimütiger Schilderungen über Homosexualität fügte sich auch John Lehmanns Autobiografie *In the Purely Pagan Sense* aus dem Jahr 1976, das einen Bericht darüber enthält, wie der Autor von Isherwood mit den Berliner Lokalitäten bekannt gemacht wurde.[17]

Dialog der Kulturen

Folgt man den Spuren englischer Schriftsteller*innen in Berlin, so zeigt sich ein dauerhafter und von kosmopolitischer Offenheit geprägter Dialog der Kulturen. Bei ihrer Rückkehr nach Großbritannien oder, wie im Falle von Auden und Isherwood, ihrer Reise über den Atlantik führten die Schriftsteller neue Ideen und neue Erkenntnisse im Gepäck und traten offen oder unbewusst in materieller wie symbolischer Hinsicht als Mittler zwischen den Kulturen auf. Ihre Fähigkeit, in die deutsche Kultur abzutauchen, verdankten sie zum Teil ihren deutschen Sprachkenntnissen, die sich rückblickend nicht immer genau bewerten lassen. Ungeachtet möglicher Verständigungsschwierigkeiten werden zu Beginn des Jahrhunderts in vielen englischen Berichten Produktionen von Max Reinhardt und deutschsprachige Shakespeare-Aufführungen erwähnt. Dies ist ein Beleg für Berlins Ruf als Zentrum des innovativen Theaters. In den 1920er Jahren rückte das Kino mit der wachsenden internationalen Bekanntheit der Universum Film AG, der Ufa, die Berlin zur wichtigsten Kinostadt Europas machten, immer weiter in den Mittelpunkt des Interesses. T.E. Hulme, der in

the cinematic city in Europe. Expressionist aesthetics informed English modernism via T. E. Hulme, who had come into contact with Wilhelm Worringer in Berlin; while Auden and Isherwood's dramatic collaborations from the 1930s show the influence of Bertolt Brecht. Alix Strachey's translations of Freud and Stephen Spender's translations of Brecht are also connected with these writers' stays in Berlin. Equally importantly, however, Berlin acted as an international conduit for non-native, as it were, forms of culture, such as psychoanalysis and Soviet cinema, which was subjected to heavy censorship in Britain in the interwar years.

With the rise of Nazism and the growing danger of persecution, some English writers paved the way for Germans or Austrians to escape the horrors at home. Thus, in the mid 1920s, Alix and James Strachey helped the Austrian-born psychoanalyst Melanie Klein to relocate to London, where she became one of the best-known specialists on child analysis. Storm Jameson brought the left-wing writer Lilo Linke to Britain, where she was in exile for a while, before proceeding to Latin America. Isherwood also tried to help a former Berlin lover to emigrate and later wrote about this episode in *Christopher and His Kind*. Most notably, Auden married Erika Mann when her life was in danger under Nazi rule. A remarkable photograph taken in America in 1939 shows a reunion of Thomas Mann's family, which includes his somewhat dishevelled son-in-law Auden, the

Berlin mit Wilhelm Worringer in Kontakt gekommen war, führte dessen expressionistische Ästhetik in den englischen Modernismus ein. Auden und Isherwood schrieben gemeinsam Theaterstücke, die den Einfluss von Bertolt Brecht anklingen lassen. Alix Stracheys Freud-Übersetzungen und Stephen Spenders Brecht-Übersetzungen können ebenfalls mit ihren Berlin-Aufenthalten in Verbindung gebracht werden. Eine vergleichbare Bedeutung kam der Rolle Berlins als Zentrum der Vermittlung kultureller Ausdrucksformen zu, die ihren Ursprung nicht in Deutschland hatten, darunter die Psychoanalyse oder das sowjetische Kino, das in Großbritannien in den Jahren zwischen den Kriegen einer strengen Zensur unterlag.

Angesichts des Machtzuwachses der Nationalsozialisten und der wachsenden Gefahr einer Verfolgung halfen einige englische Schriftsteller*innen Deutschen oder Österreicher*innen dabei, den Schrecken in der Heimat zu entfliehen. So unterstützten Alix und James Strachey Mitte der 1920er Jahre die in Österreich geborene Psychoanalytikerin Melanie Klein bei ihrem Umzug nach London, wo sie eine der bekanntesten Spezialistinnen für Kinderanalyse wurde. Storm Jameson brachte die linke Schriftstellerin Lilo Linke nach Großbritannien, wo sie einige Jahre im Exil lebte, bevor es sie nach Lateinamerika zog. Auch Isherwood versuchte, einem ehemaligen Berliner Geliebten bei der Emigration zu helfen und schrieb darüber später eine Episode in *Christopher und die Seinen*. Ein weiteres bekanntes Beispiel war auch die Eheschließung zwischen Auden und Erika Mann, als ihr Leben unter der Nazi-Herrschaft in Gefahr geriet. Auf einer eindrucksvollen Fotografie von einem Treffen der Familie von Thomas Mann, die 1939 in Amerika aufgenommen wurde, sind auch sein etwas zerzauster Schwiegersohn Auden, dessen On-Off-Geliebter Isherwood und die beiden homosexuel-

latter's on-and-off lover Isherwood, and the German writer's queer literary children Erika and Klaus. Klaus Mann, also a Berlin chronicler and myth-maker, became a friend and collaborator of Isherwood. The ties of cosmopolitan literary collaboration and queer affect that connect this group are an apt image of the complex legacy of Berlin on English writers' lives and careers.

English writers and artists are still in the city today, and still trying to find out 'how to be happy in Berlin'. Recent English

len Kinder des deutschen Schriftstellers, Erika und Klaus, zu sehen. Klaus Mann, ein weiterer Chronist und Mythen-Macher, wurde zum Freund und literarischen Weggefährten von Isherwood. Die Bande der kosmopolitischen literarischen Zusammenarbeit und des queeren Begehrens, die diese Gruppe zusammenhielten, belegen auf eindrucksvolle Weise, das Berlin in den Lebensentwürfen und Laufbahnen englischer Schriftsteller*innen ein vielfältiges Vermächtnis hinterließ.

Auch heute noch leben englische Schriftsteller*innen und Künstler*innen in der Stadt und begeben sich noch immer auf die Suche nach dem

[Fig. 11: The Mann family with Christopher Isherwood and W.H. Auden (left), photograph by Carl Mydans, 1939]

[Abb. 11: Die Mann-Familie mit Christopher Isherwood und W. H. Auden (links), Fotografie von Carl Mydans, 1939]

migrants, whose numbers have surged with the prospect of Brexit, inhabit the city in the wake of their literary predecessors. The Berlin myth is thus an open history. Every new generation of writers and artists rewrites Berlin for themselves, looking back to the 1920s and 1930s, while at the same time using the lens of more recent art forms, most notably popular music and fine art, to shape their own response to the city. The ambivalence often remains, as can be seen in David Bowie, Nick Cave, or the Pet Shop Boys from the realm of music. The same might be said of recent English fiction and art set and produced in Berlin. The range of artists is now much broader than it used to be. And, while class remains a key marker—it is mostly middle-class and highly educated Britons who write about Berlin—there is a greater number of influential women writers, and perhaps more strikingly, it is no longer only white writers who seek out Berlin to explore their often troubled relationship with their home country. With them, Berlin remains an open space of exploration, a place where writers and artists engage with the past and the present simultaneously, as if through a palimpsest. They rewrite the city and, in so doing, rewrite themselves.

Glück in Berlin. Die englischen Migrant*innen der heutigen Zeit, deren Zahl mit der Aussicht auf den Brexit in die Höhe geschnellt ist, sind ihren literarischen Wegbereiter*innen in die Stadt gefolgt. Der Berliner Mythos ist damit zu einer unendlichen Geschichte geworden. Jede neue Generation von Schriftsteller*innen und Künstler*innen entwirft ein eigenes Bild von ihrem Berlin. Dabei blicken sie zum einen zurück auf die 1920er und 1930er Jahre. Zum anderen betrachten sie die Stadt aus der Perspektive modernerer Kunstformen, darunter vor allem die Popmusik und die Bildenden Künste, um ihre eigene Antwort auf die Stadt zu finden. In vielen Fällen bleibt ein ambivalentes Verhältnis zurück, wie es bei Musikern wie David Bowie, Nick Cave oder den Pet Shop Boys zu beobachten ist. Dasselbe ließe sich über zeitgenössische englische Belletristik und Kunst sagen, die Berlin zum Thema hat und auch in der Stadt entstanden ist. Die künstlerische Bandbreite ist heute viel größer als zur damaligen Zeit. Obwohl die Klassenzugehörigkeit noch immer ein wichtiges Merkmal ist – in der Mehrzahl schreiben Brit*innen aus der Mittelklasse mit hohem Bildungsstand über Berlin –, gibt es inzwischen deutlich mehr Frauen unter den Schriftsteller*innen. Und, was womöglich noch bemerkenswerter ist, es sind nicht mehr nur weiße Schriftsteller*innen, die sich nach Berlin begeben, um sich mit ihrem oftmals gestörten Verhältnis zu ihrem Heimatland auseinanderzusetzen. Sie tragen dazu bei, dass Berlin noch immer ein weites Experimentierfeld bietet, auf dem sich Schriftsteller*innen und Künstler*innen wie auf einem Palimpsest gleichzeitig mit der Vergangenheit und der Gegenwart beschäftigen können. Sie erfinden die Stadt und auf diese Weise auch ihr eigenes Leben neu.

Notes

1 John Chancellor: How to be Happy in Berlin, London, Arrowsmith 1929, p. 102.
2 E.M. Forster: The Journals and Diaries of E.M. Forster, ed. by Philip Garner, 3 vols, London, Pickering and Chatto 2011, vol. I, p. 134.
3 Vita Sackville-West to Virginia Woolf, 31 January 1929, in: The Letters of Vita Sackville-West to Virginia Woolf, ed. by Louise DeSalvo and Mitchell Leaska, New York, Morrow repr. 1985, p. 311.
4 Chancellor: How to be Happy in Berlin, p. 10.
5 Elizabeth Wiskemann: The Europe I Saw, London, Collins 1968, p. 18.
6 Curt Moreck: Ein Führer durch das lasterhafte Berlin, Berlin, be.bra (1931) 2018, p. 12.
7 Georg Simmel: The Stranger, in: The Sociology of Georg Simmel, translated by Kurt Wolff, New York, Free Press 1950, pp. 402–408; German original 1908.
8 Harold Nicolson: The Charm of Berlin, in: Der Querschnitt 9/5, May 1929, pp. 345f., here p. 345.
9 See Alison E. Martin: Bloomsbury in Berlin: Vita Sackville-West's *Seducers in Ecuador* on the German Literary Marketplace, in: Modernist Cultures 13/1, 2018, pp. 77–95.
10 Alix Strachey to James Strachey, 23 February 1925, in: Bloomsbury/Freud: The Letters of James and Alix Strachey, 1924–1925, ed. by Perry Meisel and Walter Kendrick, New York, Basic Books 1985, pp. 213–215.
11 Christopher Isherwood: Introduction, in: Mr. Norris and I: An autobiographical Sketch, by Gerald Hamilton, London, Wingate 1956, p. 10.
12 Moreck: Ein Führer durch das lasterhafte Berlin, p. 14.
13 See Aydan Greatrick, 'Goodbye to Berlin': Sexuality, Modernity, and Exile, *Refugee History*, http://refugeehistory.org/blog/2017/10/19/goodbye-to-berlin-sexuality-modernity-and-exile.
14 Wiskemann: The Europe I Saw, p. 13.

Anmerkungen

1 John Chancellor: How to be Happy in Berlin, London, Arrowsmith 1929, S. 102.
2 E.M. Forster: The Journals and Diaries of E.M. Forster, hg. von Philip Garner, 3 Bände, London, Pickering and Chatto 2011, Bd. I, S. 134.
3 Vita Sackville-West an Virginia Woolf, 31. Januar 1929, in: Geliebtes Wesen. Die Briefe von Vita Sackville-West und Virginia Woolf, hg. von Louise DeSalvo und Mitchell A. Leaska, aus dem Englischen von Sybill und Dirk Vanderbeke, Frankfurt a.M., S. Fischer 1995, S. 304.
4 Chancellor: How to be Happy in Berlin, S. 10.
5 Elizabeth Wiskemann: Erlebtes Europa. Ein politischer Reisebericht 1930–1945, Bern und Stuttgart, Verlag Hallwag 1969, S. 18.
6 Curt Moreck: Ein Führer durch das lasterhafte Berlin, Berlin, be.bra (1931) 2018, S. 12.
7 Georg Simmel: Soziologie. Untersuchungen über die Formen der Vergesellschaftung, Berlin, Duncker & Humblot 1908, Kapitel IX: Der Raum und die räumlichen Ordnungen der Gesellschaft, Exkurs über den Fremden, S. 509–512.
8 Harold Nicolson: The Charm of Berlin, in: Der Querschnitt 9/5, Mai 1929, S. 345f., hier S. 345.
9 Siehe Alison E. Martin: Bloomsbury in Berlin: Vita Sackville-West's *Seducers in Ecuador* on the German Literary Marketplace, in: Modernist Cultures 13/1, 2018, S. 77–95.
10 Alix Strachey an James Strachey, 25. Februar 1925, in: Kultur und Psychoanalyse in Bloomsbury und Berlin. Die Briefe von James und Alix Strachey 1924–1925, hg. von Perry Meisel und Walter Kendrick, aus dem Englischen übersetzt von Rotraut De Clerck, Stuttgart, Verlag Internationale Psychoanalyse 1995, S. 328–330.
11 Christopher Isherwood: Einleitung, in: Mr. Norris and I: An autobiographical Sketch, by Gerald Hamilton, London, Wingate 1956, S. 10.
12 Moreck: Ein Führer durch das lasterhafte Berlin, S. 14.
13 Siehe Aydan Greatrick, ›Goodbye to Berlin‹: Sexuality, Modernity, and Exile, *Refugee History*, http://refugeehistory.org/blog/2017/10/19/goodbye-to-berlin-sexuality-modernity-and-exile.
14 Wiskemann: Erlebtes Europa, S. 9.

15 Alix Strachey to James Strachey, 2 February 1925; 25 February 1925, in: Bloomsbury/Freud: The Letters of James and Alix Strachey, p. 194, 218.
16 Christopher Isherwood: Christopher and His Kind, London, Vintage (1976) 2012, p. 3.
17 John Lehmann: In the Purely Pagan Sense, London, GMP (1976) 1989, p. 44.

a Vita Sackville-West to Virginia Woolf, 6 February 1929, in: The Letters of Vita Sackville-West to Virginia Woolf, ed. by Louise DeSalvo and Mitchell Leaska, New York, Morrow repr. 1985, p. 318.
b Christopher Isherwood: Goodbye to Berlin, in: The Berlin Novels, London, Vintage 1999, p. 383.

15 Alix Strachey an James Strachey, 2. Februar 1925; 25. Februar 1925, in: Kultur und Psychoanalyse in Bloomsbury und Berlin, S. 298, 329.
16 Christopher Isherwood: Willkommen in Berlin. Christopher und die Seinen, aus dem Englischen von Stefan Troßbach, 1. Auflage dieser Ausgabe, Berlin, Bruno Gmünder Verlag 2014, S. 9.
17 John Lehmann: In the Purely Pagan Sense, London, GMP (1976) 1989, S. 44.

a Vita Sackville-West an Virginia Woolf, 6. Februar 1929, in: Geliebtes Wesen. Die Briefe von Vita Sackville-West und Virginia Woolf, hg. von Louise DeSalvo und Mitchell A. Leaska, aus dem Englischen von Sybill und Dirk Vanderbeke, Frankfurt a.M., S. Fischer 1995, S. 312f.
b Christopher Isherwood: Lebwohl Berlin, aus dem Englischen von Kathrin Passig und Gerhard Henschel, 3. Auflage, Hamburg, Hoffmann und Campe (1939) 2019, S. 157.

Stefano Evangelista

Writing Decadent Berlin
Literarische Erkundungen der Berliner Dekadenz

Cities are physical spaces constructed by architects and urban planners. But they are also, at the same time, imaginary places shaped by artists and writers: novels and poems, films or, more humbly, postcards and advertisements constantly re-invent the city by making it legible in new ways, opening up paths through the urban maze, fixing points of view for future spectators. To walk the city, to inhabit it, and to write about it involve engaging with this double—material and immaterial—heritage. When we look back to the Berlin of one hundred years ago, we must therefore picture the city maps of old guide books as being overlaid with an intangible literary topography. British writers participated in this 'production' of the city long before Christopher Isherwood's novels fixed a popular image of Berlin for audiences in Britain and around the world. In particular, starting from the end of the nineteenth century, several writers attempted to capture the decadent fascination of Berlin, manifested in its mixture of hedonism, cosmopolitanism, sexual transgression, and stark juxtaposition of glamour and

Städte als physische Räume werden von Architekt*innen und Stadtplaner*innen gestaltet. Doch auch Künstler*innen und Schriftsteller*innen bilden Städte als imaginäre Orte ab. In Romanen und Gedichten, Filmen oder, in noch einfacherer Form, auf Postkarten und Werbeplakaten werden Städte unaufhörlich neu erfunden: mit alternativen Darstellungen, durch die Erkundung neuer Wege im Labyrinth der Stadt, oder indem der Blick künftiger Besucher*innen auf bestimmte Aspekte gelenkt wird. Will man sich eine Stadt erschließen, sie bewohnen und über sie schreiben, muss man sich mit diesem doppelten – materiellen und immateriellen – Erbe auseinandersetzen. Für diesen Rückblick auf das Berlin der 1920er Jahre muss man sich daher vorstellen, dass sich eine literarische Topografie wie ein Schatten über die Stadtpläne alter Reiseführer legt. Schon lange bevor Christopher Isherwood mit seinen Romanen bei seiner britischen und internationalen Leserschaft ein populäres Image von Berlin prägte, leisteten britische Schriftsteller*innen ihren Beitrag zu einer solchen »Inszenierung« der Stadt. Insbesondere seit dem Ende des 19. Jahrhunderts versuchten viele von ihnen, in Worte zu fassen, was ihre Faszination für diese Dekadenz ausmachte, die in der Berliner Melange aus Hedonismus, Weltbürgertum, sexuellen Ausschweifungen und in dem harten Kontrast

squalor. Indeed, decadence became one of the key ingredients, as it were, of the Berlin myth associated with the period of the Weimar Republic. This essay unravels some of the literary layers of decadent Berlin that accrued before the 'golden' twenties, sometimes in the form of fragments and false starts, as British authors followed in each other's footsteps in their efforts to read and write the German capital.

We could trace the start of the British fascination with decadent Berlin to 1891, the year in which English writer Arthur Symons spent two months getting to know the city in the company of Josiah Flynt, an American anthropologist who was studying at the Friedrich Wilhelm University. Symons was fast becoming England's leading decadent poet. Flynt was famous for his habit of disappearing off for long periods in order to live among homeless people. The two writers planned to work together on a sociological study of the nocturnal goings-on in Berlin cafés, which they intended to observe from 10:30 at night till 6:00 in the morning.[1] Their findings were to appear as a luxurious illustrated volume, complete with portraits and autographs, half scientific record, half tantalising invitation to explore the nightlife of this up-and-coming European metropolis of which the British still knew relatively little. The integrated use of the literary and photographic mediums, still rare at the time, was to create a sense of documentary realism but also map a human geography of Berlin's bohemian scene.

zwischen Glanz und Elend zum Ausdruck kam. Tatsächlich entwickelte sich die Dekadenz zu einem der Hauptmerkmale des Berliner Mythos im Berlin der Weimarer Epoche. Mit diesem Essay sollen einige der literarischen Schichten dieser großstädtischen Dekadenz aufgedeckt werden, die sich vor den »Goldenen Zwanzigern« bildeten. Dabei handelt es sich mitunter um Fragmente oder erste Entwürfe. Zu dieser Zeit beflügelten sich britische Autor*innen gegenseitig in ihrem Bestreben, das Leben in der deutschen Hauptstadt literarisch zu erfassen und zu beschreiben.

Die Spur der britischen Faszination für die Dekadenz in Berlin lässt sich bis in das Jahr 1891 zurückverfolgen. In diesem Jahr kam der britische Schriftsteller Arthur Symons für einen zweimonatigen Aufenthalt in die Stadt. Auf seinen Erkundungstouren begleitete ihn der amerikanische Anthropologe Josiah Flynt, der an der Friedrich-Wilhelm-Universität studierte. Symons war Englands führender Dichter der Dekadenz. Flynt war bekannt dafür, immer wieder für längere Zeit zu verschwinden und unter Obdachlosen zu leben. Die beiden Schriftsteller planten eine gemeinsame Studie zum nächtlichen Treiben in den Berliner Cafés. Dafür wollten sie sich in der Zeit zwischen 22.30 Uhr nachts und 6.00 Uhr morgens auf Beobachtungstour begeben.[1] Sie beabsichtigten, ihre Ergebnisse in einem reich illustrierten Band mit Portraits und Autogrammen zu veröffentlichen. Das Buch sollte wissenschaftliche Fakten liefern und zugleich als Anregung dienen, das Nachtleben dieser in Großbritannien noch immer relativ unbekannten aufstrebenden europäischen Metropole zu erkunden. Durch die zu dieser Zeit noch seltene intermediale Verbindung von Literatur und Fotografie sollte zum einen der Eindruck eines dokumentarischen Realismus, zum anderen aber auch ein demografischer Überblick über die Angehörigen der Berliner Bohème vermittelt werden.

However, something must have gone wrong in Berlin. For the book never materialised and all that came out of the trip was a single poem titled "Emmy", after a Polish girl Symons met during one of his amblings around the pleasure quarters. Set in a seedy Berlin dancing-hall, "Emmy" adopts an uncharacteristically moralistic tone for Symons, who condemns society and the man who first wronged the young girl, dooming her to a life of prostitution. As the only Berliner—significantly, a foreign migrant—to have emerged out of the aborted book, Symons's Emmy is a suitably haunting emanation of the Berlin night:

> Emmy's laughter rings in my ears, as bright,
>   Fresh and sweet as the voice of a mountain brook,
> And still I hear her telling us tales that night,
>   Out of Boccaccio's book.[2]

A vulnerable being who has fallen prey to the sex industry of the modern metropolis, Emmy is also an articulate voice who mesmerises the older listeners who congregate around her with strings of obscene tales. She is the debased bard of decadent Berlin.

Published many years later, the notes that Symons took in 1891 may hold a clue for his failure to write about the city. There, he recounts a typical night spent with his bohemian male friends, going from bar to increasingly squalid bar in the area around Friedrichstraße station: the evening started in the elegant Concert de

Noblesse on Friedrichstraße and ended in the seedy Preinitz on Leipziger Straße. The impressions are punctuated by a series of uncanny encounters: Emmy, an "enormous *décolletée* woman with the face of a man …", etc.[3] The title that Symons gave to his recollections is telling: "Berlin's Discomforts". The idea of discomfort has a heavy proto-psychoanalytic flavour that anticipates Freud's "Unbehagen" in *Civilisation and its Discontents* ("Das Unbehagen in der Kultur", 1930). To Symons, Berlin lays bare the clash between civilisation and the basest desires of the individual. Indeed, with its atmosphere of militaristic authority and surveillance, the city tests the very notions of civilisation and civility associated with metropolitan life. Symons vividly remembers being challenged by an army officer in a tram just for having his legs stretched out, and constantly being told off for having done something wrong.

Symons's fragmented impressions of Berlin are typical of a generation of cosmopolitan English writers who identified strongly with Paris and were outspokenly Francophile in their tastes. In "Berlin's Discomforts", Symons almost takes pride in his ignorance of the German language, as if he wanted to be perfectly clear about his lack of sympathy with German culture. Symons approached Berlin as a sensation-hungry *flâneur* who followed in the literary footsteps of Baudelaire and the French decadents. To the English writers of the turn of the century, however, there

schäbiger: Der Abend begann im eleganten *Concert de Noblesse* an der Friedrichstraße und endete in einer Kaschemme mit dem Namen *Preinitz* an der Leipziger Straße. Seine Berichte stecken voller merkwürdiger Begegnungen. Wenn er beispielsweise Emmy darstellt, beschreibt er eine »Frau mit einem ausladenden Dekolleté und dem Gesicht eines Mannes«.[3] Symons gab seinen Erinnerungen den aussagekräftigen Titel *Berlin's Discomforts* (Berliner Unannehmlichkeiten). Die Idee der Unannehmlichkeit hat einen starken proto-psychoanalytischen Beigeschmack, der Freuds Begriff des »Unbehagens« in *Das Unbehagen in der Kultur* (1930) vorwegnimmt. Aus Symons' Sicht tritt in Berlin der Konflikt zwischen der Zivilisation und den niedersten Bedürfnissen des Individuums deutlich zutage. Tatsächlich stellt die Stadt angesichts ihrer militaristischen, durch Autorität und Überwachung geprägten Atmosphäre die mit dem großstädtischen Leben assoziierten Begriffe der Zivilisation und des zivilen Verhaltens auf die Probe. Symons erinnert sich lebhaft daran, wie ihn ein Armeeoffizier in der Straßenbahn nur deshalb zur Ordnung rief, weil er seine Beine ausgestreckt hatte, und wie er auch sonst immerzu auf sein Fehlverhalten hingewiesen wurde.

Symons' bruchstückhafte Berliner Impressionen sind charakteristisch für seine Generation weltgewandter englischer Schriftsteller, die sich stark mit Paris identifizierten und in Stilfragen ausdrücklich an Frankreich orientierten. In *Berlin Discomforts* brüstet sich Symons fast schon mit seinen mangelhaften Deutschkenntnissen, als wolle er seine Geringschätzung für die deutsche Kultur mit aller Deutlichkeit zum Ausdruck bringen. Symons erkundete Berlin gleich einem sensationshungrigen Flaneur, der in die literarischen Fußstapfen Baudelaires und der Vertreter der dekadenten Bewegung in Frank-

was no German Baudelaire, who could lead them through the underworld of the German capital and teach them how to see poetry in its squalor. In the absence of such a literary guide, Symons's tour of the nightspots of decadent Berlin collapses into note form: it fails to take shape as a piece of literature.

An even more extreme response to the discomforts of Berlin came from Rupert Brooke. The photogenic Brooke, whose photographs always seem to burst with youth and polymorphous sexuality, has enjoyed lasting popularity in Britain as a romantic poet-hero after his untimely death in the First World War. In 1912, Brooke spent some time in Berlin staying with his friend, the journalist Dudley Ward. We know from his letters that he visited art exhibitions and enjoyed a performance of Wedekind's *Spring Awakening*. Otherwise, he reported to his friends back home, he spent most days sitting in cafés and consorting with English journalists.

It was in the Café des Westens that Brooke composed one of his most famous poems, "The Old Vicarage, Grantchester". Grantchester is a village just outside Cambridge, where Brooke went to university. Brooke's verses depict it as a sanctuary of unspoilt nature and time-honoured traditions: ancient chestnut trees make shady tunnels above clean streams and every stone tells stories of old poets and honest country folk. Now and then, the reality of Berlin breaks the spell of this nostalgic

reich tritt. Doch für die englischen Schriftsteller der Jahrhundertwende gab es keinen deutschen Baudelaire, der ihnen auf einer Führung durch die Unterwelt der deutschen Hauptstadt die Poesie des Berliner Elends nahegebracht hätte. In Ermangelung eines solchen literarischen Stadtführers beschränken sich Symons Berichte über seine Besuche in den Nachtlokalen des dekadenten Berlins auf kurze Notizen, die sich nicht zu einem literarischen Werk zusammenfügen ließen.

Eine noch extremere Reaktion auf die Unannehmlichkeiten des Berliner Lebens lieferte Rupert Brooke. Aufnahmen des fotogenen Brooke zeigen ihn, als würde er stets überschäumen vor Jugendlichkeit und polymorpher Sexualität. Trotz seines verfrühten Tods im Ersten Weltkrieg erfreut er sich in Großbritannien einer anhaltenden Beliebtheit als romantischer Dichterheld. Im Jahr 1912 verbrachte Brooke einige Zeit in Berlin bei seinem Freund, dem Journalisten Dudley Ward. Seinen Briefen ist zu entnehmen, dass er Kunstausstellungen und eine Aufführung von Wedekinds *Frühlingserwachen* besuchte. Darüber hinaus verbrachte er die meiste Zeit in Cafés und traf sich mit englischen Journalisten, wie er seinen Freund*innen in der Heimat berichtete.

Im Café des Westens verfasste Brooke eines seiner berühmtesten Gedichte, *The Old Vicarage, Grantchester* (Das alte Pfarrhaus in Grantchester). Grantchester ist ein Dorf vor den Toren von Cambridge, wo Brooke seine Studienzeit verbrachte. In seinen Versen beschreibt Brooke das Dorf als einen Ort der altehrwürdigen Traditionen und der Zuflucht inmitten unberührter Natur: Alte Kastanien bilden schattige Tunnel über dem klaren Wasser der Bäche und jeder Stein erzählt eine Geschichte von alten Dichtern und ehrlichen Landbewohnern. Immer wieder wird der Zauber dieser nostalgischen Träumereien von der

[Fig. 12: Café des Westens, Ernst Pauly, Kurfürstendamm 26, postcard, photographer and date unknown]

[Abb. 12: Café des Westens, Ernst Pauly, Kurfürstendamm 26, Postkarte, Fotograf und Datum unbekannt]

reverie as the voice of other customers of the Café des Westens is interpolated into the fabric of the poem:

> Du lieber Gott!
> Here am I, sweating, sick, and hot,
> And there the shadowed waters fresh
> Lean up to embrace the naked flesh.
> Temperamentvoll German Jews
> Drink beer around;—and there the dews
> Are soft beneath a morn of gold.[4]

Berliner Wirklichkeit durchbrochen, wenn sich die Stimmen anderer Gäste im Café des Westens unter die Verse mischen:

> Du lieber Gott!
> Here am I, sweating, sick, and hot,
> And there the shadowed waters fresh
> Lean up to embrace the naked flesh.
> Temperamentvoll German Jews
> Drink beer around; — and there the dews
> Are soft beneath a morn of gold.[4]

Orte
Café des Westens

Autorencafés waren eine wichtige Besonderheit im Berlin des frühen 20. Jahrhunderts. Sie übten eine große Anziehungskraft auf britische Reisende aus, die solche halböffentlichen Schauplätze des kreativen Lebens nicht kannten. Die Mehrzahl dieser Cafés befand sich auf dem Kurfürstendamm oder am Potsdamer Platz. Im Café des Westens verkehrte vor dem Ersten Weltkrieg auch der berühmte englische Dichter Rupert Brooke. Er schrieb dort krank vor Heimweh sein bekanntes Gedicht »The Old Vicarage, Grantchester«, in dem auch das Café eine Rolle spielt. Der Kontrast zwischen dieser Klagehymne auf das englische Wesen und den vielfach schillernden Verheißungen des urbanen Berliner Nachtlebens hätte größer nicht sein können. Dieser berühmte Künstler*innen-Treffpunkt befand sich auf dem Kurfürstendamm.

Places
Café des Westens

Writers' cafés were an important feature of early 20th-century Berlin and highly attractive to British travellers, who were unfamiliar with this particular kind of semi-public space from back home. Most of the cafés could be found on Kurfürstendamm or on Potsdamer Platz. The Café des Westens, which the poet Rupert Brooke visited before the First World War, suffering from home-sickness, features in his well-known poem, "The Old Vicarage, Grantchester", an elegiac evocation of Englishness which could not stand in greater contrast with the ambivalent multifaceted attractions of Berlin's urban nightlife. This famous meeting place for artists was situated on Kurfürstendamm.

Brooke was in Berlin during the height of the expressionist movement. His friend T.E. Hulme, with whom he spent time in Berlin, was personally acquainted with Wilhelm Worringer and introduced the latter's aesthetic theories into England. Brooke's poem "The Night Journey", also written in Berlin, flirts with a staccato expressionist style to describe the overhead railway crossing at Zoo station, which the poet reputedly came across during a walk with Hulme. But "The Old Vicarage, Grantches-

Brooke kam auf dem Höhepunkt der expressionistischen Bewegung nach Berlin. Sein Freund T.E. Hulme, den er dort traf, war mit Wilhelm Worringer bekannt und brachte dessen ästhetische Theorien nach England. In seinem Gedicht *The Night Journey* (»Die nächtliche Reise«), das ebenfalls in Berlin entstand, spielt Brooke mit stakkatoartigen, expressionistischen Stilmitteln. Er will auf diese Weise das Geräusch der vorbeifahrenden Hochbahn am Bahnhof Zoo wiedergeben, das er vermutlich auf einem Spaziergang mit Hulme vernommen hatte. *The Old Vicarage, Grantchester* dagegen bleibt vom Stil der *Avantgarde* voll-

ter" is conspicuously untouched by the style of the *avant garde* even as Brooke writes from one of the locations most beloved by the expressionists. That very year, Else Lasker-Schüler published her epistolary novel *Mein Herz*, also written from the Café des Westens, which celebrates the transformative aesthetics of urban modernity and its effect on gender relations. By contrast, Brooke's pastoral fantasy, with its clichés about rural life and sentimental reverie about Little England, is the antitype of the cosmopolitan expressionist café poetry exemplified by Lasker-Schüler.

Despite all this, however, "The Old Vicarage, Grantchester" is still, very self-consciously, a Berlin poem. Brooke is careful to underscore the importance of the setting by including the place and time of composition as a subtitle: "Cafe des Westens, Berlin, 1912". The Berlin café—full of foreign voices and unfamiliar faces—is where English domesticity suddenly becomes overwhelmingly appealing to the home- and love-sick Brooke, who in an early draft of the poem styled himself as a "Sentimental Exile". "The Old Vicarage, Grantchester" is a poem of contrasts. As with Symons, Berlin stands for an inhospitable and somewhat uncanny modernity that is hard to decipher and write about. England, by contrast, is expansive, sun-flooded, legible, soft-edged, and welcoming:

oh! yet
Stands the Church clock at ten to three?
And is there honey still for tea?

kommen unberührt, auch wenn Brooke das Gedicht an einem unter Expressionisten ganz besonders beliebten Ort schrieb.

Im selben Jahr veröffentlichte Else Lasker-Schüler ihren Briefroman *Mein Herz*, der ebenfalls im Café des Westens entstand. Er ist eine Lobeshymne auf die transformative Ästhetik der urbanen Moderne und ihre Auswirkungen auf die Beziehungen zwischen den Geschlechtern. Im Gegensatz dazu bildet Brookes pastorale Fantasie mit ihren klischeehaften Vorstellungen vom Leben auf dem Lande und ihren sentimentalen Träumereien von Klein-England den literarischen Gegenentwurf zur weltgewandten expressionistischen Kaffeehaus-Lyrik einer Lasker-Schüler.

Und doch ist *The Old Vicarage, Grantchester* auf seine ganz eigene Weise ein Berlin-Gedicht. Brooke will unter allen Umständen die Bedeutung der besonderen Atmosphäre hervorheben, wenn er Ort und Zeit der Entstehung in einem Untertitel erwähnt: »Café des Westens, Berlin, 1912«. In diesem Berliner Café mit seinem Gewirr unterschiedlicher Sprachen und unbekannter Gesichter überkommt den von Heimweh und Liebeskummer geplagten Brooke, der sich in einer früheren Fassung des Gedichts als »sentimentalen Exilanten« bezeichnet hatte, mit einem Mal eine überwältigende Sehnsucht nach englischer Häuslichkeit. *The Old Vicarage, Grantchester* ist ein Gedicht der Gegensätze. Wie auch bei Symons steht Berlin für eine ungastliche und auf gewisse Weise auch bedrohliche Moderne, die sich nur schwer ergründen und in Worte fassen lässt. Im Gegensatz dazu ist England ein sonnendurchfluteter Ort, der viel Platz bietet, keine Rätsel aufgibt und eine weiche und angenehme Ankunft garantiert:

oh! yet
Stands the Church clock at ten to three?
And is there honey still for tea?[5]

The famous closing gambit of the poem captures an ideal of timelessness, identified with England, that is extremely reassuring to Brooke and is quite the opposite of the expressionists' fascination with movement. In fact, against the backdrop of Berlin, Brooke managed to create the myth of Grantchester as an unspoilt haven of Englishness—a myth that thrives to this day as visitors to the village easily find out. A suspicious reader, however, may well feel more drawn to the unglamorous, cosmopolitan, grotty city glimpsed between the lines. For there is something cloying and even claustrophobic in Brooke's English pastoral, exacerbated by the casual anti-Semitism.

After the First World War, the revolution that transformed the monarchy led by Kaiser Wilhelm to the democratic Weimar Republic softened the Prussian gruffness that grated on Symons and Brooke; and the inflation and its aftermath made the city a cheap destination for English visitors with pounds in their pockets. One of these was the young writer and music critic, Edward Sackville-West. Eddy, as he was known, was a cousin of the writer Vita Sackville-West. His stunning ancestral home, Knole, was used by Virginia Woolf as the setting for her experimental, gender-bending *Orlando* (1928). Eddy, who was spending time in Dresden pursuing his musical interests, came to Berlin via his Bloomsbury connections, notably Vita's husband Harold Nicolson, who was then *chargé d'affaires* in the British Embassy.

Mit dem berühmten Schlussvers des Gedichts soll ein Ideal der Zeitlosigkeit vermittelt werden, das England zugeschrieben wird. Auf Brooke hat es eine ausgesprochen beruhigende Wirkung und bildet einen klaren Kontrast zu Bewegung und Fortschritt, der die Expressionisten faszinierte. Brooke ist es tatsächlich gelungen, vor dem Hintergrund Berlins den Mythos von Grantchester als unberührten Zufluchtsort für das englische Wesen zu begründen – ein Mythos, der sich bis heute gehalten hat, wie Besucher*innen des Dorfes schnell feststellen werden. Misstrauische Leser*innen werden sich womöglich mehr von der unglamourösen, weltoffenen, heruntergekommenen Stadt angezogen fühlen, die zwischen den Zeilen durchscheint. Denn Brookes Beschreibung des englischen Landlebens wirkt bisweilen sentimental und beklemmend, ein Eindruck, der sich durch vereinzelte antisemitische Anklänge zusätzlich verstärkt.

Nach dem Ersten Weltkrieg und der anschließenden Revolution, in deren Folge die Monarchie unter Kaiser Wilhelm durch die Weimarer Republik abgelöst wurde, nahm die preußische Schroffheit, unter der Symons und Brooke gelitten hatten, ein wenig ab. Darüber hinaus entwickelte sich die Stadt durch die Inflation und ihre Folgen zu einem günstigen Reiseziel für englische Besucher*innen mit Pfundnoten in der Tasche. Einer von ihnen war der junge Schriftsteller und Musikkritiker Edward Sackville-West. Eddy, wie er genannt wurde, war ein Cousin der Schriftstellerin Vita Sackville-West. Das prächtige Stammhaus seiner Familie, Knole House, inspirierte Virginia Woolf zum Schauplatz ihres experimentellen Romans *Orlando* (1928), in dem sie die Geschlechtergrenzen auslotete. Eddy, der wegen seines Musikinteresses eine Zeit lang in Dresden gelebt hatte, folgte seinen Bloomsbury-Bekannten nach Berlin. Darunter war vor allem Vitas Ehemann

[Fig. 13: Edward ("Eddy") Sackville-West, photograph by Bassano Ltd, 1930]

[Abb. 13: Edward (»Eddy«) Sackville-West, Fotografie von Bassano Ltd, 1930]

Nicolson, who had written a biography of Paul Verlaine, shared Eddy's fascination with decadent literature. A photograph from this period shows an ethereal Sackville-West almost as a ghost from the *fin de siècle* or a caricature by Max Beerbohm.

Like Auden and many other English men of his class and generation, Sackville-West first went to Germany in order to be cured of his homosexuality. What he found instead was a place where his sexual tastes could be expressed more freely than at home. After taking him to the Embassy Club, Nicolson introduced Sackville-West to the more colourful side of the Berlin nightlife, including the Eldorado and various gay bars. In a letter to E.M. Forster, whom he vainly tried to lure to the city,

Harold Nicolson, der 1927 zum *Chargé d'Affaires* an die britische Botschaft berufen worden war. Nicolson, der eine Biografie über Paul Verlaine verfasst hatte, teilte Eddys Begeisterung für dekadente Literatur. Auf einer Fotografie aus dieser Zeit ist ein der Welt entrückter Sackville-West zu sehen, der etwas von einem Geist des *Fin de Siècle* oder einer Karikatur von Max Beerbohm hat.

Sackville-West zog es wie Auden und viele andere Engländer seiner sozialen Schicht und Generation zunächst nach Deutschland, um sich von seiner Homosexualität heilen zu lassen. Stattdessen fand er mit Berlin jedoch einen Ort vor, an dem er sich seinen sexuellen Vorlieben viel freier als in der Heimat widmen konnte. Nach einem Besuch im Embassy Club machte Nicolson seinen Freund Sackville-West mit der schillernden Seite des Berliner Nachtlebens vertraut, zu der das Eldorado und zahlreiche Schwulenbars gehör-

Eddy wrote about the astonishing openness of the Berlin gay life:

> There are even large dance places for inverts. And some of the people one sees—huge men with breasts like women & faces like Ottoline [Morrell], dressed as female Spanish dancers—are really quite unintelligible ... They just moon about like great question marks ...[5]

Aside from showing us how knowledge about the permissiveness of Berlin circulated among the male homosexual literary elite in Britain, this letter is striking for posing the problem of how to understand and how to represent the gender transgressions of Berlin from the point of view of a culture, such as the British, that was still extremely squeamish about sex. In his diaries and letters Sackville-West broods again and again over his fascination with the squalor and the ugliness of the city, which he overlays with records of his sexual exploits. Writing to Virginia Woolf, who had recently published her classic modernist urban novel, *Mrs Dalloway* (1925), he compared living in Berlin to "a Lear nonsense rhyme re-written by Joyce".[6] The epigram is too self-conscious to be brilliant. But it is a perfect expression of the city as literary text: Sackville-West translates Berlin into an unlikely hybrid of Victorian light verse and experimental modernism, reflecting perhaps its perceived parvenu status as a cosmopolitan metropolis. The attempt to frame the city through an avant-garde style would be left to Stevie Smith

ten. In einem Brief an E.M. Forster, den er erfolglos in die Stadt zu locken versuchte, beschrieb Eddy die erstaunliche Offenheit des schwulen Lebens in Berlin:

> Hier gibt es sogar große Tanzbars für Invertierte. Und man bekommt unglaubliche Gestalten zu sehen – riesige Männer mit Brüsten wie Frauen & Gesichtern wie Ottoline [Morrell], im Gewand spanischer Tänzerinnen –, die sich beim besten Willen nicht einordnen lassen [...] Wie große Fragezeichen schweben sie durch den Raum ...[6]

Dieser Brief zeigt zum einen, wie sich die Kunde von der sexuellen Freizügigkeit Berlins in der schwulen literarischen Elite Großbritanniens verbreitete. Zum anderen macht er deutlich, wie schwierig es aus der Perspektive einer in sexuellen Dingen nach wie vor ausgesprochen verklemmten Kultur wie der britischen sein musste, die fließenden Geschlechtergrenzen in Berlin zu verstehen und in Worte zu fassen. In seinen Briefen und Tagebüchern verliert sich Sackville-West wieder und wieder in Grübeleien über seine Faszination für das Elend und die Hässlichkeit der Stadt, die er mit Berichten über seine sexuellen Abenteuer ausschmückt. In einem Brief an Virginia Woolf, die zu dieser Zeit gerade ihren klassischen Stadtroman der Moderne, *Mrs Dalloway* (1925), veröffentlicht hatte, verglich er das Leben in Berlin mit einem »von Joyce umgeschriebenen Nonsens-Vers von Lear«.[7] Um wirklich brillant zu sein, kommt diese epigrammatische Aussage zu affektiert daher. Doch sie beschreibt auf eindrückliche Weise die Stadt als literarischen Text: Sackville-West überträgt das Berliner Leben in eine ungewöhnliche Mischform aus heiteren viktorianischen Versen und experimentellem Modernismus. Möglicherweise

and Djuna Barnes, who would both include Berlin scenes in their 1936 modernist novels *Nightwood* and *Novel on Yellow Paper*.

Sackville-West's own Berlin fiction was rather tame compared to Joyce, Woolf, and the modernists, although his short story "Hellmut lies in the Sun" was included by Elizabeth Bowen in the 1937 *Faber Book of Modern Stories* and has since won some critical acclaim. By that point in the 1930s, however, Christopher Isherwood was already gaining his reputation as the British authority on decadent Berlin. Like Symons, Brooke, and Eddy Sackville-West, Isherwood approached Berlin with the attitude of a *flâneur*—granted, a modernised *flâneur* in the more casual post-war style—at a time in which the global epicentre of *flânerie* was shifting from Paris to Berlin. Franz Hessel's *Walking in Berlin* (*Spazieren in Berlin*, 1929), which was published the year of Isherwood's first visit, gave a stylish and incredibly vivid picture of Berlin as a perpetually unfolding, variegated spectacle. Hessel showed Berliners how to practise the art of city-living that his friend Walter Benjamin was exploring critically in the sprawling *Passagenwerk* or *Arcades Project*, which also started appearing around this time. Eugene Szatmari's *Was nicht im Baedeker steht* (1927) and Curt Moreck's (pseud. for Konrad Hämmerling) *Führer durch das 'lasterhafte' Berlin* (1931) provided a more specialised coverage, where the emphasis was on the quirky and debauched sectors of the city's nightlife that gave Berlin its transgressive reputation.

will er darauf anspielen, dass Berlin den Status als weltoffene Stadt noch nicht allzu lange genießt. Der Versuch, ein avantgardistisches Bild von der Stadt zu zeichnen, sollte Djuna Barnes und Stevie Smith vorbehalten bleiben, deren modernistische Romane *Nachtgewächs* (»Nightwood«) und *Roman auf gelbem Papier* (»Novel on Yellow Paper«) aus dem Jahr 1936 beide ebenfalls zum Teil in Berlin spielen.

Sackville-Wests eigene Berlin-Prosa war im Vergleich zu Joyce, Woolf und den Vertreter*innen der Moderne eher zahm. Trotzdem wurde seine Kurzgeschichte *Hellmut lies in the Sun* 1937 von Elizabeth Bowen in das *Faber Book of Modern Stories* aufgenommen und fand seitdem lobende Erwähnung bei Kritiker*innen. Allerdings war Christopher Isherwood zu diesem Zeitpunkt der 1930er Jahre bereits damit beschäftigt, seinen Ruf als britischer Fachmann für Berliner Dekadenz zu festigen. Wie Symons, Brooke und Eddy Sackville-West erkundete auch er Berlin mit der Haltung des Flaneurs – wenn auch des modernen Flaneurs im lässigen Nachkriegsstil – zu einer Zeit, in der sich der weltweite Mittelpunkt der *Flânerie* stetig von Paris nach Berlin verlagerte. In seinem Buch *Spazieren in Berlin* (1929), das im Jahr von Isherwoods erstem Berlin-Besuch veröffentlicht wurde, zeichnete Franz Hessel ein stilvolles und ausgesprochen lebhaftes Bild von Berlin als Schauplatz eines wechselhaften und abwechslungsreichen Spektakels. Er gab Berliner*innen praktische Hinweise zur Kunst des Stadtlebens, mit der sich auch sein Freund Walter Benjamin in seinem umfangreichen *Passagenwerk* oder *Arkaden-Projekt*, von dem Teile ebenfalls zu dieser Zeit erschienen, kritisch auseinandersetzte. Eugene Szatmaris *Was nicht im Baedeker steht* (1927) und Curt Morecks (Pseudonym für Konrad Hämmerling) *Führer durch das »lasterhafte« Berlin* (1931) widmeten sich spezielleren Themen und vor allem

Isherwood was one of the first British writers to enter the deep relationship with city space that characterised the German literature of *flânerie*. Hessel wrote that "[t]he flaneur reads the street, and human faces, displays, window dresses, café terraces, trains, cars, and trees become letters that yield the words, sentences, and pages of a book that is always new."[7] Isherwood's Berlin stories convey a similar sense of the city's facility to display itself as literature. His autobiographical narrators—one of whom is named Christopher Isherwood—are attentive observers of the city-as-spectacle, amplified by frequent references to cinema, advertising, songs and, later on, by the grotesque spectacle of Nazism. In a famous passage from *Goodbye to Berlin*, Isherwood describes himself as "a camera with its shutter open, quite passive, recording, not thinking."[8] But of course Isherwood's literary photography, far from being passive, is in fact the product of a highly self-conscious literary technique. It is significant that, while he was in Berlin, Isherwood was busy translating Baudelaire, the author who inspired Walter Benjamin with some of his most powerful insights on urban modernity. There is something profoundly, and studiedly, Baudelairean in Isherwood's photographic outlook: he recoils from passing moral judgements on what the city presents to him—be it poverty, alienation, or sexual excess—retaining the blasé outlook of the worldly *flâneur*.

In his first Berlin novel, *Mr Norris Changes Trains* (1935), while "young men auch der extravaganten Seite des zügellosen Berliner Nachtlebens, die ihren Ruf als Stadt der sexuellen Freizügigkeit begründete.

Isherwood ging als einer der ersten britischen Schriftsteller das intensive Verhältnis mit dem städtischen Raum ein, das die deutsche Flaneur-Literatur kennzeichnet. Hessel schrieb dazu: »Flanieren ist eine Art Lektüre der Straße, wobei Menschengesichter, Auslagen, Schaufenster, Caféterrassen, Bahnen, Autos, Bäume zu lauter gleichberechtigten Buchstaben werden, die zusammen Wörter, Sätze und Seiten eines immer neuen Buches ergeben.«[8] In seinen Berliner Geschichten nimmt Isherwood die Stadt auf ähnliche Weise als einen Ort wahr, der sich selbst als Lektüre anbietet. Seine autobiografischen Erzähler – einer von ihnen trägt den Namen Christopher Isherwood – sind aufmerksame Beobachter des städtischen Spektakels, das durch wiederholte Verweise auf Kinofilme, Werbeplakate, Songs und später auch auf das groteske Schauspiel der Nationalsozialisten betont wird. In einer berühmten Passage aus *Leb wohl, Berlin* beschreibt sich Isherwood selbst als »eine Kamera mit offenem Verschluss, ganz passiv, ich nehme auf, ich denke nicht«.[9] Doch natürlich erweist sich Isherwoods Form der literarischen Fotografie als alles andere als passiv und ist in Wirklichkeit das Ergebnis einer bewusst eingesetzten literarischen Technik. Es ist bezeichnend, dass Isherwood während seiner Berliner Zeit Baudelaire übersetzte, der Walter Benjamin zu einigen seiner wichtigsten Erkenntnisse über die Großstadtmoderne inspirierte. Isherwoods Kameraperspektive trägt nicht zufällig die eindeutige Handschrift Baudelaires: Er fällt keine moralischen Urteile über seine Erfahrungen in der Stadt – ob Armut, Entfremdung oder sexuelle Exzesse – und hält an seinem gleichgültigen Blick des weltgewandten Flaneurs fest.

were waking up to another empty day to be spent as they could best contrive; selling boot-laces, begging, playing draughts in the hall of the Labour Exchange, hanging about urinals, opening the doors of cars, helping with crates in the markets, gossiping, lounging, stealing, overhearing racing tips, sharing stumps of cigarette-ends picked up in the gutter",[9] the narrator and his friends sip cocktails in the bar of the Eden Hotel, observing the collapse of society with cynical detachment, wondering whether the Communists or the Nazis will eventually hold the day. The switch between worlds is performed with a clean precision that leaves no time to psychologise or philosophise. Berlin in Isherwood's writings is a city of juxtapositions, fast movement, cinematic montage.

In the passage from *Mr Norris*, the reference to urinals—blink and you might miss it—reveals the important role that mercenary sex plays in Isherwood's Berlin. Sex is the only stable currency in this fast shifting world where the value of everything is being called into question. This is another echo of Baudelaire and the nineteenth-century decadents, who looked on the prostitute as the female counterpart to the male *flâneur*: both were creatures of the street who shared the deepest knowledge of the metropolis and embodied the ephemeral and transient nature of its social transactions. Switching genders, Isherwood ascribes to the Berlin rent boy an equivalent mythic function. In *Christopher and His Kind* (1976), he would look back on the commercialisa-

In seinem ersten Berlin-Roman *Mr Norris steigt um* (1935) nippen der Erzähler und seine Freunde in der Bar des Hotels Eden an ihren Cocktails, während »junge Männer zu einem weiteren Tag ohne Arbeit [erwachten], den sie auf irgendeine Weise herumbringen mussten – indem sie Schuhbänder verkauften, bettelten, in der Eingangshalle des Arbeitsamts Dame spielten, in Pissoirs herumlungerten, Wagentüren offenhielten, auf dem Markt Kisten schleppten, große Reden schwangen, herumlungerten, stahlen, Wetttipps aufschnappten, im Rinnstein aufgelesene Kippen teilten«. Den Zusammenbruch der Gesellschaft verfolgen sie aus zynischer Distanz und sinnieren darüber, ob am Ende die Kommunisten oder die Nazis siegen werden.[10] Der Wechsel zwischen den Welten erfolgt mit einem klaren Schnitt und lässt keine Zeit für psychologische oder philosophische Betrachtungen. Berlin ist in Isherwoods Werken eine filmisch montierte, schnelllebige Stadt der Gegensätze.

In der Passage aus *Mr Norris* steht der klitzekleine Hinweis auf die »Pissoirs« für die wichtige Rolle von käuflichem Sex in Isherwoods Berlin. Sexuelle Dienstleistungen sind die einzige stabile Währung in dieser Welt des rasanten Wandels, die den Wert aller Dinge infrage stellt. Auch hier klingen Baudelaire und andere Vertreter der Dekadenz des 19. Jahrhunderts an, die Prostituierte als weibliches Pendant zum männlichen Flaneur betrachteten: Beide waren auf den Straßen der Stadt unterwegs, mit dem Geschehen in der Metropole aufs Beste vertraut und lebender Beweis für die Vergänglichkeit und Kurzlebigkeit der sozialen Wechselbeziehungen. Isherwood schreibt dem Berliner Stricherjungen eine ähnlich mythische Rolle zu. In *Christopher und die Seinen* (1976) erinnert er sich mit einem gewissen Schuldbewusstsein an die Vermarktung von Sex in

tion of sex in Berlin with a measure of guilt, describing it as a "colonial situation" and admitting that he participated in the exploitation of working-class boys.[10] Yet, there even more than in earlier writings the boy is the foremost protagonist of the Berlin myth. "To Christopher, Berlin meant Boys":[11] the Boy (by which Isherwood meant an uninhibited working-class young man who sometimes doubled as hustler in order to earn some extra cash) is like those winged figures in ancient myths that transported characters between worlds—between repressed England and freer Germany, in this case, but also across the class boundary, something of which Isherwood was extremely conscious in his peregrinations around Berlin.

The feeling of discomfort that previous English writers experienced in Berlin survives in Isherwood in his encounters with working-class life. As for Auden before him, the thrill of venturing into this alien territory was as exhilarating as the new sensation of sexual promiscuity. The combined political and erotic appeal of the working-class male body on the British writers is captured in G. W. Pabst's film *Kameradschaft* (1931), which greatly impressed Isherwood and Stephen Spender.

Goodbye to Berlin contains a fictional account of Isherwood's experience of lodging with the family of one of his working-class lovers in Kreuzberg, which powerfully exemplifies the "colonial situation" that he identified later on. The Nowaks, as Isherwood names them, lived in a crammed, leaky attic in Simeonstraße that smelt of

Berlin, die er als »Kolonialverhalten« bezeichnet, und räumt ein, sich an der Ausbeutung der Arbeiterjungen beteiligt zu haben.[11] Doch noch viel mehr als in seinen früheren Werken sind Jungs hier die wichtigsten Protagonisten des Berliner Mythos. »Für Christopher war Berlin gleichbedeutend mit ›Jungs‹.«[12] Diese Jungs – aus Isherwoods Sicht ungenierte junge Männer aus der Arbeiterklasse, die hin und wieder auch kleine Gaunereien übernahmen, um sich etwas dazuzuverdienen – sind wie die geflügelten Wesen antiker Mythen, die zwischen den Welten vermitteln: in diesem Fall zwischen dem verklemmten England und dem freizügigeren Deutschland. Aber auch zwischen Klassengrenzen, deren sich Isherwood auf seinen Wanderungen durch Berlin sehr bewusst war.

Das Gefühl des Unbehagens, das englische Schriftsteller vor Isherwoods Zeiten in Berlin beschlich, findet sich auch in seinen Werken wieder, und zwar immer dann, wenn er mit dem Leben der Arbeiterklasse in Berührung kommt. Wie zuvor bereits Auden faszinierte es ihn, in dieses unbekannte Terrain vorzudringen. Er empfand dieses Erlebnis als ebenso aufregend wie seine neu gewonnene sexuelle Freizügigkeit. Die politische und erotische Anziehungskraft des männlichen Arbeiterkörpers auf englische Autoren wird in G. W. Pabsts Film *Kameradschaft* (1931) besonders gut sichtbar – ein Film, der Isherwood und Stephen Spender sehr beeindruckt hatte.

Leb wohl, Berlin enthält eine fiktive Episode, in der Isherwood bei der Familie eines seiner Geliebten aus der Arbeiterklasse in Kreuzberg unterkommt. Sie spiegelt auf eindrückliche Weise das »Kolonialverhalten« wider, das er später beschreiben würde. Die Familie Nowak, wie Isherwood sie nannte, lebte in der Simeonstraße in beengten Verhältnissen in einer Mansardenwohnung mit undichtem Dach, in der es

[Fig. 14: Film still from G.W. Pabst's *Kameradschaft*, 1931]

[Abb. 14: Standbild aus G.W. Pabsts *Kameradschaft*, 1931]

cooking and bad drains. Spending the night here, Isherwood recalls, was "alien and mysterious and uncanny, like sleeping out in the jungle alone".[12] The act of comparing one of the most densely populated parts of the city to the jungle powerfully reveals Isherwood's class prejudice. What most readers might well find uncanny is the way that the city is emptied out of its human content, and that working-class culture is projected outside the sphere of civilisation as the upper-class Isherwood conceived it.

"Alone" in Kreuzberg, Isherwood was free to observe the alien world of the urban proletariat. His Berlin photo albums, which are now in the Huntington Library in California, contain striking portraits of working-class men in unmistakable Berlin tenement settings. The mixture of complicity and voyeurism evoked by these images is amplified by the fact that, in

nach Kochgerüchen und aus dem Ausguss stank. In Isherwoods Erinnerung waren die Nächte in dieser Wohnung: »[...] fremdartig, geheimnisvoll und unheimlich, als schliefe man alleine im Dschungel.«[13] Der Vergleich, den Isherwood an dieser Stelle zwischen dem Dschungel und einem der am dichtesten bevölkerten Stadtviertel Berlins zieht, macht seine Klassenvorurteile auf eindrucksvolle Weise deutlich. Was die meisten Leser*innen als »unheimlich« empfinden könnten, ist die Art und Weise, wie Isherwood die Stadt ihres menschlichen Inhalts beraubt und es der Kultur der Arbeiterklasse abspricht, zur – nach seiner Ansicht von der Oberklasse definierten – zivilisierten Welt zu gehören.

»Allein« in Kreuzberg hatte Isherwood Gelegenheit, die für ihn fremde Welt des städtischen Proletariats zu erkunden. Seine Berliner Fotoalben, die heute in der Huntington Library in Kalifornien verwahrt werden, enthalten eindrucksvolle Portraitaufnahmen von Männern der Arbeiterklasse vor der typischen Kulisse der Berliner Mietskasernen. Die

the same albums, Isherwood pasted in photographs of his Berlin working-class lovers, sometimes obsessively reproduced in multiple copies on the same page. The famous refrain, "I am a camera", takes on a new resonance after seeing the albums, which show Isherwood as a portrait collector. Without knowing it, Isherwood was following in the footsteps of Arthur Symons in his desire to map and preserve the city by means of photographic portraits of the inhabitants of its underworld.

It was not to Symons, however, but to Oscar Wilde that Isherwood turned in his effort to create a decadent geography of Berlin. The Francophile Wilde never ventured to the German capital but Isherwood exploited the fact that, to the English, Wilde's name was virtually synonymous with decadence. In *Mr Norris Changes Trains*, the yellow '90s and the golden '20s are so close they almost rub shoulders: the fictional Mr Norris, whose habit of speaking in epigrams recalls Wilde, declares to be a former friend of Frank Harris, an actual Irish-American writer who was, in his turn, a friend and biographer of Wilde's. In *Goodbye to Berlin*, the titles of Wilde's plays provide the names for some of the city's dingiest nightclubs: Sally Bowles works in a cabaret called the "Lady Windermere" and the "Salomé" is a glitzy tourist trap where "stage lesbians and some young men with plucked eyebrows" perform for the benefit of queer-curious customers from out of town.[13] By writing Wilde into his imaginary topography of the city, Isherwood paid

Mischung aus Komplizenschaft und Voyeurismus, die diese Bilder vermitteln, wird dadurch verstärkt, dass Isherwood in dieselben Alben auch Fotografien seiner Berliner Liebschaften aus der Arbeiterklasse klebte, in einigen Fällen sogar mehrere Exemplare auf einer einzigen Seite. Die berühmte Aussage »Ich bin eine Kamera« erhält nach einem Blick in diese Alben, die Isherwood als Portraitsammler zeigen, eine neue Bedeutung. Mit seinem Bedürfnis, die Stadt zu dokumentieren und in Fotoportraits ihre Bewohner aus der Unterwelt festzuhalten, trat Isherwood unbewusst in die Fußstapfen von Arthur Symons.

Doch in seinen Bemühungen, einen Überblick über die Berliner Dekadenz zu vermitteln, orientiert sich Isherwood nicht an Symons, sondern an Oscar Wilde. Der frankophile Wilde hatte der deutschen Hauptstadt zwar nie einen Besuch abgestattet, doch Isherwood machte sich die Tatsache zunutze, dass der Name Wilde bei seiner englischen Leserschaft nahezu gleichbedeutend mit Dekadenz war. In *Mr Norris steigt um* liegen die »Yellow Nineties« und die »Goldenen Zwanziger« derart nah beieinander, dass sie fast ineinander übergehen: Der fiktive Charakter des Mr Norris, dessen Angewohnheit, in Aphorismen zu sprechen, an Oscar Wilde erinnert, gibt sich als ehemaliger Freund des irisch-amerikanischen Schriftstellers Frank Harris aus, der im wahren Leben wiederum Freund und Biograf von Oscar Wilde war. In *Leb wohl, Berlin* sind einige der schäbigsten Nachtclubs der Stadt nach Wildes Dramen benannt: Sally Bowles arbeitet in einem Kabarett namens »Lady Windermere«, und das »Salomé« ist eine pompöse Touristenfalle, in der »Bühnenlesbierinnen und junge Männer, die sich die Augenbrauen ausgezupft hatten«, Schaulustigen aus der Provinz das homosexuelle Nachtleben vorspielen.[14] Indem er Wilde einen Platz in seiner imaginären Topografie der Stadt einräumt, will Isherwood der

homage to the Irish writer's actual, enduring presence in the cultural landscape of early twentieth-century Berlin. For it was in Berlin's Kleines Theater that Max Reinhardt first staged an experimental production (1902) of *Salomé* that launched the international success of Wilde's Symbolist play, at a time when that work was still banned from British stages (it is sobering to think that the British ban on *Salomé* was only lifted in 1931, when Isherwood was in Berlin). *Salomé* was a strong influence also on Curt Moreck, the author of the *Führer durch das 'lasterhafte' Berlin*, who published a German translation (1919) of the play, complete with Aubrey Beardsley's illustrations. And even Frank Harris had an important connection with the city: earlier in the 1920s, he published the first volume of his scandalous autobiography, *My Life and Loves* (1922–27), in Berlin. Isherwood deploys these literary references to depict Berlin as hospitable to decadents and sexual outsiders, showing that Wilde's name was now even being used as a brand by the entrepreneurs of alternative nightlife; one of the city's most famous gay and lesbian clubs was indeed called the "Dorian Gray".

The many references to Wilde are also Isherwood's way of acknowledging the influence of English literary decadence on the distinctive atmosphere of his Berlin novels, which combine camp, dandyism, and sexual ambiguity. One of his favourite adjectives to describe Berlin characters and situations is the word "queer", which he

tatsächlichen und anhaltenden Präsenz des irischen Schriftstellers in der kulturellen Landschaft der frühen 1920er Jahre in Berlin gedenken. Denn Max Reinhardt brachte 1902 in Berlins Kleinem Theater eine erste experimentelle Inszenierung von Wildes *Salomé* auf die Bühne. Sie sollte den internationalen Erfolg dieses symbolistischen Dramas in einer Zeit begründen, als das Aufführungsverbot für britische Bühnen noch nicht aufgehoben war. (Es ist ausgesprochen ernüchternd, dass *Salomé* erst 1931, als Isherwood bereits in Berlin weilte, auf britischen Bühnen gespielt werden durfte.) Auch auf Curt Moreck, den Verfasser des *Führers durch das »lasterhafte« Berlin*, übte *Salomé* einen starken Einfluss aus. Im Jahr 1919 brachte er eine deutsche Übersetzung des Dramas mit Zeichnungen von Aubrey Beardsley heraus. Und sogar Frank Harris verfügte über eine wichtige Verbindung zu Berlin: Zu Beginn der 1920er Jahre hatte er hier den ersten Band seiner skandalträchtigen Autobiografie *Mein Leben und Lieben* (»My Life and Loves«, 1922–27) veröffentlicht. Isherwood machte sich diese literarischen Referenzen zunutze, um Berlin als verlockenden Ort für Dekadente und sexuelle Außenseiter*innen zu präsentieren. Er verwies darauf, dass Wildes Name inzwischen sogar von den Entrepreneuren des alternativen Nachtlebens als Markenzeichen eingesetzt wurde. Einer der bekanntesten Berliner Schwulen- und Lesbenclubs hieß tatsächlich »Dorian Gray«.

Mit den zahlreichen Wilde-Bezügen wollte Isherwood zudem zeigen, dass die englische Dekadenzliteratur einen maßgeblichen Einfluss auf die besondere Atmosphäre seiner Berlin-Romane hatte, in denen er mit einer Melange aus affektierten Verhaltensweisen, Dandyismus und sexuellen Doppeldeutigkeiten spielt. Eines seiner liebsten Adjektive für die Beschreibung Berliner Figuren oder Situationen war das Wort »queer«, dessen doppelter Bedeutung als

[Fig. 15: Heinz Neddermeyer and four unidentified young men, from Christopher Isherwood's photo album, photographer unknown, 1930s]

[Abb. 15: Heinz Neddermeyer und vier unbekannte junge Männer, aus Christopher Isherwoods Fotoalbum, unbekannter Fotograf, 1930er]

[Fig. 16: A set of images of a young man, taken in Berlin, from Christopher Isherwood's photo album, photographer unknown, 1930s]

[Abb. 16: Eine Fotoserie eines jungen Mannes in Berlin, aus Christopher Isherwoods Fotoalbum, unbekannter Fotograf, 1930er]

uses with the full force of its double meaning as devious or odd, and homosexual:

'Say,' he asked Fritz, 'what's going on here?'
'Men dressed as women,' Fritz grinned.
The little American simply couldn't believe it.
'Men dressed as *women*? As *women*, hey?
Do you mean they're *queer*?'
'Eventually we're all queer,' drawled Fritz solemnly, in lugubrious tones. The young man looked us over very slowly. [...]
'You *queer*, too, hey?' demanded the little American, turning suddenly on me.
'Yes,' I said, 'very queer indeed.'¹⁴

As a figure of speech, the *double entendre* captures something essential to Isherwood's Berlin: here straight and queer ways of looking at the world exist side by side, without asking people to choose between them. It is fitting that this exchange should take place in the fictional Salomé cabaret, where the city stages its own decadence for a mixed audience of impressionable tourists and cosmopolitan *flâneurs*. By the end of the Weimar Republic, decadent Berlin had become self-conscious, performative, commercialised. Isherwood's stories reflected this complex heritage, which had in turn fascinated and daunted British writers since the turn of the twentieth century.

»abwegig oder merkwürdig« und »homosexuell« er sich sehr wohl bewusst war:

»Sag mal«, fragte er Fritz, »was wird denn hier geboten?«
»Männer als Frauen verkleidet« sagte Fritz grinsend.
Der kleine Amerikaner konnte es schlicht nicht glauben.
»Männer als *Frauen* verkleidet? Als *Frauen*, hey?
Heißt das, die sind *andersrum*?«
»*Eventually* sind wir alle andersrum«, sagte Fritz feierlich und düster. Der junge Mann betrachtete uns eingehend. [...]
»Du bist wohl auch *andersrum*, was?« wandte sich der kleine Amerikaner plötzlich herausfordernd an mich.
»Ja«, sagte ich, »vollkommen andersrum, allerdings.«¹⁵

Dieses Stilmittel der Doppeldeutigkeit ist ein wesentliches Merkmal von Isherwoods Berlin: Hier existieren hetero- und homosexuelle Perspektiven auf die Welt gleichberechtigt nebeneinander. Niemand muss sich für eine Seite entscheiden. Passenderweise findet dieses Gespräch im fiktiven Kabarett Salomé statt, in dem die Stadt ihre eigene Dekadenz für ein gemischtes Publikum aus schaulustigen Tourist*innen und weltgewandten Flaneur*innen inszeniert. Zum Ende der Weimarer Republik wurde diese Dekadenz nur noch bewusst zur Schau gestellt und vermarktet. Isherwood hat in seinen Geschichten dieses vielfältige Erbe festgehalten, das bei britischen Schriftsteller*innen seit dem Beginn des 20. Jahrhunderts sowohl Faszination als auch Verunsicherung auslöst.

Notes

1   Arthur Symons: Letter to Ernest Rhys. 9 September 1891, in: Arthur Symons: Selected Letters, 1880–1935, ed. by Karl Beckson and John M. Munro, Basingstoke, Macmillan 1989, p. 83.

Anmerkungen

1   Brief von Arthur Symons an Ernest Rhys, 9. September 1891, in: Arthur Symons: Selected Letters, 1880–1935, hg. von Karl Beckson und John M. Munro, Basingstoke, Macmillan, 1989, S. 83.

2 Arthur Symons: Emmy, in: Selected Early Poems, ed. by Jane Desmarais and Chris Baldick, Cambridge, Modern Humanities Research Association 2017, p. 53.
3 Arthur Symons: Berlin's Discomforts, in: Wanderings, London, Dent 1931, pp. 134–140, here 137.
4 Rupert Brooke: The Old Vicarage, Grantchester, in: Collected Poems, London, Sidgwick and Jackson 1918, p. 53.
5 Edward Sackville-West to E. M. Forster, 7 January 1928, in: Michael De-la-Noy: Eddy. The Life of Edward Sackville-West, London, Arcadia 1999, p. 117.
6 Edward Sackville-West to Virginia Woolf, 14 January 1928, in: De-la-Noy: Eddy, p. 118.
7 Franz Hessel: Walking in Berlin. A Flaneur in the Capital, trans. by Amanda DeMarco, Melbourne and London, Scribe 2018, p. 127.
8 Christopher Isherwood: Goodbye to Berlin, in: The Berlin Novels, London, Vintage 1999, p. 243.
9 Christopher Isherwood: Mr Norris Changes Trains, in: The Berlin Novels., p. 109.
10 Christopher Isherwood: Christopher and His Kind, London, Vintage 2012, p. 33.
11 Ibid., p. 3.
12 Isherwood: Goodbye to Berlin, p. 387.
13 Ibid., p. 471.
14 Ibid., p. 472.

2 Arthur Symons: Emmy, in: Selected Early Poems, hg. von Jane Desmarais und Chris Baldick, Cambridge, Modern Humanities Research Association 2017, S. 53. [Emmys Lachen klingt in meinen Ohren, so hell, / Frisch und süß wie das Rauschen eines Bergbachs / Und ich höre noch immer, wie sie uns in dieser Nacht Erzählungen / Aus Boccaccios Buch vorlas]
3 Arthur Symons: Berlin's Discomforts, in: Wanderings, London, Dent 1931, S. 134–140, hier S. 137.
4 Rupert Brooke: The Old Vicarage, Grantchester, in: Collected Poems, London, Sidgwick and Jackson 1918, S. 53. [*Du lieber Gott!* / Hier schwitze ich, mir ist elend und heiß, / Und dort am schattigen Gewässer / läuft mir das kühle Wasser über die nackte Haut. / Um mich herum deutsche Juden, *temperamentvoll* / mit einem Bier in der Hand – und dort legt sich der Tau / ganz sacht über das goldene Licht des Morgens.]
5 oh! da / Die Kirchturmuhr steht schon auf zehn vor drei? / Und gibt es noch Honig zum Tee?
6 Brief von Edward Sackville-West an E.M. Forster, 7. Januar 1928, in: Michael De-la-Noy: Eddy. The Life of Edward Sackville-West, London, Arcadia 1999, S. 117.
7 Edward Sackville-West an Virginia Woolf, 14. Januar 1928, zitiert in: De-la-Noy: Eddy, S. 118.
8 Franz Hessel: Spazieren in Berlin, 6. Auflage, München und Berlin, Berlin Verlag in der Piper Verlag GmbH (2012) Januar 2019, S. 156.
9 Christopher Isherwood: Leb wohl, Berlin, aus dem Englischen von Kathrin Passig und Gerhard Henschel, 3. Auflage, Hamburg, Hoffmann und Campe 2019, S. 13.
10 Christopher Isherwood: Mr Norris steigt um, aus dem Englischen von Georg Deggerich, Hamburg, Hoffmann und Campe 2016, S. 88f.
11 Christopher Isherwood: Willkommen in Berlin. Christopher und die Seinen, aus dem Englischen von Stefan Troßbach, 1. Auflage dieser Ausgabe, Berlin, Bruno Gmünder Verlag 2014, S. 39.
12 Ebd., S. 9. Die »« Anführungszeichen sind ebenfalls Teil des Zitats.
13 Isherwood: Leb wohl, Berlin, S. 161.
14 Ebd., S. 250.
15 Ebd., S. 251.

Heike Bauer

The Institute of Sexual Science and Sexual Subcultures in 1920s Berlin

Das Institut für Sexualwissenschaft und sexuelle Subkulturen im Berlin der 1920er Jahre

The sexual subcultures of 1920s Berlin are commonly envisioned as flamboyantly nocturnal. Many of the city's queer inhabitants—those whose gender and/or sexual desires did not match the norms of the time—gathered in bars and clubs such as the famous Eldorado, home to transvestite performers, homosexual and lesbian patrons, and the straight people who liked to watch and mingle with them. For instance, the gender-nonconforming bisexual actor Marlene Dietrich performed at the club and its patrons included visitors from around the world such as Christopher Isherwood, whose description of Berlin's demi-monde in the autobiographically inspired novel *Goodbye to Berlin* (1939) famously helped to shape the image of Weimar Berlin in the Anglophone imagination. The queer crowds at places such as the Eldorado played an important and highly visible role in Berlin's cultural life. Alongside cabaret, varieté, and circus performers and all kinds of sex workers, these crowds embody the promises of sexual freedom and erotic possibility of Weimar

Die sexuellen Subkulturen im Berlin der 1920er Jahre werden gemeinhin mit einem ausschweifenden Nachtleben assoziiert. Viele der queeren Stadtbewohner*innen – deren geschlechtliche Identität und/oder sexuelles Begehren nicht den Normen der damaligen Zeit entsprachen – trafen sich in Bars und Clubs wie dem berühmten Eldorado, in dem Travestiekünstler*innen, homosexuelle und lesbische Kundschaft, aber auch Heterosexuelle verkehrten, die sich als Zuschauer*innen gern unter die Menge mischten. So kam beispielsweise auch die nicht den gängigen Geschlechtsnormen entsprechende bisexuelle Schauspielerin Marlene Dietrich für Auftritte in den Club. Zu seinen Kund*innen gehörten zudem Besucher*innen aus aller Welt wie Christopher Isherwood, dessen Beschreibungen von Berlins Halbwelt in seinem autobiografisch geprägten Roman *Leb wohl, Berlin* (»Goodbye to Berlin«, 1939) bekanntermaßen dazu beitrugen, in der englischsprachigen Welt das Image Berlins in der Weimarer Zeit nachhaltig zu prägen. Das queere Publikum an Orten wie dem Eldorado übte durch seine starke Präsenz einen entscheidenden Einfluss auf das kulturelle Leben in der Hauptstadt aus. Neben Kabarett-, Varieté- und Zirkuskünstler*innen und Sexarbeiter*innen aller Art standen auch diese Gruppen für das Versprechen sexueller Freiheit und eroti-

Berlin, a subject of fascination for writers such as Isherwood, who had been drawn to Berlin by the accounts of the city's homosexual life by friend and on-off lover, the English poet W. H. Auden, whose letters led Isherwood to imagine that "Berlin meant Boys".[1] But sexual pursuits were only one aspect of queer life in Weimar Berlin and its sexual subcultures were not just nocturnal. They were part of everyday life in a metropolis ravaged by the impact of the First World War, a paradoxical, multifaceted city that was both a place of economic hardship and thriving cultural life, the home of repressive anti-homosexuality legislation and sexual freedom alike.

scher Möglichkeiten im Berlin der Weimarer Republik. Dieses Thema faszinierte Schriftsteller wie Isherwood, den die Berichte seines Freundes und On-Off-Geliebten W. H. Auden nach Berlin gelockt hatten: Der englische Dichter hatte in seinen Briefen bei Isherwood die Vorstellung geweckt, dass »Berlin gleichbedeutend mit ›Jungs‹« war.[1] Allerdings war das Ausleben sexueller Neigungen nur ein Merkmal des queeren Lebens im damaligen Berlin, und die sexuellen Subkulturen beschränkten sich nicht nur auf das Nachtleben. Sie bestimmten den Alltag in einer von den verheerenden Folgen des Ersten Weltkriegs gezeichneten Metropole. Berlin war ein widersprüchlicher Ort mit vielen Gesichtern. Wirtschaftliche Not und kulturelle Blüte lagen hier nah beieinander, und sexuelle Freiheiten konnten repressiven Anti-Homosexuellen-Gesetzen zum Trotz ausgelebt werden.

[Fig. 17: The Eldorado, unknown photographer, 1932]

[Abb. 17: Das Eldorado, unbekannter Fotograf, 1932]

Places
The Eldorado Cabaret

In his 1931 book *Hitler*, the leading avant-garde English writer Wyndham Lewis left a striking description of the queer and transgender scene at the Eldorado on Motzstraße. Appalled by what he saw, Lewis railed against Berlin as "the Perverts' Paradise, the Mecca of both Lesb and So".[a] Lewis became a great admirer of Hitler after visiting Berlin, although he was later to change his mind. In describing the "perversions" of the Eldorado, he was making the point that the Nazis tolerated such things because they rose above petty bourgeois morality. He was wrong of course. For the Nazis would immediately shut down the Eldorado as part of their attempt to eradicate Berlin's queer subcultures. Lewis followed on the footsteps of many male English writers, including Christopher Isherwood, Harold Nicolson, and Eddy Sackville-West, who stepped into the glitzy bubble of the Eldorado in the 1920s and early 1930s, often as the first stop on a tour of the city's nightlife. Cabaret more than any other art form embodied the heady mix of high and popular culture of Weimar Berlin. It provided the setting for several novels, paintings, and songs from this period, and eventually became an international symbol of the city with Bob Fosse's film *Cabaret* (1972). Even before Liza Minnelli and the Oscars, however, Berlin cabarets were hardly undiscovered places. Many of the large cabaret venues, including the Eldorado, were tourist attractions and were recommended in guidebooks: they were stages where the city put on a show of its transgressive reputation for the benefit of curious bourgeois patrons, foreign visitors, and bona fide members of the queer community. More than meccas of "perversion" they were temples of voyeurism. Most of all, they reveal the theatricality of Weimar Berlin and its intertwining of sexual transgression and commercialism.

Orte
Das Kabarett Eldorado

Einer der bekanntesten englischen Schriftsteller der Avantgarde, Wyndham Lewis, liefert in seinem Buch *Hitler* eine eindrucksvolle Beschreibung der queeren und transgender Szene im Eldorado an der Motzstraße. Lewis zeigte sich angewidert von dem, was er dort sah, und wetterte gegen Berlin als »das Hauptquartier der entschiedenen Perversität, das Paradies und Mekka der Lesbierin und des Sodomiten«.[a] Nach seinem Besuch in der Stadt wurde er zunächst zum großen Hitler-Verehrer, sollte seine Meinung jedoch später revidieren. Mit seiner Beschreibung der »Perversionen« im Eldorado wollte er deutlich machen, dass die Nazis derartige Erscheinungen duldeten, weil sie sich über kleingeistige bürgerliche Moralvorstellungen hinwegsetzten. Natürlich lag er damit falsch. Die Schließung des Eldorado gehörte zu den ersten Amtshandlungen der Nazis, die die queeren Subkulturen Berlins im Keim ersticken wollten. Lewis trat in die Fußstapfen etlicher englischer Schriftsteller, darunter Christopher Isherwood, Harold Nicolson, und Eddy Sackville-West, die in den 1920er und frühen 1930er Jahren in der glitzernden Parallelwelt des Eldorado verkehrt hatten. Dort begann in vielen Fällen ihre Tour durch das Berliner Nachtleben. Das Kabarett stand mehr als jede andere Kunstform für die berauschende Mischung aus Hoch- und Populärkultur im Berlin der Weimarer Zeit. Es wurde zum Schauplatz mehrerer Romane, Gemälde und Songs aus dieser Epoche. Und mit Bob Fosses Film *Cabaret* (1972) wurde es schließlich auch international zum Symbol für Berlin. Doch bereits vor Liza Minnelli und den Oscars waren die Berliner Kabaretts kein Geheimtipp. Viele der großen Bühnen wie das Eldorado gehörten zu den Touristenattraktionen und wurden in Reiseführern empfohlen. Sie inszenierten den Ruf der unangepassten Stadt für schaulustige Kleinbürger*innen, ausländische Besucher*innen und tatsächliche Mitglieder der queeren Gemeinschaft. Sie waren kein »Mekka der Perversität«, sondern Tempel des Voyeurismus. Und vor allem brachten sie die Theatralik Berlins und die Vermarktung sexueller Grenzüberschreitungen deutlich zum Vorschein.

A space that arguably encapsulates the complexities of Berlin's sexual subcultures better than any other appears at first glance rather sombre: Isherwood's one-time home in Berlin, the Institute of Sexual Science. It was founded in the immediate aftermath of the First World War as the first of its kind worldwide by the Jewish sexologist and sexual rights activist Magnus Hirschfeld (1868–1935) and his reform colleagues. The Institute was dedicated to the study of sex (encompassing bodies, desires, and gender), related medical advancements (ranging from the treatment of venereal diseases to pioneering "sex change" operations), sex education (including marital and eugenics counselling for heterosexual couples), and political advocacy (it campaigned, for instance, against Paragraph 175 of the German Penal Code which criminalised homosexuality, and also supported transgender people). It occupied a desirable position right in the heart of the city, at the meeting point of two streets, In den Zelten 10 and Beethovenstr. 3, near the northern side of the famous Tiergarten Park and not too far from the Reichstag. The impressive mansion building was the former home of the French ambassador to Germany which Hirschfeld had bought in the reshuffling of property and power after the war. It ranged over several floors, providing space for working, meeting, and living.

The Institute officially opened its doors to the public on 6 July 1919, a Sunday, with an evening soirée that foreshadowed its subsequent role as a space that brought

Ein Ort, der wie wohl kein anderer für die Vielfalt der Berliner Subkulturen steht, mutet auf den ersten Blick eher düster an: Das Institut für Sexualwissenschaft, in dem auch Isherwood eine Zeit lang logierte. Als weltweit erstes Institut dieser Art wurde es unmittelbar nach dem Ersten Weltkrieg durch den jüdischen Sexualforscher und Sexualrechtsaktivisten Magnus Hirschfeld (1868–1935) und seine reformorientierten Mitstreiter*innen gegründet. Das Institut widmete sich der Sexualforschung (in den Bereichen Körper, Begehren und Geschlecht), damit zusammenhängenden medizinischen Fortschritten (von der Behandlung von Geschlechtskrankheiten bis hin zu den ersten »Geschlechtsumwandlungen«), der Sexualerziehung (einschließlich Eheberatung und eugenischer Beratung für heterosexuelle Paare) und der politischen Lobbyarbeit (beispielsweise führte es Kampagnen gegen den Paragrafen 175 des deutschen Strafgesetzbuches, der Homosexualität unter Strafe stellte, und unterstützte transsexuelle Menschen). Sein Standort befand sich in prominenter Lage im Herzen der Stadt an der Kreuzung zweier Straßen, In den Zelten 10 und Beethovenstraße 3, nahe des nördlichen Teils des berühmten Tiergartens und in nicht allzu weiter Entfernung vom Reichstag. Hirschfeld hatte die herrschaftliche Villa des ehemaligen französischen Botschafters in Deutschland in der Nachkriegszeit erworben, als sich die Besitz- und Machtverhältnisse neu ordneten. Sie bot über mehrere Stockwerke Platz zum Arbeiten und Leben und für Veranstaltungen.

Offiziell öffnete das Institut am Sonntag, den 6. Juli 1919 seine Tore für die Öffentlichkeit. Die zu diesem Anlass veranstaltete Soirée sollte einen Vorgeschmack auf die künftige Rolle des Instituts als Begegnungsort von Wissenschaft und Kultur, Arbeit und häuslichem Leben bieten. Sowohl auf Einheimi-

[Fig. 18: Fancy dress party at the Institute of Sexual Science, unknown photographer, 1920s]

[Abb. 18: Maskenball im Institut für Sexualwissenschaften, unbekannter Fotograf, 1920er]

together science and culture, work and domesticity—a place that attracted both locals and visitors from around the world, and quickly established itself as part of Berlin's queer scene.

At its heart was Magnus Hirschfeld. Born in 1868 in a small town on the German Baltic coast, Hirschfeld was a trained doctor who had started off studying literature and languages before embarking on a medical degree, graduating from Berlin's Friedrich-Wilhelm University in 1892 with a dissertation on influenza. Berlin would become intrinsic to his life and work, the

sche als auch auf Besucher*innen aus aller Welt übte es eine große Anziehungskraft aus und etablierte sich schon bald als fester Bestandteil der queeren Szene Berlins.

Zentrale Figur des Instituts war Magnus Hirschfeld. Der ausgebildete Arzt, der 1868 in einer Kleinstadt an der deutschen Ostseeküste geboren wurde, hatte zunächst Literatur und Sprachen studiert, bevor er sein Medizinstudium aufnahm und 1892 mit einer Dissertation zur Influenza an der Berliner Friedrich-Wilhelms-Universität promovierte. Berlin sollte sich zum Mittelpunkt seines Lebens und seiner Arbeit entwickeln. Die Stadt diente Hirschfeld als Inspirationsquelle für die meisten seiner Studien zu

source and inspiration for much of his studies of gender and sexuality, and the locale that benefitted most directly from the sexual reform initiatives he set up. Hirschfeld first publicly turned his attention to matters of sex in 1896 with the publication of a pamphlet on love between men and love between women, *Sapho und Socrates*. This short treatise and Hirschfeld's subsequent work built on and took in a new direction the writings of those earlier nineteenth-century doctors and lawyers who had first devoted sustained scientific interest to questions of sex. The most famous of them was the Vienna-based psychiatrist Richard von Krafft-Ebing, author of an influential medico-forensic textbook, *Psychopathia Sexualis*, which was first published in 1886, and expanded over 12 editions until 1902. *Psychopathia Sexualis* is considered a foundational text of the new science of sex. It was intended for use in the clinic and courtroom to aid the identification and classification of perceived sexual perversions and real sexual crimes, which at the time included sex between men (sex between men remained criminalised in many European countries and in North America until well into the postwar years). Despite the book's medico-forensic focus the new vocabulary of sex popularised by *Psychopathia Sexualis* was drawn from the worlds of literature and culture. It included words such as "homosexuality" and its lesser discussed but equally newly invented opposite "heterosexuality", both coined by the Austrian-born Hungarian writer and

Geschlecht und Sexualität und profitierte als Schauplatz seines Wirkens ganz unmittelbar von seinen sexuellen Reforminitiativen. Hirschfeld beschäftigte sich erstmals mit Fragen des Geschlechts, als er seine Abhandlung zur Liebe zwischen Männern und Liebe zwischen Frauen, *Sappho und Sokrates*, veröffentlichte. In diesem kurzen Aufsatz und in weiteren Untersuchungen berief sich Hirschfeld auf die Schriften von Ärzten und Juristen aus dem früheren neunzehnten Jahrhundert, die sich zum ersten Mal wissenschaftlich mit Geschlechtsfragen auseinandergesetzt hatten, und entwickelte diese weiter. Zu deren berühmtesten Vertretern gehörte der Wiener Psychiater Richard von Krafft-Ebing. Sein Werk *Psychopathia Sexualis*, das zum ersten Mal 1886 erschien und 1902 seine 12. und letzte Auflage erreichte, war ein einflussreiches klinisch-forensisches Lehrbuch, das als Grundlagenwerk für die neue Sexualwissenschaft galt. Es sollte im klinischen Umfeld und vor Gericht als Handbuch für die Identifizierung und Einordnung angeblicher sexueller Perversionen und tatsächlicher Sexualverbrechen dienen, die zu dieser Zeit auch sexuelle Handlungen zwischen Männern einschlossen (Sex unter Männern war in vielen europäischen Ländern und in Nordamerika noch lange Zeit nach dem Zweiten Weltkrieg strafbar). Trotz seines klinisch-forensischen Schwerpunkts stammte das neue einschlägige Vokabular, das mit *Psychopathia Sexualis* größere Verbreitung fand, aus der Welt der Literatur und der Kultur. Dazu gehörten Begriffe wie »Homosexualität« sowie der weniger diskutierte, aber ebenfalls neue gegenteilige Begriff der »Heterosexualität«, die beide durch den österreichisch-ungarischen Schriftsteller und Journalisten Karl-Maria Kertbeny geprägt wurden. Auch Krafft-Ebings eigene Wortschöpfungen »Sadismus« und »Masochismus« kamen darin vor, die jeweils aus den Werken des

journalist Karl-Maria Kertbeny; it also featured Krafft-Ebing's own neologisms of "sadism" and "masochism", which were derived from the writings of the Marquis de Sade and Leopold von Sacher-Masoch respectively. These new categories associated sexual acts and desires with certain types of people—a mode of thinking that helped to shape the modern notion of sexual identity. After Krafft-Ebing's death, sex research in Vienna turned primarily towards unconscious sexual desires under the steadily growing influence of Sigmund Freud and his fledgling psychoanalytic movement. Berlin, in contrast, became a hotbed for a new kind of politically motivated sex research promoted by Hirschfeld and his colleagues at the Institute. It favoured sociological and anthropological approaches to understanding sexuality and had a particular medical interest in endocrinology and related sex change technologies. Moving away from the earlier emphasis on crime and sexual pathology, the Berlin-based sex researchers pursued sexual reform, inspired by challenges faced by sexual misfits from Berlin and abroad.

Hirschfeld was himself a well-known member of the city's queer subcultures. A lover of men (although he did not publicly identify as homosexual, perhaps so as not to jeopardise his professional standing), he made two radical conceptual contributions to sexual politics. 1: he put forward the notion of "sexual intermediaries" or "sexuelle Zwischenstufen", which challenged binary ideas about sex and gender, arguing

Marquis de Sade und von Leopold von Sacher-Masoch abgeleitet waren. Mit diesen neuen Kategorien wurden sexuelle Handlungen und Begehrlichkeiten bestimmten Menschentypen zugeordnet, eine Denkweise, auf deren Grundlage das moderne Konzept der sexuellen Identität entwickelt wurde. Nach dem Tod von Krafft-Ebing konzentrierte sich die Wiener Sexualforschung unter dem stetig wachsenden Einfluss Sigmund Freuds und seiner noch jungen psychoanalytischen Bewegung vornehmlich auf unbewusste Formen des sexuellen Verlangens. Berlin dagegen entwickelte sich zur Brutstätte einer neuen Form der politisch motivierten Sexualforschung, die von Hirschfeld und seinen Kolleg*innen am Institut vorangetrieben wurde. Dort wurde Sexualität vor allem auf der Grundlage soziologischer und anthropologischer Konzepte erkundet. Zudem pflegte man ein ausgeprägtes medizinisches Interesse an der Endokrinologie und den damit verbundenen Methoden der Geschlechtsumwandlung. Die Berliner Sexualforscher vollzogen eine Abkehr von der gängigen Lehrmeinung, die den Schwerpunkt auf strafbare Handlungen und Sexualpathologie legte, und setzten sich für eine Sexualreform ein, die sich an den Herausforderungen orientierte, mit denen sich sexuelle Außenseiter*innen in Berlin und aller Welt konfrontiert sahen.

Hirschfeld selbst war innerhalb der sexuellen Subkulturen Berlins kein Unbekannter. Als Mann, der Männer liebte (auch wenn er sich öffentlich nie zu seiner Homosexualität bekannte, vermutlich weil er seinem beruflichen Ansehen nicht schaden wollte), leistete er zwei radikale inhaltliche Beiträge zur Sexualpolitik. Erstens entwickelte er den Begriff der »sexuellen Zwischenstufen«, der binäre Vorstellungen von Sexualität und Geschlecht hinterfragte. Hirschfeld war davon überzeugt, dass es unendliche

that there exist near infinite variations in gender and that all humans contain to varying degrees masculine and feminine parts. And 2: Hirschfeld decoupled ideas about the relatedness of gender expression and sexual object choice. That is to say, he pointed out that sexuality and gender are not the same thing and that particular kinds of gender expression—such as effeminacy or female masculinity—are not tied to specific sexual desires. In 1910 he coined the term "transvestite", which took "cross-dressing" as its starting point to examine more broadly gender expressions that do not match the one assigned at birth. It was followed in 1923 by "transsexualism", published in an article on intersex, which focused more specifically on people wishing to change sex. The term was made famous by Hirschfeld's Berlin born and raised friend and colleague Harry Benjamin, an endocrinologist who permanently moved to the United States during the First World War. In America, Benjamin started to work with transgender people, publishing an influential book, *The Transsexual Phenomenon*, in 1966. Hirschfeld's own support for transgender people was not merely theoretical. It was directly linked to life in the metropolis: he offered help to those who applied to Berlin's police for so-called "transvestite passes" that would allow them to wear in public clothes commonly reserved for what was considered the "opposite sex". The Institute furthermore offered counselling and pioneering medical treatments, and it employed some

Variationen des Geschlechts gab und alle Menschen männliche und weibliche Eigenschaften in unterschiedlicher Ausprägung in sich trugen. Zweitens löste er den Kausalzusammenhang zwischen dem Ausdruck der Geschlechtlichkeit und der sexuellen Orientierung auf. Damit wollte er zum Ausdruck bringen, dass Sexualität und Geschlecht einander nicht bedingen und dass bestimmte Ausdrucksformen der Geschlechtlichkeit – wie Effemination oder weibliche Maskulinität – nicht an ein spezifisches sexuelles Begehren gebunden sind. Im Jahr 1910 prägte er den Begriff »Transvestit«, der sich ausgehend vom »Transvestismus« ausführlicher mit geschlechtlichen Ausdrucksformen beschäftigte, die nicht den qua Geburt zugeordneten entsprechen. Darauf folgte 1923 der Begriff der »Transsexualität«, der in einem Artikel über Intersexualität erschien, in dem es insbesondere um Menschen ging, die sich eine Geschlechtsumwandlung wünschten. Größere Bekanntheit erlangte der Begriff durch Hirschfelds in Berlin geborenen und aufgewachsenen Freund und Kollegen, den Endokrinologen Harry Benjamin, der während des Ersten Weltkriegs in die Vereinigten Staaten übergesiedelt war. In Amerika arbeitete Benjamin mit transsexuellen Menschen und veröffentlichte 1966 sein einflussreiches Werk *The Transsexual Phenomenon*. Hirschfeld selbst unterstützte transsexuelle Menschen auch durch sein praktisches Engagement, das sich unmittelbar an den Lebensrealitäten in der Großstadt orientierte: Er bot Menschen seine Hilfe an, die bei der Berliner Polizei so genannte »Transvestitenscheine« beantragen wollten, um in der Öffentlichkeit Kleidung tragen zu können, die üblicherweise dem so genannten »anderen Geschlecht« vorbehalten war. Darüber hinaus offerierte das Institut Beratungen und fortschrittliche medizinische Behandlungsmöglichkeiten und beschäftigte

transgender people as domestic staff. Yet, although transgender people were highly visible both at the Institute and in Berlin's sexual subcultures during the 1920s—the Austrian writer Stefan Zweig famously claimed that the city's transvestite balls were evidence of a collapse in values—sexual activism in the city was directed elsewhere: it focused primarily on either feminist efforts or homosexual rights.

Berlin was the epicentre of the German homosexual rights movement. In 1897 the so-called Scientific-Humanitarian Committee, or Wissenschaftlich-humanitäres Kommittee, the first homosexual rights activism group, was co-founded by Hirschfeld in Berlin, followed in 1899 by the related *Yearbook for Sexual Intermediaries*, or *Jahrbuch für sexuelle Zwischenstufen*, the first journal dedicated to same-sex sexuality and gender variation. Much of these political efforts were concerned with male homosexuality, specifically the revocation of Paragraph 175 of the German Penal Code. Most famously, Hirschfeld spearheaded a campaign against the oppressive legislation, leading a petition that was signed by many prominent scientists, politicians, philosophers, and artists including Albert Einstein, August Bebel, Martin Buber, and Käthe Kollwitz and writers such as Thomas Mann, Heinrich Mann, Reiner Maria Rilke, and Leo Tolstoy. Whilst Berlin's queer subcultures inspired and supported the campaign, the wider support it received makes clear that these subcultures did not persist in isolation but were connected to

auch einige transsexuelle Menschen als Hausangestellte. Doch obwohl Transsexuelle sowohl im Institut als auch in Berlins sexuellen Subkulturen der 1920er Jahre ausgesprochen präsent waren – vom österreichischen Schriftsteller Stefan Zweig stammt das berüchtigte Zitat, dass die Transvestitenbälle der Stadt ein Zeichen für den Sturz aller Werte seien – konzentrierte sich das Engagement in der Stadt vor allem auf feministische Forderungen oder Homosexuellenrechte.

Berlin war das Epizentrum der deutschen Homosexuellenrechtsbewegung. Im Jahr 1897 gehörte Hirschfeld zu den Mitbegründern der ersten Aktivistengruppe für Homosexuellenrechte in Berlin, die als *Wissenschaftlich-humanitäres Komitee* (WhK) ab 1899 mit einem eigenen *Jahrbuch für sexuelle Zwischenstufen* das erste Fachblatt zu gleichgeschlechtlicher Sexualität und Geschlechtsvariationen veröffentlichte. Das damit verbundene politische Engagement war vornehmlich auf die männliche Homosexualität und in diesem Zusammenhang insbesondere auf die Abschaffung des Paragrafen 175 des Deutschen Strafgesetzbuches gerichtet. Besondere Berühmtheit erlangte Hirschfeld durch seinen Einsatz an der Speerspitze einer Kampagne gegen repressive Gesetze, die eine von zahlreichen prominenten Wissenschaftler*innen, Politiker*innen, Philosoph*innen und Künstler*innen wie Albert Einstein, August Bebel, Martin Buber und Käthe Kollwitz und Schriftstellern wie Thomas Mann, Heinrich Mann, Reiner Maria Rilke und Leo Tolstoi unterzeichnete Petition ins Leben rief. Die Kampagne wurde von den queeren Subkulturen Berlins inspiriert und unterstützt. Die weitreichende Zustimmung, auf die sie stieß, zeugt zudem davon, dass diese Subkulturen nicht in ihrer eigenen Blase agierten, sondern mit zahlreichen wichtigen kultu-

many major cultural, scientific, and political figures and movements of the time. In 1904 Hirschfeld published a study, *Berlins Drittes Geschlecht* (Berlin's Third Gender), which documented the richness of what we would now call LGBTQI+ life in the city, including numerous photographs of its queer inhabitants and the places where they socialised. *Berlins Drittes Geschlecht* was part of a major book series, *Großstadt-dokumente* (Documents of the Metropolis), edited by the writer Hans Ostwald and dedicated to exploring the sociology of modern city life in Berlin and Vienna. The series focused on overlooked urban subcultures and those living on the margins of society. It published, for example, Ostwald's own studies of pimps (1905), coffee houses (1905), and gambling (1907), a book about unmarried mothers (1906) by the sexual reformer Max Marcuse, and one on "tribadism" (1906) by Wilhelm Hammer, which was the only book in the series to be banned immediately. It was published alongside a study of leading feminist figures (1906) by Ella Mensch, which rejected the idea that lesbians could or should play a role in the feminist movement. Mensch's work indicates the tensions between Berlin's lesbian subcultures and the feminist movement at the time, with many feminists rejecting lesbian involvement.

Political conflicts notwithstanding, lesbian subcultures were thriving in Berlin throughout the 1920s. Sex between women was not criminalised in Germany, reflecting a long history of denying both women's

rellen, wissenschaftlichen und politischen Persönlichkeiten und Bewegungen der damaligen Zeit in Verbindung standen. Im Jahr 1904 veröffentlichte Hirschfeld seine Studie *Berlins Drittes Geschlecht*, in der er die vielfältigen Lebenswelten der heute als LGBTQI+ bezeichneten Menschen in der Großstadt beschrieb. Sie enthält zahlreiche Fotografien von queeren Stadtbewohner*innen und ihren Treffpunkten. *Berlins Drittes Geschlecht* erschien im Rahmen der umfangreichen Veröffentlichungsreihe *Großstadt-Dokumente* des Schriftstellers Hans Ostwald, die der soziologischen Erkundung der modernen städtischen Lebensverhältnisse in Berlin und Wien gewidmet war. Im Mittelpunkt dieser Reihe standen unbeachtete städtische Subkulturen und Menschen am Rande der Gesellschaft. Sie enthielt beispielsweise Ostwalds eigene Abhandlungen über Zuhältertum (1905), Kaffeehäuser (1905) und Spielertum (1907), ein Buch über uneheliche Mütter (1906) des Sexualreformers Max Marcuse und eines über »Tribadie« (1906) von Wilhelm Hammer, das als einziges Buch dieser Reihe unmittelbar nach Erscheinen verboten wurde. Der Verfasser ging darin auf eine Studie über führende Vertreterinnen der feministischen Bewegung (1906) von Ella Mensch ein, in der sich diese dagegen verwahrte, dass Lesben eine Rolle in der Frauenbewegung spielen könnten oder sollten. Menschs Beitrag zeugt von den Spannungen, die zu dieser Zeit zwischen den lesbischen Subkulturen und der Frauenbewegung in Berlin herrschten, denn viele Feministinnen lehnten die Beteiligung von Lesben an ihrem Kampf ab.

Ungeachtet der politischen Konflikte erlebten lesbische Subkulturen im Berlin der 1920er Jahre ihre Blütezeit. Die Tatsache, dass sexuelle Handlungen zwischen Frauen in Deutschland nicht unter Strafe standen, zeugt von einer langen Geschichte, in der

citizenship and the existence of female sexual desire and pleasure per se. However, women whose sexual object choice and gender expression did not conform to the norm nevertheless frequently experienced social isolation and ostracisation. Berlin offered an opportunity to find community and live a freer life, as books such as *Berlins lesbische Frauen* (Berlin's Lesbian Women, 1928) by the writer and editor Ruth Margarete Roellig indicate. The city was furthermore home to lesbian magazines such as *Die Freundin* (The Girlfriend), which published literary writings, some contemporary commentary, and many personal ads. *The Girlfriend* was distributed throughout Germany, initially on a monthly basis and soon weekly, presenting the queer possibilities of the city to women throughout the country. But Berlin was not just a magnet for German lesbians. Whilst the city did not attract quite as many British and American women as Paris—the undisputed capital of Sapphic modernity whose scene revolved around figures such as the American Natalie Clifford Barney and her compatriots Djuna Barnes, Gertrude Stein, and Alice B. Toklas—it certainly featured on the itineraries of prominent modernists. The English writer Virginia Woolf, for instance, visited the city during the late 1920s. At the time Woolf's lover Vita Sackville-West briefly lived in Berlin with her husband, the diplomat Harold Nicolson, who was stationed in the metropolis. Sackville-West wrote to Woolf about the city's thriving sexual subcultures, explaining that she

Frauen weder Bürgerrechte noch das Empfinden von sexuellem Begehren oder Lust an sich zugestanden wurden. Trotzdem wurden Frauen, deren sexuelle Orientierung und Ausdruck ihrer Geschlechtlichkeit nicht der Norm entsprach, in vielen Fällen isoliert und gesellschaftlich ausgegrenzt. In Berlin hatten sie die Möglichkeit, sich einer Gemeinschaft anzuschließen und ein freieres Leben zu führen, wie es in Büchern wie *Berlins lesbische Frauen* (1928) der Schriftstellerin und Publizistin Ruth Margarete Roellig beschrieben wird. In der Stadt wurden zudem lesbische Magazine wie *Die Freundin* publiziert, die literarische Texte, Kommentare zum aktuellen Zeitgeschehen und zahlreiche Kontaktanzeigen enthielten. *Die Freundin* wurde in ganz Deutschland zunächst monatlich und später wöchentlich vertrieben und zeigte Frauen im ganzen Land die queeren Möglichkeiten in der Stadt. Doch Berlin übte nicht nur auf deutsche Lesben eine große Anziehungskraft aus. Wenngleich die Stadt nicht so viele britische und amerikanische Frauen anlocken konnte wie Paris – das als unumstrittene Hauptstadt der sapphischen Moderne galt, in der die Szene um Persönlichkeiten wie die Amerikanerin Natalie Clifford Barney und ihre Landsfrauen Djuna Barnes, Gertrude Stein und Alice B. Toklas kreiste –, gehörte sie ohne Zweifel zu den Reisezielen namhafter Vertreterinnen der Moderne. Beispielweise stattete die englische Schriftstellerin Virginia Woolf der Stadt Ende der 1920er Jahre einen Besuch ab. Ihre Geliebte Vita Sackville-West lebte damals für kurze Zeit in Berlin, da ihr Ehemann, der Diplomat Harold Nicolson, in die Metropole entsandt worden war. Sackville-West berichtete Woolf in ihren Briefen von blühenden sexuellen Subkulturen und »Sodomiten-Bällen«, die für sie »[e]in sehr seltsamer Anblick« waren.[2] Wie Gesa Stedman in ihrem Kapital erläutert, stieß der Berlin-Besuch

had witnessed "sodomites' balls" and other "very queer things".² As Gesa Stedman explains in her chapter, the visit to Berlin by the Bloomsbury set was not a success; but other women writers like Alix Strachey and the modernist author Bryher were less ambivalent. In 1931, the latter wrote to her American lover, the poet and writer H.D. with whom she was in an open relationship for over forty years, that she loved the city "like a person".³

Woolf, Bryher, and their compatriots commented more extensively on Berlin's sexual subcultures rather than the city's political movements, although the two spheres frequently overlapped. Hirschfeld, who tracked the impact of homosexual rights activism on the city, argued in an article in the homosexual magazine *Die Freundschaft* (Friendship) that the number of gay bars in Berlin had grown from around half a dozen in 1896, the year he published *Sapho and Sokrates*, to around 90–100 twenty-five years or so later because of the efforts of the homosexual rights movement. Whilst Hirschfeld makes it sound as if there was just the one homosexual rights movement, Berlin's homosexual activists were in fact divided. The Scientific-Humanitarian Committee's (SHC) greatest rival was the so-called *Gemeinschaft der Eigenen* (GdE), a name that is often translated as "community of the self-determined" in an attempt to capture the connotations of self-ownership inherent in the expression. Founded in 1903, it supported the SHC's fight for the abolition of anti-homosexuality

des Bloomsbury Sets allerdings auf wenig Begeisterung. Andere Schriftstellerinnen wie Alix Strachey und die modernistische Autorin Bryher brachten ihre Zuneigung dagegen deutlicher zum Ausdruck. Im Jahr 1931 schrieb Bryher ihrer amerikanischen Geliebten, der Dichterin und Schriftstellerin H.D., mit der sie seit über vierzig Jahren eine offene Beziehung führte, dass sie die Stadt »wie einen Menschen« liebe.³

Woolf, Bryher und ihre Landsleute beschäftigten sich weitaus ausführlicher mit den sexuellen Subkulturen Berlins als mit den politischen Bewegungen in der Stadt, obwohl beide Sphären häufig miteinander in Berührung kamen. Hirschfeld verfolgte aufmerksam die Auswirkungen des Engagements der Homosexuellenrechtsaktivist*innen auf das städtische Leben. In einem Artikel für die Homosexuellenzeitschrift *Die Freundschaft* wies er darauf hin, dass dank der Bemühungen der Homosexuellenrechtsbewegung die Zahl der Schwulenbars in Berlin innerhalb von 25 Jahren von etwa einem halben Dutzend im Jahr 1896, als er *Sappho und Sokrates* veröffentlichte, auf rund 90–100 gestiegen war. Obwohl es bei Hirschfeld so klingt, als hätte es nur eine einzige Homosexuellenrechtsbewegung gegeben, verteilten sich die Aktivist*innen in diesem Bereich auf mehrere Gruppen. Größter Widersacher des *Wissenschaftlich-humanitären Komitees* (WhK) war die so genannte *Gemeinschaft der Eigenen* (GdE), die in englischer Übersetzung häufig als »community of the self-determined« (Gesellschaft der Selbstbestimmten) bezeichnet wird, um die in diesem Ausdruck enthaltene Konnotation des Selbsteigentums zu vermitteln. Die im Jahr 1903 gegründete Gesellschaft unterstützte den Kampf des WhK für die Abschaffung der Anti-Homosexuellen-Gesetze, verwahrte sich jedoch gegen Hirschfelds Führungsanspruch

legislation but rejected both Hirschfeld's leadership and his theorisation of sexual intermediaries. The GdE was led by the writer and anarchist Adolf Brand and the scientist and philosopher Benedict Friedländer. It was heavily influenced by the writings of the Scottish-born but German-raised writer John Henry Mackay who had moved to Berlin in the 1890s, attracted by the city's promise of sexual freedom. Mackay, an anarchist arguably most famous for his autobiographically inspired political novel *Die Anarchisten* (1891), also published a number of books on homosexuality under the pseudonym "Sagitta". They include a collection of pro-homosexuality works, *Die Bucher der namenlosen Liebe* (The Books of the Nameless Love, 1913), and the novel *Der Puppenjunge* (1926), set in Berlin's gay bars and brothels, which was translated into English by Hubert Kennedy in 1985 as *The Hustler*. These works focused on love and sex between men and adolescent boys. They stand in marked contrast to the views of Hirschfeld and others who campaigned for the age of consent to be raised for everyone to sixteen and for homosexual sex to be legalised at the same time. Mackay was against the regulation of sex altogether. He argued for individual freedom to pursue sexual pleasure, partly deriving his model of homosexuality from classical debates about pederasty. Mackay's focus on man-boy relationships fitted well the philosophy of the GdE, which also drew on Hellenic masculine ideals. The GdE promoted physical pursuits, outdoor

und seine Theorie der sexuellen Zwischenstufen. An der Spitze der GdE standen der Schriftsteller und Anarchist Adolf Brand und der Wissenschaftler und Philosoph Benedict Friedländer. Die Organisation orientierte sich vorrangig an den Texten des in Schottland geborenen und in Deutschland aufgewachsenen Schriftstellers John Henry Mackay, den die Aussicht auf sexuelle Freiheiten in den 1890er Jahren nach Berlin gelockt hatte. Größte Bekanntheit erlangte der Anarchist Mackay zweifellos durch seinen autobiografisch inspirierten politischen Roman *Die Anarchisten* (1891). Unter dem Pseudonym »Sagitta« brachte er zudem eine Reihe von Büchern zur Homosexualität heraus. Darunter findet sich eine Sammlung mit Werken, die sich auf positive Weise mit dem Thema auseinandersetzen, wie *Die Bücher der namenlosen Liebe* (1913) und der Roman *Der Puppenjunge* (1926), der in den Schwulenbars und Bordellen Berlins spielt und von Hubert Kennedy 1985 unter dem Titel *The Hustler* ins Englische übersetzt wurde. Diese Werke behandeln Liebe und Sex zwischen Männern und Halbwüchsigen. Sie stehen im deutlichen Kontrast zu den Ansichten Hirschfelds und anderer Aktivisten, die sich dafür einsetzten, das Schutzalter generell auf 16 Jahre anzuheben und gleichgeschlechtliche Liebe ab demselben Alter zu legalisieren. Mackay sprach sich gegen jede Form der Regulierung sexueller Beziehungen aus. Er plädierte für die persönliche Frciheit des sexuellen Lustgewinns. Sein Modell der Homosexualität beruhte zum Teil auf Debatten über Knabenliebe aus der Antike. Dass Mackays hauptsächliches Interesse den Beziehungen zwischen Männern und Knaben galt, fügte sich gut in die Philosophie der GdE, die sich ebenfalls an hellenistischen Männlichkeitsidealen orientierte. Die GdE propagierte körperliche Ertüchtigung, Freiluftkultur und eine idealisierte homosexuelle Männ-

culture, and an idealised homosexual virility that also appealed to writers such as W. H. Auden, whose early poems similarly favour strong masculinity. Auden and Isherwood were both familiar with *Der Puppenjunge*. Indeed, towards the end of his life, Isherwood wrote an endorsement for the English translation in which he spoke about his love of the book and praised its authentic portrayal of the Berlin sexual underworld. In 1906 Friedländer founded another splinter group, the *Bund für männliche Kultur* (League for Manly Culture). The League did not last long, although its emphasis on manliness and argument that homosexuality was part of virile masculinity rather than a distinct manifestation of desire retained currency within some parts of male homosexual subcultures at the time that were opposed to Hirschfeld's ideas about gender and sexuality variation.

These quarrels about homosexuality were largely played out within Berlin's homosexual subcultures. It was the Institute of Sexual Science with its respectably scientific set-up yet thriving queer life that reached wider audiences and became for many a symbol of their hopes and aspirations. For example, many of Berlin's cross-dressers and other "sexual deviants" visited the Institute and had their picture taken there. These portraits were then displayed alongside images of the Institute's transgender and intersex visitors and patients, and a collection of paintings and objects relating to sex.

lichkeit, die auch Schriftstellern wie W. H. Auden zusagte, der in seinen frühen Gedichten auf ähnliche Weise einer ausgeprägten Männlichkeit gefrönt hatte. Sowohl Auden als auch Isherwood waren mit *Der Puppenjunge* vertraut. Kurz vor seinem Lebensende schrieb Isherwood sogar in einer Empfehlung der englischen Übersetzung, dass er das Buch liebe und darin ein authentisches Bild der sexuellen Unterwelt Berlins gezeichnet werde. Im Jahr 1906 gründete Friedländer eine weitere Splittergruppe, den *Bund für männliche Kultur*, dem nur ein kurzes Leben beschert sein sollte. Und dies, obwohl er den Aspekt der Männlichkeit in den Vordergrund stellte und die These vertrat, dass mit Homosexualität echte Männlichkeit und keine bestimmte Form des Begehrens zum Ausdruck gebracht wird – eine Haltung, die in dieser Zeit bei einigen männlichen Vertretern der homosexuellen Subkulturen, die Hirschfelds Vorstellungen von Geschlecht und Geschlechtsvariationen nicht teilten, hoch im Kurs stand.

Derartige Auseinandersetzungen über die Frage der Homosexualität fanden größtenteils innerhalb der homosexuellen Subkulturen Berlins statt. Als anerkannte wissenschaftliche Einrichtung konnte vor allem das Institut für Sexualwissenschaft, das gleichzeitig auch ein lebhafter Treffpunkt des queeren Lebens war, ein breiteres Publikum erreichen und wurde für viele zum Symbol ihrer Hoffnungen und Wünsche. So kamen beispielsweise viele Berliner Cross-Dresser und andere Menschen mit »abweichendem Sexualverhalten« in das Institut, um sich fotografieren zu lassen. Ihre Portraits wurden anschließend zusammen mit weiteren Aufnahmen der transsexuellen und intersexuellen Besucher*innen und Patient*innen des Instituts und einer Sammlung von Gemälden und Gegenständen zum Thema Sexualität ausgestellt.

[Fig. 19: Interior of the Institute of Sexual Science, in Magnus Hirschfeld, *Geschlechtskunde*, 4, 1930, unknown photographer, 1920s]

[Abb. 19: Interieur des Instituts für Sexualwissenschaft, in Magnus Hirschfeld, *Geschlechtskunde*, 4, 1930, unbekannter Fotograf, 1920er]

The Institute and its collections attracted visitors from around the world. They included doctors, scientists, and campaigners such as the American birth control activist Margaret Sanger who visited the Institute in 1920 because of its sex education work. The French writer André Gide visited the Institute and "was taken on a tour of the premises personally conducted by Hirschfeld", meeting many the of the queer and transgender people from Germany and beyond who met, received

Das Institut lockte mit seinen Sammlungen Besucher*innen aus aller Welt an. Dazu gehörten auch Ärzt*innen, Wissenschaftler*innen und Aktivist*innen wie die Amerikanerin Margaret Sanger, die sich für Geburtenkontrolle einsetzte und dem Institut 1920 einen Besuch abstattete, um sich über die dortige Arbeit im Bereich der sexuellen Aufklärung zu informieren. Als der französische Schriftsteller André Gide das Institut besuchte, führte Hirschfeld ihn persönlich durch die Räumlichkeiten. Dabei traf er auf viele der queeren und transsexuellen Menschen aus Deutschland und aller Welt, die an diesem

treatments, and occasionally lived in the imposing yet also decidedly domestic space in central Berlin.⁴

Hirschfeld himself lived at the Institute with his partner Karl Giese. Other rooms were rented out to permanent and temporary staff, and visitors from around the world such as Isherwood, for whom it provided a space of self-realisation. In his autobiographical *Christopher and His Kind*, which was written in the third person and only published in 1976, he writes that when he was first shown around the Institute's museum he felt that he was at last "being brought face to face with his tribe".⁵ Although he remained ambivalent about the Institute in this later work, Isherwood's time there was formative. It was there that he met his friend, the British archaeologist Francis Turville-Petre, famous for his excavations in Galilee, with whom he later left the city under the threat of rising Nazism. Turville-Petre, also known as Der Franni or Fronny, would provide the basis for the character of Ambrose in Isherwood's *Down there on a Visit* (1962). Other residents included Hirschfeld's widowed eldest sister, Recha Tobias. Recha in turn sublet rooms to the philosopher Walter Benjamin who stayed for around three months, after which another philosopher, the recently widowed Ernst Bloch, moved in. Whilst neither of the two famous men wrote about the Institute's activities, a record of the experiences of another prominent Institute occupant, the communist Willi Münzenberg, survives to-

Ort zusammenkamen, Behandlungen erhielten oder für einige Zeit in diesem imposanten und gleichzeitig ausgesprochen behaglichen Domizil im Zentrum Berlins logierten.⁴

Hirschfeld selbst lebte mit seinem Partner Karl Giese im Institut. Andere Zimmer wurden an ständige oder temporäre Mitarbeiter*innen und Besucher*innen aus aller Welt wie Isherwood vermietet, der dort einen Ort der Selbstverwirklichung fand. In seinem autobiografischen Werk *Christopher und die Seinen*, das er in der dritten Person verfasste und erst 1976 veröffentlichte, schreibt er, dass er bei seiner ersten Führung durch das Museum des Instituts den Eindruck hatte, »[h]ier konfrontierte man ihn endlich mit seinen Artgenossen«.⁵ Obwohl er in späteren Werken an seinem zwiespältigen Verhältnis zu diesem Ort festhielt, verbrachte er doch eine prägende Zeit am Institut. Dort lernte er auch seinen Freund, den für seine Ausgrabungen in Galiläa bekannten britischen Archäologen Francis Turville-Petre kennen, mit dem er später angesichts der wachsenden Bedrohung durch die Nationalsozialisten gemeinsam die Stadt verließ. Turville-Petre, auch bekannt als »Der Franni« oder »Fronny«, diente Isherwood später als Vorbild für die Figur des Ambrose in seinem Roman *Down there on a Visit* (1962). Eine weitere Bewohnerin war Hirschfelds verwitwete älteste Schwester Recha Tobias. Recha wiederum hatte etwa drei Monate lang ein Zimmer an den Philosophen Walter Benjamin vermietet, in das im Anschluss ein weiterer Philosoph, der kurz zuvor verwitwete Ernst Bloch, ziehen sollte. Während die Aktivitäten des Instituts in den Werken dieser beiden berühmten Männer keinerlei Erwähnung finden, sind die Berichte eines weiteren bekannten Institutsbewohners, des Kommunisten Willi Münzenberg, heute überliefert. Münzenberg war Pressebeauftragter und

day. Münzenberg was the press officer of the German communist party and one of its members of parliament. According to his partner, the political activist and publicist Babette Gross, Münzenberg and his comrades relished life at the Institute, not necessarily because they were interested in queer life and politics but because the busy environment enabled them to conduct many clandestine meetings including with visitors from abroad keen to fly under the radar of the German state.[6] Yet if the Institute may appear as a quasi-utopian space, it is also important to remember that not everyone was included equally. The working-class transgender maid Dora, for instance, who was employed at the Institute where she underwent a number of medical procedures, remained somewhat separate from its social life. In contrast, Turville-Petre's servant, a man named Erwin Hansen, and "a boy" called Heinz Neddermeyer, were more integrated. As Isherwood's and Turville-Petre's lovers as well as servants they regularly frequented Berlin's gay nightlife with their employers. Isherwood got to know Heinz in Mohrin, a village near the Polish border (and now in Poland) where Turville-Petre had rented a holiday house, and the two became long-term partners. After the Nazis came to power, Isherwood desperately tried to help Heinz flee Germany—a picaresque tale of migration from one European country to another that is also recorded in *Christopher and His Kind*—but his efforts proved vain.

Reichstagsabgeordneter der Deutschen Kommunistischen Partei. Nach Angaben seiner Lebensgefährtin, der politischen Aktivistin und Publizistin Babette Gross, genossen Münzenberg und seine Kameraden das Leben am Institut nicht so sehr, weil sie sich für queere Lebenswelten und Politik interessierten, sondern weil sie in diesem geschäftigen Umfeld – unbemerkt von der deutschen Obrigkeit – zahlreiche geheime Treffen, auch mit Besuchern aus dem Ausland, abhalten konnten.[6] Doch obwohl das Institut den Anschein eines nahezu utopischen Orts vermittelte, darf nicht vergessen werden, dass dort nicht alle Bewohner*innen gleichermaßen integriert waren. So nahm beispielsweise das aus der Arbeiterklasse stammende transsexuelle Hausmädchen Dora, das am Institut arbeitete und dort auch einige medizinische Behandlungen erhielt, nicht an allen Bereichen des sozialen Lebens teil. Im Gegensatz dazu waren sowohl der Diener von Turville-Petre, ein Mann namens Erwin Hansen, als auch »ein Knabe« mit dem Namen Heinz Neddermeyer deutlich besser integriert. Als Geliebte und Diener von Isherwood und Turville-Petre verkehrten sie gemeinsam mit ihren Arbeitgebern regelmäßig im schwulen Berliner Nachtleben. Isherwood hatte Heinz in Mohrin kennengelernt, einem Dorf nahe der polnischen Grenze (das heute in Polen liegt), wo Turville-Petre ein Ferienhaus gemietet hatte. Die beiden blieben lange Zeit ein Paar. Nach der Machtübernahme der Nazis versuchte Isherwood verzweifelt, Heinz bei der Flucht aus Deutschland zu helfen – die pikareske Geschichte einer Wanderung von einem europäischen Land in das nächste, die auch in *Christopher und die Seinen* behandelt wird –, doch seine Bemühungen sollten sich als erfolglos erweisen.

Mit der Machtübernahme der Nazis kam das Aus, sowohl für das Institut, das 1933 zerstört und

The Nazi rise to power spelled an end for both the Institute, which was raided in 1933, and Weimar Berlin's extrovertly queer scene. Hirschfeld was already in exile by the time of the Nazi attack (he died in France in 1935) and many of his colleagues, a considerable number of whom were, like Hirschfeld, Jewish, had also left Berlin. After the war the centre of sex research shifted from Europe to the United States with the rise of Alfred Kinsey's large-scale studies of sexual behaviours. Berlin, meanwhile, rebuilt its queer subcultures, developing once more into a destination for those whose bodies and desires were at odds with the ideals of the nuclear family that took hold in the postwar period. Today, the Institute of Sexual Science is but a—well-remembered—memory in the city's history, although its founder Hirschfeld is once more a figurehead of part of the German homosexual rights movement. Unlike in the early twentieth century, however, Hirschfeld is no longer positioned as an outsider but commemorated by many, including a society that carries his name and by the German state itself, which has named a foundation after him. Traces of queer Weimar thus survive in Berlin including its place names, museums, and memorials. But the "Berlin myth" of sexual freedom and liberation between the world wars has also come under scrutiny as scholars and activists are turning their attention to the historical whiteness of Germany's homosexual rights movement and its emergence during the

geplündert wurde, als auch für die extrovertierte Berliner Homosexuellenszene der Weimarer Republik. Hirschfeld befand sich zum Zeitpunkt des Nazi-Angriffs bereits im Exil (er starb 1935 in Frankreich), und viele seiner Kolleg*innen, die wie Hirschfeld selbst oftmals jüdisch waren, hatten Berlin ebenfalls verlassen. Nach Kriegsende verlagerte sich das Zentrum der Sexualforschung mit dem zunehmenden Erfolg von Alfred Kinsey, der umfangreiche Studien über das Sexualverhalten durchführte, von Europa in die Vereinigten Staaten. Unterdessen formierten sich die queeren Subkulturen Berlins neu, und die Stadt entwickelte sich einmal mehr zum Ziel für all diejenigen, deren Körper und Begehren nicht den Idealen der Kernfamilie entsprachen, die sich in der Nachkriegszeit durchgesetzt hatten. Das Institut für Sozialwissenschaft ist heute nur mehr eine – wenn auch gute – Erinnerung an die Geschichte der Stadt. Und das, obwohl sein Gründer Hirschfeld für einen Teil der deutschen Homosexuellenrechtsbewegung einmal mehr zu einer Gallionsfigur geworden ist. Im Gegensatz zum frühen 20. Jahrhundert gilt Hirschfeld heute allerdings nicht mehr als Außenseiter. Sein Andenken wird von vielen gewürdigt, so von einer Gesellschaft, die seinen Namen trägt, und vom deutschen Staat selbst, der eine Stiftung nach ihm benannte. In Berlin sind noch immer Spuren der queeren Weimarer Zeit zu finden, darunter die Namen von Orten oder Museen und Gedenkstätten. Doch der »Berliner Mythos« der sexuellen Freiheit und Befreiung in der Zeit zwischen den beiden Weltkriegen gerät auch unter Beschuss, denn Wissenschaftler*innen und Aktivist*innen machen darauf aufmerksam, dass die Geschichte der Homosexuellenrechtsbewegung in Deutschland vornehmlich von weißen Menschen geprägt wurde und dass sich diese Bewegung während der Blütezeit der deutschen Kolonialherrschaft ent-

country's colonial heyday. While Weimar Berlin is thus once more at the heart of modern debates about gender and sexuality, the city remains an important home for LGBTIQ+ culture, activism, and everyday life in the twenty-first century.

wickelte. Während das Berlin der Weimarer Republik also einmal mehr im Mittelpunkt moderner Debatten über Gender und Sexualität steht, bietet die Stadt im 21. Jahrhundert noch immer ein wichtiges Zuhause für die Kultur, den Aktivismus und das Alltagsleben von LGBTIQ*-Menschen.

Notes

1 Christopher Isherwood: Christopher and His Kind, 1976, London, Vintage 2012, p. 3.
2 Vita Sackville-West to Virginia Woolf, 12 January 1929, in: The Letters of Vita Sackville-West, ed. by Louise de Salvo and Mitchell A. Leaska, London, Virago 1992, p. 324.
3 Cited in Laura Marcus: The Tenth Muse. Writing about Cinema in the Modernist Period, Oxford, Oxford University Press 2007, p. 496.
4 Isherwood: Christopher and His Kind, p. 17.
5 Ibid., p. 16.
6 Heike Bauer: The Hirschfeld Archives. Violence, Death, and Modern Queer Culture, Philadelphia, Temple University Press 2017, p. 81.

a Wyndham Lewis: Hitler, London, Chatto & Windus 1931, p. 21.

Anmerkungen

1 Christopher Isherwood: Willkommen in Berlin. Christopher und die Seinen, aus dem Englischen von Stefan Troßbach, 1. Auflage dieser Ausgabe, Berlin, Bruno Gmünder Verlag 2014, S. 9.
2 Vita Sackville-West an Virginia Woolf, 12. Januar 1929, in: Geliebtes Wesen. Die Briefe von Vita Sackville-West und Virginia Woolf, hg. von Louise DeSalvo und Mitchell A. Leaska, aus dem Englischen von Sybill und Dirk Vanderbeke, Frankfurt a.M., S. Fischer 1995, S. 300.
3 Zitat aus Laura Marcus: The Tenth Muse. Writing about Cinema in the Modernist Period, Oxford, Oxford University Press 2007, S. 496.
4 Isherwood: Willkommen in Berlin, S. 23.
5 Ebd., S. 22.
6 Heike Bauer: The Hirschfeld Archives. Violence, Death, and Modern Queer Culture, Philadelphia, Temple University Press 2017, S. 81.

a Wyndham Lewis: Hitler und sein Werk in englischer Beleuchtung, Berlin, Verlag Reimar Hobbing 1932, S. 19.

Gesa Stedman

English Women Writers in Berlin: From the Cage of Diplomacy to the Gestapo Prison

Englische Schriftstellerinnen in Berlin: Vom Käfig der Diplomatie bis zum Gestapo-Gefängnis

Even if no English women writers produced the equivalent of Isherwood's Berlin novels, in their memoirs, letters, novels, articles, and essays, they created a nuanced, astute, and often surprising representation of Berlin. Some of the elements of the Berlin myth are put into question by these texts, and certainly let the reader ponder Isherwood's role as the sole important English authority on Berlin.

Auch wenn keine englische Schriftstellerin einen Berlin-Roman verfasst hat, der sich mit Isherwoods *Berliner Geschichten* vergleichen lässt, so finden sich in den Memoiren, Briefen, Romanen, Artikeln und Essays dieser Autorinnen doch differenzierte, scharfsichtige und oft auch überraschende Beobachtungen zu Berlin. Durch die Lektüre ihrer Texte geraten einige Aspekte des Berliner Mythos und mit Sicherheit auch Isherwoods Rolle als einzig bedeutsamer englischer Berlin-Kenner ins Wanken.

Why did women writers come to Berlin?

Warum kamen Schriftstellerinnen nach Berlin?

In the years following the First World War, and even continuing into the 1930s and the early years of the Nazi regime, Berlin was exciting, it was comparatively cheap, and it promised otherness. It was the opposite of London or Paris, and just like male travellers and writers, women were attracted and intrigued. They came to seek pleasure and adventure, or for professional reasons as psychoanalysts in training, or as journalists. There is one difference, however, in why some English women travelled

In den Jahren nach dem Ersten Weltkrieg und sogar noch bis in die 1930er Jahre und die frühen Jahre der Nazi-Herrschaft war Berlin ein aufregender Ort. Das Leben in der Stadt war vergleichsweise günstig und verhieß die Möglichkeit der Andersartigkeit. Berlin war das genaue Gegenteil von London oder Paris und übte auf männliche wie weibliche Reisende und Schriftsteller*innen eine große Faszination und Anziehungskraft aus. Frauen kamen auf der Suche nach Vergnügen und Abenteuer oder auch aus beruflichen Gründen in die Stadt, für eine Ausbildung zur Psychoanalytikerin oder als Journalistin. Im Vergleich zu ihren männlichen

[Fig. 20: Evelyn Blücher, frontispiece of *An English Wife in Berlin*, 1920, based on the portrait by an unknown photographer, c. 1896]

[Abb. 20: Evelyn Blücher, Frontispiz von *An English Wife in Berlin*, 1920, unter Verwendung eines Porträts eines unbekannten Fotografen, ca. 1896]

to Berlin, and then often not out of choice: they had to accompany their husbands. Evelyn Countess Blücher joined her German husband Count Blücher when he was sent into exile in Berlin at the beginning of the First World War.

Lady Helen D'Abernon prepared the British Embassy shortly after the war and held the fort when her husband was away negotiating Eastern European peace talks.

Landsleuten machten sich einige Engländerinnen allerdings häufig nicht aus eigenen Stücken auf den Weg, sondern mussten ihre Ehemänner nach Berlin begleiten. Evelyn Fürstin Blücher kam an der Seite ihres deutschen Ehemannes, Fürst Blücher, der zu Beginn des Ersten Weltkriegs ins Berliner Exil geschickt wurde.

Lady Helen D'Abernon traf kurz nach Kriegsende die ersten Vorbereitungen in der Britischen Botschaft und hielt dort Stellung, während ihr Ehemann noch zu Verhandlungen über einen Friedensvertrag in Ost-

Vita Sackville-West, writer and lover of Virginia Woolf, very unwillingly spent part of her time in Berlin as wife to the embassy's *chargé d'affaires* Harold Nicolson. Yet, the majority of English women writers came of their own accord and have left memorable and multiple written records of their stay.

On class terms

Not surprisingly, in class terms the women writers all came from the upper middle or the upper classes. Although Berlin was not expensive, a stay in the city did still depend on disposable income to spend on luxurious hotels, dining out, going clubbing, or simply visiting the many modern sights Berlin had to offer, such as the Wellenbad in Luna Park, the newly erected radio tower, the opera, theatre or concert halls, or the six-day cycle races. The last of these attracted commentary from several writers—all of them unfavourable. The presence of working-class men in the race was scathingly described by psychoanalyst and Bloomsbury author Alix Strachey, who spent nearly a year in Berlin: "And the Public! They simply sat & roared, hypnotised by 30 pairs of stumpy, dirty lower-class legs in old Jaeger combinations, going round & round on the bicycle treadles".[1] Four years later, Vita Sackville-West heartily agreed with her. And nothing could mask Evelyn Countess Blücher's shock and distaste at being confronted with the revolutionary masses she observed from the window of

europa weilte. Vita Sackville-West, die Schriftstellerin und Geliebte von Virginia Woolf, musste gegen ihren ausdrücklichen Willen einen Teil ihres Lebens als Ehefrau des stellvertretenden Botschafters Harold Nicolson in Berlin verbringen. Doch die Mehrzahl der englischen Schriftstellerinnen kam aus eigenem Antrieb, und von ihren Aufenthalten sind zahlreiche eindrucksvolle Berichte überliefert.

Eine Frage der Klasse

Es ist nicht überraschend, dass diese Schriftstellerinnen allesamt aus der oberen Mittelklasse oder der Oberklasse stammten. Das Leben in Berlin war zwar alles andere als kostspielig, doch für einen Aufenthalt in der Stadt brauchte man dennoch das nötige Kleingeld, um luxuriöse Hotels, Restaurants, Clubabende oder einfach nur den Besuch einer der zahlreichen Sehenswürdigkeiten Berlins finanzieren zu können, wie das Wellenbad im Luna Park, den neu errichteten Funkturm, Opern, Theater oder Konzerthäuser oder das Sechstagerennen. Über Letzteres fanden mehrere Schriftstellerinnen keine freundlichen Worte. Die Psychoanalytikerin, Autorin und Angehörige der Bloomsbury Group, Alix Strachey, die fast ein Jahr lang in Berlin gelebt hatte, äußerte sich vernichtend über die Rennteilnehmer aus der Arbeiterklasse: »Und das Publikum! Sie saßen nur & grölten, hypnotisiert von 30 Paar stämmiger, schmutziger Proletarierbeinen in alten Jaeger-Kombinationen, die sich rund und rund auf den Pedalen drehten«.[1] Vier Jahre später stimmte ihr Vita Sackville-West aus vollem Herzen zu. Und Evelyn Fürstin Blücher brachte völlig unverblümt ihre Bestürzung und Abscheu angesichts der revolutionären Massen zum Ausdruck, die sie durch die Fenster ihres Palais erblickte. Lady D'Abernon übertrug ihr britisches Klassendenken auf

her Palais. British class terms were transferred to Berlin, as Lady D'Abernon made clear in her haughty comments on the first German president Friedrich Ebert, his wife, and their lower middle-class origins:

> The President is a rough diamond, coarse and heavy, but one feels at once that he has a strong personality and is no mere figurehead. Frau Ebert is a hefty upstanding lady from Danzig, said to be the daughter of a saddler. Both are unused to social amenities ...[2]

Virginia Woolf was equally scathing when she described her return journey from Berlin to Vita Sackville-West: "There were two Germans in the carriage—fat, greasy, the woman with broken nails. The man peeled an orange for her. She squeezed his hand. It was repulsive".[3]

This tells us more about the class habitus the women shared than about Berlin. But it points to one significant difference between Isherwood, Auden, and Spender and their female compatriots: in contrast to the intrepid male explorers of Schöneberg and Kreuzberg nightlife, the women writers' interest in Berlin did not extend beyond the affluent West and its equally well-off inhabitants, cafés, theatres, and bars. And if they did venture out to the masses, this was usually as part of chaperoned visits to charitable institutions such as soup kitchens or nurseries for orphaned children. Even in the later 1920s and 1930s, when fashion constraints and impractical

Berlin, als sie in hochnäsigem Ton über den ersten deutschen Reichspräsidenten Friedrich Ebert, seine Ehefrau und ihre Herkunft aus der unteren Mittelklasse feststellte:

> Der Reichspräsident ist ein ungeschliffener Diamant, ungehobelt und grobschlächtig im Auftreten, doch ohne Zweifel von starker Persönlichkeit und mehr als nur eine Gallionsfigur. Frau Ebert ist eine robuste und aufrechte Danziger Dame, angeblich Tochter eines Sattlers. Beide haben keinerlei Gespür für gesellschaftliche Umgangsformen ...[2]

Und Virginia Woolf berichtete Vita Sackville-West nicht minder abfällig von den Erlebnissen ihrer Heimreise aus Berlin: »Mit mir saßen zwei beleibte, ungepflegte Deutsche im Abteil, die Frau mit brüchigen Nägeln. Der Mann schälte ihr eine Orange. Sie drückte seine Hand. Es war widerwärtig.«[3]

Dies sagt mehr über den Klassenhabitus aus, den die Frauen gemein hatten, als über Berlin. Doch es deutet auch auf einen wesentlichen Unterschied zwischen Isherwood, Auden und Spender und ihren weiblichen Landsfrauen hin: Im Gegensatz zu den Männern, die sich furchtlos in das Schöneberger und Kreuzberger Nachtleben stürzten, beschränkte sich das Interesse der Schriftstellerinnen auf den wohlhabenden Westen der Stadt und seine ebenfalls begüterten Bewohner*innen sowie die dort angesiedelten Cafés, Theater und Bars. Sollten sie sich doch einmal unter die Massen mischen, handelte es sich in der Regel um organisierte Besuche von Wohlfahrtseinrichtungen wie Suppenküchen oder Waisenhäusern. Und sogar in den späten 1920er Jahren und den 1930er Jahren, als unpraktische Bekleidung die Frauen nicht mehr behinderte, bevorzugten eng-

[Fig. 21: Vita Sackville-West, photograph by Howard Coster, c. 1927]

[Abb. 21: Vita Sackville-West, Fotografie von Howard Coster, ca. 1927]

dresses no longer proved such a problem, female English visitors to Berlin kept to middle-class environments and places.

lische Berlin-Besucherinnen weiterhin bürgerliche Milieus und Treffpunkte.

From the *voyeuse* to the *flâneuse*

When one reads the many written records of both unwilling and voluntary stays in early 20th-century Berlin in chronological order, one aspect stands out: the earlier texts posit the women writers merely as *voyeuses*, as observers behind windows, and only later do they venture into the increasingly modern, fast-paced city on their own as *flâneuses*, taking on different spaces out of choice, and inhabiting these

Von der Voyeurin zur Flaneurin

Liest man die unzähligen Berichte über ungewollte und freiwillige Aufenthalte im Berlin des frühen 20. Jahrhunderts in chronologischer Reihenfolge, fällt ein Aspekt sofort ins Auge: In früheren Texten nimmt die Schriftstellerin vor allem die Position einer Voyeurin ein, einer Beobachterin hinter geschlossenen Fenstern. Erst später wagt sie selbst den Schritt in die immer modernere, rastlose Stadt. Als Flaneurin erkundet sie verschiedene Orte ihrer Wahl und erobert sich diese Räume selbstständig und in

spaces independently and often without male accompaniment. This development mirrors the ambivalent emancipation of German women, whose greater scope of movement, occupations, and political and public possibilities nevertheless did not apply to all classes, and certainly did not change their role as mothers and wives if they happened to be married with children. This is an aspect of the Berlin myth that is perhaps less well known in a British context.

vielen Fällen ohne männliche Begleitung. Diese Entwicklung spiegelt wider, wie es um die Emanzipation in Deutschland bestellt war. Nicht alle Frauen aus allen sozialen Klassen profitierten von dem damaligen Zugewinn an Bewegungsfreiheit, beruflichen, politischen und staatlichen Möglichkeiten, die zudem mit Sicherheit nichts an ihrer Rolle als Mütter und Ehefrauen änderten, sofern sie verheiratet waren und Kinder hatten. Dies ist ein Aspekt des Berliner Mythos, der in britischen Kreisen vermutlich weniger bekannt ist.

Watching from enclosed spaces

When the English Catholic Evelyn, Countess Blücher, arrived in Berlin in 1914, shortly after the outbreak of the First World War, she observed events evolving from the Hotel Esplanade, and later the Palais Blücher near Pariser Platz. As her husband Count Blücher was German, they were forced to leave London as so-called enemy-aliens and just made it across the Channel without being torpedoed. From her window, Countess Blücher first watched impoverished Berliners as the war progressed, and later the soldiers, workers, and sailors spear-heading the November Revolution which followed the war and led to the end of the German monarchy. If she wanted to go out, she could only do that in disguise, or with a man accompanying her. She was frightened, but her privilege shines through in the memoir which she wrote during the events and had published shortly afterwards.

Beobachterin hinter geschlossenen Fenstern

Als die englische Katholikin Evelyn Fürstin Blücher 1914 kurz nach Ausbruch des Ersten Weltkriegs nach Berlin kam, verfolgte sie die dortigen Ereignisse zunächst aus dem Hotel Esplanade und später aus dem Palais Blücher nahe dem Pariser Platz. Weil ihr Ehemann Fürst Blücher Deutscher war, wurden sie gezwungen, London als sogenannte feindliche Ausländer zu verlassen und schafften es knapp, den Torpedoangriffen im Ärmelkanal zu entgehen. Von ihrem Fenster aus beobachtete Fürstin Blücher zunächst die mit dem Fortschreiten des Krieges zunehmende Verarmung der Berliner*innen und später nach Kriegsende die Soldaten, Arbeiter und Matrosen an der Speerspitze der November-Revolution, die das Ende der Monarchie in Deutschland einläutete. Wenn sie ausgehen wollte, konnte sie dies nur in einer Verkleidung oder in männlicher Begleitung tun. Sie war voller Angst, und doch zeugen die Erinnerungen, die sie während dieser Ereignisse niederschrieb und wenig später veröffentlichen ließ, von ihrer privilegierten Stellung:

> There we sat crouched together in the darkness, for we dared not turn on a light, listening to the fierce fighting going on all around us from the Bradenburger (sic) Tor away over to the Reichstag [...] At the end of an hour the firing died away, and Frau von Derenthall suggested we should have a cup of coffee; and two maids set to work and made us some.[4]

> Da saßen wir nun dicht beieinander in der Dunkelheit, weil wir es nicht wagen konnten, Licht zu machen, und lauschten dem heftigen Kampf, der vom Brandenburger Tor aus bis zum Reichstag uns umtobte [...] Nach einer Stunde hörte das Schießen auf, und Frau von Derenthall lud uns zu einer Tasse Kaffee ein, den uns die beiden Mädchen bereiteten.[4]

The discrepancy between the downtrodden masses and the cosmopolitan aristocratic elite at the Hotel Esplanade and in the Palais Blücher could not be greater.

Der Kontrast zwischen den unterdrückten Massen und der kosmopolitischen aristokratischen Elite im Hotel Esplanade und im Palais Blücher hätte größer nicht sein können.

Venturing beyond the window

The next English writer to observe events mostly from the window, and only in an escorted fashion if in the city itself, was Lady Helen D'Abernon, wife of the first British ambassador to Germany after the First World War. Berlin was crippled economically by the war and the Treaty of Versailles, many were forced into homelessness and prostitution, and in the early years after the war, hunger was widespread. This situation only improved after 1924, when the economy had stabilised somewhat with Weimar social reform acts taking effect and hyperinflation having been stopped by the introduction of a new currency. The American Dawes plan helped to tie the payment of war reparations to the overall German economic performance, which improved until the Great Depression set in during the 1930s.

Die Welt auf der anderen Seite des Fensters

Eine weitere englische Autorin, die die Ereignisse vornehmlich von ihrem Fenster aus beobachtete und die Stadt selbst nie ohne Begleitung besuchte, war Lady Helen D'Abernon, die Ehefrau des ersten britischen Botschafters in Deutschland nach dem Ersten Weltkrieg. Berlins Wirtschaft lag nach dem Krieg und dem Vertrag von Versailles am Boden. Viele Menschen sahen sich zu einem Leben auf der Straße und in die Prostitution gezwungen. In den ersten Nachkriegsjahren war Hunger weit verbreitet. Die Situation besserte sich erst nach 1924, als sich die Wirtschaft mit der Sozialreform der Weimarer Republik langsam stabilisierte und die Hyperinflation durch die Einführung einer neuen Währung gestoppt werden konnte. Mit dem amerikanischen Dawes-Plan wurden die Reparationszahlungen an die wirtschaftliche Leistungsfähigkeit Deutschlands geknüpft, die bis zum Beginn der Weltwirtschaftskrise stetig zunahm.

Places
The British Embassy

The British Embassy on Wilhelmstraße close to the boulevard Unter den Linden, the Brandenburg Gate, Pariser Platz, and the Hotel Adlon was housed in an impressive palais—the Palais Strousberg, which the British government had bought in the late 19th century. During the First World War it had stood empty, but was restored to its former glory after the war. Its interior was even more impressive than its façade, and used for extensive balls, dinners, and parties. After the First World War, it soon became a hub of political meetings and cultural exchange. Depending on the interests of the ambassador in residence, his wife, and the political climate, these meetings and exchanges took on a different character. Lady Helen D'Abernon, society hostess and wife of the first ambassador after the war to reopen the embassy, was intent on showing Berlin that pre-war splendour and parties were still possible. As their aristocratic visitor Lady Violet Bonham-Carter comments: "I can't tell you what admiration I felt for your *masterly* performance on that most difficult stage".[a] Harold Nicolson, *chargé d'affaires* under Sir Horace Rumbold in the late 1920s, was more interested in inviting other important authors and speakers. Thus, the actor and singer Ivor Novello came for a visit, and the writer H.G. Wells found his way to Berlin to address the Reichstag. Nicolson's friends from England such as the writers and critics Maurice Bowra, Cyril Connolly, and Raymond Mortimer enjoyed the combination of intellectual debate and entertainment:

> The candles lit up the polished table, the dark glow of port, the lighter one of brandy in our glasses. The night air smelt of lake-water and smoke from our cigars. … We were all going over our pasts to see if they contained moments as happy as this one. I thought of our security, our freedom from worries, our friendship and free play of ideas and intelligences, and what a good setting we were in for the end of the world.[b]

Under the Nazi regime, diplomacy, parties, and receptions had to continue but became even more politically fraught. Britons who fell foul of the regime had to be rescued and the embassy turned into a refuge, not least for the left-wing historian and political journalist Elizabeth Wiskemann, who only escaped lasting Gestapo imprisonment with the help of embassy staff, as well as her own intellect.

[Fig. 22: The British Embassy in Berlin, unknown photographer, 1937]

[Abb. 22: Die Britische Botschaft in Berlin, unbekannter Fotograf, 1937]

Orte
Die Britische Botschaft

Die Britische Botschaft an der Wilhelmstraße befand sich in unmittelbarer Nachbarschaft zum Boulevard Unter den Linden, dem Brandenburger Tor, dem Pariser Platz und dem Hotel Adlon. Sie war im Palais Strousberg untergebracht, einem beeindruckenden Palast, den die britische Regierung im späten 19. Jahrhundert erworben hatte. Nachdem der Palast während des Ersten Weltkriegs leer gestanden hatte, erstrahlte er nach Kriegsende erneut im alten Glanz. Die Innenräume waren noch prächtiger als die Fassade und wurden für große Bälle, Abendessen und Feste genutzt. Nach dem Ersten Weltkrieg entwickelte sich die Botschaft schon bald zur Schaltstelle des politischen und kulturellen Lebens. Je nach Vorlieben des amtierenden Botschafters und seiner Gattin und abhängig vom politischen Klima nahmen die politischen Begegnungen und der kulturelle Austausch unterschiedliche Formen an. Lady Helen D'Abernon, Dame der gehobenen Gesellschaft und Ehefrau des ersten Botschafters der Nachkriegszeit, der die Botschaft wiedereröffnete, wollte den Berliner*innen beweisen, dass die prunkvollen Feste der Vorkriegszeit noch nicht der Vergangenheit angehörten. Unter ihren Gästen befand sich auch die Aristokratin Lady Violet Bonham-Carter, die über ihre Erlebnisse in der Botschaft schrieb: »Ich kann Ihnen gar nicht sagen, wie sehr ich ihre *meisterhafte* Leistung unter diesen ausgesprochen schwierigen Bedingungen bewundere«.[a] Harold Nicolson, der in den späten 1920er Jahren als *Chargé d'Affaires* unter Sir Horace Rumbold in der Berliner Botschaft weilte, empfing besonders gern namhafte Autor*innen und Redner*innen. Seiner Einladung folgte auch der Schauspieler und Sänger Ivor Novello. Der Schriftsteller H.G. Wells kam für eine Rede vor dem Reichstag nach Berlin. Nicolsons Freunde aus England, darunter die Schriftsteller und Kritiker Maurice Bowra, Cyril Connolly und Raymond Mortimer, genossen die Verbindung aus intellektuellem Austausch und Unterhaltung:

> Das Licht der Kerzen beleuchtete die polierten Tische und unsere Gläser, in denen der Port im dunklen, der Brandy im etwas helleren Glanz erstrahlten. Die Nachtluft roch nach Seewasser und war vom Rauch unserer Zigarren erfüllt. […] Wir alle forschten in unserer Vergangenheit nach Momenten, in denen wir ein solches Glück empfunden hatten. Ich dachte an unser sicheres und sorgenfreies Leben, unsere Freundschaft und unser freies Spiel der Ideen und Ansichten. Und daran, in welch guter Gesellschaft wir doch waren, falls das Ende der Welt bevorstand.[b]

Während der Nazi-Herrschaft mussten die diplomatischen Treffen, Feste und Empfänge weiter stattfinden, doch die politische Lage war deutlich angespannter. Es galt, Brit*innen zu retten, die beim Regime im Ungnade gefallen waren. Die Botschaft entwickelte sich zum Zufluchtsort; nicht nur für die linke Historikerin und politische Journalistin Elizabeth Wiskemann, die nur mit Hilfe von Botschaftsmitarbeiter*innen und dank ihres eigenen Scharfsinns einem längeren Aufenthalt in den Gefängnissen der Gestapo entgehen konnte.

Like Countess Blücher, D'Abernon observed the differences between the Berlin population and her own social standing as a London society hostess, an ambassador's wife, and a political mediator in her own right.

But in spite of her awareness of Berlin's poverty, she set the embassy to rights and held glamorous parties—sparking Harry

Wie auch Fürstin Blücher hatte D'Abernon einen Blick für die Unterschiede zwischen ihrem eigenen sozialen Status als Dame der Londoner Gesellschaft, Botschaftergattin und selbst ernannte politische Vermittlerin und der Berliner Bevölkerung.

Doch trotz ihres Wissens um die Armut in der Stadt war in der Botschaft davon nichts zu spüren: Sie veranstaltete rauschende Feste, die Harry Graf

Englische Schriftstellerinnen in Berlin

Count Kessler to remark that this might have been in poor taste, given the tense political situation.⁵ The same discrepancy can be found in the hand-written diary of one of the D'Abernon's visitors, Lady Violet Bonham-Carter, who came to stay at the embassy and alternated parties and visiting diplomats and politicians, with shopping in Leipziger Straße. The contrasts and odd juxtapositions of two worlds in her Berlin diary resemble similar instances in Helen D'Abernon's memoir. One scene Helen D'Abernon comments on is particularly striking as it is a very early instance of cross-dressing and poverty-induced prostitution which predates Isherwood's descriptions of the city's flamboyant underworld by more than a decade. He, of course, was immersed in this world himself, while D'Abernon could only adopt the stance of the *voyeuse*, with the text seeming to oscillate between fascination and a suppressed desire to leave the position behind the window:

> I spend hours at the window, watching the lumbering conveyances and the unusual pedestrians that pass to and fro. Sometimes the sights are peculiar and intriguing. Last night a woman (as at first sight I took the figure to be) dressed in a light coat and skirt, a large hat and a floating veil, stood ever so long on the opposite side of the street in a dark doorway. At last she was joined by a man. After exchanging a few words they strolled away toward Unter den Linden. Then it was that the

Kessler zu der Frage verleiteten, »warum gerade Diplomaten in diesem Augenblick, wo die internationale Lage so gespannt und ernst ist, als Bauern und Bäuerinnen tanzen müssen«.⁵ Derselbe Zwiespalt lässt sich auch im handschriftlichen Tagebuch einer Besucherin von D'Abernon, Lady Violet Bonham-Carter, nachlesen, die eine Zeit lang in der Botschaft weilte und ihre Tage im Wechsel mit Festen, Besuchen bei Diplomaten und Politikern und Einkaufstouren an der Leipziger Straße verbrachte. Die Unterschiede und kuriosen Gegenüberstellungen der beiden Welten in ihrem Berlin-Tagebuch lassen sich mit ähnlichen Episoden in Helen D'Abernons Memoiren vergleichen. Eine Szene in D'Abernons Beschreibungen sticht dabei besonders hervor, denn es ist ein früher Bericht über Cross-Dressing und armutsbedingte Prostitution, den sie mehr als ein Jahrzehnt vor Isherwoods Schilderungen der extravaganten Berliner Unterwelt niedergeschrieben hatte. Natürlich war Isherwood selbst Teil dieser Welt, während D'Abernon lediglich die Position der Voyeurin einnehmen konnte. In ihren Notizen scheint sie zwischen Faszination und dem unterdrückten Wunsch, die Position am Fenster verlassen zu können, hin- und hergerissen:

> Ich stand stundenlang am Fenster, schaute den rumpelnden Fuhrwerken nach und hielt Ausschau nach ungewöhnlichen Passanten. Manchmal gab es merkwürdige und verblüffende Dinge zu sehen. Vergangene Nacht stand in einem dunklen Türeingang auf der anderen Straßenseite lange Zeit eine Frau (zumindest sah diese Person auf den ersten Blick so aus) im dünnen Mantel und Rock, mit großem Hut und flatterndem Schleier. Schließlich gesellte sich ein Mann zu ihr. Sie wechselten einige Worte und schlenderten dann in Richtung Unter den Linden davon.

flat feet and heavy silhouette made me realize that this was a man dressed like a woman. When the figure advanced into the glare of the lamplight I saw that round the waist of the jacket was strapped a military belt from which hung a scabbard. It was not the first time that from my window I have seen men street-walkers dressed up as women, but never before one with a cavalry belt and sabre superadded.[6]

Slightly later, English women writers began travelling to Germany and Berlin, following in the footsteps of their male counterparts, often out of an interest in the British occupation of the Rhineland. Journalists and writers like Vera Brittain and Winifred Holtby stopped briefly in Berlin on their German tour.[7] They did this of their own accord of course, and were far less circumscribed than the aristocratic ladies had been. They prefigure a trend which was to become dominant in the later 1920s, namely, the independent female traveller, professional, or visitor whose freedom of movement in Berlin was virtually without limits. The feminist playwright and travel writer Cicely Hamilton is an example of this new type of writer.

Erst da erkannte ich an den flachen Füßen und der kräftigen Silhouette, dass es sich um einen Mann in Frauenkleidern handeln musste. Und als sie den Schein der Straßenlaterne erreicht hatten, sah ich, dass der Mantel in der Taille mit einem Militärgürtel mit Schwerthalter geschnürt war. Nicht zum ersten Mal erblickte ich auf der Straße einen Mann in Frauenkleidern. Doch dies war der Erste, der noch dazu einen Kavalleriegürtel mit Schwert trug.[6]

Wenig später folgten die ersten englischen Schriftstellerinnen ihren männlichen Kollegen nach Deutschland und Berlin, häufig aus Interesse an der britischen Besatzung des Rheinlands. Journalist*innen und Schriftsteller*innen wie Vera Brittain und Winifred Holtby legten auf ihren Reisen durch Deutschland kurze Zwischenstopps in Berlin ein.[7] Sie hatten sich natürlich aus eigenem Antrieb auf den Weg gemacht und waren auf ihren Reisen im Vergleich zu den aristokratischen Ladys weitaus weniger eingeschränkt. Sie sollten einen Trend begründen, der sich in den späten 1920er Jahren durchsetzte, nämlich den der unabhängigen weiblichen Reisenden, die beruflich oder touristisch unterwegs war und deren Bewegungsfreiheit in Berlin nahezu keine Grenzen kannte. Die feministische Dramatikerin und Reiseschriftstellerin Cicely Hamilton ist ein weiteres Beispiel für diesen neuen Typus Autorin.

Enjoying the freedom of the *flâneuse*

The role of the *flâneuse* can perhaps best be illustrated by the case of psychoanalyst and member of the Bloomsbury group Alix Strachey.

Die wunderbare Freiheit der Flaneurin

Eine besonders eindrucksvolle Vertreterin dieser Gruppe der Flaneurinnen ist womöglich die Psychoanalytikerin und Angehörige der Bloomsbury Group Alix Strachey.

[Fig. 23: Alix Strachey, photograph by Barbara Ker-Seymer, 1930s]

[Abb. 23: Alix Strachey, Fotografie von Barbara Ker-Seymer, 1930er]

Alix was married to James Strachey, with whom she translated the works of Freud. She came to Berlin in 1924, to be analysed by Karl Abraham at the newly founded and hugely important Berlin Psychoanalytical Institute and, after initial hesitation, took to Berlin. In contrast to Auden, Spender, and Isherwood, she kept to the affluent western parts of the city. She enjoyed dances and balls, moving in the kind of social milieus, hospitable to emancipated women, that are familiar to us through the works of Jeanne Mammen.

Alix war mit James Strachey verheiratet, mit dem sie gemeinsam die Werke Sigmund Freuds übersetzte. Sie kam 1924 nach Berlin, um sich im neu gegründeten und ausgesprochen einflussreichen Berliner Psychoanalytischen Institut einer Analyse bei Karl Abraham zu unterziehen. Nach anfänglichem Zögern fand sie Gefallen an der Stadt. Im Unterschied zu Auden, Spender und Isherwood beschränkte sich ihr Radius auf den wohlhabenden Berliner Westen. Mit großer Freude nahm sie an Tanzveranstaltungen und Bällen teil und bewegte sich in jenen für emanzipierte Frauen offenen gesellschaftlichen Milieus, die uns aus Jeanne Mammens Werk bekannt sind.

She also attended radio concerts, theatre performances, films, and ballets. She spent hours at the writers' café Romanisches Café, and there met journalists, writers, artists, psychoanalysts, and people from many European countries. They hotly discussed psychoanalysis, politics, art, and writing. Her letters were only published in 1985 but they are a rich source of both the unfolding of psychoanalysis, images of Berlin, Anglo-German relations, cultural exchange, and of the act of writing the city itself. They testify to the great freedom of movement now possible for women, from the entertainment venue Luna Park to the theatres, from the Grunewald lakes to the nightlife of all shades, but they also bear witness to the serious nature of the Berlin Psychoanalytical Institute.

> I have a terrible week before me, as I find I've let myself in for a Ball on Tuesday, tomorrow (Fast-Nacht) as well as Saturday. On Saturday I'm again in Cleopatra's tow [Melanie Klein, G.S.], who's got a rage for 'em. It is a Kunst Akademie dance, very large & official. Tomorrow's affair is connected with the Romanisches Café & altogether cheap, Communistic & perhaps low. It is in the "Schall u. Rauch" & preceded by a Cabaret Show.[8]

Alix Strachey, who was seminal in enabling the famous Austrian child psychoanalyst Melanie Klein to make her way from Berlin to London, where her career really took off,

Alix Strachey besuchte auch Radiokonzerte, Theateraufführungen, Kinovorstellungen und Ballettdarbietungen. Stundenlang saß sie in dem bei Schriftsteller*innen beliebten Romanischen Café, wo sie Journalist*innen, Schriftsteller*innen, Künstler*innen, Psychoanalytiker*innen und Menschen aus zahlreichen Ländern Europas traf. Man führte lebhafte Diskussionen über Psychoanalyse, Politik, Kunst und Schriftstellerei. Ihre Briefe, die erst 1985 veröffentlicht wurden, enthalten aufschlussreiche Details zur Entwicklung der Psychoanalyse sowie Beschreibungen Berlins und Berichte über die deutsch-englischen Beziehungen, den kulturellen Austausch und das Schreiben über die Stadt im Allgemeinen. Sie zeugen von der großen Freizügigkeit, die Frauen zu dieser Zeit genossen und die sich vom Vergnügungsort Luna Park bis zu den Theatern, von den Seen im Grunewald bis in das Nachtleben mit all seinen Facetten erstreckte. Doch sie sind auch ein Beleg für die Seriosität des Berliner Psychoanalytischen Instituts.

> Ich habe eine schreckliche Woche vor mir, da mir klargeworden ist, daß ich mich auf zwei Bälle eingelassen habe, einen am Dienstag, also morgen (Fast-Nacht) sowie einen am Samstag. Am Samstag bin ich wieder in Cleopatras Schlepptau [Melanie Klein, G.S.], die ganz wild darauf ist. Ein Ball in der Kunstakademie, sehr groß & offiziell. Die Angelegenheit morgen ist verbunden mit dem Romanischen Café & durch & durch billig, kommunistisch & vielleicht ordinär. Es ist im »Schall u. Rauch« & wird von einer Kabarettdarbietung eingeleitet.[8]

Alix Strachey, die einen wichtigen Anteil daran hatte, dass die berühmte österreichische Kinderpsychoanalytikerin Melanie Klein Berlin in Richtung London

[Fig. 24: Jeanne Mammen, *Sie repräsentiert!* In: *Simplicissimus* 32. Jg. Nr. 47, 1928, Munich, paper, three colour print]

[Abb. 24: Jeanne Mammen, *Sie repräsentiert!*, in: *Simplicissimus* 32. Jg. Nr. 47, 1928, München, Papier, Dreifarbdruck]

was not the only English person to travel to Berlin because of an interest in psychoanalysis. A number of burgeoning psychoanalysts from Britain were trained in Berlin, or underwent analysis there, most notably perhaps the modernist writer Bryher, who accidentally met Hanns Sachs at Babelsberg Film Studios and returned for several months each year to be analysed. She first visited Berlin with her group of like-minded film enthusiasts who gathered around the British film journal *Close Up*. Others had come for professional reasons such as setting up a dancing school—as the famous modern dancer and choreographer Isadora Duncan had done in 1904—or in order to let their daughters attend the latter, as was the case with the modernist poet Mina Loy. In her autobiography *My Life* (1927), Duncan describes the school enthusiastically:

> We acted exactly as though we were people in Grimm's Fairy Tales. We went down to Wertheimer's and actually bought forty little beds, each covered with white muslin curtains, drawn back with blue ribbons. We set about to make of our villa a real children's Paradise.[9]

No overview of English women writers travelling or staying in Berlin could do without the more ambivalent members of the Bloomsbury group whose experience of the city was much less positive than Alix Strachey's. She also had her reservations and thought Bloomsbury parties much more entertaining than Berlin's

verließ, wo ihre Karriere erst richtig beginnen sollte, war nicht die einzige Engländerin, die wegen ihres Interesses an der Psychoanalyse nach Berlin gekommen war. Eine ganze Reihe aufstrebender britischer Psychoanalytiker*innen wurde in Berlin ausgebildet oder unterzog sich hier einer Analyse. Die bekannteste von ihnen war womöglich die modernistische Autorin Bryher, die in den Babelsberger Filmstudios zufällig Hanns Sachs getroffen hatte und anschließend alljährlich für mehrere Monate zur Analyse in die Stadt kam. Bei ihrem ersten Berlin-Besuch reiste sie gemeinsam mit einer Gruppe gleichgesinnter Filmliebhaber*innen an, die sich um das britische Filmmagazin *Close up* versammelten. Andere hatten sich aus beruflichen Gründen auf den Weg in die Stadt gemacht, beispielsweise um eine Tanzschule zu gründen – wie die berühmte moderne Tänzerin und Choreografin Isadora Duncan es bereits 1904 getan hatte – oder damit ihre Töchter diese Schulen besuchen konnten, wie im Falle der modernistischen Lyrikerin Mina Loy. In ihren Memoiren aus dem Jahr 1927 berichtet Duncan enthusiastisch:

> Wie in einem Grimmschen Märchen spielt sich jetzt alles ab: wir gingen zu Wertheim und kauften dort 40 kleine Bettchen mit Musselinvorhängen und blauen Bändern. Unsere Villa sollte ein Paradies für Kinder werden.[9]

Kein Bericht über englische Schriftstellerinnen, die Berlin einen Besuch abstatteten oder dort lebten, wäre vollständig ohne diejenigen Mitglieder der Bloomsbury Group, die ein deutlich gespalteneres Verhältnis zur Stadt hatten und dort weniger positive Erfahrungen als Alix Strachey machten. Doch auch sie hatte ihre Vorbehalte und beurteilte die Bloomsbury-Partys als weitaus unterhaltsamer als

balls—"sub-sub-subissimo Bloomsbury"[10] as she put it—but on the whole, her letters are less lugubrious than their counterparts from other Bloomsbury visitors.

Virginia Woolf and her lover Vita Sackville-West were frank in their shared distrust or almost hatred of Berlin in their exchange of letters. Vita Sackville-West had to accompany her husband, Harold Nicolson, *chargé d'affaires* at the British Embassy, to Berlin, and she abhorred it. "Berlin for 3 years! Good Lord deliver us!"[11] The "cage"[12] of diplomacy made her yearn for greater freedom in England, but she did spend several months in Berlin each year. And although her relationship with Virginia Woolf was important to both women, it did not hinder her from beginning an affair with the German-American novelist Margaret Goldsmith-Voigt, and writing about it in her letters to Virginia. Meanwhile, Harold Nicolson explored Berlin's gay scene, taking Vita's cousin, the writer and critic Eddy Sackville-West to clubs such as the famous Eldorado.[13]

Virginia Woolf, her husband the publisher Leonard Woolf, Virginia's sister, the painter Vanessa Bell, and painter Duncan Grant all travelled to Berlin in January 1929. By that time, Berlin was 'the' modern city to see. Accordingly, the Bloomsbury group followed a punishing programme of tourist sites (the radio tower, the planetarium, the indoor swimming pool), evening entertainments at the opera, watching avant-garde Soviet films unavailable in London, visiting art galleries and museums, and meeting people.

die Berliner Bälle, die sie für »sub-sub-subissimo Bloomsbury«[10] hielt. Alles in allem zeichnet sie in ihren Briefen jedoch ein wesentlich weniger düsteres Bild von Berlin als andere Mitglieder der Bloomsbury Group, die Berlin besuchten.

Virginia Woolf und ihre Geliebte Vita Sackville-West nahmen in ihrem Briefwechsel kein Blatt vor den Mund, wenn es um ihre geteilte Skepsis, ja fast schon um ihren Hass gegenüber Berlin ging. Vita Sackville-West musste ihren Ehemann, Harold Nicolson, *Chargé d'Affaires* an der Britischen Botschaft, nach Berlin begleiten, und ihr grauste davor. »Drei Jahre lang Berlin! Gütiger Gott, bewahre uns!«[11] In ihrem diplomatischen »Käfig«[12] sehnte sie sich nach der größeren Freiheit, die England ihr bot, und verbrachte doch alljährlich mehrere Monate in Berlin. Und obwohl ihre Beziehung mit Virginia Woolf auch ihr viel bedeutete, hinderte sie dies nicht daran, eine Affäre mit der deutsch-amerikanischen Romanautorin Margaret Goldsmith-Voigt einzugehen und Virginia in ihren Briefen davon zu berichten. In der Zwischenzeit erkundete Vitas Ehemann Harold Nicolson die Berliner Schwulenszene und besuchte gemeinsam mit Vitas Cousin, dem Schriftsteller und Kritiker Eddy Sackville-West, Clubs wie das berühmte Eldorado.[13]

Virginia Woolf, ihr Ehemann – der Verleger Leonard Woolf –, Virginias Schwester – die Malerin Vanessa Bell – und der Maler Duncan Grant unternahmen im Januar 1929 eine gemeinsame Berlin-Reise. Zu dieser Zeit galt Berlin als moderne Stadt, die man gesehen haben musste. Entsprechend absolvierte die Bloomsbury Group ein strapaziöses Touristenprogramm (mit dem Funkturm, dem Planetarium und dem Wellenbad), besuchte Abendveranstaltungen in der Oper oder Kinovorführungen sowjetischer Avantgardefilme, die man in London nicht zu sehen bekam, ging in Kunstgalerien und Museen und pflegte soziale Kontakte.

[Fig. 25: Luna Park Berlin Halensee – having a good time in the indoor swimming pool, unknown photographer, 1927]

[Abb. 25: Luna Park Berlin Halensee – Freizeitspaß im Wellenbad, unbekannter Fotograf, 1927]

Vanessa Bell gives a succinct account of the short and rather fated visit in which Eddy Sackville-West also features:

> Altogether tempers waxed so hot that they hardly felt the bitter cold as we stood helplessly in the slush afterwards, waiting for Eddy to carry Duncan off to see the night life in Berlin *without* getting involved also with Harold and the rest of the party. In

Vanessa Bell schildert in knappen Worten diesen kurzen und eher unglücklichen Besuch, bei dem sie auch Eddy Sackville-West trafen:

> Insgesamt war die Stimmung so aufgeheizt, dass sie die bittere Kälte kaum wahrnahmen, als wir im Anschluss hilflos im Schneematsch herumstanden und warteten. Eddy *hatte Duncan angeboten, ihm ein bisschen das Berliner Nachtleben zu zeigen, wollte aber um keinen Preis, daß Harold und die anderen mitkamen. Vergeblich, denn schließ-*

Englische Schriftstellerinnen in Berlin

vain, for Harold did accompany them in the end. Also there has been a terrible storm brewing ever since we came, for Leonard refuses to go to a lunch party specially got up by Harold in his honour, on the ground that Virginia told them beforehand (but did she?) that they wouldn't go to any parties. Altogether a lot of quiet amusement is to be got by those who are happily not embroiled. The Germans are ugly, incredibly badly dressed, kind. The food tasteless. I begin to long for France.[14]

Woolf was exhausted by Berlin and following a case of flu and a sea-sickness potion which had adverse effects, she had a breakdown on her return to England and spent the next couple of weeks in bed. Nevertheless, her time in Berlin did not hinder her from writing, when back in London, among other things, the new novel "The Moths", later to be entitled *The Waves*, and memorable letters to numerous friends about her experience. She wrote to Vita on 28 January 1929:

> Well anyhow it was worth the week with you. I think of the tower [the radio tower where Virginia and Vita had dined] and the lights and the waves [Wellenbad, indoor swimming pool] and the shell room at Sans Souci [the whole party visited that one afternoon] and you—Next week is Feb. 1st, so there's really not long to wait. But Lord! What a horror Berlin and diplo-

lich *hatte er ihn doch am Hals*. Zudem braute sich seit unserer Ankunft ein schrecklicher Sturm zusammen, denn Leonard weigert sich, zu einem Mittagessen zu gehen, das Harold speziell zu seinen Ehren organisiert hatte. Und zwar mit der Begründung, Virginia hätte ihnen zuvor gesagt, sie würden keine Feste besuchen (doch hatte sie das wirklich?). Aber da ich ganz unbeteiligt war, habe ich mich doch ziemlich amüsiert. Die Deutschen sind hässliche und unglaublich schlecht gekleidete Menschen. Das Essen ist fade. Langsam sehne ich mich nach Frankreich.[14]

Virginia Woolf war von Berlin vollkommen überfordert. Nach einer Grippe und der Einnahme einer Arznei gegen Seekrankheit, die sie nicht vertrug, erlitt sie auf der Rückreise nach England einen Zusammenbruch und musste in den kommenden beiden Wochen das Bett hüten. Nichtsdestotrotz hinderte ihre Zeit in Berlin sie nicht daran, im Anschluss an ihre Rückkehr nach London unter anderem ihren neuen Roman »The Moths« zu schreiben, der später unter dem Titel *Die Wellen* (»The Waves«) erscheinen sollte, und zahlreichen Freund*innen ihre Erlebnisse in eindrucksvollen Briefen zu schildern. Vita schrieb sie am 28. Januar 1929:

> Auf jeden Fall war es die Woche mit dir wert. Ich denke an den Turm [den Funkturm, wo Virginia und Vita miteinander zu Abend aßen] und die Lichter und die Wellen [das Wellenbad] und den Muschelsaal in Sanssouci [den die Gruppe an einem Nachmittag gemeinsam besuchte] und an dich. – Nächste Woche ist schon der 1. Februar, wir müssen also nicht mehr lange warten. Aber ach, mein Gott! Was für ein Graus Berlin und die diplomatischen Kreise doch sind! Ich hatte ja gar keine Vorstellung davon, bevor ich es mit eigenen

macy are! I'd no idea till I'd seen it. And I shiver at the thought of our behavior about that lunch. You and Harold were such angels. My love to him. Write. (Here's Leonard, so I must stop.) V.[15]

A few days later, she commented on having to stay in bed and summed up her visit to Berlin in another letter to Vita: "Berlin was great fun in many ways—humans and pictures. Never again though. Even what I see of London from the window has an incredible distinction. Lord! How nice to see you again!"[16]

The 1930s: "Germany is settling down quite nicely"?

The panorama of English women writers in Berlin takes on a more sinister note at the beginning of the 1930s. The historian and left-wing journalist Elizabeth Wiskemann used her knowledge of German and frequently alternated between teaching history at Cambridge and spending several months a year in Germany. She observed how the university in Berlin allowed itself to become run by "a vet about thirty-five, because none of the ordinary professors were sufficiently tough to please the regime"[17] and reported her increasingly worrying impressions to British politicians whenever she returned to England, but to no avail. In contrast to the social freedom which members of the Bloomsbury group had enjoyed, her activities were observed

Augen gesehen habe. Und bei dem Gedanken an unsere Reaktion auf dieses Mittagessen überkommt mich ein Zittern. Ihr wart wahre Engel, du und Harold. Sag ihm liebe Grüße. *Und schreib mir.* (Leonard kommt, ich muss aufhören.) V.[15]

Einige Tage später berichtete sie Vita in einem weiteren Brief davon, dass sie nach wie vor ans Bett gefesselt sei, und fasste ihren Berlin-Besuch erneut zusammen: »Der Besuch in Berlin hat mir große Freude bereitet – wegen der Menschen und der Bilder. Doch einmal und nie wieder. Selbst das, was ich nur aus dem Fenster von London sehen kann, ist von weitaus größerer Vornehmheit. Mein Gott! Wie schön es war, dich wiederzusehen!«[16]

Die 1930er Jahre: Normalisiert sich die Lage in Deutschlands zusehends?

Zu Beginn der 1930er Jahre verfinstert sich der Blick englischer Schriftstellerinnen auf Berlin. Die Historikerin und linke Journalistin Elizabeth Wiskemann verbrachte dank ihrer deutschen Sprachkenntnisse neben ihrer Arbeit als Geschichtsdozentin in Cambridge alljährlich mehrere Monate in Deutschland. Sie beobachtete, wie sich die Berliner Universität gezwungen sah, »einen etwa 35 Jahre alten Veterinär als Rektor zu akzeptieren, da keiner der ordentlichen Professoren ›tatkräftig‹ genug war, um dem Regime genehm zu sein«,[17] und berichtete britischen Politikern nach jeder Rückkehr in England vergeblich von ihren immer besorgniserregenderen Eindrücken. Im Unterschied zu den gesellschaftlichen Freiheiten, die die Mitglieder der Bloomsbury Group hatten genießen können, wurden ihre Aktivitäten von der Geheimen Staatspolizei verfolgt. In ihren Memoiren

by the secret police. She explains in her memoir that she only returned to Germany in March 1936:

> I was grimly aware that the remilitarization of the Rhineland was Hitler's first decisive victory by aggression, that it could have been resisted, but that British public opinion was determined to shut its eyes to the danger. It was obviously increasingly perilous for a person like myself to go to Germany and it might be increasingly thankless to write articles which people at home found unpalatable. I do not remember doubting that it had to be done.[18]

In her article for the *New Statesman and Nation* from 1935, she set up a stark contrast between received English opinion and her own observations based on her Berlin experience:

> The general line in England to-day is, it seems, to feel that Germany is settling down quite nicely—a few little un-Englishnesses, but then foreigners will be foreign. One's first superficial impression of Berlin, round about the glorious anniversary of June 30th, 1934, seems to tell the same tale; there are so few Brown Shirts and so many Jews that one might almost be back in Weimar Germany. Nothing could be more disastrously deceptive than this impression.[19]

beschreibt sie, dass sie erst im März 1936 nach Deutschland zurückkehrte:

> Ich war mir der unangenehmen Tatsache vollauf bewusst, dass Hitler mit der Remilitarisierung des Rheinlandes seinen ersten entscheidenden Sieg durch Aggressionstaktik errungen hatte und dass dieser Sieg zu verhindern gewesen wäre; doch schien die öffentliche Meinung Englands entschlossen, ihre Augen weiterhin vor der Gefahr zu verschließen. Für mich und meinesgleichen wurden Reisen nach Deutschland immer gefährlicher, und es wäre eine höchst undankbare Aufgabe, Artikel zu schreiben, deren Tendenz man in meinem Heimatland als peinlich empfand. Trotzdem dachte ich nicht einen Augenblick daran, damit aufzuhören.[18]

In einem Artikel für den *New Statesman and Nation* aus dem Jahr 1935 verwies sie auf den augenfälligen Kontrast zwischen der in England herrschenden Meinung und ihren eigenen Betrachtungen, die sie anhand ihrer Erlebnisse in Berlin formulierte:

> In England scheint man heutzutage allgemein der Ansicht zuzuneigen, dass sich die Lage in Deutschland zusehends normalisiere – zwar entspreche manches nicht gerade dem englischen Wesen, aber Ausländer seien nun mal Ausländer. Der erste flüchtige Eindruck, den man von Berlin zur Zeit des ruhmvollen Jahrestages vom 30. Juni 1934 erhält, scheint diese Ansicht zu bestätigen. Man sieht so wenig Braunhemden und so viele Juden, dass man sich beinahe in das Deutschland der Weimarer Tage zurückversetzt glaubt. Nichts könnte jedoch trügerischer sein als dieser Eindruck.[19]

[Fig. 26: Elizabeth Wiskemann, photographer and date unknown]

[Abb. 26: Elizabeth Wiskemann, Fotograf und Datum unbekannt]

Only with the help of the Berlin correspondent of *The Times*, Norman Ebbut, and the British Embassy in Berlin, which by this time had become a safe haven rather than a hub of Anglo-German exchange, was she able to escape from the Gestapo prison to which she was taken in 1935. A both harrowing and ironic account of this can be found in her post-war memoir. "Altogether, the Gestapo had been pretty incompetent. After all if they had arrested me on the frontier it would have taken much longer for Ebbutt or the Embassy to find me."[20]

Wiskemann went on to become the first woman to hold a chair at Edinburgh University but her intrepid reporting for the *New Statesman* is less well known today.

From the other end of the political spectrum comes a much more famous

Nur mithilfe des Berliner Korrespondenten der *Times*, Norman Ebbut, und der Britischen Botschaft in Berlin, die sich zu diesem Zeitpunkt mehr zu einem sicheren Hafen denn zu einem Drehpunkt der englisch-deutschen Beziehungen entwickelt hatte, konnte sie aus dem Gestapo-Gefängnis entkommen, in das man sie 1935 gebracht hatte. Ihre Nachkriegsmemoiren enthalten einen erschütternden und zugleich ironischen Bericht über diese Zeit. »Im grossen und ganzen hatte sich die Gestapo ziemlich dilettantisch benommen; denn wenn sie mich an der Grenze verhaftet hätte, wären Ebbutt und die Britische Botschaft bestimmt nicht so bald dahintergekommen.«[20]

Wiskemann erhielt als erste Frau einen Lehrstuhl an der Universität von Edinburgh. Ihre furchtlosen Reportagen für den *New Statesman* sind heute dagegen weit weniger bekannt.

Am anderen Ende des politischen Spektrums fand sich mit Diana Mosley, einer der vornehmen,

author, namely Diana Mosley, one of the posh, well-connected, and prolific Mitford sisters. Diana married the leader of the British fascists, Oswald Mosley, and travelled to Germany with her younger sister Unity, a Hitler-groupie. Her description of home life with the Goebbels family during her visit to Berlin in 1936 is chilling. Even more so when one learns that her memoirs were serialised on the BBC, lauded by critics as being "witty and amusing" and are still in print today:

> … I left for Berlin where Unity and I went to the Olympic Games. Hitler gave us tickets and we stayed with the Goebbels at their lake-side villa at Schwanenwerder. I became very fond of Magda Goebbels and her children. […] Dr Goebbels was intelligent, witty and sarcastic; he had an exceptionally beautiful speaking voice. Magda called him "Engel". We taught them to play Analogies. Dr. Goebbels was being questioned: "What colour does he remind you of?" "Fiery red!" said Goebbels. He had chosen the Führer for his subject.[21]

Conclusion

The varied experience of women writers in Berlin did not, of course, end with the rise of the Nazi party in the 1930s. A number of British travellers continued to visit Berlin, and wrote about their time in the German capital in guidebooks, memoirs, or even novels. Stevie Smith published her *Novel*

on *Yellow Paper*, which contains a substantial Berlin chapter, in 1936. That same year, the American Djuna Barnes published her modernist novel *Nightwood*, which also has a famous Berlin underworld part. While both novels were and are acclaimed in academic circles and form part of the modernist canon, they did not find a mass readership nor were they adapted for film like Isherwood's Berlin novels, therefore failing to feed into the Berlin myth to a comparable extent.

The freedom of movement which, for a brief time, English women writers had enjoyed in Berlin, became more and more circumscribed during the Nazi regime, and ended at the latest with the beginning of the Second World War. When the Berlin myth continued with different stories after the end of the Nazi period, it was again mainly written by men in the form of espionage novels during the Cold War. In this different version of the myth, Berlin is posited as the archetypal frontier space between opposing forces of "good" and "bad", between capitalism and communism. In contrast, in 21st-century Berlin, there are once again women writers with close ties to Britain re-inventing the city from diverse angles, as the recent Berlin novels and stories of Kate McNaughton, Sharon Dodua-Ottoo, or Deborah Levy testify.

1936 ihren *Roman auf gelbem Papier* (Novel on Yellow Paper), der ein umfangreiches Berlin-Kapitel enthält. Womöglich war es dem experimentellen Charakter dieses Buchs geschuldet, dass es keine größere Leserschaft fand und auch nicht wie Isherwoods Berliner Geschichten verfilmt wurde. Dies traf auch auf den im selben Jahr veröffentlichten modernistischen Roman *Nachtgewächs* (Nightwood) der amerikanischen Schriftstellerin Djuna Barnes zu, der ebenfalls eine bekannte Episode aus der Berliner Unterwelt enthält.

In akademischen Kreisen erfreuen sich beide Texte allerdings nach wie vor einer großen Anerkennung und gehören zum Kanon der literarischen Moderne. Da sie weder verfilmt wurden, noch eine große Leserschaft fanden, haben beide Romane den Mythos Berlin allerdings sehr viel weniger als Isherwoods Berlin Romane befördert.

Die Freizügigkeit, die englische Schriftstellerinnen für kurze Zeit in Berlin genossen, wurde während der Nazi-Herrschaft immer weiter eingeschränkt und fand ihr Ende spätestens mit dem Beginn des Zweiten Weltkriegs. Als sich der Mythos Berlin nach der Nazi-Zeit mit anderen Geschichten fortsetzte, stammten diese Spionageromane aus der Zeit des Kalten Krieges in der Mehrzahl von Männern. In dieser Neuauflage des Mythos wird Berlin als archetypisches Grenzgebiet zwischen den gegensätzlichen Kräften des »Guten« und des »Bösen«, zwischen Kapitalismus und Kommunismus dargestellt. Im Gegensatz dazu gibt es im Berlin des 21. Jahrhunderts erneut Schriftstellerinnen mit engem Bezug zu Großbritannien, die die Stadt aus unterschiedlichen Perspektiven neu erfinden, wie die aktuellen Romane und Erzählungen von Kate McNaughton, Sharon Dodua-Ottoo oder Deborah Levy belegen.

Notes

1. Alix Strachey to James Strachey, 10 March 1925, in: Bloomsbury/Freud: The Letters of James and Alix Strachey, 1924–1925, ed. by Perry Meisel and Walter Kendrick, New York, Basic Books 1985, p. 231.
2. Helen D'Abernon, 8 December 1920, in: Red Cross and Berlin Embassy 1915–1926. Extracts from the Diaries of Viscountess D'Abernon, London, John Murray 1946, p. 80.
3. Virginia Woolf to Vita Sackville-West, 1 February 1929, in: A Reflection of the Other Person. The Letters of Virginia Woolf, vol. IV: 1929–1931, ed. by Nigel Nicolson, London, The Hogarth Press 1978, p. 12.
4. Evelyn Princess Blücher, 10 November 1918, in: An English Wife in Berlin. A Private Memoir of Events, Politics, and Daily Life in Germany Throughout the War and the Social Revolution of 1918, London, Constable and Co. 1920, pp. 284 f.
5. Harry Graf Kessler, 26 May 1925, in: Tagebücher 1918–1937, ed. by Wolfgang Pfeiffer-Belli, 7. Auflage, Frankfurt a. M., Insel-Verlag (1996) 2017, p. 466.
6. Helen D'Abernon, 4 August 1920, in: Red Cross and Berlin Embassy, p. 61 f.
7. Colin Storer: Weimar Germany as Seen by an Englishwoman: British Women Writers and the Weimar Republic, in: German Studies Review 32/11, February 2009, pp. 129–147.
8. Alix Strachey to James Strachey, 25 February 1925, in: Bloomsbury/Freud, p. 215.
9. Isadora Duncan: My Life, New York, Boni and Liveright 1927, p. 126.
10. Alix Strachey to James Strachey, 14 June 1925, in: Bloomsbury/Freud, p. 282.
11. Vita Sackville-West to Virginia Woolf, 14 October 1927, in: The Letters of Vita Sackville-West to Virginia Woolf, ed. by Louise DeSalvo and Mitchell Leaska, New York, Morrow repr. 1985, p. 240.

Anmerkungen

1. Alix Strachey an James Strachey, 10. März 1925, in: Kultur und Psychoanalyse in Bloomsbury und Berlin. Die Briefe von James und Alix Strachey 1924–1925, hg. von Perry Meisel und Walter Kendrick, aus dem Englischen übersetzt von Rotraut De Clerck, Stuttgart, Verlag Internationale Psychoanalyse 1995, S. 345.
2. Helen D'Abernon, 8. Dezember 1920, in: Red Cross and Berlin Embassy 1915–1926. Extracts from the Diaries of Viscountess D'Abernon, London, John Murray 1946, S. 80.
3. Brief von Virginia Woolf an Vita Sackville-West, 1. Februar 1929, in: A Reflection of the Other Person. The Letters of Virginia Woolf, vol. IV: 1929–1931, hg. von Nigel Nicolson, London, The Hogarth Press 1978, S. 12. Dieser Brief ist in der deutschen Ausgabe der Briefe von Virginia Woolf nicht enthalten.
4. Evelyn Blücher Fürstin von Wahlstatt: Tagebuch, München, Verlag für Kulturpolitik 1924, S. 309 f.
5. Harry Graf Kessler, 26. Mai 1925, in: Tagebücher 1918–1937, hg. von Wolfgang Pfeiffer-Belli, 7. Auflage, Frankfurt a. M., Insel-Verlag (1996) 2017, S. 466.
6. Helen D'Abernon, 4. August 1920, in: Red Cross and Berlin Embassy, S. 61 f.
7. Colin Storer: Weimar Germany as Seen by an Englishwoman: British Women Writers and the Weimar Republic, in: German Studies Review 32/1, Februar 2009, S. 129–147.
8. Alix Strachey an James Strachey, 25. Februar 1925, in: Psychoanalyse in Bloomsbury und Berlin, S. 326.
9. Isadora Duncan: Memoiren, nach dem englischen Manuskript von C. Zell, Zürich, Leipzig und Wien, Almathea-Verlag 1928, S. 170.
10. Alix Strachey an James Strachey, 14. Juni 1925, in: Psychoanalyse in Bloomsbury und Berlin, S. 411.
11. Vita Sackville-West an Virginia Woolf, 14. Oktober 1927, in: Geliebtes Wesen. Die Briefe von Vita Sackville-West und Virginia Woolf, hg. von Louise DeSalvo und Mitchell A. Leaska, aus dem Englischen von Sybill und Dirk Vanderbeke, Frankfurt a. M., S. Fischer 1995, S. 238.
12. »Der Käfig öffnet sich«, in: De Salvo und Leaska, Geliebtes Wesen, S. 312. Woolf verwendete ebenfalls das Bild eines Käfigs, in dem Vita leben musste, verglich es mit

12 Vita Sackville-West to Virginia Woolf, 5 February 1929, in: The Letters of Vita Sackville-West to Virginia Woolf, p. 317. Woolf also used the image of the cage in which Vita had to live, likening it to the Albert Memorial in London and thus emphasising both the size, the pomp and what they both referred to as the 'ugliness' of Berlin. Virginia Woolf to Vita Sackville-West, 31 January 1928, in: A Reflection of the Other Person, p. 11.
13 Nino Strachey: Rooms of their Own, London, Pitkin Publishing 2018, p. 127.
14 Vanessa Bell to Julian Bell, 22 January 1929, in: Selected Letters of Vanessa Bell, ed. by Regina Marler, London, Bloomsbury 1993, p. 342.
15 Virginia Woolf to Vita Sackville-West, 29 January 1929, in: A Reflection of the Other Person, p. 8 f.
16 Virginia Woolf to Vita Sackville-West, 2 February 1929, in: A Reflection of the Other Person, p. 15.
17 Elizabeth Wiskemann: The Europe I Saw, Appendix I, 1968, p. 243 (reprint of her article in The New Statesman and Nation, 13 July 1935).
18 Ibid., p. 51 f.
19 Ibid., Appendix II, p. 242.
20 Ibid., p. 58.
21 Diana Mosley: A Life of Contrasts. The Autobiography, London, Gibson Square 2009, p. 130.

a Violet Bonham-Carter, quoted in: Helen D'Abernon: Red Cross and Berlin Embassy 1915–1926. Extracts from the Diaries of Viscountess D'Abernon, London, John Murray 1946, p. 106.
b Cyril Connolly, Conversations in Berlin, in: Life and Letters, ed. by Desmond MacCarthy, Vol. IV, No. 22, March 1930, pp. 206–212, here p. 211.

dem Albert Memorial in London und hob auf diese Weise sowohl die Größe und Pracht als auch die von beiden genannte »Hässlichkeit« Berlins hervor.
13 Nino Strachey: Rooms of their Own, London, Pitkin Publishing 2018, S. 127.
14 Kursive Passagen übernommen aus Quentin Bell: Virginia Woolf. Eine Biographie, 3. Auflage, Frankfurt a.M., Insel (1977) 1980, S. 409. Vanessa Bell an Julian Bell, 22. Januar 1929, in: Selected Letters of Vanessa Bell, hg. von Regina Marler, London, Bloomsbury 1993, S. 342.
15 Brief von Virginia Woolf an Vita Sackville-West, 29. Januar 1929, in: A Reflection of the Other Person, S. 8 f. Dieser Brief ist in der deutschen Ausgabe der Briefe von Virginia Woolf nicht enthalten.
16 Virginia Woolf an Vita Sackville-West, 2. Februar 1929, in: A Reflection of the Other Person, S. 15. Dieser Brief ist in der deutschen Ausgabe der Briefe von Virginia Woolf nicht enthalten.
17 Elizabeth Wiskemann: Erlebtes Europa. Ein politischer Reisebericht 1930–1945, Bern und Stuttgart, Verlag Hallwag 1969, S. 241.
18 Ebd., S. 51 f.
19 Ebd., Anlage II, S. 242.
20 Ebd., S. 58.
21 Diana Mosley: A Life of Contrasts. The Autobiography, London, Gibson Square 2009, S. 130.

a Violet Bonham-Carter, zitiert in: Helen D'Abernon: Red Cross and Berlin Embassy 1915–1926. Extracts from the Diaries of Viscountess D'Abernon, London, John Murray 1946, S. 106.
b Cyril Connolly, Conversations in Berlin, in: Life and Letters, hg. von Desmond MacCarthy, Bd. IV, Nr. 22, March 1930, S. 206–212, hier S. 211.

Laura Marcus

"Never be anchorage / never be safety / only be the kino." Weimar Berlin Cinema and British Connections

»Never be anchorage / never be safety / only be the kino.«[1] Das Kino im Berlin der Weimarer Republik und seine Verbindungen zu Großbritannien

The German film industry was already well established by the beginning of the Weimar period. Foreign film imports were banned for a short period from 1916 onwards, giving protection to the plethora of small German film companies. Universum Film Aktiengesellschaft (Ufa), founded in 1917, came to dominate production after WW1, buying up a number of firms and, in 1921, taking over and developing a massive studio complex (*Filmstadt*) at Babelsberg near Potsdam which out-classed the other film studios in Berlin. After 1923, British film-makers often shot there or elsewhere in Germany, where the facilities were better than at home.[1] Ufa followed the model of teams linked to directors rather than the producer-centred approach emerging in Hollywood, thus offering a context in which the creative vision of individual directors was paramount. The British film director Alfred Hitchcock co-directed

Die deutsche Filmindustrie war zu Beginn der Weimarer Zeit bereits ein etablierter Wirtschaftszweig. Mit einem vorübergehenden Verbot ausländischer Filmimporte sollten ab 1916 die unzähligen kleinen Filmunternehmen in Deutschland geschützt werden. Nach dem Ersten Weltkrieg beherrschte die 1917 gegründete Universum Film Aktiengesellschaft (Ufa) durch den Aufkauf mehrerer Gesellschaften zunehmend das Produktionsgeschehen. In Babelsberg nahe Potsdam übernahm sie ein riesiges Studiogelände (*Filmstadt*), das nach einer Erweiterung alle übrigen Filmstudios in den Schatten stellte. Wegen der besseren Ausstattung im Vergleich zu heimischen Studios verlegten nach 1923 zahlreiche britische Regisseure ihre Dreharbeiten an diese oder andere deutsche Produktionsstätten.[2] Bei der Ufa arbeiteten Filmteams unter der Leitung von Regisseuren. Hier stand vor allem die kreative Vision einzelner Regisseure im Mittelpunkt, während in Hollywood die Produzenten immer mehr Gewicht erhielten. Der britische Regisseur Alfred Hitchcock kam in den Jahren 1924–25 als Co-Regisseur von *Die Prinzessin und der Geiger*

his film *The Blackguard* at Babelsberg in 1924–25 and said that he learned there everything he knew; his films of the 1920s, including *The Lodger* and *Blackmail*, were strongly influenced by the style and camerawork of German Expressionist cinema.

Berlin was exceptionally well provided with cinemas, with 336 in 1929. Emblematic picture palaces included the Mozartsaal and the windowless concrete Cines (built in 1913 and later renamed the Ufa-Pavillon) on the Nollendorfplatz (just down the street from Christopher Isherwood's apartment at Nollendorfstraße 17), the Gloria-Palast on the Kurfürstendamm, the nearby Tauentzienpalast and Capitol, and the Titania Palast in Steglitz. There were also numerous smaller district cinemas or "Kinos im Kiez", often located in housing blocks and known as "Hinterhofkinos" or "Pantoffelkinos".

What did Berlin, and in particular its cinema culture, mean to the numerous British writers who visited or lived in the city in the 1920s? Among them were journalist and critic Huntly Carter, who wrote extensively on European and Soviet film, art, and theatre, Alix Strachey, co-translator of Freud, who lived in Grunewald for a year in 1924–25 while being analysed by Karl Abraham, and Harold Nicolson, *chargé d'affaires* and Counsellor from 1928 to 1929. Well-known literary figures and film enthusiasts included W. H. Auden, Christopher Isherwood, and Stephen Spender. Those making shorter visits included Leonard and Virginia Woolf, who travelled to Berlin in

(»The Blackguard«) nach Babelsberg. Rückblickend sagte er, dass er sich sein gesamtes Wissen in dieser Zeit angeeignet hätte. Seine Filme aus den 1920er Jahren, darunter *Der Mieter* (»The Lodger«) und *Erpressung* (»Blackmail«), waren deutlich vom Stil und von der Kameraführung des deutschen expressionistischen Films beeinflusst.

Im Jahr 1929 gab es in Berlin nicht weniger als 336 Kinos. Darunter waren legendäre Filmpaläste wie der Mozartsaal, der 1913 erbaute und später in Ufa-Pavillon umbenannte fensterlose Betonbau Cines am Nollendorfplatz (gleich um die Ecke von Christopher Isherwoods Wohnung in der Nollendorfstraße 17), der Gloria-Palast am Kurfürstendamm, die nahegelegenen Kinos Tauentzienpalast und Capitol und der Titania-Palast in Steglitz. Außerdem gab es zahlreiche kleinere Kinos in den einzelnen Stadtvierteln oder »Kinos im Kiez«, die sich häufig innerhalb von Häuserblocks befanden und als »Hinterhofkinos« oder »Pantoffelkinos« bezeichnet wurden.

Welche Bedeutung hatte Berlin, und vor allem auch seine Kinokultur, für die vielen britischen Schriftsteller*innen, die die Stadt in den 1920er Jahren besuchten oder zu ihrem Domizil machten? Zu ihnen gehörte auch der Journalist und Kritiker Huntly Carter, der sich in seinen Beiträgen ausführlich mit Film, Kunst und Theater aus Europa und Sowjetunion befasste. Die Freud-Co-Übersetzerin Alix Strachey lebte zwischen 1924 und 1925 für eine Analyse bei Karl Abraham ein Jahr lang in Berlin-Grunewald. Und von 1928 bis 1929 weilte Harold Nicolson als *Chargé d'Affaires* und Botschaftsrat in der Stadt. Zu den bekannten Literat*innen und Filmbegeisterten zählten W.H. Auden, Christopher Isherwood und Stephen Spender. Leonard und Virginia Woolf kamen 1929 für einen kürzeren Aufenthalt in die Stadt. Eine Freundin Isherwoods, die Schauspielerin Beatrix Lehmann,

1929. Isherwood's friend, the actor Beatrix Lehmann, visited in 1932 while hoping to break into the German film industry. Her brother John, who was centrally involved in the running of the Woolfs' Hogarth Press, also came on a visit in 1933, "in the midst of the last agony of the Weimar Republic", lodging near Isherwood "off the Nollendorfplatz".[2]

Some British residents were casual about their regular cinema-going. Alix Strachey wrote of spending a day "in Konditoreis and cinemas"[3] and of "sometimes … nestling in a warm, dark hole, with soft music playing & a movie showing the latest Ufa luxus"[4] if she had "the physical energy to rattle into town & visit a Kino".[5] The only films she describes by name are the "rotten" *Zur Chronik von Grieshuus*[6] and a historical film about Frederick the Great "at the Zoo-Ufa Palast (most instructive & not too boring)".[7]

For others, film-going in Berlin was a central activity. Those with direct involvement with film and the cinema world included Ivor Montagu, who became a major figure in British film culture, as critic, director, and producer, with strong links to the U.S.S.R. and Soviet cinema. In 1925 Montagu, newly graduated from the University of Cambridge, co-founded the London-based Film Society (whose Sunday screenings were the forum in which many of England's writers and artists, including the members of the Bloomsbury Group, first engaged with "film as an art") after spending some time in Berlin in that year and watching the new German

folgte ihm 1932, um sich in der deutschen Filmindustrie einen Namen zu machen. Und auch ihr Bruder John, einer der wichtigsten Mitarbeiter beim Verlag der Eheleute Woolf, The Hogarth Press, stattete Berlin 1933 einen Besuch ab, »als die Weimarer Republik ihre letzten Atemzüge tat«, und wohnte wie Isherwood unweit vom Nollendorfplatz.[3]

Einige englische Stadtbewohner*innen betrachteten den Kinobesuch als willkommenen Zeitvertreib. Alix Strachey schrieb dazu: »Die Folge war, daß wir uns den ganzen Tag in Konditoreien & Kinos herumtrieben«[4] […]; »allerdings muß ich zugeben, daß ich mich manchmal in eine warme, dunkle Höhle gekuschelt wiederfinde, mit sanfter Musik & einem Film mit dem neuesten Ufa-Luxus«,[5] sofern sie »die Energie [hatte], in die Stadt zu rasen & ein Kino zu besuchen«.[6] Als einzigen Filmtitel nannte sie einen »miserablen« Film zur »Chronik des Haus/Burg (?) Giessheuss«[7] und berichtete von »einem Kurs über Filmgeschichte im Ufa-Palast am Zoo […] (höchst lehrreich & nicht allzu langweilig), alles über Friedrich den Großen«.[8]

Für andere wiederum gehörte der Kinobesuch zu den Hauptaktivitäten ihrer Zeit in Berlin. So beispielsweise auch für Ivor Montagu, der über direkte Kontakte zur Film- und Kinowelt verfügte und als Kritiker, Regisseur und Produzent mit engen Verbindungen zu Filmschaffenden aus der Sowjetunion zu einer zentralen Figur der britischen Filmkultur wurde. Im Jahr 1925 gehörte Montagu als frischgebackener Absolvent der Universität Cambridge zu den Mitbegründern der Londoner Film Society (die mit ihren Sonntagsvorführungen ein Forum schuf, bei dem viele Schriftsteller*innen und Künstler*innen aus England, darunter auch die Mitglieder der Bloomsbury Group, zum ersten Mal mit »Filmen als Kunstwerken« in Berührung kamen).

films: "films medieval, rococo, contemporary, expressionist, and futurist".⁸ In 1928 the musicologist Eric Walter White, a recent Oxford graduate, came to work in Berlin and Potsdam as an English tutor, developing a close friendship with the Berlin-born silhouette-film artist Lotte Reiniger and her husband Carl Koch, a film cameraman. White collaborated with Reiniger on a number of films and published, with Leonard and Virginia Woolf's Hogarth Press, the first discussion in English of Reiniger's work, *Walking Shadows* (1931), following another short book, *Parnassus to Let. An Essay about Rhythm in the Films* (1928).

White also formed a lasting friendship with the American-born poet H.D. whom he met, through Reiniger, during the brief period at the beginning of the 1930s during which H.D. was undertaking analysis in Berlin with Hanns Sachs, before she began her analysis with Sigmund Freud in Vienna. H.D. was the life-long companion of the writer Bryher (born Winifred Ellerman, the daughter of the immensely wealthy industrialist and shipping magnate Sir John Ellerman), who, along with the young Scottish artist Kenneth Macpherson, had started a film journal, *Close Up*, which they ran from their home in Switzerland between 1927 and 1933, the charged years of the transition from silent to sound film.

Huntly Carter, writing in 1930, recalled his stays in Germany in 1919 and in 1922, during which he found social conditions which "were almost beyond description".⁹

Im selben Jahr verbrachte er einige Zeit in Berlin, um sich neue Filme aus Deutschland anzuschauen: »mittelalterliche, rokokohafte, zeitgenössische, expressionistische und futuristische Filme«.⁹ Der junge Oxford-Absolvent und Musikwissenschaftler Eric Walter White kam 1928 für eine Anstellung als Englischlehrer nach Berlin und Potsdam und entwickelte eine enge Freundschaft mit der in Berlin geborenen Scherenschnitt-Filmkünstlerin Lotte Reiniger und ihrem Ehemann Carl Koch, der als Kameramann beim Film arbeitete. White und Reiniger arbeiteten gemeinsam an zahlreichen Filmen. Bei Leonard und Virginia Woolfs Hogarth Press veröffentlichte er die erste englischsprachige Abhandlung zu Reinigers Werken, *Walking Shadows* (1931), nachdem er bereits ein Heft mit dem Titel *Parnassus to Let. An Essay about Rhythm in the Films* (1928) herausgebracht hatte.

Zudem verband White eine lange Freundschaft mit der in Amerika geborenen Dichterin H.D., die er Anfang der 1930er Jahre über Reiniger kennenlernte. H.D. weilte damals für eine Analyse bei Hanns Sachs für kurze Zeit in Berlin, bevor sie für eine Analyse bei Sigmund Freud nach Wien weiterreiste. Sie war die lebenslange Gefährtin der Schriftstellerin Bryher (der als Winifred Ellerman geborenen Tochter des wohlhabenden Industriellen und Großreeders Sir John Ellerman). Diese wiederum hatte gemeinsam mit dem jungen schottischen Künstler Kenneth Macpherson die Filmzeitschrift *Close Up* ins Leben gerufen, die sie in der durch den Übergang vom Stumm- zum Tonfilm turbulenten Phase zwischen 1927 und 1933 in ihrem Schweizer Domizil produzierten.

Huntly Carter erinnerte sich 1930 an seine Deutschlandaufenthalte der Jahre 1919 und 1922. In dieser Zeit habe er nahezu unbeschreibliche soziale

[Fig. 27: Cover of Eric Walter White, *Walking Shadows*, 1931]

[Abb. 27: Umschlag von Eric Walter White, *Walking Shadows*, 1931]

The poverty and destitution had, he wrote, "cinema consequences"; two students whom he met admitted that to them and many thousands of poor students the Cinema was an economic necessity. It cost less to sit huddled in a cinema of an evening deriving what heat they could from each other's body and the badly-heated auditorium, and what instruction they could from the picture, than to buy a pint of oil to keep them from freezing to death in their icy cold attics. The Cinema was, in fact, light and heat and entertainment to them.[10]

Bedingungen vorgefunden.[10] Armut und Not, so schrieb er, hätten sich auf das Verhalten der Kinobesucher*innen ausgewirkt. Er traf zwei Studenten, die ihm gestanden, dass der Kinobesuch für sie und Tausende armer Student*innen eine wirtschaftliche Notwendigkeit sei. Es sei günstiger, sich einen Abend lang gemeinsam in den Kinosessel eines schlecht beheizten Kinosaals zu kuscheln, gegenseitig Wärme zu spenden und etwas aus dem Film zu lernen, als Geld in das Heizen ihrer Öfen zu investieren, um in ihren eiskalten Mansarden nicht zu erfrieren. Das Kino habe ihnen daher Licht und Wärme und Unterhaltung geboten.[11]

[Fig. 28: The Berlin Psychoanalytical Institute, on the left-hand side of Potsdamer Straße, photograph by Hans G. Casparius, 1930s]

[Abb. 28: Das Berliner Psychoanalytische Institut auf der linken Seite der Potsdamer Straße, Fotografie von Hans G. Casparius, 1930er]

Like many writers after him, Carter saw the Expressionist cinema of the end of the 1910s and the early 1920s as a reflection of the social and political conditions of the times, including responses to the First World War and its immediate aftermath. One of the most influential films in this context was *The Cabinet of Dr Caligari*, which had its Berlin premiere on February 27, 1920 at the Marmorhaus Lichtspiele on Kurfürstendamm: a large and ornate cinema, designed by Hugo Pal, dating from 1913. Advertisements, including neon-lit sign-writing, and posters for the film appeared across Berlin, with the enigmatic slogan "Du musst Caligari werden!". *Caligari*'s painted sets, use of shadows, and geometric architecture and sightlines were intertwined with its themes

Wie zahlreiche Schriftsteller*innen nach ihm betrachtete Carter das expressionistische Kino Ende der 1910er und Anfang der 1920er Jahre als Spiegelbild der sozialen und politischen Verhältnisse der damaligen Zeit und auch als Reaktion auf den Ersten Weltkrieg und seine unmittelbaren Folgen. Einer der einflussreichsten Filme war in diesem Zusammenhang *Das Cabinet des Dr. Caligari*. Er feierte seine Premiere am 27. Februar 1920 im Marmorhaus am Kurfürstendamm, einem von Hugo Pal im Jahr 1913 erbauten großen und prächtigen Filmpalast. Damals erschienen überall in Berlin Werbeanzeigen, darunter auch neonbeleuchtete Schriftzüge, und Filmplakate mit einem geheimnisvollen Slogan: »Du musst Caligari werden!«. Die in *Caligari* behandelten Themen Horror und Wahnsinn kommen auch durch die gemalten Filmsets, das Schattenspiel, die geometrische Architektur und die filmischen

Places
The Berlin Psychoanalytical Institute

Next to Vienna, Berlin was the up-and-coming hub for psychoanalysts from all over Europe, who flocked to the newly opened Berlin Psychoanalytical Institute and its *Poliklinik* on Potsdamer Straße. Lectures, meetings, joint trips to the psychoanalytical congresses held in Würzburg, Salzburg, and Weimar, training analysis, as well as seeing regular patients, all went on under the guidance of Karl Abraham and his colleagues. The majority of them had to go into exile once the Nazi Party came into power, but in the 1920s, this was a meeting place which attracted numerous Britons, some of whom became famous psychoanalysts themselves. The English translator of Freud's work, Alix Strachey, frequented it, and there met the Austrian analyst Melanie Klein who later established herself in London with the Stracheys' help. The modernist writer Bryher, having encountered the Berlin analyst Hanns Sachs by chance, returned to Berlin regularly for her analysis with him. One of the leading female British analysts, Sylvia Payne, was trained here, as well as Ernest and James Glover. Not all of them became famous writers, but all of them found the institute a modern and inspiring place without which their careers would have taken a very different course. It is one of many Berlin places whose energy and impact was cut off brutally by Nazi intervention and enforced exile.

Orte
Das Berliner Psychoanalytische Institut

Neben Wien entwickelte sich auch Berlin zu einem vielversprechenden Treffpunkt für Psychoanalytiker*innen aus ganz Europa, die in Scharen in das neu eröffnete Berliner Psychoanalytische Institut und seine Poliklinik an der Potsdamer Straße strömten. Unter Leitung von Karl Abraham und seinen Kolleg*innen wurden hier Vorträge, Versammlungen, gemeinsame Reisen zu Psychoanalytischen Kongressen in Würzburg, Salzburg und Weimar, Lehranalysen und Sitzungen mit Patient*innen veranstaltet. Mit der Machtübernahme der NSDAP sah sich die Mehrheit der Mitarbeiter zur Flucht ins Exil gezwungen. Doch in den 1920er Jahren war das Institut ein Treffpunkt, der auch zahlreiche Brit*innen anlockte. Einige von ihnen wurden später selbst bekannte Psychoanalytiker*innen. Auch die englische Freud-Übersetzerin Alix Strachey kam oft in das Institut. Sie traf dort die österreichische Analytikerin Melanie Klein, die sich später mit Unterstützung der Stracheys in London niederließ. Die Schriftstellerin der Moderne Bryher traf zufällig den Berliner Analytiker Hanns Sachs. Sie kehrte anschließend regelmäßig nach Berlin zurück, um sich bei ihm einer Analyse zu unterziehen. Eine der führenden britischen Analytiker*innen, Sylvia Payne, aber auch Ernest und James Glover absolvierten ihre Ausbildung am Institut. Nicht alle von ihnen wurden später berühmte Autor*innen. Doch sie alle nahmen das Institut als modernen und inspirierenden Ort wahr, ohne den ihre Karrieren in ganz anderen Bahnen verlaufen wären. Das Institut ist einer von zahlreichen Berliner Orten, dessen Energie und Einfluss durch das Eingreifen der Nazis und ein erzwungenes Exil ein jähes Ende fanden.

of horror and madness. For some, the film was a wrong turning in film's development, "flatly photographing eccentric sets, instead of achieving surprises through camera work", in the words of the French artist and film-maker Jean Cocteau.[11] It was, however, received by many contemporary commentators as, in the Bloomsbury critic Clive Bell's words, "the first attempt to create an art of the cinema",[12] while its screening at London's Film Society in 1926 was the starting-point for Virginia Woolf's essay "The Cinema", in which she attempted to define the properties and potential of the new medium.[13] *Caligari* was an enormous success amongst Berlin's audiences, selling out for many weeks at the Marmorhaus before moving into Berlin's repertory theatres and then gaining national and international distribution.

As the advertising for *Caligari* suggests, Berlin presented itself as a cinematic spectacle, a dimension reinforced by the popularity of city films, including Walther Ruttmann's immensely influential documentary film *Berlin. Symphony of a Great City* (1927), and the so-called "street films", such as Karl Grune's *Die Straße* and Joe May's *Asphalt*. In an article, "Berlin aus der Landschaft gesehen" ("Berlin seen from the countryside"), the philosopher and cultural commentator Ernst Bloch described the city as a kind of stage projection against the background of the surrounding countryside.[14] A striking feature of the larger cinemas which came to predominate in the later part of the decade was the use of light on their facades: there was

Perspektiven zum Ausdruck. Für manche war der Film der »erste Schritt zu einem schlimmen Fehler. Hier wird ganz simpel exzentrische Ausstattung fotografiert, statt daß man Überraschungseffekte durch die Kamera erzielt«, wie der französische Künstler und Filmemacher Jean Cocteau es ausdrückte.[12] Allerdings wurde der Film von vielen Kommentatoren der damaligen Zeit, wie es der Bloomsbury-Kunstkritiker Clive Bell formulierte, als erster Versuch gewertet, ein filmisches Kunstwerk zu erschaffen.[13] Virginia Woolf ließ sich 1926 von einer Vorführung des Films in der Londoner Film Society zu ihrem Essay »The Cinema« inspirieren, in dem sie versuchte, das Wesen und das Potenzial des neuen Mediums zu erfassen.[14] *Caligari* wurde zum Kassenschlager beim Berliner Publikum. Im Marmorhaus lief der Film wochenlang vor ausverkauften Reihen, bevor er weiter durch die Berliner Programmkinos zog und schließlich einen nationalen und internationalen Verleih fand.

Wie die Werbekampagne für *Caligari* zeigt, sollte Berlin als filmisches Spektakel präsentiert werden. Zusätzlich befördert wurde diese Perspektive durch die damalige Popularität von Stadtfilmen, darunter Walther Ruttmanns äußerst einflussreicher Dokumentarfilm *Berlin. Die Sinfonie der Großstadt* (1927), und sogenannten »Straßenfilmen«, wie Karl Grunes *Die Straße* and Joe Mays *Asphalt*. Der Philosoph und Kulturwissenschaftler Ernst Bloch beschrieb die Stadt in seinem Artikel »Berlin aus der Landschaft gesehen« als eine Art Bühnenprojektion vor dem Hintergrund der umliegenden Landschaft.[15] Ein besonderes Merkmal größerer Kinos waren die beleuchteten Fassaden der Filmpaläste, die sich vor allem zum Ende des Jahrzehnts großer Beliebtheit erfreuten: Das Lichtspiel fand sowohl in den Innenräumen als auch an den Außenfassaden statt.

a Lichtspiel both inside and outside. One of the most dramatic displays was on the Ufa Palast am Zoo for Fritz Lang's *Frau im Mond* (1929), with an image of a rocket travelling through starlit space. This form of light-show reinforced the impression made on foreign visitors, including Bryher and Macpherson, of Berlin as a quintessentially cinematic city and as a city of modernity. The city's pride in its use of light as spectacle, and its engagement with the aesthetics of light, were strikingly apparent in the *Berlin im Licht* festival that took place in October 1928.

Bryher and Macpherson had first gone together to Berlin in 1927, having formed a "marriage of convenience" earlier that year. H.D. had recently begun a relationship with Macpherson, and the marriage served to provide a cover for that liaison. Their visits were crucial to the formation of *Close Up*, which developed into one of the most important and influential film publications of the period, publishing, for example, the first English-language translations of the great Russian film director Sergei Eisenstein's writings. It was intended to bring new developments in European and world cinema to the attention of British audiences and to those in the British film industry, of whose work the group were frequently highly critical. They also made their own films, directed by Macpherson, only one of which has survived in a complete form: *Borderline*, which "starred" H.D. along with the African-American actor Paul Robeson and his wife Eslanda, and in which Bryher appeared as a cigar-smoking hotel proprietor.

Eine besonders beeindruckende Attraktion bot die Darstellung einer Rakete, die an der Fassade des Ufa Palasts am Zoo für Fritz Langs *Frau im Mond* (1929) in den Sternenhimmel schoss. Ausländische Besucher*innen wie Bryher und Macpherson fühlten sich durch derartige Lichtinstallationen in ihrem Eindruck bestätigt, dass Berlin eine einzigartige Kinostadt und eine Stadt der Moderne war. Wie stolz Berlin auf seine Lichtspektakel und Kunstlichtspiele war, machte das Festival *Berlin im Licht* im Oktober 1928 auf eindrucksvolle Weise deutlich.

Bryher und Macpherson, die 1927 eine »Zweckehe« eingingen, statteten Berlin in diesem Jahr ebenfalls ihren ersten Besuch ab. Für die noch frische Liebesbeziehung zwischen Bryher und H.D. sollte ihre Ehe als Deckmantel dienen. Ihre Besuche hatten einen maßgeblichen Einfluss auf die Gründung von *Close Up*, das sich zu einem der wichtigsten und einflussreichsten Filmmagazine der damaligen Zeit entwickelte. In der Zeitschrift erschienen beispielsweise die ersten englischen Übersetzungen der Schriften des großen russischen Regisseurs Sergei Eisenstein. Sie enthielt Informationen über neue Filme aus Europa und aller Welt für britische Leser*innen und Vertreter*innen der britischen Filmbranche, deren Werke die Gruppe in vielen Fällen äußerst kritisch kommentierte. Darüber hinaus drehten sie auch eigene Filme unter der Regie von Macpherson, von denen nur ein einziger vollständig erhalten ist: *Borderline* mit H.D., dem afroamerikanischen Schauspieler Paul Robeson und seiner Ehefrau Eslanda in den Hauptrollen. Bryher hat in dem Film einen Auftritt als Zigarre rauchende Hotelbesitzerin.

Berlin war das Zentrum ihrer filmischen Aktivitäten. In der Schweiz gab es zwar die Möglichkeit, wie Bryher schrieb, in einer Woche sowohl französische

[Fig. 29: Portrait of Bryher, photograph by Gisèle Freund, 1930s]

[Abb. 29: Portrait von Bryher, Fotografie von Gisèle Freund, 1930er]

Berlin was a centre for their film activity, and while Switzerland offered opportunities, as Bryher wrote, "to see French, German, American and English films all in one week",[15] it was in Berlin that she found the excitement, energy, and, in her word, "danger" for which she was seeking at this time. "I fell in love with Berlin at once to my own amazement", Bryher writes. "We were conscious that we were standing near the centre of a volcano, it was raw, dangerous, explosive but I have never encountered before or since so vital a response to experimental art."[16]

Recalling the years between 1927 and 1932, during which she and Macpherson made regular visits to Berlin to see new als auch deutsche, amerikanische und englische Filme zu sehen.[16] Doch in Berlin fand sie die Aufregung, die Energie und auch die »Gefahr«, wie sie es nannte, nach der es sie in dieser Zeit verlangte. »Zu meiner eigenen Überraschung verliebte ich mich sofort in Berlin«, so Bryher. »Uns war bewusst, dass wir auf einem Vulkan tanzten. Die Stimmung war rau, gefährlich, explosiv. Doch niemals zuvor oder danach hatte ich eine derart lebendige Reaktion auf experimentelle Kunst erlebt.«[17]

In ihren Erinnerungen an die Jahre zwischen 1927 und 1932, als sie Berlin gemeinsam mit Macpherson regelmäßig besuchte, um neue Filme zu sehen und Menschen aus der Filmwelt zu treffen, beschreibt Bryher auch ihre immer engeren Kontakte zur psychoanalytischen Bewegung in der Stadt.

films and to meet up with people in the film world, Bryher also wrote of her increasing involvement with Berlin psychoanalysis. At the house of the director G.W. Pabst she met Hanns Sachs, a Viennese analyst, based in Berlin from 1922 to 1934, who was part of Freud's special circle of psychoanalysts, the "Secret Ring", and who became editor of the psychoanalytic journal *Imago*. Sachs, who had been invited to the Berlin Psychoanalytical Institute to initiate training analyses there, also worked with British analysts Ella Freeman Sharpe, Sylvia Payne, Barbara Low, and Mary Chadwick.[17] This followed a pattern in which those entering the profession, or developing their work within it, travelled to the European centres for psychoanalysis: Berlin, Vienna, and Budapest. Sharpe, who returned to Berlin regularly to continue her training with Sachs, arranged for him to give a series of lectures in London in 1924 in Adrian and Karin Stephen's house; Melanie Klein, with Alix and James Strachey's support, gave the series the following year and moved permanently to Britain in 1926. Adrian Stephen, Virginia Woolf's brother, was analysed by Sharpe from 1926 onwards.

Sachs had been involved in the making of the 1926 film *Secrets of a Soul*, directed by Pabst, which represented the workings of phobias and obsessions and of psychoanalytic treatment, and which, along with Pabst's other films of the 1920s, was an important influence on *Borderline*. Pabst's form of "psychological realism" was an immense draw for Bryher and H.D., as were his complex representations of women and

Im Haus des Regisseurs G.W. Pabst traf sie den Wiener Psychoanalytiker Hanns Sachs, der von 1922 bis 1934 in Berlin lebte. Er gehörte dem engen Kreis von Psychoanalytikern an, die sich in Freuds »Geheimem Komitee« zusammengeschlossen hatten, und wurde später Herausgeber der psychoanalytischen Zeitschrift *Imago*. Auf Einladung des Berliner Psychoanalytischen Instituts bildete Sachs Psychoanalytiker*innen aus und arbeitete dabei auch mit den Britinnen Ella Freeman Sharpe, Sylvia Payne, Barbara Low und Mary Chadwick.[18] Die Ausbildung erfolgte nach einem bestimmten Modell. Menschen, die neu in diesem Beruf waren oder sich weiterbilden wollten, begaben sich in die europäischen Zentren für Psychoanalyse in Berlin, Wien und Budapest. Ella Freeman Sharpe kehrte regelmäßig nach Berlin zurück, um ihre Ausbildung bei Sachs fortzusetzen. Im Jahr 1924 veranstaltete sie im Haus von Adrian und Karin Stephen in London eine Vortragsreihe mit ihrem Lehrmeister. Melanie Klein übernahm im Folgejahr die Organisation dieser Reihe mit Unterstützung von Alix und James Strachey und siedelte 1926 endgültig nach Großbritannien über. Virginia Woolfs Bruder Adrian Stephen unterzog sich ab 1926 einer Analyse bei Sharpe.

Sachs war 1926 an den Dreharbeiten zum Film *Geheimnisse einer Seele* unter der Regie von Pabst beteiligt. Der Film hatte die Wirkung von Phobien und Zwangsvorstellungen und psychoanalytische Behandlungsmöglichkeiten zum Thema. Wie alle weiteren Filme, die Pabst in den 1920er Jahren drehte, hatte auch dieser Film einen entscheidenden Einfluss auf die Entstehung von *Borderline*. Auf Bryher und H.D. übte die von Pabst eingesetzte Form des »psychologischen Realismus« eine große Anziehungskraft aus. Dasselbe traf auch auf seine komplexen Darstellungen von Frauen und weiblicher Sexualität in

female sexuality, in films including *Joyless Street* (an early Greta Garbo film) and *Pandora's Box* (1929), starring Louise Brooks.

Bryher entered an analysis with Sachs, with a view (not ultimately fulfilled) to becoming an analyst herself. "Films and psychoanalysis", she writes, "in those experimental days they were twins, some directors were trying to 'make thoughts visible'".[18] Her "circle" in Berlin included, in addition to Pabst, Sachs and Lotte Reiniger, the designer and film director Ernst Metzner and the actor and photographer Hans G. Casparius. There were also the actor Elisabeth Bergner (for whom Bryher developed a passion) and the Berlin architect Hermann Henselmann, whom Bryher commissioned to build a Bauhaus dwelling in Switzerland, which she called 'Kenwin' and which became her permanent home.

While Bryher was later to write that psychoanalysis was for her a greater draw than cinema,[19] her extensive writings on film, for *Close Up* and in other publications, indicate how fully involved she was with "the new art" at this time, meeting "film people" and gathering information about films in production and on release in Berlin. Visits to the city also gave opportunities to collect the film stills that were one of *Close Up*'s attractions, giving readers, in Britain and elsewhere, a degree of visual access to films that they were unable to view. Letters that she and Macpherson wrote during their first visits in 1927, many of them to H.D., provide vivid descriptions of life in Berlin, which, in their first visits, they

Filmen wie *Die freudlose Gasse* (ein früher Film mit Greta Garbo) und *Die Büchse der Pandora* (1929) mit Louise Brooks in der Hauptrolle zu.

Bryher begann eine Analyse bei Sachs mit dem Wunsch, selbst Analytikerin zu werden, konnte dieses Ziel jedoch nie ganz verwirklichen. »Filmschaffen und Psychoanalyse«, so schreibt sie, »gingen in diesen experimentellen Zeiten Hand in Hand, und einige Regisseure wollten ›Gedanken sichtbar machen‹«.[19] Zu ihrem Berliner »Kreis« gehörten neben Pabst, Sachs und Lotte Reiniger auch der Designer und Regisseur Ernst Metzner und der Schauspieler und Fotograf Hans G. Casparius. Weitere Mitglieder waren die Schauspielerin Elisabeth Bergner (für die Bryher schwärmte) und der Berliner Architekt Hermann Henselmann, den Bryher mit dem Bau einer Bauhaus-Villa in der Schweiz beauftragte, die sie »Villa Kenwin« nannte und zu ihrem Hauptwohnsitz machte.

Obwohl Bryher später schrieb, dass sie die Psychoanalyse weitaus mehr fasziniert habe als das Kino,[20] sind ihre umfangreichen Artikel zum Thema Film für *Close Up* und andere Publikationen ein Beleg dafür, wie ausführlich sie sich zu dieser Zeit mit »dieser neuen Kunstform« auseinandersetzte. Sie traf sich mit »Filmleuten« und trug Informationen über Filme zusammen, die in Berlin produziert oder veröffentlicht wurden. Bei ihren Berlin-Besuchen konnte sie außerdem Standbilder aus Filmen organisieren. Sie waren eine der Attraktionen von *Close Up* und boten Leser*innen in Großbritannien und aller Welt einen kleinen Einblick in Filme, die in ihrer Heimat nicht in den Kinos liefen. Die Briefe, die Bryher und Macpherson während ihrer ersten Besuche im Jahr 1927 in vielen Fällen auch an H.D. schrieben, enthalten lebhafte Beschreibungen des Lebens in Berlin, das sie in dieser Zeit immer wie-

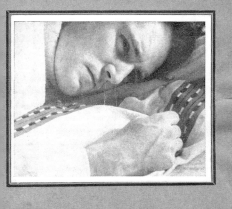

[Fig. 30: Cover of the English film journal *Close Up*, 1930]

[Abb. 30: Titelbild des englischen Filmmagazin *Close Up*, 1930]

repeatedly compared to New York: "Miles and miles of electric lights".[20] Film-going was a central activity, at cinemas small and large, the latter including the Ufa Palast am Zoo ("about the size of Regents Park another gold beehive, with *red plush* walls and red carpets. And miles and miles of entrances and exits and disappearances and cabinets") and the Beba Palast, "where they were showing Heimweh with Mady Christians".[21] Bryher writes of this occasion:

> Cinemas open at five on Sundays so we went to the five oclock show and coming out there was a crowd to fill the whole vast place but arranged cir-

der mit New York verglichen: »Meilenweit elektrisches Licht, wohin das Auge blickt«.[21] Zu ihren Hauptaktivitäten gehörten Kinobesuche in kleinen und großen Lichtspielhäusern, darunter auch der Ufa Palast am Zoo –»etwa so groß wie der Regent's Park, ein weiterer goldener Bienenstock mit *rotem Plüsch* an den Wänden und roten Teppichen. Und mit unzähligen Eingängen und Ausgängen und Verstecken und Wandschränken« und der Beba Palast, »wo sie Heimweh mit Mady Christians zeigten«.[22] »Die Kinos«, schreibt Bryher in diesem Zusammenhang,

> öffnen sonntags um fünf. Wir gingen also zur Fünf-Uhr-Vorstellung. Als wir wieder hinauskamen, hatten sich draußen auf dem Vorplatz

cular wise and in perfect grouping as if for a movie. You cant get the German movies till you've been here.²²

"Berlin", Macpherson writes, "is one big movie, like an impossible dream".²³

For many, the powerful sense of living in a film-world became linked to an involvement in film-making and performance. This found one outlet in the active amateur film movement, as well as the trend towards the use of amateur actors in Germany at this time, as in Robert Siodmak's pioneering film *Menschen am Sonntag* (1930), set in Berlin and at the Wannsee. Eric Walter White's letters described the "home movies" made at Lotte Reiniger's house in Potsdam, while Spender's autobiographical novel *The Temple* (written in 1930 though not published, in revised form, until the 1980s) gives an account of a party in which an amateur film is projected:

> Now on the screen there was a party held in this very studio, with boys and girls dancing. Some of them were there then, some of them here now—dancing. The camera sauntered among twisting and turning figures ... Suddenly they all fell on top of each other on the floor, some of them now present in this room.²⁴

The doubled world of the screen becomes a hall of mirrors as the partygoers watch the film images which, in part, replicate their current reality. Past time and present time merge, while spectators are also actors,

Menschenmassen versammelt, die sich wie für einen Filmdreh perfekt kreisförmig gruppiert hatten. Das deutsche Kino kann man nur verstehen, wenn man es selbst erlebt hat.²³

»Berlin«, schreibt Macpherson, »ist ein einziger großer Film, wie ein unerfüllbarer Traum«.²⁴

Für viele verband sich das intensive Gefühl, in einer Filmwelt zu leben, mit dem Wunsch nach eigenen Filmarbeiten und Filmauftritten. Davon zeugen die aktive Amateurfilm-Bewegung sowie der im damaligen Deutschland zunehmende Einsatz von Laiendarsteller*innen – beispielsweise in Robert Siodmaks wegweisendem Film *Menschen am Sonntag* (1930), der in Berlin und am Wannsee spielt. Eric Walter White beschreibt in seinen Briefen die »Amateurfilme«, die in Lotte Reinigers Haus in Potsdam gedreht wurden. Spenders autobiografischer Roman *Der Tempel* (1930 verfasst, aber in überarbeiteter Form erst in den 1980er Jahren veröffentlicht) enthält eine Episode mit einer Party, auf der ein Amateurfilm gezeigt wird:

> Jetzt war auf der Leinwand eine Party zu sehen, in diesem Studio, die Jungen und Mädchen tanzten. Einige von ihnen hatten damals dort getanzt, einige von ihnen tanzten an diesem Abend hier. Die Kamera bewegte sich lässig zwischen sich drehenden und windenden Gestalten [...] Plötzlich fielen sie alle zu Boden, alle übereinander, auch einige, die sich jetzt in diesem Raum befanden.²⁵

Die Parallelwelt auf der Leinwand übernimmt die Funktion eines Spiegelsaals, wenn die Partygäste Filmbilder betrachten, die zum Teil ihre aktuelle Realität nachbilden. Vergangenheit und Gegenwart verschmelzen miteinander, Zuschauer*innen werden

enacting and projecting their own desires onto the world of the screen. The images of sexual freedoms depicted by Spender relate also to the relative absence of film censorship on sexual grounds, with sexual relations often to the fore and same-sex desire, explicit or implied, portrayed in films such as Pabst's *Pandora's Box* and Leontine Sagan's *Mädchen in Uniform* (1931).

"Life and the films must not be separated", H.D. wrote in her *Close Up* article on "Russian Films": "people and things must pass across the screen naturally like shad-

zu Schauspieler*innen, die ihre eigenen Sehnsüchte inszenieren und auf die Welt auf der Leinwand projizieren. Die von Spender geschilderten Darstellungen sexueller Freiheit weisen zudem darauf hin, dass die Filmzensoren in der Regel kein Interesse an sexuellen Inhalten hatten. In Filmen wie Pabsts *Die Büchse der Pandora* und Leontine Sagans *Mädchen in Uniform* (1931) standen sexuelle Beziehungen im Vordergrund und gleichgeschlechtliches Begehren wurde explizit oder implizit dargestellt.

»Leben und Film dürfen nicht voneinander getrennt werden«, schrieb H.D. in einem Artikel in *Close Up* über »Russische Filme«: »Menschen und

[Fig. 31: A homoerotic moment in G.W. Pabst's film *Pandora's Box*, film still, 1928/29]

[Abb. 31: Ein homoerotischer Moment in G.W. Pabsts Film *Die Büchse der Pandora*, Standbild, 1928/29]

ows of trees on grass or passing reflections in a crowded city window".²⁵ Soviet cinema was the great film-excitement of the later 1920s and Berlin was one of the few places in western and central Europe where it was possible to see Soviet films at a time when they were censored on political grounds in Britain, with the exception of private cinema clubs, and even there with difficulty of access. Eisenstein's *Battleship Potemkin* (1926) was only briefly banned in Germany, and in fact the Lichtspielgesetz of 1920 had specified that no film could be banned because of its politics: "Die Zulassung darf wegen einer politischen, sozialen, religiösen, ethischen oder Weltanschauungstendenz als solcher nicht versagt werden."²⁶ As Huntly Carter wrote:

> Several revolutionary pictures have been established in Berlin which have not been permitted to be shown in this country [Britain]. Owing to the fairly large number of Bolshevist pictures exhibited in Berlin, that city has of late become the Mecca of the aesthete in search of adventures among revolutionary films, and of evidence by which he may slay the British censor.²⁷

Spender writes in his autobiography of his time in Berlin, when he was living near Isherwood:

> Whenever we could, we went to see those Russian films which were shown often in Berlin at this period: *Earth*, *The*

Dinge müssen sich natürlich über die Leinwand bewegen, wie die Schatten von Bäumen auf dem Gras oder flüchtige Spiegelungen auf den Fensterscheiben einer belebten Stadt«.²⁶ In den späten 1920er Jahren stieß das sowjetische Kino bei Filmliebhaber*innen auf große Begeisterung. Berlin war in Mittel- und Westeuropa einer der wenigen Orte, an dem sowjetische Filme gezeigt werden durften. In Großbritannien waren sie zu dieser Zeit aus politischen Gründen verboten und liefen nur in privaten Kinoklubs, die jedoch nicht für jedermann zugänglich waren. Eisensteins *Panzerkreuzer Potemkin* (1926) fiel in Deutschland nur für kurze Zeit der Zensur zum Opfer. Gemäß dem Lichtspielgesetz von 1920 durften Filme nicht aus politischen Gründe verboten werden: »Die Zulassung darf wegen einer politischen, sozialen, religiösen, ethischen oder Weltanschauungstendenz als solcher nicht versagt werden«.²⁷ Dazu schrieb Huntly Carter:

> In Berlin sind mehrere Revolutionsfilme entstanden, die in unserem Land [Großbritannien] nicht gezeigt werden durften. Da in den Berliner Kinos recht viele bolschewistische Filme laufen, hat sich die Stadt inzwischen zu einem Mekka für Filmästheten entwickelt. In Revolutionsfilmen begeben sie sich auf die Suche nach Abenteuer und nach Anhaltspunkten, um den britischen Zensoren das Handwerk zu legen.²⁸

Spender schreibt in seiner Autobiografie über seine Zeit in Berlin, in der er ganz in der Nähe von Isherwood wohnte:

> Wo es einen russischen Film zu sehen gab, und es gab damals viele in Berlin zu sehen, gingen wir hin: *Erde, Die Mutter, Panzerkreuzer Potemkin,*

General Line, *The Mother*, *Ten Days that Shook the World*, *The Way into Life*, etc. These films which form a curiously isolated episode in the aesthetic history of this century, excited us because they had the modernism, the aesthetic sensibility, the satire, the visual beauty, all those qualities we found most exciting in other forms of modern art, but they also conveyed a message of hope [...]. We used to go long journeys to little cinemas in the outer suburbs of Berlin, and there among the grimy tenements we saw the images of the New Life of the workers [...].²⁸

Soviet films, Spender suggested, played a central role in their "restless and awakening mood", projecting images of a "socially just world" in, and onto, the decaying facades of Berlin. Isherwood himself did not write at length about his Berlin film-going, although frequent comments on having visited the cinema abound in his texts, but "camera vision" shaped his writing about Berlin and he became fully involved in the film-world on his return to Britain, working with the Austrian director Berthold Viertel in the making of the film *Little Friend* (1934). Isherwood, in his 1946 autobiographical novel *Prater Violet*, describes meeting him: "I knew that face. It was the face of a political situation, an epoch. The face of Central Europe."²⁹

In 1929, Bryher published her book *Film Problems of Soviet Russia* under the POOL imprint, which encompassed *Close Up* and other publications in film, litera-

Zehn Tage, die die Welt erschütterten, Der Weg ins Leben und andere mehr. Diese Filme, die eine sonderbar vereinzelte Episode im Kunstgeschmack dieses Jahrhunderts bilden, erregten uns, denn in ihnen fanden wir den modernen Standpunkt, die poetische Einfühlung, die Satire, die augenfällige Schönheit, kurz, alles wieder, was uns in anderen zeitgenössischen Werken so aufgewühlt hatte; zugleich aber brachten sie eine Hoffnungsbotschaft. [...] Wir gingen den weiten Weg in kleine Vorstadtkinos und sahen, mitten unter schmutzigen Mietskasernen, Bilder vom neuen Leben der Arbeiter [...].²⁹

Sowjetische Filme, so Spender, hatten einen maßgeblichen Einfluss auf ihre »unruhige[n] Stimmung vor dem Erwachen« und projizierten Bilder einer »Welt der sozialen Gerechtigkeit« in und auf die verfallenden Fassaden Berlins. Isherwood selbst ging nicht besonders ausführlich auf seine Berliner Filmerlebnisse ein, obwohl seine Texte unzählige Hinweise auf Kinobesuche enthalten. Allerdings nahm er in seinen Berliner Geschichten eine Art »Kameraperspektive« ein. Nach seiner Rückkehr nach Großbritannien beteiligte er sich zudem aktiv am Filmschaffen und unterstützte den österreichischen Filmemacher Berthold Viertel bei der Arbeit an seinem Film *Little Friend* (1934). Isherwood beschreibt ihr Zusammentreffen in seinem autobiografischen Roman *Praterveilchen* aus dem Jahr 1946 wie folgt: »Ich kannte das Gesicht. Es war das Gesicht einer politischen Situation, einer ganzen Epoche. Es war das Gesicht Mitteleuropas«.³⁰

Im Jahr 1929 veröffentlichte Bryher (bei der POOL Group, die *Close Up* und andere Publikationen in den Bereichen Film, Literatur und Kultur herausgab) ihr Buch *Film Problems of Soviet Russia*. Mit

ture, and culture. One of the earliest English-language studies of Soviet film, it was a major achievement, covering a substantial number of films, many of which she viewed in Berlin in under a year, and was substantially concerned with questions of international distribution, as well as with the details of individual film directors and genres. She wrote:

> Up to last summer I had seen only four Russian films, three in Switzerland and one in Germany. But we took the aeroplane service to Berlin last July, having been promised that we could see there the output of a whole season. … I saw a dozen of these films last summer in a small projection room without music at nine in the morning, and they were art—as the Elizabethans were art—and they were truth.[30]

Film Problems of Soviet Russia was written to introduce British readers to a film culture to which they were denied access and, in tandem with *Close Up*'s anti-censorship petition, to promote a reform of British censorship laws as they applied to cinema. Bryher returned throughout the study to the argument that no revolution had fomented in Germany and Austria, despite the relative ease of access to Soviet film. At the end of the book, she offered "suggestions" to those travelling to Germany, including advice on modes of travel and on where to see films, at kinos large and central as well as small and "outlying".[31]

diesem umfassenden Werk legte sie eine der ersten englischsprachigen Untersuchungen zum sowjetischen Film vor. Darin fanden sich zahlreiche Artikel über Filme, die sie zum größten Teil innerhalb nur eines Jahres in Berlin gesehen hatte. Auch Fragen des internationalen Vertriebs sowie zu einzelnen Filmregisseuren und Genres wurden darin ausführlich behandelt. Sie schrieb:

> Bis zum vergangenen Sommer hatte ich lediglich vier russische Filme gesehen, drei in der Schweiz und einen in Deutschland. Doch im vergangenen Juli kamen wir mit dem Flugzeug nach Berlin, da man uns versprochen hatte, dass wir dort die Filmproduktion einer ganzen Saison zu sehen bekämen. […] In einem kleinen Vorführraum schaute ich mir in diesem Sommer um neun Uhr morgens Dutzende von Filmen ohne Musikbegleitung an. Und ich bekam wahre Kunst zu sehen – die der Elisabethanischen Kunst in nichts nachkam – und noch dazu das wahre Leben.[31]

Mit *Film Problems of Soviet Russia* sollten britische Leser*innen an eine Filmkultur herangeführt werden, zu der sie keinen Zugang hatten. Außerdem zielte das Buch zusammen mit der Anti-Zensur-Petition der *Close Up* auf eine Reform der britischen Zensurgesetze für Kinofilme ab. Bryher wies in ihrer Studie wiederholt darauf hin, dass in Deutschland und Österreich trotz des relativ leichten Zugangs zu sowjetischen Filmen noch keine Revolution ausgebrochen sei. Am Ende des Buchs gab sie einige »Tipps« für Deutschlandreisende, darunter auch Empfehlungen zur Anreise und zu den Möglichkeiten, Filme in großen Kinos im Zentrum sowie in kleinen Vorortkinos anzusehen.[32]

Both *Film Problems of Soviet Russia* and *Close Up* devoted significant space to Pudovkin's film *Storm over Asia*, which was as great a success in Berlin as *Battleship Potemkin* had been two years earlier. "Newspapers forgot their politics and united in praising it as a work of art", Bryher writes. "Police were called out to control the crowds trying to get tickets. Performances were sold out days beforehand."[32] At the close of January 1929, the Marmorhaus had enjoyed fifty sold-out screenings of *Storm over Asia*, and the film was, it was reported, being shown in two hundred further cinemas in Berlin. Leonard and Virginia Woolf saw the film during a not altogether successful ten-day stay in Berlin in mid-January 1929 in the company of Woolf's artist sister Vanessa Bell and her artist-lover Duncan Grant, Harold Nicolson (then Counsellor at the British Embassy), his wife Vita Sackville-West, and her cousin, the writer and music critic Eddy Sackville-West. In a letter to the art critic Roger Fry, Vanessa Bell described the experience of watching the film and its stormy aftermath:

> The film seemed to me extraordinary—there were the most lovely pictures of odd Chinese types, very well done. I enjoyed it immensely & was under the impression that everyone else did too until we got out on into the street when it appeared that feeling was very high on the question whether it was anti-British propaganda. No doubt it was—at least the feeblest part of it consisted of the flight of soldiers in British uniforms

Sowohl *Film Problems of Soviet Russia* als auch *Close Up* gingen ausführlich auf Pudowkins Film *Sturm über Asien* ein, der – wie *Panzerkreuzer Potemkin* zwei Jahre zuvor – in Berlin zum Kassenschlager wurde. »Zeitungen vergaßen ihre politische Linie und priesen den Film einhellig als Kunstwerk«, schreibt Bryher. »Die Polizei musste die Massen, die für Tickets anstanden, unter Kontrolle bringen. Die Vorführungen waren Tage im Voraus ausverkauft«.[33] Bis Ende Januar 1929 liefen im Marmorhaus bereits über fünfzig ausverkaufte Vorstellungen von *Sturm über Asien*. Der Film stand Berichten zufolge in zweihundert weiteren Filmtheatern in Berlin auf dem Programm. Leonard und Virginia Woolf sahen sich den Film während eines nicht allzu gelungenen zehntägigen Aufenthalts Mitte Januar 1929 in Berlin an. Begleitet wurden sie bei diesem Kinobesuch von Woolfs Schwester, der Künstlerin Vanessa Bell, ihrem Geliebten, dem Künstler Duncan Grant, sowie von Harold Nicolson (zu dieser Zeit *Chargé d'Affaires* an der britischen Botschaft), seiner Ehefrau Vita Sackville-West und ihrem Cousin, dem Schriftsteller und Musikkritiker Eddy Sackville-West. In einem Brief an den Kunstkritiker Roger Fry beschreibt Vanessa Bell das Filmerlebnis und die anschließenden Turbulenzen wie folgt:

> Der Film schien mir ganz außerordentlich – es gab darin wunderschöne Aufnahmen von eigenartigen Chinesen, ausgezeichnet gemacht. Ich habe den Film ausgesprochen genossen, und ich dachte, die anderen auch, bis sich draußen auf der Straße die Gemüter erhitzten über die Frage, ob der Film antibritische Propaganda sei. Natürlich war er das – zumindest in seinem schwächsten Teil, wo gezeigt wird, wie Soldaten in britischen Uniformen vor Asiaten davonlaufen. Vita brachte Leonard von neuem in Rage,

flying from Asiatics. Vita again enraged Leonard by asking him 6 times whether he thought they were meant for Englishmen—she and Harold both thought they weren't but managed to quarrel with each other all the same. The discussions went on & on, all standing in the melting snow, & the general rage & uneasiness was increased by Eddy who was also of the party .... Never have I spent quite such a thundery evening.[33]

A number of British visitors and residents saw the film, expressing little doubt in their comments about its anti-British sentiment. Eric Walter White wrote to his close friend Thorold Dickinson (who would become a highly regarded film-director): "it is the British army and officers which grow horns. Of course, at times one wants to shout out that not every every every British officer is like that".[34] Bryher notes that, when watching the film in a private projection context, they were asked "if we would see the Russian version with Russian sub-titles, but added, doubtfully, when we said yes, 'it is anti-English'".[35] Accepting the film's critique of imperialism, she writes ruefully of "the realisation that we have lost the one reputation abroad"—the sense of justice—"of which we might well have been proud".[36] Like White, she also argues, however, that while the English as portrayed in *Storm over Asia* are not exaggerated, "they are rare".[37]

There was another thundery Berlin evening when Macpherson's film *Borderline* was screened in May 1931, first in a small

indem sie ihn sechsmal fragte, ob er glaube, daß man damit habe Engländer darstellen wollen – sie und Harold meinten, nein, aber sie brachten es trotzdem fertig, sich in die Haare zu geraten. Der Streit ging weiter und weiter; wir standen in dem Schneematsch herum, und die allgemeine schlechte Laune wurde noch vermehrt durch Eddy, der auch mit war [...] Ich habe noch nie einen so turbulenten Abend erlebt.[34]

Für etliche Brit*innen, die auf Besuch in Berlin waren oder dort lebten und den Film gesehen hatten, bestand so gut wie kein Zweifel daran, dass dieser eine antibritische Haltung vertrat. Eric Walter White schrieb an seinen engen Freund Thorold Dickinson (der später ein angesehener Regisseur war): »die britische Armee und die britischen Offiziere sind hier die Teufel. Natürlich möchte man bisweilen ausrufen, dass nicht jeder einzelne britische Offizier so ist«.[35] Bryher berichtet, dass man sie bei einer Privatvorführung des Films gefragt habe, »ob wir uns auch die russische Fassung mit russischen Untertiteln anschauen würden, nachdem wir bejahten, allerdings hinterhergeschoben wurde, dass der Film ›englandfeindlich‹ sei«.[36] Der im Film geäußerten Imperialismuskritik kann sie sich anschließen und schreibt reumütig von ihrer »Erkenntnis, dass wir im Ausland ausgerechnet den Ruf eingebüßt haben« – es geht um den Gerechtigkeitssinn – »der uns durchaus mit Stolz hätte erfüllen können«.[37] Wie auch White merkt sie an, dass die in *Sturm über Asien* portraitierten Engländer zwar nicht übertrieben dargestellt, aber doch »eine Seltenheit sind«.[38]

Zu einem weiteren turbulenten Abend kam es im Mai 1931 in Berlin anlässlich der Aufführung von Macphersons Film *Borderline*, der zuerst in der Roten Mühle, einem kleinen Kino in Halensee, und anschließend in der Kamera, Unter den Linden, gezeigt

[Fig. 32: A British imperial officer in Vsevolod Pudovkin's film *Storm over Asia*, 1929]

[Abb. 32: Ein Britischer Kolonialbeamter in Vsevolod Pudovkins Film *Sturm über Asien*, 1929]

cinema in Halensee, the Rote Mühle, and then in the Kamera, Unter den Linden.[38] After an enthusiastic review in the *Film-Kurier* on 15 April, which described it as pushing back the borders of film art, the first public showing, very late at night and preceded by Germaine Dulac's surrealist film *Mussel*, dramatically polarised the audience between supporters, who included Sachs, Pabst, Metzner, and Lotte Reiniger, and a critical mass who whistled, booed, and, in some cases, walked out. The *Film-Kurier*'s second review, by the film theorist and novelist Walter J. Bloem, praised its experimen-

wurde.[39] In einer begeisterten Rezension schrieb der *Film-Kurier* bereits am 15. April, dass in *Borderline* die Grenzen der Filmkunst neu definiert würden. Doch im Publikum bildeten sich bei der ersten öffentlichen Vorführung, spätnachts und im Anschluss an Germaine Dulacs surrealistischen Film *Die Muschel und der Kleriker*, zwei harte Fronten. Auf der einen Seite waren die Unterstützer*innen, zu denen Sachs, Pabst, Metzner und Lotte Reiniger gehörten, auf der anderen Seite befand sich eine große Gruppe, die pfiff, buhte oder sogar das Kino verließ. In der zweiten Kritik im *Film-Kurier* zeigte sich der Filmtheoretiker und Schriftsteller Walter Bloem zwar begeistert vom experimentellen Charakter und von der eindringlichen

tal character and penetrating expression of emotional processes, but criticised its length and repetition.

Bryher herself attended the premiere, after an early evening spent at a psychoanalytic lecture by the analyst and anthropologist Géza Róheim. She wrote to H. D. and Macpherson of the *Borderline* screening:

> ... there was uproar. It hit their unconscious too badly. Turtle [their nickname for Sachs] said it was not a typical Berlin audience, Metzner yelled furiously at them "ruhe" and wanted to fight them. If I had been on my own, I too would have joined in. We had a real surrealist evening. Half of them yelled, whistled, not straight but in a kind of hysterical way ...
>
> Personally I consider it highly successful. Turtle says he is ashamed of Berlin but that's silly because you cannot expect an ordinary audience to take such an onslaught on their unc[onscious] quietly.

The letter, which links the showing with surrealism, psychoanalysis (including the gory initiation rituals described by Róheim), and sexuality, concludes with a mention of her analytic hour with Sachs the following morning, at which she "Got a lot of interesting material up ...".[39]

Under National Socialism, when some 2,000 film-workers lost their jobs, Bryher helped Jews and others under attack to leave Germany. In 1933, as *Close Up* came

Darstellung emotionaler Prozesse, äußerte sich jedoch kritisch über die Länge und die vielen Wiederholungen.

Bryher selbst war bei der Premiere anwesend. Zuvor hatte sie am frühen Abend einen psychoanalytischen Vortrag des Analytikers und Anthropologen Géza Róheim besucht. In einem Brief berichtete sie H. D. und Macpherson von der *Borderline*-Vorführung:

> ...es kam zu tumultartigen Szenen. Ihr Unterbewusstsein wurde zu stark angesprochen. Turtle [ihr Spitzname für Sachs] sagte, dies sei kein typisches Berliner Publikum. Metzner brüllte wütend um »Ruhe« und drohte ihnen Prügel an. Wäre ich allein gewesen, hätte ich mich ebenfalls beteiligt. Es war ein surrealistischer Abend. Die eine Hälfte johlte und pfiff, nicht geradeheraus, sondern irgendwie hysterisch ...
>
> Ich persönlich sehe darin einen großen Erfolg. Turtle sagt, er schäme sich für Berlin. Doch das ist Quatsch, denn man kann nicht von einem normalen Publikum erwarten, dass es einen derartigen Angriff auf sein Unterbewusstsein mit Fassung trägt.

Der Brief, in dem die Vorführung mit Surrealismus, Psychoanalyse (einschließlich der von Róheim beschriebenen schaurigen Initiationsrituale) und Sexualität in Verbindung gebracht wird, schließt mit einer Bemerkung zu ihrer Analysestunde bei Sachs am folgenden Morgen, während der sie »viele interessante Erkenntnisse zutage fördern konnte«.[40]

Unter den Nationalsozialisten verloren fast 2000 Mitarbeiter*innen der Filmwirtschaft ihre Arbeit. Bryher half jüdischen Menschen und anderen Verfolgten bei der Flucht aus Deutschland. Als *Close Up* 1933 eingestellt wurde, schrieb sie, dass es nun

to an end, she wrote of needing to turn from involvement in film culture to "[helping] to raise respect for intellectual liberty".[40] Despite the horrors that followed, she remembered Berlin for, in the words of a poem she wrote in the 1920s, "all the sharp, white, overreaching promise we call life".[41] In a letter to Macpherson in 1970, she wrote: "I'm delighted that you are working on Berlin. The church, the Gedächtniskirche. Gedächtnis means memory [...] Berlin was a great moment, I think films have never been so rich nor so adventurous since, [though] naturally improved beyond recognition in technique."[42] In the words of her poem, a love song to Weimar Berlin:

Never be anchorage
never be safety
only be the kino.
where the truant boy
and the old knitting-cook
watched shadows
with carrots in her basket
and a cabbage.
And I between them knowing …

Notes

1 Rachael Low: The History of the British Film. 1918–1929, London, George Allen and Unwin 1971, p. 224.
2 John Lehmann: The Whispering Gallery. Autobiography I, London, Longmans 1955, p. 209.
3 Bloomsbury/Freud. The Letters of James and Alix Strachey 1924–1925, ed. by Perry Meisel and Walter Kendrick, New York, Basic Books 1985, p. 163.

4 Ibid., p. 203.
5 Ibid., p. 212.
6 Ibid., p. 215.
7 Ibid., p. 287.
8 Ivor Montagu: The Youngest Son, London, George Allen and Unwin 1971, p. 267.
9 Huntly Carter: The New Spirit in the Cinema, London, Harold Shayler 1930, p. 242.
10 Ibid., p. 243.
11 René Clair: Reflections on the Cinema, trans. Vera Traill, London, William Kimber 1953, p. 15.
12 Clive Bell: Art and the Cinema: A Prophecy that the Motion Pictures, in Exploiting Imitation Art, will Leave Real Art to the Artist, Vanity Fair, November 1922, p. 39.
13 The question of cinema as an art form was substantially addressed in Germany in the "Kino-Debatte" in the 1910s. Many British writers and intellectuals showed an indifference to films, perceived as popular entertainment, until they became familiar with the 'art' cinema of Europe, in particular Germany and France.
14 Frankfurter Zeitung, 7 July 1932.
15 Bryher: The Heart to Artemis. A Writer's Memoirs, London, Collins 1963, p. 248.
16 Ibid., p. 249.
17 See Laura Marcus: European Witness: Analysands Abroad in the 1920s and 1930s, in: Laura Marcus, Dreams of Modernity, New York, Cambridge University Press 2014, pp. 151–177.
18 Unpublished two-page manuscript, headed BERLIN, Beinecke archive, Box 72.
19 On the previous page, she writes that she told Sachs "that psychology meant far more to me as a would be writer than pictures …".
20 Letter from Bryher to H.D. 23 October 1927. Beinecke H.D. Papers YCAL MSS 24 I Box 3, Folder 83.
21 Macpherson in joint letter to H.D. 27 October 1927. Beinecke H.D. Papers, loc.cit.
22 Ibid.
23 Macpherson, 23 October 1927.

und Walter Kendrick, aus dem Englischen übersetzt von Rortraut De Clerck, Stuttgart, Verlag Internationale Psychoanalyse 1995, S. 256.
5 Ebd., S. 309.
6 Ebd., S. 321.
7 Ebd., S. 325.
8 Ebd., S. 418.
9 Ivor Montagu: The Youngest Son, London, George Allen and Unwin 1971, S. 267.
10 Huntly Carter: The New Spirit in the Cinema, London, Harold Shayler 1930, S. 242.
11 Ebd., S. 243.
12 René Clair: Kino. Vom Stummfilm zum Tonfilm, aus dem Französischen von Eva Fehsenbecker, Zürich, Diogenes Verlag AG 1995, S. 17.
13 Clive Bell: Art and the Cinema: A Prophecy that the Motion Pictures, in Exploiting Imitation Art, will Leave Real Art to the Artist, Vanity Fair, November 1922, S. 39.
14 Über Kino als Kunstform wurde in Deutschland im Rahmen der »Kino-Debatte« der 1910er Jahre ausführlich diskutiert. Viele britische Schriftsteller*innen und Intellektuelle zeigten sich gleichgültig gegenüber dem Medium Film, das sie als populäre Unterhaltung wahrnahmen, bevor sie mit der »Kinokunst« aus Europa und insbesondere aus Deutschland und Frankreich in Berührung kamen.
15 Frankfurter Zeitung 7.7.32.
16 Bryher: The Heart to Artemis. A Writer's Memoirs, London, Collins 1963, S. 248.
17 Ebd., S. 249.
18 Siehe Laura Marcus: European Witness: Analysands Abroad in the 1920s and 1930s, in: Laura Marcus, Dreams of Modernity, New York, Cambridge University Press 2014, S. 151–177.
19 Unveröffentlichtes zweiseitiges Manuskript mit der Überschrift BERLIN, Beinecke archive, Box 72.
20 Auf der vorherigen Seite schreibt sie, dass für sie als Möchtegern-Schriftstellerin »Psychologie weitaus wichtiger gewesen sei als Film …«.
21 Brief von Bryher an H.D. vom 23. Oktober 1927. Beinecke H.D. Papers YCAL MSS 24 I Box 3, Folder 83.
22 Macpherson in einem gemeinsamen Brief an H.D. vom 27. Oktober 1927. Beinecke H.D. Papers, a.a.O.

24 Stephen Spender: The Temple, London, Faber & Faber 1988, p. 44.
25 H. D.: Russian Films, Close Up 3, 3 September 1928, pp. 18–29, here 28.
26 Lichtspielgesetz, Prüfung von Bildstreifen, paragraph 1, http://www.documentarchiv.de/wr/1920/lichtspielgesetz.html.
27 Carter: The new spirit, p. 277.
28 Stephen Spender: World Within World, London, Hamish Hamilton 1951, pp. 132 f.
29 Christopher Isherwood: Prater Violet, Harmondsworth, Penguin 1961, p. 20.
30 Bryher: Film Problems of Soviet Russia, Territet, Switzerland, Pool 1929, p. 9, p. 12.
31 Ibid., p. 134 f.
32 Ibid., p. 69.
33 19 January 1929. Charleston Papers, Kings College Cambridge Library. Cited in: Quentin Bell: Virginia Woolf. A Biography, volume 2, London, Hogarth Press 1972, pp. 142 f.
34 Potsdam, January 1929. Dickinson papers, Special Collections, British Film Institute, London.
35 Bryher: Film Problems, p. 61.
36 Ibid.
37 Ibid., p. 69.
38 *Borderline* had premiered in the Academy Cinema, Oxford Street, London in 1930 and was subsequently shown in Brussels, Birmingham, and Catalonia. It was impounded by the US customs because of its inter-racial content. The Berlin screenings appear to have been the last public showings for many decades.
39 Bryher: Letter to H. D. and Macpherson, dated 26 April 1931, Beinecke, Rare Book and Manuscript Library, Uncat. MS. Vault Pearson/Bryher, Yale University, New Haven.
40 Bryher: What Shall You Do in the War?, Close Up x, 2 June 1933, p. 192.
41 Bryher: Diary (1927–47), Bryher Papers, General Collection, Beinecke Rare Book and Manu-

23 Ebd.
24 Macpherson, 23. Oktober 1927.
25 Stephen Spender: Der Tempel, aus dem Englischen von Sylvia List, München und Zürich, Piper Verlag 1991, S. 66.
26 H. D.: Russian Films, Close Up 3, 3. September 1928, S. 18–29; hier S. 28.
27 Lichtspielgesetz, Prüfung von Bildstreifen, Paragraph 1 http://www.documentarchiv.de/wr/1920/lichtspielgesetz.html.
28 Carter: The New Spirit, S. 277.
29 Stephen Spender: Welt in der Welt, aus dem Englischen von Andreas Sattler, München, R. Piper GmbH & Co. KG 1992, S. 169.
30 Christopher Isherwood: Praterveilchen, Deutsch von Hansi Bochow-Blüthgen, Hamburg, Rowohlt 1953, S. 22.
31 Bryher: Film Problems of Soviet Russia, Territet, Switzerland, Pool 1929, S. 9, 12.
32 Ebd., S. 134 f.
33 Ebd., S. 69.
34 Vanessa Bell an Roger Fry, 19. Januar 1929, in: Quentin Bell: Virginia Woolf. Eine Biographie, aus dem Englischen von Arnold Fernberg, 3. Auflage, Frankfurt a.M., Insel Verlag (1977) 1980, S. 409.
35 Potsdam, January 1929. Dickinson papers, Special Collections, British Film Institute, London.
36 Bryher: Film Problems, S. 61.
37 Ebd.
38 Ebd., S. 69.
39 *Borderline* feierte seine Premiere 1930 in London im Academy Cinema an der Oxford Street und wurde anschließend in Brüssel, Birmingham und Katalonien gezeigt. Wegen seiner interkulturellen Inhalte wurde er vom US-Zoll beschlagnahmt. Die Berliner Vorführungen waren offenbar die letzten für mehrere Jahrzehnte.
40 Bryher: Brief an H. D. und Macpherson vom 26. April 1931, Beinecke, uncat. ms. vault Pearson/Bryher.
41 Bryher: What Shall You Do in the War?, Close Up x, 2. Juni 1933, S. 192.
42 Beinecke: Bryher papers, Box 149, Folder 5064. Diary (1927–47).
43 Bryher, Feb 16, 1970. ms. vault uncat. Pearson.

script Library, Box 149, Folder 5064, Yale University, New Haven.

42 Bryher, Feb 16, 1970, Beinecke Rare Book and Manuscript Library, Uncat. MS. Vault Pearson, Yale University, New Haven.

44 Sei niemals ein Ankerplatz / niemals der sichere Hafen / sei einfach nur das Kino / Wo der Schulschwänzer / und die alte Köchin mit ihrem Strickzeug / und Karotten und Kohl / in ihrem Korb / Schatten vorbeihuschen sehen / Und ich sitze zwischen ihnen und weiß Bescheid [...].

Annabel Williams

Touring Political Berlin: War, Revolution, and Fascism

Eine Tour durch das politische Berlin: Krieg, Revolution und Faschismus

When in October 1945 the British poet and essayist Stephen Spender travelled through a war-devastated Berlin, the sight of the ruined Kaiser Wilhelm Memorial Church triggered an unsettling memory of clairvoyance at the site fourteen years earlier. It had been the summer of 1931, Berlin was currently Spender's home, and he was walking with fellow writer Edward Upward, who was soon to join the Communist Party of Great Britain. Passing the church, which looked to Spender "like an absurdly ornate over-large inkstand set down in the middle of the traffic", they contemplated the city's poverty, its unemployment crisis, and its increasingly emboldened fascists. The street scene seemed to dissolve before them, giving way to the desolation Spender was to witness in 1945. It was "as though [they] looked through the transparent traffic on to the ruin".[1] This ripple in time marked the beginning of a deepening political awareness for Spender; a combination of Upward's revolutionary talk, and the clear evidence of emergency in everyday life, seemed to indicate that Berlin's and Europe's future ca-

Als der britische Dichter und Essayist Stephen Spender im Oktober 1945 während einer Reise in das vom Krieg verwüstete Berlin die Ruinen der Kaiser-Wilhelm-Gedächtniskirche erblickte, entstand vor seinem inneren Auge ein beängstigend klares Bild von diesem Ort vierzehn Jahre zuvor. Damals, im Sommer 1931, hatte Spender für einige Zeit sein Domizil in Berlin aufgeschlagen. Er erkundete die Stadt gemeinsam mit seinem Schriftstellerkollegen Edward Upward, der schon bald der Kommunistischen Partei Großbritanniens beitrat. Auf ihrem Spaziergang kamen sie auch an der Gedächtniskirche vorbei, die Spender »damals wie ein lächerlich verschnörkeltes Riesentintenfaß vorgekommen war«, und sprachen über die Armut, die Arbeitslosenkrise und die immer dreister nach der Macht strebenden Faschisten in der Stadt. Die Straßenszene schien vor ihrem inneren Auge zu dem desolaten Bild zu verschwimmen, das Spender schließlich 1945 erblickte. Es war, »als ob wir beide schon hinter dem durchsichtig gewordenen Verkehr die Ruine erblickten«.[1]

In dieser Zeitenwende entwickelte Spender sein ausgeprägtes politisches Bewusstsein, das sich aus Upwards revolutionären Vorträgen und der Alltäglichkeit des Ausnahmezustands nährte. Offenbar prägten die Verluste, die man in Berlin und Europa

sualties were somehow already contained within the fabric of the city.

In the early twentieth century, few British writers travelled to Berlin for exclusively political reasons, and fewer predicted its immediate political future. Yet collectively their work invites us to view the city's tensions, traumas, and opportunities as though through a series of transparencies that slide across one another, revealing social and political structures in coexistence with their past and future states. The patterns they form are arresting and unreliable, filtered by a prism of political outlooks ranging from radical to apathetic, short-sighted to prescient, Communist to Nazi-sympathising. A traveller's slideshow, they draw us into and around the political realities and fantasies of Berlin, and throw light on important transformations in British literary culture. They form a tour of political Berlin that telescopes time and space.

I.

The tour might begin with two luxury hotels, the Adlon and the Esplanade, which opened in 1907 and 1908 respectively, announcing Berlin's arrival as one of the world's great metropolises and its new attractiveness to wealthy travellers. Countess Evelyn Blücher, an English aristocrat remembered now for her memoirs of the period, checked in at the Hotel Esplanade on Potsdamer Platz in August 1914. As Gesa Stedman explains in her article, Blücher

beklagen sollte, schon damals den Charakter der Stadt.

Zu Beginn des 20. Jahrhunderts kamen nur wenige britische Schriftsteller*innen aus rein politischem Interesse nach Berlin. Eine noch geringere Zahl von ihnen wagte eine Vorhersage über die unmittelbare politische Zukunft der Stadt. Allerdings lassen sich aus ihren Werken die in Berlin erlebten Spannungen, Traumata und Möglichkeiten ablesen. Ganz so, als würde man eine Reihe von Dias übereinanderlegen, auf denen die sozialen und politischen Strukturen der aktuellen und künftigen Verhältnisse abgebildet sind. Auf diese Weise bilden sich eindrucksvolle und veränderliche Muster gebrochen durch ein Prisma politischer Ansichten, die von radikal bis gleichgültig, kurzsichtig bis vorausschauend, kommunistisch bis nationalsozialistisch reichen. Wie bei der Diashow einer Reise entführen uns ihre Werke in die politischen Realitäten und Fantasien Berlins und werfen ein Licht auf bedeutende Umbruchphasen der britischen Literatur. Sie laden ein zu einer Tour durch das politische Berlin, bei der sich Zeit und Raum überlagern.

I.

Beginnen könnte diese Tour in den beiden Luxushotels Adlon und Esplanade, die in den Jahren 1907 bzw. 1908 eröffnet wurden. Sie kündeten davon, dass Berlin mittlerweile zu den größten internationalen Metropolen zählte und sich unter wohlhabenden Reisenden inzwischen großer Beliebtheit erfreute. Die englische Aristokratin Evelyn Fürstin Blücher, die heute für ihre Memoiren aus dieser Zeit bekannt ist, zog im August 1914 in das Hotel Esplanade am Potsdamer Platz. Wie Gesa Stedman in ihrem Artikel erläutert, kam Blücher nicht als Touristin, sondern als Exilantin nach Berlin.

did not travel to Berlin as a tourist but as an exile forced to leave England with her German husband, Gebhard von Blücher, when war was declared. In palatial settings, here, and later in her apartment on the exclusive Pariser Platz, Blücher dined and talked with other wartime "birds of passage".[2] It was a remarkable viewpoint from which to see and record the major events of Germany's war years.

It was also a striking location for witnessing the eruptions of social unrest that had simmered in the city for decades. Since Germany's unification in 1871, rapid industrialisation in Berlin made it a haven for Marxist thought, trade unionism, and the various factions within the social-democratic camp—all of which meant friction with the Prussian aristocracy that still held the balance of power. In the harsh winter of 1915, Blücher heard the discontent of the workers: "We are forced to keep silence now; but wait till the war is over, then our turn will come".[3] Her diary records a face, smouldering with resentment, pressed to the glass doors of the Esplanade where, inside, officers drank champagne with their pheasant and pineapple.[4] It was clear to her that a Socialist uprising was coming.

Meanwhile, Bolshevik ideology was rampant; its leading representatives in Germany—Karl Liebknecht and Rosa Luxemburg—bookended the First World War with their revolutionary movements, founding the Spartacus League in 1914, and in 1919 the Communist Party of Ger-

Nach Kriegsausbruch musste sie England gemeinsam mit ihrem deutschen Ehemann, Gebhard von Blücher, verlassen. In den palastartigen Räumlichkeiten des Hotels und später dann in ihrem Quartier am exklusiven Pariser Platz empfing Blücher andere »Zugvögel«[2] des Krieges zum gemeinsamen Abendessen und Gespräch. Von dort hatte man einen einmaligen Ausblick und konnte die wichtigsten Ereignisse der deutschen Kriegsjahre verfolgen und aufzeichnen.

Auch die sozialen Unruhen, die seit Jahrzehnten in der Stadt schwelten, ließen sich von diesem Posten hervorragend beobachten. Seit der deutschen Einigung im Jahr 1871 hatte sich Berlin im Zuge einer raschen Industrialisierung zum Sammelbecken für marxistisches Gedankengut, Gewerkschaftsbewegungen und verschiedene Strömungen innerhalb des sozialdemokratischen Lagers entwickelt. All dies führte zu Spannungen mit der preußischen Aristokratie, die nach wie vor die Machtverhältnisse bestimmte. Im strengen Winter des Jahres 1915 vernahm Blücher die Unzufriedenheit der Arbeiterklasse: »Wir müssen jetzt schweigen, aber wenn der Krieg vorüber ist, dann gehen wir los«.[3] In ihrem Tagebuch beschreibt sie ein hasserfülltes Gesicht, das gegen die Glastüren des Esplanade gepresst Offiziere erblickt, die sich an Fasan mit Ananas und Champagner gütlich tun.[4] Für sie stand fest, dass ein Aufstand der Sozialisten nicht mehr zu verhindern war.

In der Zwischenzeit griff bolschewistisches Gedankengut immer weiter um sich. Die führenden deutschen Vertreter*innen dieser Richtung – Karl Liebknecht und Rosa Luxemburg – riefen ihre revolutionären Bewegungen jeweils vor und nach dem Ersten Weltkrieg ins Leben. Im Jahr 1914 gründeten sie den Spartakusbund und 1919 die Kommunistische Partei Deutschlands (KPD). Blücher verfolgte diese Entwicklung angesichts ihres aristokratischen Habi-

Places
The Adlon and Esplanade Hotels

The Adlon Hotel, one of the prime social, diplomatic, and political sites of the Weimar Republic, was opened on 7 October 1907 with great pomp by the German Kaiser and his family. The most modern hotel in Berlin to that date, it had cost the equivalent of 400 million euros, and was frequented by the great and the good from all over the world. Upper-class English writers often mention the splendid hotel in passing only, their memoirs include entries such as "dined at the Adlon". It was situated around the corner from the British embassy on Wilhelmstraße, and was thus ideal for sensitive political meetings held on neutral ground. The hotel was known as "little Switzerland" for this reason. In the early 1920s, tempers were still fraught, as we learn from Violet Bonham-Carter's diary who reports on an encounter with a waiter. He objected to being spoken to in French as the French occupation of parts of Germany after World War One obviously still smarted. Over the years, the hotel became a tourist attraction in its own right. The hotel was large, it contained 450 rooms, which started at 12–35 marks for a single room, and went up to 36–50 marks for a double. Breakfast could be had for 3 marks and a longer stay "en pension" started at 30 marks. By contrast, the cheaper hotels and pensions would cost from 2 marks upwards—for the room, rather than breakfast. The Hotel Esplanade on Bellevuestraße, where the Anglo-German couple Count and Countess Blücher had spent part of the First World War, was only slightly smaller with 400 rooms, and only very slightly cheaper. Most British visitors stayed in pensions rather than hotels. However, the prestigious and the famous would not of course have stood for any other type of accommodation than the best.

Orte
Das Adlon und das Hotel Esplanade

Das Hotel Adlon, eine der ersten Adressen des gesellschaftlichen, diplomatischen und politischen Lebens der Weimarer Republik, wurde am 7. Oktober 1907 in einer prunkvollen Zeremonie durch den deutschen Kaiser und seine Familie eröffnet. Der Bau des zu diesem Zeitpunkt modernsten Hotels in Berlin hatte den damaligen Gegenwert von 400 Millionen Euro verschlungen. Hier gaben sich die Großen und Mächtigen aus aller Welt die Klinke in die Hand. Englische Schriftsteller*innen aus der Oberklasse erwähnen das noble Hotel häufig nur am Rande. Ihre Memoiren enthalten Notizen wie »Abendessen im Adlon«. Das Hotel befand sich ganz in der Nähe der Britischen Botschaft an der Wilhelmstraße und eignete sich damit hervorragend für vertrauliche politische Zusammenkünfte auf neutralem Boden. Aus eben diesem Grund war es auch als »die kleine Schweiz« bekannt. In den frühen 1920er Jahren war die Stimmung hier noch angespannt, wie wir aus einem Eintrag in Violet Bonham-Carters Tagebuch über die Begegnung mit einem Kellner erfahren. Er verwahrte sich dagegen, auf Französisch angesprochen zu werden, da ihn die französische Besatzung deutscher Landesteile nach dem Ersten Weltkrieg offenbar noch immer schmerzte. Mit den Jahren entwickelte sich das Hotel zu einer Touristenattraktion. Es war mit 450 Zimmern sehr groß. Die Preise lagen zwischen 12 und 35 Mark für ein Einzelzimmer und 36 und 50 Mark für ein Doppelzimmer. Ein Frühstück gab es für 3 Mark, und ein längerer Aufenthalt »mit Pension« kostete 30 Mark oder mehr. Die Preise für günstigere Hotels starteten im Vergleich bei 2 Mark für ein Zimmer, nicht nur für ein Frühstück. Das Hotel Esplanade in der Bellevuestraße, in dem das deutsch-englische Ehepaar Fürst und Fürstin Blücher einen Teil des Ersten Weltkriegs verbrachte, war mit 400 Zimmern nur etwas kleiner und nur unbedeutend günstiger. Die Mehrzahl der britischen Besucher*innen kam in Pensionen und nicht in Hotels unter. Doch die Reichen und Berühmten wählten selbstverständlich nur die bestmögliche Art der Unterbringung.

[Fig. 33: A summer evening on the new restaurant terrace of the Adlon Hotel, Berlin, coloured postcard after a watercolour by Karl Lindegreen, c. 1928]

[Abb. 33: Eine Sommernacht auf der neuen Restaurant-Terrasse des Hotel Adlon, Berlin, farbige Postkarte nach einem Aquarell von Karl Lindegreen, ca. 1928]

many (KPD). Blücher, given her aristocratic habitus, looked on with suspicion. On May Day 1916, her hotel was besieged by Liebknecht's demonstrating supporters, and she reported with relief when "the notorious quarreller in Parliament" was arrested.[5] Two years later, the war was over and the crowds returned. From her precarious eyrie, Blücher watched revolutionaries stream along Unter den Linden, and post machine guns outside the Hotel Adlon.

Other revolutionary enterprises escaped Blücher's notice. Virendranath Chattopadhyaya, the Indian nationalist and brother of the poet Sarojini Naidu, found Berlin conducive for anti-colonial

tus mit Argwohn. Am Maifeiertag des Jahres 1916 besetzten demonstrierende Liebknecht-Anhänger ihr Hotel und sie notierte voller Erleichterung, dass man »Liebknecht wegen öffentlicher Ruhestörung arretiert« habe.[5] Zwei Jahre später war der Krieg vorüber und die Massen kehrten zurück. Von ihrem unsicheren Aussichtspunkt beobachtete Blücher, wie Revolutionäre über die Linden auf das Adlon zuströmten und Maschinengewehre vor dem Hotel postierten.

Andere revolutionäre Bestrebungen gingen unbemerkt an Blücher vorüber. Der indische Nationalist und Bruder der Dichterin Sarojini Naidu, Virendranath Chattopadhyaya, hatte Berlin während des Kriegs zum geeigneten Ort für seinen Kampf gegen die Kolonialherrschaft erkoren. In diesem Schulterschluss mit dem Feind seines Feindes machte er sich den Wunsch

activism during the war. Making a friend of his enemy's enemy, he took advantage of the German Foreign Office's desire to weaken Britain's colonial power. In 1914, Chattopadhyaya established the Indian Independence Committee, which rallied sympathisers and smuggled arms to India. By 1927, he was a Marxist and, still devoted to Indian independence, established the League Against Imperialism with Willi Münzenberg—the KPD's leading propagandist. Chattopadhyaya's association with anarchists and communists made Berlin increasingly unsafe for him, and he narrowly survived an assassination attempt when poison was slipped into his drinking chocolate at a restaurant.[6] Forced into hiding at last, he was pursued, ironically, both by British spies and German police.

Blücher encountered another notorious revolutionary in Berlin: the Irish na-

des deutschen Außenministeriums zunutze, die Kolonialmacht Großbritannien zu schwächen. Im Jahr 1914 gründete Chattopadhyaya das Indische Unabhängigkeitskomitee (*Indian Independence Committee*), in dem sich seine Anhänger versammelten und Waffen nach Indien schmuggelten. Gemeinsam mit dem führenden Propagandisten der KPD, Willi Münzenberg, gründete der inzwischen zum Marxismus übergetretene Aktivist, der noch immer für die indische Unabhängigkeit kämpfte, im Jahr 1927 die Liga gegen Imperialismus. Aufgrund seiner Nähe zu Anarchisten und Kommunisten war Chattopadhyaya in Berlin inzwischen nicht mehr sicher und entging knapp einem Mordanschlag, als ihm in einem Restaurant Gift in seine Trinkschokolade gemischt wurde.[6] Letzten Endes sah er sich zu einem Leben im Untergrund gezwungen und wurde paradoxerweise sowohl vom britischen Geheimdienst als auch von der deutschen Polizei verfolgt.

Blücher traf in Berlin auf einen weiteren berüchtigten Anhänger der Revolution: Der irische Nationalist Roger Casement war 1914 im Rahmen einer Kampagne gegen die britische Herrschaft über Irland

[Fig. 34: Revolutionaries on Unter den Linden during the November Revolution of 1918, unknown photographer and date]

[Abb. 34: Revolutionäre auf dem Boulevard Unter den Linden, Novemberrevolution 1918, Fotograf und Datum unbekannt]

tionalist Roger Casement, who travelled to Germany in 1914 on a campaign against English imperialism in Ireland. In her diary, Blücher records meeting her old friend, and she is careful to describe her efforts to dissuade him from treason. She does not mention the letters they exchanged. In one, Blücher asked Casement how she might improve her writing, and his reply encouraged her to prioritise sincerity and self-revelation. Her diary "should tell things but still more of the writer and his (or her) outlook on those things".[7] Lessons in honesty from a fugitive; statecraft conducted between fading ballrooms and barricades; glass windows with a view onto angry eyes staring back. Such paradoxes shaped Blücher's life, and diary, during the war.

II.

A few paces' walk from the Hotel Adlon, on Wilhelmstraße, is a building left empty during the war, and thrown open again in 1919: the Palais Strousberg, which housed the British Embassy. When Ramsay MacDonald, the Labour politician and later Prime Minister, travelled to Berlin in 1920, the Palais stood out among the revolution-scarred facades as the only building with a fresh coat of paint. Here, in 1927, the aspiring writer and diplomat Harold Nicolson joined the embassy as a *chargé d'affaires*. Though his work brought him into contact with leading political figures including President Hindenburg and Kon-

nach Deutschland gekommen. Blücher berichtet in ihrem Tagebuch von einem Treffen mit dem alten Freund. Darin beschreibt sie ausführlich, wie sie Casement von seinem Landesverrat abhalten wollte. Auf ihren Briefwechsel geht sie nicht weiter ein. In einem dieser Briefe bat sie Casement um Rat, wie sie ihren Schreibstil verbessern könnte. In seiner Antwort ermutigte er sie dazu, vor allem aufrichtig zu schreiben und ihr Inneres zu offenbaren. Sie solle in ihrem Tagebuch »zwar Erlebnisse beschreiben, aber vor allem auch auf sich als Verfasserin und ihre eigene Sicht auf diese Dinge eingehen«.[7] Ein Mann auf der Flucht ermahnt zur Aufrichtigkeit; die Kunst der Staatsführung gerät ins Spannungsfeld zwischen den Ballsälen der Vergangenheit und den Barrikaden der Gegenwart; beim Blick aus dem Fenster starren hasserfüllte Augen zurück: Dies sind nur einige der eigentümlichen Erlebnisse, die Blüchers Alltag und Tagebucheinträge in Kriegszeiten prägten.

II.

Wenige Schritte vom Hotel Adlon entfernt befand sich an der Wilhelmstraße ein Gebäude, das zu Kriegszeiten leer stand und sich im Jahr 1919 erneut mit Leben füllte: Der Palais Strousberg, in dem die britische Botschaft ihren Sitz hatte. Als der Labour-Politiker und spätere Premierminister Ramsay MacDonald 1920 für einen Besuch nach Berlin kam, stach der Palais zwischen den von den Revolutionskämpfen gezeichneten Fassaden als einziges frisch gestrichenes Gebäude hervor. Hier trat der aufstrebende Schriftsteller und Diplomat Harold Nicolson 1927 seine Position als Botschaftsrat an. Obwohl er durch seine Arbeit mit führenden Politikern wie Reichspräsident Paul von Hindenburg und Konrad Adenauer (der erste Bundeskanzler Westdeutschlands nach

rad Adenauer (later the first Chancellor of West Germany), Nicolson claimed to have learned most about Weimar politics at the bar of the Adlon, where journalists first brought to his attention the threat of the Nazi movement.

Nicolson's presence in Berlin drew over from England a stream of acquaintances, many of whom were writers keen to experience the city's famed decadence, and in doing so found it easy to ignore the volatile political situation. Among Nicolson's visitors was Cyril Connolly, who became an influential editor and journalist a decade later, but was for now laying down a stock of experiences in travelling Europe. The young man was "not perhaps the ideal guest", Nicolson wrote with restraint to his wife, the writer Vita Sackville-West, but he was entertaining—discussing French literature with verve, and pestering Nicolson to treat him to the plovers' eggs at Pelzer's restaurant.[8]

Had Connolly been interested to form an opinion of the city's political affairs, he would have had the expertise of those at the embassy to call upon. Instead, he passed the time composing comic sketches to be performed in Nicolson's apartment. Friends and embassy attachés were recruited to act, with the Ambassador, Sir Horace Rumbold, as their guest of honour. Connolly's essay about his hedonistic German excursion describes a scene outside of time: walking along the tree-lined Kurfürstendamm, or dining by the lake in Potsdam, were chances to indulge in a

dem Krieg) in Verbindung stand, konnte er sich nach eigenen Angaben vor allem an der Bar des Adlon mit der Weimarer Politik vertraut machen. Dort berichteten ihm Journalisten auch zum ersten Mal von der drohenden Gefahr durch die nationalsozialistische Bewegung.

Während seiner Zeit in Berlin erhielt Nicolson Besuch von zahlreichen Bekannten. Darunter waren auch viele Schriftsteller*innen, die sich selbst einen Eindruck von der berühmten Dekadenz der Stadt machen wollten, wobei ihnen die politische Instabilität nur allzu leicht entgehen konnte. Unter Nicolsons Gästen befand sich auch Cyril Connolly, der ein Jahrzehnt später als einflussreicher Redakteur und Journalist arbeiten sollte, zu dieser Zeit jedoch noch damit beschäftigt war, auf Reisen durch Europa umfangreiche Erfahrungen zu sammeln. Der junge Mann sei vielleicht nicht der ideale Gast, schrieb Nicolson verhalten an seine Ehefrau, die Schriftstellerin Vita Sackville-West, dafür aber unterhaltsam. Über französische Literatur diskutiere er leidenschaftlich gern und dränge Nicolson dazu, ihn auf Kiebitzeier ins Restaurant Pelzer einzuladen.[8]

Hätte Connolly ein Interesse daran gehabt, sich eine eigene Meinung über die politische Lage in der Stadt zu bilden, dann hätte er auf das Sachverständnis der Botschaftsmitarbeiter zurückgreifen können. Stattdessen vertrieb er sich die Zeit mit dem Schreiben lustiger Sketche, die in Nicolsons Wohnung aufgeführt wurden. Für die verschiedenen Rollen gewann er Freunde und Botschaftsmitarbeiter. Der Botschafter, Sir Horace Rumbold, wurde als Ehrengast geladen. Connollys Essay über seine hedonistischen Streifzüge durch Deutschland enthält Szenen, die aus der Zeit gefallen scheinen: Bei Spaziergängen mit seinen Freunden entlang des von Bäumen gesäumten Kurfürstendamms oder Abendessen am Potsdamer

premature nostalgia with his friends, and to test their wits on each other. Unapologetic about his political apathy, Connolly hated "well-informed people with fluent general knowledge and vivid curiosity about contemporary problems, they drove [him] to the Dark Ages".[9] The elegiac note in his Berlin writing is sounded for himself and the transience of his happiness, not for the possibility that unimaginably worse awaited Berliners than a large bill at the Adlon.

A fellow *bon vivant* and bracing influence from Connolly's studies at Oxford, the classical scholar Maurice Bowra began to visit Berlin regularly in the same period, but the attractions of its nightlife didn't preclude his sharp sense of social and political catastrophe. On the one hand, Bowra kept up a busy social round of operas, cinemas, and (before they were forced shut) homosexual bars, and on the other hand curiosity drew him to rallies and speeches across the political spectrum. Hearing Heinrich Brüning of the Centre Party campaign for President Hindenburg in the 1932 election, Bowra was struck by the deflating effect of the Chancellor's talk of austerity, in contrast with Hitler's frenzied speeches at the same venue—the massive Sportpalast. Bowra met Hitler briefly, and this disturbing encounter, alongside his reading of *Mein Kampf*, convinced him that the barbaric manifesto of Nazism was in earnest.

Bowra's visits to Germany ended in 1938 after the horrors of the pogrom

Seeufer blickte man gemeinsam nostalgisch in die Zukunft oder vergnügte sich mit Rätselspielen. Connolly machte keinerlei Hehl aus seinem Desinteresse für Politik und verabscheute gut informierte Menschen mit einer ausgezeichneten Allgemeinbildung und einem ausgeprägten Interesse für aktuelle Themen, weil sie ihn in dunkle Zeiten zurückversetzten.[9] Der elegische Unterton seiner Berliner Schriften bezog sich ausschließlich auf seine eigene Person und die Vergänglichkeit seines Glücks, nicht jedoch auf die Möglichkeit, dass den Berliner*innen weitaus Schlimmeres bevorstehen könnte als nur eine hohe Rechnung im Adlon.

Ein weiterer *Bonvivant*, der Connolly in seiner Studienzeit in Oxford nachhaltig geprägt hatte, war der Altphilologe Maurice Bowra, der Berlin zu dieser Zeit ebenfalls regelmäßige Besuche abstattete. Allerdings konnten die Attraktionen des Nachtlebens sein scharfes Gespür für die bevorstehende soziale und politische Katastrophe nicht schmälern. Bowra führte zwar ein reges gesellschaftliches Leben mit Besuchen von Opern, Kinos und (vor ihrer Zwangsschließung) Homosexuellenbars, doch seine Neugier trieb ihn auch dazu, Kundgebungen und Reden aller Parteien des politischen Spektrums zu besuchen. Als Heinrich Brüning von der Zentrumspartei 1932 eine Wahlkampfrede für Reichspräsident Hindenburg hielt, zeigte sich Bowra erstaunt, wie ernüchternd die Ausführungen des Reichskanzlers zur Sparpolitik im Vergleich zu den feurigen Reden waren, die Hitler am selben Ort – im riesigen Sportpalast – gehalten hatte. Bowra traf Hitler nur kurz. Doch nach dieser verstörenden Begegnung und der Lektüre von *Mein Kampf* war er überzeugt davon, dass es die Nazis mit ihrem grausamen Plan ernst meinten.

Bowras Besuche in Deutschland endeten 1939 mit den schrecklichen Pogromen gegen die jüdische

against Jews, known by its Nazi term "Kristallnacht", but he remained engaged with the situation in Berlin. Back in Oxford, and along with many of the University's younger fellows and undergraduates, Bowra was outspoken against arguments for appeasing Hitler, and against the apathy towards Nazi brutality that this entailed. When British fascists came to speak in Oxford in 1936, he joined in the undergraduates' protests.

III.

We travel now southwest out of central Berlin, beyond the Grunewald forest to the suburb of Nikolassee and a smart modern villa modelled on an English country house. The poet W.H. Auden arrived here as a paying guest in August 1928, the first of a group of friends and literary collaborators impressed by the potential in Berlin's young democracy for a thrilling new cultural experiment. It wasn't long before Auden moved again, into the working-class district of Hallesches Tor where he could drop the bourgeois decorum and pursue more determinedly his real social and romantic interests. Auden's stay heralded a new kind of British literary visitor. He was followed by the novelist Christopher Isherwood, who was followed in turn by Spender—all three being friends who, as Sandra Meyer explains, loosely formed a coterie. Like Nicolson's guests, they had the material freedom to come and go between England and Germany.

Bevölkerung, die auch unter der Nazi-Bezeichnung »Kristallnacht« bekannt sind. Die Lage in Berlin beschäftigte ihn jedoch weiterhin. Nach seiner Rückkehr nach Oxford sprach sich Bowra gemeinsam mit vielen jüngeren Kolleg*innen und Student*innen an der Universität entschlossen gegen eine Appeasement-Politik gegenüber Hitler und die damit einhergehende Teilnahmslosigkeit gegenüber den Gräueltaten des NS-Regimes aus. Als 1936 britische Faschisten für eine Vortragsreihe nach Oxford kamen, schloss er sich den Protesten der Studierenden an.

III.

An dieser Stelle verlassen wir das Berliner Zentrum in Richtung Südwesten vorbei am Grunewald und gelangen schließlich im Vorort Nikolassee zu einer eleganten modernen Villa im englischen Landhausstil. Hier mietete sich der Dichter W.H. Auden im August 1928 ein. Er war der erste Vertreter einer Gruppe von Freunden und literarischen Weggefährten, die sich vom Potential der jungen Berliner Demokratie für ein neues kulturelles Experiment beeindruckt zeigten. Auden verlegte seinen Wohnort schon bald in den Arbeiterbezirk rund um das Hallesche Tor, wo er sich von bürgerlichen Anstandsregeln befreien und besser auf seine wahren gesellschaftlichen und romantischen Interessen konzentrieren konnte. Mit Auden kam eine neue Gruppe von Besuchern aus dem britischen Literaturbetrieb in die Stadt – zuerst der Romanautor Christopher Isherwood, später auch Stephen Spender. Die drei Freunde bildeten laut Sandra Meyer einen losen Zusammenschluss von Gleichgesinnten. Wie auch Nicolsons Gäste befanden sie sich in der glücklichen finanziellen Lage, ihren Aufenthaltsort zwischen England und Deutschland frei wählen zu können. In Abhängigkeit von

They variously toured Berlin according to their fluctuating fortunes, driven also by a developing sense of where it was worth a writer's time to linger.

Their movements between the different parts of the city reflected their social fluidity, but this was not sufficient to bring a clear overview of their temporary home. Things that, in retrospect, might have seemed transparent about the city's future were obscured by the beguiling way in which the structures and solidities of their middle-class upbringings shifted before them.

Auden claimed ignorance of international politics while a student at Oxford. It was his sojourn in Berlin that drew European affairs firmly into his purview, shaping the landscape of his poetry for a decade. By 1929, the Weimar Republic's period of relative stability had come to an end, and tensions between the Social Democratic Party (SPD) and Communists were prominent in the neighbourhoods Auden frequented. On May Day of that year, the police, under orders from the president of police, opened fire on a Communist demonstration and triggered days of rioting. Auden captured the mood in his poem "It was Easter as I walked in the public gardens":

All this time was anxiety at night,
Shooting and barricade in street.
Walking home late I listened to a friend
Talking excitedly of final war
Of proletariat against police[10]

ihren jeweiligen Lebensumständen hielten sie sich in verschiedenen Stadtvierteln auf und entwickelten mit der Zeit ein Gespür dafür, wo sich aus schriftstellerischer Sicht ein Aufenthalt besonders lohnte.

Ihre Bewegungen zwischen den unterschiedlichen Stadtteilen waren auch ein Spiegelbild ihrer sozialen Mobilität. Allerdings konnten sie sich allein dadurch kein vollständiges Bild von ihrem vorübergehenden Zuhause verschaffen. Es gab Dinge, die rückblickend ganz klar auf die Ereignisse hindeuteten, die der Stadt noch bevorstanden. Doch sie wurden überlagert von der verführerischen Verwandlung der Strukturen und Gewissheiten ihrer bürgerlichen Herkunft.

Als Student an der Universität Oxford gab sich Auden gleichgültig gegenüber dem internationalen politischen Geschehen. Während seiner Zeit in Berlin dagegen entwickelte er ein ausgeprägtes Interesse für europäische Fragen, das sich im kommenden Jahrzehnt in seinem lyrischen Werk wiederfinden sollte. Im Jahr 1929 endete die Phase der relativen Stabilität in der Weimarer Republik. Von nun an bestimmten Spannungen zwischen der Sozialdemokratischen Partei (SPD) und der Kommunistischen Partei (KPD) das Geschehen in den Stadtvierteln, in denen auch Auden verkehrte. Am Maifeiertag desselben Jahres eröffnete die Polizei auf Befehl des SPD-Polizeipräsidenten das Feuer auf die Teilnehmer*innen einer kommunistischen Kundgebung. Tagelange Unruhen waren die Folge. Auden fing die damalige Stimmung in seinem Gedicht »It was Easter as I walked in the public gardens« auf:

All this time was anxiety at night,
Shooting and barricade in street.
Walking home late I listened to a friend
Talking excitedly of final war
Of proletariat against police[10]

The poet is an observer, a listener, here—it is his friend who is carried away by prophecies of cataclysm—yet the struggle has encroached into daily routine and conversation. Political awakening, and the choosing of sides, seemed unavoidable.

Auden's solidarity was with the proletariat, but how to express this was complicated by the counter-intuitive relations between Centre, Left, and Right. At the extreme wings of Weimar politics, the Communists and Nazis found common ground in seeing the Socialist party as the greater enemy. The official Soviet line in the late 1920s was that the SPD were "social fascists", which led the KPD to sometimes collaborate with Nazi demonstrations. The confusion generated by such arrangements can be seen in Auden's strange poetic work *The Orators* (1932), featuring a revolutionary airman hero who could easily be mistaken for a fascist leader. The work was intended to mock the fascist position, but Auden later admitted that the text's obvious bewitchment by the airman figure made the author sound like somebody contemplating conversion to Nazism. By the 1940s, Auden expressed scepticism about the poet's role in making political judgments at all: it was more than some writers could resist to adopt extreme positions, and more than some readers could resist to swallow their seductive rhetoric.

Arthur Koestler, the Hungarian journalist and intellectual, who was a KPD member in Berlin when the Nationalsocialists won their first landslide in the Reichstag,

Der Dichter tritt hier als Beobachter, als Zuhörer auf. Sein Freund ist es, der sich von den Warnungen vor einer Katastrophe mitreißen lässt. Doch der Kampf hatte nun auch seinen Alltag und seine Gespräche erfasst. Ein politisches Erwachen und eine politische Positionierung schienen unvermeidlich.

Auden konnte seine Solidarität mit dem Proletariat angesichts der widersprüchlichen Beziehungen zwischen Angehörigen der Zentrumspartei, der Rechten und der Linken nur schwer in Worte fassen. Die KPD und die NSDAP hatten sich als radikale Flügelparteien der Weimarer Politik auf die SPD als größten Feind einigen können. In den späten 1920er Jahren galt die SPD nach offizieller sowjetischer Linie als »sozialfaschistische« Partei, was wiederum die KDP dazu veranlasste, sich wiederholt an Nazi-Aufmärschen zu beteiligen. Die Verwirrung, die derartige Arrangements hervorriefen, lässt sich in Audens befremdlichem lyrischen Werk *The Orators* (1932) nachvollziehen. Die Hauptfigur des revolutionären Fliegerhelden könnte hier gut und gerne auch als faschistischer Führer durchgehen. Auden wollte sich mit seinem Text über die politische Haltung der Faschisten lustig machen. Später räumte er jedoch ein, dass die darin vermittelte Begeisterung für die Figur des Fliegers den Eindruck erwecken könnte, dass der Verfasser einen Wechsel zum Nationalsozialismus in Erwägung ziehe. Mit Beginn der 1940er Jahre zeigte sich Auden grundsätzlich skeptisch in der Frage, ob Dichter ein politisches Urteil fällen sollten: So manche Schriftsteller*innen könnten sich dazu verleitet fühlen, extreme Standpunkte zu vertreten, und so manche Leser*innen dazu, ihrer verführerische Rhetorik zu erliegen.

Während des ersten Erdrutschsiegs der NSDAP bei den Reichstagswahlen war der ungarische Journalist und Intellektuelle Arthur Koestler Abgeordneter der Berliner KPD. Er fand treffende Worte für die

found an eloquent analogy for the Left's political blindness in the period. They were living through a magnetic storm caused by "cosmic disturbances", which made their political compasses faulty: "We fought our battle of words and did not see that the familiar words had lost their bearing and pointed in the wrong directions".[11]

Political polarisation in Germany intensified after the Reichstag elections of September 1930, when the National Socialist German Workers party soared from twelve seats in parliament to 107, the Communists increased their count by 40 percent, and the Centrist parties were effectively destroyed. Popular faith in the Republic was dead. A series of elections in the following two years saw the Nazi party take steps both forward and back, but astonishingly the KPD still sometimes aided them, greedy to see the Social Democrats demolished for good.

Christopher Isherwood's writings engaged with this turmoil more concertedly than those of his friends. The first of his Berlin novels, *Mr. Norris Changes Trains* (1935), follows William Bradshaw's brushes with the city's political and criminal underworld, guided by the shady Norris who was modelled on Gerald Hamilton, a Berlin acquaintance. (Hamilton, the sometime fraud, memoirist, and political intriguer, shared an unlikely connection with Evelyn Blücher in being another of Roger Casement's Berlin correspondents. The similarity ends there though, as Hamilton approved Casement's cause.) Where Norris's

politische Blindheit, von der die Linke zu dieser Zeit erfasst war. Sie durchlebte einen magnetischen Sturm, der durch »kosmische Störungen« hervorgerufen wurde und ihren politischen Kompass in die falsche Richtung weisen ließ: »Wir fochten unsere Redeschlachten und merkten nicht, daß die vertrauten Begriffe, deren wir uns bedienten, ihren Sinn geändert hatten und trügerisch geworden waren wie die Kompaßnadel«.[11]

Mit den Reichstagswahlen vom September 1930 nahm die politische Polarisierung in Deutschland weiter zu. Die Nationalsozialistische Partei konnte die Zahl ihrer Parlamentssitze mit einem Schlag von 12 auf 107 erhöhen. Die KPD verbesserte ihr Ergebnis um 40 Prozent, und die Zentrumspartei versank in der Bedeutungslosigkeit. Das Vertrauen der Bevölkerung in die Republik war zerstört. In den beiden darauffolgenden Jahren erlebten die Nationalsozialisten bei mehreren Wahlen Erfolge und Rückschläge. Erstaunlicherweise konnten sie jedoch noch immer auf eine gewisse Rückendeckung durch die Kommunisten zählen, denen es in erster Linie darum ging, die Sozialdemokraten auf den Scheiterhaufen der Geschichte zu befördern.

Christopher Isherwood beschäftigte sich in seinen Werken weitaus ausführlicher als seine Freunde mit diesen Turbulenzen. In seinem ersten Berlin-Roman *Mr. Norris Changes Trains* (»Mr. Norris steigt um«, 1935) folgt er William Bradshaw, der sich im Schlepptau des zwielichtigen Norris auf Streifzüge durch die politische und kriminelle Unterwelt der Stadt begibt. Die Figur des Norris ist angelehnt an Gerald Hamilton, einen Bekannten aus Berliner Tagen. (Hamilton, wahlweise als Betrüger, Zeitzeuge und politischer Intrigant beschrieben, verfügte über eine etwas ungewöhnliche Verbindung zu Evelyn Blücher: Auch er schrieb sich mit Roger Casement Briefe aus Berlin. Doch hier endet auch schon die Gemeinsam-

actions are fundamentally self-serving, Bradshaw has genuine sympathy for working-class Germans. He undertakes small jobs for the fictional Ludwig Bayer—a flattering portrait of Münzenberg—who lends Bradshaw contraband Communist tracts and sends him across the city with campaign posters for Ernst Thälmann, leader of the KPD.

It must be remembered that, although Isherwood drew on his diaries for the episodes and characters of his Berlin novels, he was consciously crafting fiction, as his concealment of the homosexual contexts in which he was immersed makes clear. Something Isherwood did have in common with Bradshaw was his inclination towards becoming a fellow traveller in the period. He translated material for the *Internationale Arbeiter-Hilfe* (IAH), or Workers International Relief—an organisation that attracted major left-wing intellectuals to produce propaganda for Soviet Russia. Isherwood's activities and connections led the British Secret Service to keep a file on him, and to intercept his letters to Hamilton.

But the agents that screened these learned more about the novelist's writing process than any actual subversion. One letter in Isherwood's file addressed to Hamilton in late 1933 admits: "I am not satisfied with my novel and have scrapped it. I shall start again in the Spring. [...] You must be the chief character of the book". He adds, "I wonder which foreign capital we shall be hiding in at the end of 1934?".[12]

keit, denn Hamilton gehörte zu Casements Unterstützern.) Während Norris im Grunde nur nach dem eigenen Vorteil strebt, empfindet Bradshaw echtes Mitgefühl für die deutsche Arbeiterschaft. Er übernimmt kleine Jobs für die Romanfigur des Ludwig Bayer, die ein schmeichelhaftes Porträt von Münzenberg zeichnet. Bayer lieh Bradshaw geschmuggelte kommunistische Schriften und schickte ihn mit Wahlkampfplakaten für den KPD-Vorsitzenden Ernst Thälmann durch die Stadt.

Es darf nicht vergessen werden, dass Isherwood ganz bewusst die Prosaform wählte, auch wenn er für einige Episoden und Figuren seiner Berliner Romane auf eigene Tagebucheinträge zurückgriff. Ein Beleg dafür ist die Tatsache, dass er die von ihm frequentierten homosexuellen Kontexte nicht erwähnt. Eine Tatsache, die Isherwood mit Bradshaw verband, war die politische Überzeugung als kommunistischer Sympathisant. Er übersetzte Dokumente für die *Internationale Arbeiter-Hilfe* (IAH), einer Organisation, in der bekannte linksgerichtete Intellektuelle Propaganda für die Sowjetunion betrieben. Wegen seiner Aktivitäten und Verbindungen führte der Britische Geheimdienst eine Akte über Isherwood und fing seine Briefe ab.

Allerdings erfuhren die Geheimagenten, die seine Korrespondenz überprüften, mehr über den Schreibprozess des Romanautors als über tatsächlich subversive Machenschaften. In dieser Akte findet sich auch ein Brief, in dem Isherwood Ende 1933 an Hamilton schrieb: »Ich war unzufrieden mit meinem Roman und habe ihn vernichtet. Im Frühling will ich einen neuen Versuch wagen. [...] Du sollst die Hauptfigur in meinem Buch werden.« Und er fügt hinzu: »Ich frage mich, in welcher ausländischen Hauptstadt wir uns wohl Ende 1934 verstecken müssen?«.[12] Dem Offizier, der diesen Satz las, muss Isherwoods

P.F. 42415.

ISHERWOOD, Christopher.

2.32.   Int. letter from John STRACHEY, 9, Heath-   P.F.161/39.
             cote St. London, W.C. to Gerald HAMILTON, Berlin- Vol.5.
             Charlottenberg, 9, Platanenalle 28, says:-   146b. D.735.T.
             "Tell Christopher I'm writing to him very soon."

.33.   Int. letter from Olive MANGEOT, London,   PF/161/39.V.6.
             to Gerald HAMILTON, Paris, says:- "Christopher   206b.
             is very well and full of news, its good to see him". N.303.T.

.33.   Witnessed the marriage between Gerald   P.F. 161/39.V.6.
             HAMILTON and Suzanne RENOU at the Chelsea Register (229c)
             Office on Sat. 29th, April. Name given as   SB/301/MP/2905.
             Christopher ISHERWOOD.

             A letter from "Stephen", Seeadler, Sellin-   P.F. 161/39.V.6.
             Auf-Rugen, Germany to Gerald HAMILTON, London,   233a.
             has the following postscript attached:-(22.7.32.) SB/301/MP/2905.

                 "Dear Gerald,
                         I'm sorry that I have'nt
                 written before. As regards Werner, I
                 know no more than I told you when we
                 were together. Fronny expressed
                 unwillingness that the matter should go
                 any further. I have no idea what
                 Werner's address is.
                         It looks as if I shall miss you
                 altogether this month and next. I
                 return to Berlin on August 2 and leave
                 for England about the 4th. Is there
                 any chance of seeing you either there
                 or here?
                             Best love,
                                   Christopher."

             Correspondence forwarded by S.B. who discovered
             it when searching HAMILTON'S papers.

.33.   Int. letter from Olive MANGEOT, London,   P.F. 161/39.V.6.
             to Gerald HAMILTON, Paris, says:- "no   235a. P.252.B.
             further news of Christopher."

.33.   Int. letter from C.HADEN GUEST, London, to   S.F. 452/UK.V.7.
             Dick BEECH, encloses list of authors who have   364a.
             signed the British Anti-War Movement Manifesto,   R.269.K.
             includes the name of Christopher ISHERWOOD.

.33.   Int. letter from Olive MANGEOT to Gerald   P.F. 161/39.V.6.
             HAMILTON, Paris, forwards Christopher's address   235c. P.496.K.
             c/o Thomas Cook, Athens, which she has received
             from him by p.c.

[Fig. 35: Christopher Isherwood's security file, showing intercepted letters from the early 1930s]

[Abb. 35: Christopher Isherwoods Geheimdienstakte mit abgefangenen Briefen aus den frühen 1930er Jahren]

The officer reading this sentence missed Isherwood's teasing wink, as it is marked in the margin for special notice.

In reality, Isherwood later regretted that he had not been more politically active before he left Berlin in 1933. He wished that he had met high-ranking Nazis like Joseph Goebbels, the party's propaganda chief, so as to have better understood the nature of their threat. Anxiety around the patchiness of his commitment is touched upon in his novel *Goodbye to Berlin* (1939), when a semi-autobiographical Christopher watches (as did his author) the funeral of Hermann Müller—the former Chancellor and SPD politician. As Christopher looks on from a hotel balcony with Sally Bowles and their rich American friend Clive, "the whole drab pageant of Prussian Social Democracy—trudged past under their banners towards the silhouetted arches of the Brandenburger Tor". Between Sally's indifferent yawns and Clive's promises to spirit away the three of them on a world tour, Christopher considers the wickedness of his apathy: "I've done it now" he thinks, "I am lost".[13]

Isherwood and Spender scrutinised German political affairs with increasing attention, becoming (like Auden) passionately anti-fascist after leaving the country, but the most astute records of Weimar Berlin's transition into Nazi Berlin came from the journalists who remained. Elizabeth Wiskemann first visited the city for Christmas in 1928 while a history student at Cambridge, and returned intermittently from 1930, reporting for British periodicals

scherzhafter Unterton entgangen sein, denn er versah die Passage mit einer Randnotiz.

Tatsächlich brachte Isherwood später sein Bedauern darüber zum Ausdruck, dass er sich vor seiner Abreise aus Berlin im Jahr 1933 nicht stärker politisch engagiert hatte. Im Nachhinein hätte er sich ein Treffen mit hochrangigen Nazis wie dem Propagandaleiter der Partei, Joseph Goebbels, gewünscht. Auf diese Weise hätte er sich ein besseres Bild von der Bedrohung machen können, die von dieser Bewegung ausging. Das beklemmende Gefühl eines unzureichenden Engagements deutet er in seinem Roman *Leb wohl, Berlin* (»Goodbye to Berlin«, 1939) an. In einer Szene verfolgt die halb-autobiografische Figur des Christopher (wie einst der Autor selbst) das Begräbnis des ehemaligen Reichskanzlers und SPD-Politikers Hermann Müller. Christopher steht mit Sally Bowles und ihrem reichen amerikanischen Freund Clive auf einem Hotelbalkon und beobachtet, wie »der ganze triste [...] Mummenschanz der preußischen Sozialdemokratie – mit ihren Bannern auf die Silhouette des Brandenburger Tors« zu trottete. Zwischen Sallys gleichgültigem Gähnen und Clives Versprechen, die drei auf eine Weltreise zu entführen, denkt Christopher über den boshaften Charakter seiner Gleichgültigkeit nach: »Ja, sagte ich mir, nun ist es so weit. Ich bin verloren.«[13]

Isherwood und Spender verfolgten das politische Geschehen in Deutschland mit wachsender Aufmerksamkeit und wurden (wie Auden) nach ihrer Abreise aus Deutschland zu leidenschaftlichen Antifaschisten. Doch die scharfsinnigsten Berichte über den Übergang des Weimarer Berlin zum nationalsozialistischen Berlin stammten aus der Feder derjenigen Journalist*innen, die der Stadt nicht den Rücken gekehrt hatten. Elizabeth Wiskemann kam zum ersten Mal als Geschichtsstudentin an der Universität Cambridge zum Weihnachtsfest 1928 nach Berlin. Seit 1930

until she was expelled by the Gestapo in 1936. Traversing Europe, Wiskemann gathered news from high-ranking confidantes and kept colleagues and officials at home informed, though her warnings that the air in Germany "stank of war" tended to be met with scepticism. Three years before the November Pogrom, Wiskemann warned of one of its organisers, the SS official Reinhard Heydrich, in a bold article for The New Statesman and Nation. The sinister organisation was "pledged to [...] every sort of dehumanisation".[14]

What they were witnessing, Spender later wrote, was a test case not just for Europe but for modern civilisation, which looked on course for collapse. In Britain, certain parallels with Germany's political fault-lines were emerging. In 1931, Prime Minister Ramsay MacDonald formed a coalition government with the Conservatives—an expediency regarded by many on the left as a betrayal of Labour and socialism. This, and economic crisis, made space for a local fascism to take hold. Oswald Mosley had been a Conservative, then a Labour MP, and now founded the "New Party" in answer to MacDonald's defection. He was joined by Harold Nicolson, who had returned to England. Isherwood, too, had a connection to Mosley, writing an appreciative piece on the German youth movement for the New Party's magazine. Isherwood couldn't have known that the following year Mosley would found the British Union of Fascists, from which Nicolson swiftly distanced himself.

kehrte sie als Berichterstatterin für britische Magazine immer wieder in die Stadt zurück, bis sie 1936 schließlich von der Gestapo des Landes verwiesen wurde. Auf ihren Reisen durch Europa ließ sich Wiskemann von hochrangigen Vertrauenspersonen informieren und hielt ihre Kolleg*innen und Funktionäre in der Heimat auf dem Laufenden. Allerdings begegnete man ihrer Warnung, in Deutschland liege Krieg in der Luft, eher mit Skepsis. Drei Jahre vor den Novemberpogromen hatte Wiskemann bereits in einem beherzten Artikel für *The New Statesman and Nation* vor einem der Organisatoren, dem SS-Mann Reinhard Heydrich, gewarnt. Die unheilvolle Organisation habe sich »jeder Art Enthumanisierung verschrieben«.[14]

Wie Spender später schrieb, wohnten sie damals einem Präzedenzfall nicht nur für Europa, sondern für die moderne Zivilisation bei, die offenkundig auf ihren Zusammenbruch zusteuerte. In Großbritannien konnte man Parallelen zu den politischen Konfliktlinien in Deutschland erkennen. Im Jahr 1931 bildete Premierminister Ramsay MacDonald eine Koalitionsregierung mit den Konservativen: Sein berechnendes Vorgehen wurde von vielen Vertretern der Linken als Verrat an der Labour-Partei und am Sozialismus gewertet. In Kombination mit der Wirtschaftskrise konnte sich so eine nationale Form des Faschismus weiter ausbreiten. Oswald Mosley, der zunächst Abgeordneter der Konservativen und schließlich der Labour-Partei gewesen war, gründete als Reaktion auf MacDonalds Treuebruch die »New Party«. Zu seinen Unterstützern gehörte auch Harold Nicolson, der inzwischen nach England zurückgekehrt war. Isherwood pflegte ebenfalls Verbindungen zu Mosley und schrieb für das Magazin seiner Partei einen lobenden Artikel über die deutsche Jugendbewegung. Isherwood konnte nicht wissen, dass Mosley im Jahr darauf die britische Union der

In the British government the mood was for appeasement of Hitler, but a circle of MPs—among them Nicolson—protested vocally. Denigrated by Prime Minister Neville Chamberlain as "glamour boys", they were mainly homosexuals who had enjoyed the sexual freedoms of Weimar Berlin, and now recognised the atrocities of the new regime sooner than many of their colleagues.

Back in the winter of 1932, street violence in Berlin was becoming more commonplace. In *Goodbye to Berlin*, Isherwood draws on an incident he had seen unfold after a Nazi meeting at the Sportpalast. Three SA thugs—Nazi paramilitaries—chased down a teenager and battered him with the sharpened tips of their swastika banners. Across Potsdamer Straße some policemen stood at the corner: "With their chests out, and their hands on their revolver belts, they magnificently disregarded the whole affair".[15]

IV.

The transparencies build up. A single location visited by many multiplies in its associations. Our tour has circled back to the Sportpalast, which for British writers variously inspired curiosity, horror, and admiration. In 1931, Wiskemann visited with two other renowned journalists, Frederick Voigt of the *Manchester Guardian*, and the American Dorothy Thompson, to hear Goebbels speak. His words filled them with "gloomy foreboding".[16] In the same

Faschisten gründete, von der sich Nicolson unverzüglich distanzierte.

Mit Blick auf Hitler verfolgte die britische Regierung eine Strategie des Appeasements, gegen die ein Kreis von Abgeordneten um Nicolson lautstark protestierte. Bei diesen von Premierminister Neville Chamberlain als »Glamour Boys« verunglimpften Männern handelte es sich vorwiegend um Homosexuelle, die von den sexuellen Freiheiten in Berlin zur Zeit der Weimarer Republik profitiert hatten und nun die Gräueltaten des neuen Regimes früher als viele ihrer Amtskolleg*innen erkannten.

Damals, im Winter des Jahres 1932, bestimmte die Gewalt auf den Straßen immer mehr den Berliner Alltag. In *Leb wohl, Berlin* beschreibt Isherwood einen Vorfall, den er nach einer Nazi-Versammlung im Sportpalast mit ansehen musste. Drei SA-Schläger stürzten sich auf einen jungen Mann und stachen mit den Metallspitzen ihrer Hakenkreuz-Fahnenstangen auf ihn ein. An der Ecke Potsdamer Straße stand eine Gruppe Polizisten: »Mit geschwellter Brust, die Hände am Koppel, sahen sie stolz über die ganze Angelegenheit hinweg«.[15]

IV.

Inzwischen liegen immer mehr Dias übereinander. Schließlich sind mit einem von vielen Menschen besuchten Ort stets unterschiedliche Assoziationen verbunden. Unsere Tour führt uns nun zurück in den Sportpalast, der bei britischen Schriftsteller*innen Neugier, Schrecken und Bewunderung zugleich auslöste. Im Jahre 1931 wohnte Wiskemann hier gemeinsam mit zwei weiteren bekannten Journalist*innen, Frederick Voigt vom *Manchester Guardian* und Dorothy Thompson aus den USA, einer Goebbels-Rede bei. Seine Worte erfüllten sie mit »düsteren Vorah-

year, the avant-garde writer Wyndham Lewis joined the Sportpalast's ten thousand-strong audience to hear Goebbels and Hitler. For Lewis, who has been described as protofascist, Hitler was a welcome counterpoint to the corruption of the SPD in its subservience to capitalist interests. In his book *Hitler* (1931), which makes unconvincing claims to impartiality, Lewis calls Hitler a "socialist prophet" and frames Nazi militancy as a reasonable reaction to Communist provocation.[17] A further visit to Germany in 1937 led Lewis to recant his controversial work, and his next two books criticised Hitler and anti-Semitism. Koestler's compass was still spinning.

Other British commentators were more frankly supportive of Nazism. Unity Mitford and Diana Mosley née Mitford were two of six celebrated sisters who were extraordinarily well connected in British literature, politics, and high society. Unity and Diana were fascists, and on multiple trips to Munich and Berlin developed a passion for Hitler. In 1936, Diana married Oswald Mosley at Goebbels's Berlin home, with Hitler in attendance. The newlyweds spent the evening listening to the Führer's address at the Sportpalast, and dining with him at the Reich Chancellery. Though Diana was interned in Britain during the war because of these connections, her 1977 memoir is unrepentant about her enjoyment of Hitler's company. Letters between the two sisters from the mid-1930s are thick with blithe excitement about their

[Fig. 36: Diana Mosley with her sister Unity (left) and
Nazi officer friends, unknown photographer, 1930s]

[Abb. 36: Diana Mosley mit ihrer Schwester Unity (links) und
befreundeten Nazi-Offizieren, unbekannter Fotograf, 1930er]

time in Hitler's circle, Unity tending to sign off with a "Heil Hitler".

Diana's Berlin letters are addressed from the Hotel Kaiserhof on Wilhelmstraße, which put her in convenient reach of the Chancellery for when Hitler was in the capital. One wonders what Bradshaw and Norris would have said had they crossed paths with her there. On Communist business, the co-conspirators sneak in to drink coffee in the Kaiserhof lounge—"the camp of the enemy"—morbidly hopeful of spotting some important Nazi.[18]

V.

The record of political Berlin established by these writers is indelibly shaped by the spaces through which they moved; their novels, letters, and diaries, their speeches and propaganda, their secret service files,

Schwestern Mitte der 1930er Jahre schrieben, quellen über vor heiterer Begeisterung über ihre Zeit in Hitlers innerem Kreis. Unity pflegte ihre Briefe mit einem »Heil Hitler« abzuschließen.

Dianas Adresse auf ihren Briefen aus Berlin war das Hotel Kaiserhof an der Wilhelmstraße. Wenn Hitler in der Hauptstadt weilte, war es von dort nur ein Katzensprung zur Reichskanzlei. Was hätten Bradshaw und Norris wohl gesagt, wenn sie ihr dort über den Weg gelaufen wären. In kommunistischen Angelegenheiten unterwegs, schleichen sich die beiden Verschwörer auf eine Tasse Kaffee in die Lounge des Kaiserhofs – im »Hauptquartier des Feindes« –, in der morbiden Hoffnung, eine Nazi-Größe zu erblicken.[18]

V.

Die Berichte dieser Schriftsteller*innen über das politische Berlin sind fest mit den Räumen verknüpft, in denen sie sich bewegten. Ihre Romane, Briefe und Tagebücher, ihre Vorträge und ihre propagandistischen Schriften, ihre Geheimdienstakten entstanden

were produced in the intimacies, clashes, and collaborations enabled by grand hotels and cramped boarding-houses, bureaucratic mansions, and imposing arenas. The commitments they formed in the city did not end when those spaces were closed to them. Isherwood and Bowra supported German friends, colleagues, and lovers escaping Nazi persecution. Auden married Erika Mann, the actress, writer, and dedicated anti-fascist, to provide her with a British passport when she was stripped of German citizenship.

The politicising of these figures cannot be separated from the cultural motivations that drew them to Germany, and chief among such motivations was the internationalism coursing through the arts of the Weimar Republic. For a while, some optimists perceived a grand new possibility for cosmopolitanism in Europe's artistic and political spheres, which would counteract the antagonistic nationalisms that had led the world into war once already. The novelist H.G. Wells gave a prominent speech at the Reichstag in April 1929—"The Common Sense of World Peace"—and declared that renewal in post-war Europe was to be found in a solidarity that superseded narrow loyalties to nation-states. "To become a cosmopolitan," Wells declared, "you must be born again. You must break away from the self-satisfied movement of the majority mind in the community from which you have arisen".[19]

The failure of artists to effectively realise this ideal was explored in 1942 by the

durch die Intimität, die zufälligen Begegnungen und Kollaborationen, die große Hotels und beengte Pensionen, Amtssitze und imposante Stadien ermöglichten. Die Bindungen, die sie in dieser Stadt eingingen, endeten nicht, als sich diese Orte für sie verschlossen. Isherwood und Bowra unterstützten deutsche Freund*innen, Kolleg*innen und Geliebte auf ihrer Flucht vor der Nazi-Verfolgung. Auden heiratete die Schauspielerin, Schriftstellerin und überzeugte Antifaschistin Erika Mann, um ihr nach dem Verlust ihrer deutschen Staatsbürgerschaft einen britischen Pass zu beschaffen.

Die Politisierung dieser Figuren lässt sich nicht losgelöst von der kulturellen Anziehungskraft betrachten, die diese Menschen ursprünglich nach Deutschland gebracht hatte. Einer der wichtigsten Beweggründe war der Internationalismus, der die Weimarer Kunstszene prägt. Eine Zeit lang sahen Optimist*innen das großartige neue Potenzial eines Weltbürgertums, das sich in europäischen Künstler- und Politikerkreisen eröffnete und einen Gegenpol zu den feindlichen nationalistischen Gesinnungen bilden könnte, die die Welt schon einmal in einen Krieg geführt hatten. Der Romanautor H.G. Wells hielt im April 1929 eine berühmte Rede vor dem Reichstag über »The Common Sense of World Peace« und erklärte, dass eine Erneuerung im Nachkriegseuropa eine Solidarität voraussetze, die ein strenges Festhalten am Nationalstaatsbegriff ausschließe. Um zum Weltbürger zu werden, so erklärte Wells, müsse man neu geboren werden. Man müsse sich von der selbstzufriedenen Mehrheitsmeinung der Gemeinschaft befreien, der man entspringe.[19]

Dem Unvermögen von Künstler*innen, diesem Ideal vollkommen gerecht zu werden, widmete sich 1942 der kosmopolitische Schriftsteller Klaus Mann, Bruder von Erika Mann und Freund von Auden und

cosmopolitan writer Klaus Mann, brother of Erika Mann and a friend of Auden's and Isherwood's from their time in Berlin. Remembering the "informal comradeship" of liberal, left-leaning writers in the period, Mann observed that it had not been enough to have written, lectured, launched magazines, and been "good Europeans" in the 1920s.[20] Too many underestimated Hitler, and, when the Nationalsocialists started to make serious gains in the Reichstag, were too slow to shake off their discouragement. The truth was that Spender's vision of reading the future through transparent stone was one of many myths of Weimar Berlin told in retrospect. It was hard enough at the time, in Klaus Mann's words, just to believe the "writing on the wall".[21]

Isherwood aus Berliner Zeiten. Mann erinnerte sich, dass es zu dieser Zeit eine zwanglose Kameradschaft unter liberalen, linksgerichteten Schriftstellern gegeben habe. Offenbar habe es in den 1920er Jahren nicht ausgereicht, zu schreiben, Vorträge zu halten, Magazine herauszugeben und ein »guter Europäer« zu sein.[20] Zu viele Menschen hätten Hitler unterschätzt. Und als die Nationalsozialisten immer mehr Sitze im Reichstag gewannen, seien sie viel zu sehr damit beschäftigt gewesen, ihr Gefühl der Entmutigung wieder abzuschütteln. Tatsächlich war Spenders Vision, die Zukunft durch transparentes Gestein vorhersagen zu können, eine der vielen Berliner Mythen, die man sich rückblickend erzählte. In dieser Zeit war es schon schwer genug, wie Klaus Mann schrieb, der »Schrift an der Wand« Glauben zu schenken.[21]

Notes

1 Stephen Spender: World Within World, London, Hamish Hamilton 1951, p. 133.
2 Evelyn Princess Blücher: An English Wife in Berlin, New York, Dutton 1920, p. 18.
3 Ibid., p. 95.
4 Ibid.
5 Ibid., p. 135.
6 Niroda K. Barooah: Chatto: The Life and Times of an Indian Anti-Imperialist in Europe, Oxford, Oxford University Press 2004, p. 188.
7 Roger Casement, quoted in Angus Mitchell: One Bold Deed of Open Treason, County Kildare, Merrion Press 2016, p. 8.
8 Harold Nicolson: The Harold Nicolson Diaries 1907–1964, ed. by Nigel Nicolson, London, Phoenix 2005, p. 70.
9 Cyril Connolly: Conversations in Berlin, repr. in: The Condemned Playground, London, Routledge 1946, p. 212.

Anmerkungen

1 Stephen Spender: Welt in der Welt, aus dem Englischen von Andreas Sattler, München, R. Piper GmbH & Co. KG 1992, S. 170.
2 Evelyn Fürstin Blücher von Wahlstatt, 10. November 1918, in: Tagebuch, München, Verlag für Kulturpolitik 1924, S. 23.
3 Ebd., S. 106.
4 Ebd.
5 Ebd., S. 153.
6 Niroda K. Barooah: Chatto: The Life and Times of an Indian Anti-Imperialist in Europe, Oxford, Oxford University Press 2004, S. 188.
7 Roger Casement, zitiert in Angus Mitchell: One Bold Deed of Open Treason, County Kildare, Merrion Press 2016, S. 8.
8 Harold Nicolson: The Harold Nicolson Diaries 1907–1964, hg. von Nigel Nicolson London, Phoenix 2005, S. 70.
9 Cyril Connolly: Conversations in Berlin, repr. in: The Condemned Playground, London, Routledge 1946, S. 212.
10 W. H. Auden: It was Easter as I walked in the public gardens, in: The English Auden, hg. von Edward Mendelson,

10 W. H. Auden: It was Easter as I walked in the public gardens, in: The English Auden, ed. by Edward Mendelson, London, Faber 1977, p. 38.

11 Arthur Koestler: Arrow in the Blue, London, Vintage 2005, p. 279.

12 Intercepted letter from Christopher Isherwood to Gerald Hamilton, 21 December 1933, in: The National Archives: KV 2/2587, 8a.

13 Christopher Isherwood: Goodbye to Berlin, London, Vintage 1998, pp. 59 f.

14 Elizabeth Wiskemann: The Europe I Saw, London, Collins 1968, p. 39, p. 48.

15 Isherwood: Goodbye to Berlin, p. 244.

16 Wiskemann: The Europe I Saw, p. 23.

17 Wyndham Lewis: Hitler, London, Chatto & Windus 1931, p. 49.

18 Christopher Isherwood: Mr. Norris Changes Trains, London, Vintage 1999, p. 74.

19 H. G. Wells: The Common Sense of World Peace, London, The Hogarth Press 1929, pp. 26 f.

20 Klaus Mann: The Turning Point, London, Serpent's Tail 1987 (1942), p. 123.

21 Ibid., p. 230.

London, Faber 1977, S. 38. [Zu Ostern spazierte ich durch den Park / Mit der Nacht kam stets die Angst / Schüsse und Barrikaden in den Straßen / Auf dem Heimweg lauschte ich dem Worten eines Freunds / Voller Aufregung sprach er vom letzten Krieg / der Proletarier gegen die Polizei].

11 Arthur Koestler: Pfeil ins Blaue. Bericht eines Lebens 1905–1931, Vienna etc., Verlag Kurt Desch 1953, S. 278–279.

12 Abgefangener Brief von Christopher Isherwood an Gerald Hamilton, 21. Dezember 1933, in: The National Archives, KV 2/2587, 8a.

13 Christopher Isherwood: Leb wohl, Berlin, aus dem Englischen von Kathrin Passig und Gerhard Henschel, Hamburg, Hoffmann und Campe Verlag 3. Auflage 2019, S. 71 f.

14 Elizabeth Wiskemann: Erlebtes Europa. Ein politischer Reisebericht 1930–1945, Stuttgart und Bern, Hallwag 1969, S. 243.

15 Isherwood: Leb wohl Berlin, S. 260.

16 Wiskemann: Erlebtes Europa, S. 20.

17 Wyndam Lewis: Hitler und sein Werk in englischer Beleuchtung, Berlin, Verlag Reimar Hobbing 1932, S. 45.

18 Christopher Isherwood: Mr. Norris steigt um, aus dem Englischen von Georg Deggerich, Hamburg, Hoffmann und Campe Verlag 2016, S. 62.

19 H. G. Wells: The Common Sense of World Peace, London, The Hogarth Press 1929, S. 26 f.

20 Klaus Mann: The Turning Point, London, Serpent's Tail 1987 (1942), S. 123. Die hier verwendete Passage ist in der deutschen Fassung, die Klaus Mann nach der angloamerikanischen Version veröffentlich hat, nicht enthalten.

21 Klaus Mann: Der Wendepunkt, Reinbek, Rowohlt 2019 (2006) (1952), S. 379; S. 383.

Sandra Mayer

Chronicler and Eulogist of the "Gang": Stephen Spender Writing the Berlin Myth

Chronist und Laudator der »Gruppe«: Stephen Spender schreibt den Berliner Mythos

In an essay from 1979 aptly titled "Drop Me a Name", the English poet, critic, editor, and broadcaster Stephen Spender (1909–1995) offers a tongue-in-cheek commentary on his public stature, whose "chief interest lies in the fact that I have met the great".[1] By then Spender was a 'Grand Old Man' of letters. As a former president of English PEN and Poet Laureate Consultant to the US Library of Congress, he had fully embraced his role of chronicler, witness, and eulogist, even though he would always feel ambivalent about it. Essentially an autobiographer, in whose writing public and private worlds become inseparably intertwined, Spender throughout his life maintained an impressive habit of rigorous (self-)documentation and recording. His relentless drive to relate personal experience to larger frameworks of world politics and historical transformations, paired with what his contemporary, the Irish poet Louis MacNeice, called his "lust to mythologise the world in which he walked",[2] indeed rendered him an ideal candidate for the role of keeper of the sacred flame. It was a

Der englische Dichter, Kritiker, Herausgeber und Publizist Stephen Spender (1909–1995) formulierte 1979 in einem Essay mit dem treffenden Titel »Drop Me a Name« (Nenn mir einen Namen) einen nicht ganz ernst gemeinten Kommentar zu seiner gesellschaftlichen Position, die seiner Meinung nach im Wesentlichen darauf zurückzuführen sei, dass er mit den ganz Großen verkehrt habe.[1] Zu diesem Zeitpunkt war Spender bereits ein »Großer Alter Mann« der Literatur. Dem ehemaligen Präsidenten des englischen PEN-Clubs und Berater für Lyrik der Library of Congress der Vereinigten Staaten war es gelungen, seinen Ruf als Chronist, Zeitzeuge und Laudator zu festigen, zu dem er doch stets auch ein zwiespältiges Verhältnis pflegte. Spender verfasste hauptsächlich autobiografische Werke, in denen er das Öffentliche und das Private untrennbar miteinander verknüpfte, und dokumentierte und protokollierte Zeit seines Lebens mit bemerkenswerter Routine alles, was in seinem persönlichen Umfeld und in der Welt geschah. Sein stetes Streben, persönliche Erfahrungen in übergeordnete weltpolitische Zusammenhänge und historische Umbruchprozesse einzuordnen, gepaart mit einer Eigenschaft, die sein Zeitgenosse, der irische Dichter Louis MacNeice, als einen »ausgeprägten Hang zur Mythologisierung der Welt, in der

role that he fulfilled most religiously as the ubiquitous spokesperson and, eventually, sole survivor of the "gang" of friends and fellow writers—most notably, W. H. Auden and Christopher Isherwood—whose position in cultural memory will forever be tied up with the tumultuous decade of the 1930s and their flight towards the artistic and sexual freedoms of Weimar Berlin.

Between 1930 and 1933, Spender lived in Berlin for extended periods of time after he had initially been lured to the city by Auden and Isherwood. In Spender's published and unpublished journals, voluminous correspondence, memoirs, criticism, as well as in his autobiographically inflected fiction, 1930s Berlin is constructed as a foundational myth in the self-making of a new generation of upper-middle-class young writers who abandoned their home country in search of the seductive mix of "nihilism, sophistication and primitive vitality which was so dangerously attractive in the beginning of the Weimar Republic".[3] Though less prominent than in Isherwood's Berlin novels and his memoirs, *Lions and Shadows* (1938) and *Christopher and His Kind* (1976), Berlin plays a key role in the self-mythologisation of a tightly-knit and well-connected clique with a genius for self-branding, networking, collaboration, and mutual promotion, who would faithfully dedicate their works to each other and end up writing one another's obituaries. As Spender notes, half ironically, half nostalgically, in his journal

er sich bewegte«[2] bezeichnete, machten ihn ohne Zweifel zum idealen Kandidaten für die Rolle des Gralshüters. Eine Rolle, die er als allgegenwärtiger Wortführer und schließlich auch letzter Überlebender seiner »Gruppe« aus Freunden und Schriftstellerkollegen – allen voran W.H. Auden und Christopher Isherwood – äußerst gewissenhaft erfüllte. Im kulturellen Gedächtnis wird diese Gruppe für immer mit dem turbulenten Jahrzehnt der 1930er Jahre und ihrer Flucht in die künstlerischen und sexuellen Freiheiten Berlins verhaftet bleiben.

Zwischen 1930 und 1933 kam Spender für mehrere längere Aufenthalte nach Berlin, nachdem ihn Auden und Isherwood bereits zuvor zu einem ersten Besuch in die Stadt gelockt hatten. Das Berlin der 1930er Jahre wird in seinen veröffentlichten und unveröffentlichten Tagebüchern, unzähligen Briefen, Erinnerungen und Kritiken sowie in seiner autobiografisch inspirierten Prosa zum Gründungsmythos für die Selbstfindung einer neuen Generation junger Schriftsteller der oberen Mittelklasse. Diese hatten ihrer Heimat auf der Suche nach etwas den Rücken gekehrt, das er als verführerische Mischung aus dem »Eindruck eines Auf-nichts-gestellt-Seins, der Abgebrühtheit und des Lebensüberschwanges, lauter Dinge[n], die in den ersten Jahren der Weimarer Republik so gefährlich anziehen wirkten«,[3] beschrieb. Bei Spender nimmt Berlin mit Blick auf die Selbstmythologisierung seines engen und gut vernetzten Freundeskreises, den ein besonderes Talent für Selbstvermarktung, Beziehungspflege, Zusammenarbeit und gegenseitige Förderung einte, eine wichtige, wenn auch weniger prominente Rolle ein als in Isherwoods Berlin-Romanen und Erinnerungen *Löwen und Schatten* (»Lions and Shadows«, 1938) und *Christopher und die Seinen* (»Christopher and His Kind«, 1976). In treuer Ergebenheit widmeten sich die Freunde gegenseitig ihre Werke, und die Überleben-

...ank you for the card, which I like. ...ou shall have the history-book ...ictures as soon as possible. Upward ...mes here tomorrow. I enjoyed our ...ek-end too. So did Walter. He says ...u are a lieber netter Kerl. All is ...s peace because I had a brilliant ...ea and bought some boxing gloves.
Best love and come soon
Christopher / Walter

Herrn Stephen Spender
HAMBURG 37.
Innocentiastrasse 11.

[Figs 37 and 38: Christopher Isherwood, postcard to Stephen Spender, with the signature of Isherwood's German lover, Walter Wolff, 1930]

[Abb. 37 und 38: Christopher Isherwood, Postkarte an Stephen Spender, mit der Unterschrift von Isherwoods deutschem Liebhaber Walter Wolff, 1930]

only a few months before his death at the age of 86: "A kind of comic megalomania does characterize the 1930s where the poet-novelist-intellectuals played, at any rate among the young, such a leading role. Isherwood in Berlin becomes 'Isherwood's Berlin'."⁴

The myth of Isherwood's Berlin has permanently lodged itself in the cultural imagination. This is partly thanks to its multiform appropriations in popular culture. But it is also in response to our obsession with witnessing and the deceptive promise of authenticity and immediacy that attaches to the account of those who were 'there' and experienced history in the making. As Spender became the last man standing of the generation of British writers who had known Berlin in the final years of the Weimar Republic, he increasingly settled into the part of sage-like commentator. He appears to have inhabited this persona, both self-fashioned and imposed, with a mix of the revered man of letters' mild-mannered equanimity and the gate-keeping mediator's sense of responsibility. He lived up to public expectations by generously providing testimony via lectures, TV and radio programmes, and occasional journalism. In November 1993, the octogenarian was asked to give the cast of Sam Mendes' forthcoming production of *Cabaret* at the Donmar Warehouse a flavour of "Christopher's and Jean [Ross]'s and my life in Berlin". Taken in by the "flirtatious sexy charm" of the actors, including Jane

den sollten schließlich auch die Nachrufe der Verstorbenen verfassen. Wenige Monate vor seinem Tod im Alter von 86 Jahren schrieb Spender in einer Mischung aus Ironie und Nostalgie in sein Tagebuch: »Die 1930er Jahre waren offenbar von einer Art komödiantischem Größenwahn erfasst, in dem vor allem junge Dichter, Autoren und Intellektuelle eine derart führende Rolle übernehmen konnten. Aus Isherwood in Berlin wird ›Isherwoods Berlin‹.«⁴

Dieser Mythos von Isherwoods Berlin hat sich für alle Zeiten in das kulturelle Gedächtnis eingebrannt. Dies ist zum Teil darauf zurückzuführen, dass sich die Populärkultur in vielfacher Weise mit diesem Mythos auseinandergesetzt hat. Doch es ist auch unserer Faszination für Zeitzeugenberichte geschuldet. Darüber hinaus entspringt es dem trügerischen Versprechen von Authentizität und Unmittelbarkeit, das wir mit all denjenigen verbinden, die »dabei« waren, als Geschichte geschrieben wurde. Als letzter Überlebender einer Generation von Schriftsteller*innen, die Berlin in der Endphase der Weimarer Republik erlebten, sollte sich Spender mehr und mehr in der Rolle des nahezu allwissenden Chronisten einrichten, dessen Expertise auf unmittelbaren Erfahrungen beruhte. Dieser sowohl selbstinszenierten als auch auferlegten Rolle widmete er sich offenbar mit der milden Gelassenheit eines ehrwürdigen Literaten und dem Verantwortungsgefühl eines gralshütenden Mittlers zwischen den Welten. Die Erwartungen der Öffentlichkeit erfüllte er, indem er in zahlreichen Vorträgen, Fernseh- und Radiosendungen und regelmäßigen Zeitungsartikeln umfassend über seine Erfahrungen berichtete. Im November 1993 bat man den 84-Jährigen, dem Ensemble von Sam Mendes' geplanter *Cabaret*-Inszenierung am Donmar Warehouse einen Eindruck von dem Leben zu vermitteln, das »Christopher und Jean [Ross] und ich in Berlin führten«. Spender zeigte sich

Horrocks as Sally Bowles and Alan Cumming as Emcee, who quizzed him about "our dealings with boys", he notes in his journal:

> Told them that Christopher and I could not have afforded to go to any of the bars described in the [Liza] Minnelli movie *Cabaret*. [...] I think I managed to persuade them that [the] environment of Sally Bowles was poor—though there was a still poorer level of the unemployed and real misery below us.[5]

Spender makes a similar point in "Life Wasn't a Cabaret", a short anecdotal sketch in the *New York Times*, in which he looks back on the Berlin of the late 1920s nearly fifty years after his first visit to the city. As in the early days of their friendship, Spender keeps trading on the success of Isherwood's Berlin stories, and his commentary reveals a proprietorial anxiety about who creates the most enduring version of the Berlin Myth and thus subsequently owns it. The 'real' Berlin of his recollected experience and the one immortalised by Isherwood is a far cry from the glitzy club-world portrayed by the film and musical.

The Berlin he remembers is raw and rough, riven by poverty and political unrest and yet teeming with intellectual and artistic vibrancy:

> What we mostly knew was the Berlin of poverty, unemployment, political

beeindruckt vom koketten und betörenden Charme der Schauspieler*innen, darunter Jane Horrocks als Sally Bowles und Alan Cumming als Emcee, die ihn über »unsere Beziehungen zu den Jungs« ausfragten. Spender notierte in seinem Tagebuch:

> Ich erzählte ihnen, dass Christopher und ich uns einen Besuch in einer der Bars, die in dem [Liza] Minnelli-Film *Cabaret* vorkommen, nicht hätten leisten können. [...] Ich denke, ich konnte sie davon überzeugen, dass Sally Bowles in ärmlichen Verhältnissen lebte – auch wenn es die Arbeitslosen noch härter traf und wir mit dem wahren Elend nicht in Berührung kamen.[5]

Ähnliche Gedanken formulierte Spender in einem kurzen anekdotenhaften Bericht in der *New York Times* mit dem Titel »Life Wasn't a Cabaret«. Darin blickte er fast fünfzig Jahre nach seinem ersten Besuch in der Stadt auf das Berlin der späten 1920er Jahre zurück. Wie schon zu Beginn ihrer Freundschaft machte sich Spender auch hier den Erfolg von Isherwoods Berliner Geschichten zunutze. Sein Kommentar offenbart ein ängstliches Besitzdenken in der Frage, wer von ihnen eigentlich den Anspruch darauf erheben kann, eine besonders eindrückliche Version des Berliner Mythos geschaffen zu haben. Das »wirkliche« Berlin, das Spender in seinen Erfahrungsberichten beschreibt, und das Berlin, das Isherwood unsterblich gemacht hat, haben so gut wie nichts mit der schillernden Welt der Clubs gemein, die im Film und im Musical inszeniert wurden.

Das Berlin seiner Erinnerung ist ein rauer und unbarmherziger Ort, der von Armut und politischen Unruhen bestimmt wird und zugleich doch überschäumt vor intellektueller und künstlerischer Schaffenskraft:

demonstrations and street fighting between forces of the extreme left and the extreme right. We did frequent bars, but they were very cheap ones. To us, Berlin was an immensely alive, rather common and vulgar place where there was a very active intellectual life of writers and artists whose much-photographed and publicized faces (Berlin was always a place presided over by the camera) were to be seen in the Romanisches Café.[6]

Spender's retrospective construction of Berlin rests on the idea of sexual and intellectual liberation, the conflation of the personal and the political, and an idealistic worship of youth and friendship against the background of the "*Weimardämmerung*": a sense of urgency produced by life descending into chaos and overshadowed by doom, violence, and destruction. As Spender and his friends looked towards Weimar Germany as a "kind of cure for our personal problems",[7] rooted, as they saw it, in their stifling bourgeois social milieus and repressive cultural climate of interwar Britain, the Berlin Myth became crucial in the process of shaping their own, long before the cultural hype around *Cabaret* caused them to perpetuate it.

*****

One of the prime sites of myth-making in which he dwells on the formative impact

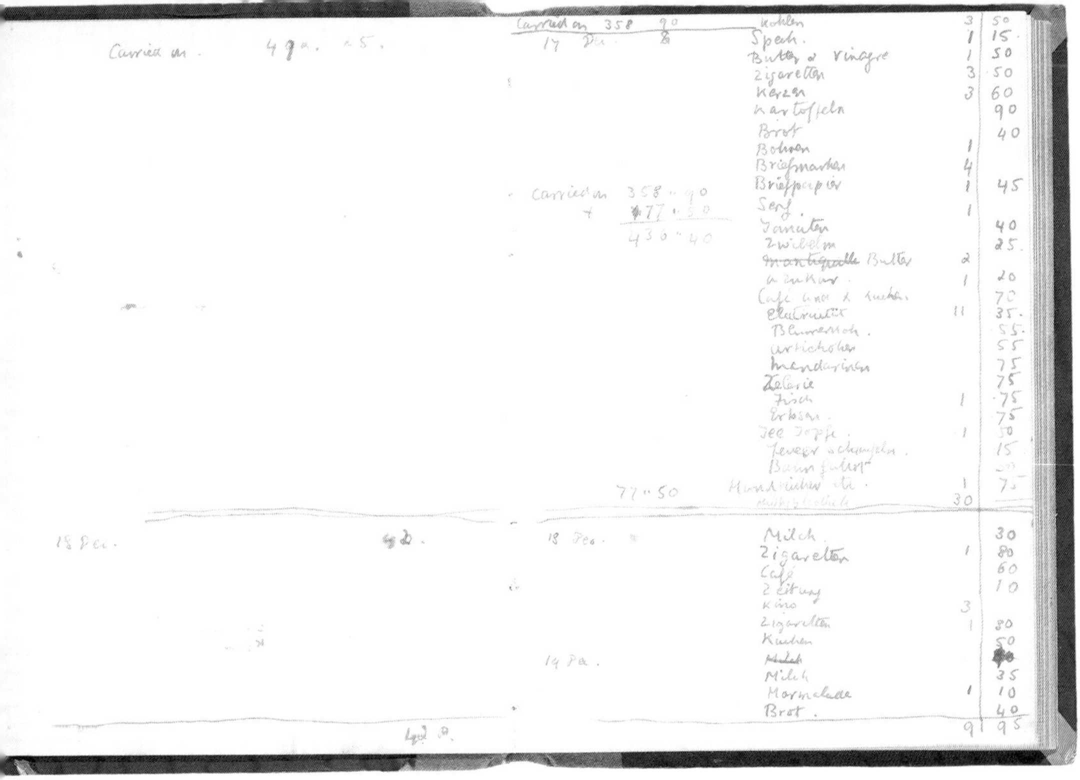

[Fig. 39: Stephen Spender, Berlin account-book, 1930s]

[Abb. 39: Stephen Spenders Berliner Haushaltsbuch, 1930er]

of Weimar Berlin is Spender's autobiography, *World Within World*. Published in 1951, the book was largely written before Spender turned 40, at a time when he was about to embark on a busy transatlantic life as a lecturer and teacher. His Berlin comrades, Isherwood and Auden, had by then become US citizens. The sense of a hiatus between his pre- and post-war lives is palpable when Spender looks back on what emerges as a decisive period in his making as a writer, largely comprising the events from 1928 until 1939. *World Within World* is both record and reflection, history

Welt (»World Within World«), in der er sich ausführlich mit der prägenden Zeit im Berlin der Weimarer Epoche auseinandersetzt. Den Großteil dieses im Jahr 1951 veröffentlichten Buchs verfasste Spender noch vor seinem 40. Geburtstag und damit kurz vor Beginn seines umtriebigen transatlantischen Lebens als Dozent und Lehrer. Zu diesem Zeitpunkt waren seine Kameraden aus Berliner Zeiten, Isherwood und Auden, bereits amerikanische Staatsbürger. Warum sich sein Leben vor dem Krieg so deutlich von seinem Leben nach dem Krieg unterscheidet, wird ersichtlich, wenn Spender über eine entscheidende Phase in seinem Werdegang als Schriftsteller berichtet, die vor allem seine Erlebnisse der Jahre 1928 bis 1939 einschließt.

and introspection, revealing the double vision of the autobiographer who locates himself as a public figure but also seeks to explore the inner self. The book is also remarkably frank in its treatment of male homosexuality at a time when homosexual acts in England still constituted a criminal offence. Less given to gossip and chatty anecdote about Berlin life, boys, and casual affairs than Isherwood's iconic autobiographical accounts, Spender's book coincidentally came out the same year that John Van Druten's play *I Am a Camera*, the first stage adaptation of Isherwood's Berlin writings, opened on Broadway.

For Spender, as for many young writers of his generation, going abroad, particularly to a former enemy nation once more in the throes of political turmoil, amounted to an act of rebellion against the liberal Edwardian milieu of their parents' generation, their stolid middle-class morality, and ideals of duty, integrity, honour, discipline, and achievement:

> The Germany of the late 1920s and early 1930s seemed, with its new architecture, its sexy air of sun and sea and nakedness, its accessible modernism, to represent what Auden called in an early poem: "New styles of architecture, a change of heart".[8]

Like Auden, Spender had a life-long affinity for German culture and literature, which expressed itself in his translation projects

Welt in der Welt enthält zugleich Aufzeichnungen und Reflexionen, historische Tatsachenberichte und innere Monologe. Es vermittelt zudem die doppelte Sicht des Autobiografen, der sich selbst als Figur des öffentlichen Lebens beschreibt, während er parallel dazu sein Innenleben erkundet. Darüber hinaus widmet sich das Buch völlig unverblümt dem Thema der männlichen Homosexualität in einer Zeit, als homosexuelle Handlungen in England noch strafbar waren. Spenders Buch, das im Vergleich zu Isherwoods Autobiografie mit Kultstatus weniger Tratsch und wortreiche Schilderungen über das Berliner Leben, Jungs und gelegentliche Affären enthält, kam zufälligerweise im selben Jahr heraus, in dem auch John Van Drutens Theaterstück *I Am a Camera* (»Ich bin eine Kamera«) als erste Bühnenproduktion von Isherwoods Berliner Geschichten am Broadway Premiere feierte.

Für Spender, wie für viele junge Schriftsteller*innen seiner Generation, kam der Schritt ins Ausland und vor allem in das Land des ehemaligen Gegners, das einmal mehr von politischen Unruhen erschüttert wurde, einem Akt des Aufbegehrens gegen das liberal edwardianisch geprägte Milieu seiner Elterngeneration mit ihren festgefahrenen bürgerlichen Moralvorstellungen und Idealen wie Pflichtbewusstsein, Redlichkeit, Ehre, Disziplin und Leistung gleich:

> Das Deutschland der späten 1920er und frühen 1930er Jahre spiegelte mit seiner neuen Architektur, seiner reizvollen Atmosphäre von Sonne und Meer und nackter Haut und seinem allgegenwärtigen Modernismus ganz offenbar das wider, was Auden in einem seiner frühen Gedichte als »neue Baustile, einen Sinneswandel« bezeichnete.[8]

Wie auch Auden fühlte sich Spender sein ganzes Leben lang zu deutscher Kultur und Literatur hin-

of Rilke's *Duino Elegies* (with J.B. Leishman, 1939) and Schiller's *Mary Stuart* (1958). His Germanophilia was also rooted in his family background: his mother, Violet Schuster, came from a Jewish banking family originally from Frankfurt-am-Main. Even though the Schuster family had converted to Christianity and blended in seamlessly with the English establishment, Spender remained acutely aware of his cultural heritage, which he held accountable for his sense of being an outsider within an upper-middle-class English environment.

What ultimately prompted Spender's departure to Berlin (via Hamburg) in 1929/30 after leaving Oxford without a degree, was a desire to join Auden and Isherwood, who, slightly older than Spender, combined the parts of hero, role model, and mentor figure. Even if Spender would eventually outgrow the master-pupil quality of their early friendship, his journals are vivid testimony to the life-long bond that united the three men in spite of geographical distance, professional rivalry, and personal animosity. In a journal entry composed only a few months before his death, Spender looks back on the relationship between the trio of friends, which in the survivor's recollection gets imbued with an almost otherworldly aura: "Such relationships—friendships—have a touch of eternity about them. 'We' are in a virtuous and all-forgiving and indulging way, 'the gang'".[9] Spender's project of memorialising the 'gang' and their close ties also becomes visible in his poem "Auden's Fu-

gezogen, was seine Übersetzungen von Rilkes *Duineser Elegien* (mit J.B. Leishman, 1939) und Schillers *Maria Stuart* (1958) belegen. Seine Liebe zu Deutschland lag auch in seiner Familiengeschichte begründet: Seine Mutter Violet Schuster entstammte einer jüdischen Bankiersfamilie aus Frankfurt am Main. Obwohl die Familie Schuster zum Christentum konvertiert war und sich unauffällig unter das englische Establishment gemischt hatte, legte Spender großen Wert auf sein kulturelles Erbe, das er für sein gefühltes Außenseitertum innerhalb der oberen englischen Mittelklasse verantwortlich machte.

Nachdem Spender sein Studium in Oxford ohne Abschluss abgebrochen hatte, reiste er 1929/30 über Hamburg nach Berlin, um Auden und Isherwood zu folgen. Er betrachtete die beiden Männer, die nur etwas älter waren, als seine Helden, Vorbilder und Lehrmeister in einer Person. Und obwohl Spender über die Jahre dem Meister-Schüler-Modell ihrer frühen Freundschaft entwachsen sollte, sind seine Tagebücher ein eindrucksvolles Zeugnis von der lebenslangen Verbindung, die trotz räumlicher Entfernungen, beruflicher Rivalitäten und persönlicher Animositäten zwischen den drei Männern bestand. Wenige Monate vor seinem Tod erinnert er sich in seinem Tagebuch an die Beziehung dieser drei Freunde, die für den Überlebenden rückblickend eine fast schon übernatürliche Qualität erhält: »Beziehungen – Freundschaften – dieser Art haben etwas Überirdisches an sich. Das ›Wir‹ vereint sich in vollendeter Form mit viel Großmut und Toleranz zu ›einer Gruppe‹.«[9] Spenders Wunsch, der »Gruppe« und ihrem engen Verhältnis ein Denkmal zu setzen, kommt auch in seinem Gedicht »Auden's Funeral« (Audens Begräbnis) zum Ausdruck. In diesen Isherwood gewidmeten Versen beschreibt er

neral", which is dedicated to Isherwood and imagines the dead Auden triumphing over his companions, who remain tethered to the world and trapped in their roles of chroniclers and public men of letters.[10]

A mere cursory glance at Spender's prose and poetry reveals the pivotal impact of his encounter with Auden during the latter's final year at Oxford. The "young bow-tied near-albino undergraduate" would invite him to his rooms at Christ Church, "blinds drawn down at midday / To shut the sun out",[11] to cross-examine him on his views on art and literature. Reimagined over and over again across genres and media throughout Spender's life, the scene gets solidified into one of his most powerful autobiographical myths that testifies to Auden's enduring intellectual influence over Spender. Auden immediately commenced to educate the willing disciple in his literary tastes and poetic self-fashioning. Regularly holding forth on a range of literary and philosophical topics in a "mixture of sense and nonsense, fun and portentousness, malice and generosity", Auden would deliver his authoritative lectures in a "secret language" that was the prime ingredient in "the witches' brew from which a literary movement is made".[12] Through Auden, Spender also met the person who would eventually become his entry ticket and guide to Berlin: Christopher Isherwood. The encounter with Isherwood, who had been sent down from Cambridge and made no secret of his disdain for the Oxbridge system, its snobbishness, and exclusivity, made a momentous impression on

Audens Triumph über seine beiden Gefährten, die weiterhin in der Welt umherirren und in ihren Rollen als Chronisten und angesehene Literaten gefangen sind.[10]

Bereits ein kurzer Blick auf Spenders Prosa und Lyrik macht die einschneidende Wirkung seiner Begegnung mit Auden in dessen Abschlussjahr in Oxford deutlich, als ihn der »junge, fast schon albinohafte Undergraduate mit Fliege« auf einen Besuch in seine Bude im Christ Church College einlud, um ihn »im abgedunkelten Zimmer hinter geschlossenen Gardinen«[11] über seine Ansichten zu Kunst und Literatur zu befragen. Spender hat sich Zeit seines Lebens immer wieder in unterschiedlichen literarischen Formen und verschiedenen Medien an diese Szene erinnert. Auf diese Weise schuf er eine seiner eindrucksvollsten autobiografischen Mythen, die auch ein Beleg für den nachhaltigen intellektuellen Einfluss sind, den Auden auf Spender ausübte. Er weihte den wissbegierigen Schüler bereitwillig in seine literarischen Vorlieben und Techniken der dichterischen Selbstinszenierung ein. In regelmäßigen Vorträgen zu literarischen und philosophischen Themen mit »ihrer Mischung aus Klugheit und Unsinn, Ironie und Heilsbotschaft, Bosheit und Wohlwollen«, wählte Auden für seine Belehrungen eine »Geheimsprache«, die als Hauptzutat dienen sollte für »das Hexengebräu, aus dem eine literarische Richtung entspringt«.[12] Durch Auden lernte Spender auch den Mann kennen, der ihn eines Tages nach und durch Berlin führen würde: Christopher Isherwood. Die Begegnung mit Isherwood, der der Cambridger Universität verwiesen worden war und keinerlei Hehl aus seiner tiefen Abneigung gegen das Oxbridge-System mit seinem Snobismus und Standesdünkel machte, hinterließ bei Spender einen bleibenden Eindruck und bestärkte ihn in seinem

Spender and hardened his resolve to "leave Oxford, to write and to live". No other place, it seemed, would lend itself so ideally to such an experiment as Berlin, where, according to Isherwood, "all the obstructions and complexities of this life were cut through".[13]

*****

Spender's experience of Berlin, when he moved there from Hamburg in 1930, was essentially filtered through Isherwood, who had settled there permanently after Auden's return to England in July 1929 to start work as a schoolteacher. The account he provides of his time in Berlin between 1930 and 1933 in *World Within World* reveals a symbiotic attachment to the older friend, whose independence, free-spirited adventurousness, and renunciation of his home country and upper-class background fascinated Spender. Embracing poverty and squalor with performative gusto and completely unshackled from convention or any standards of institutional approval, Isherwood is credited with being a catalyst in Spender's process of personal and artistic self-realisation. Once more, Spender plays the familiar part of the loyal disciple who eagerly absorbs the vibrant, morally loose, and politically charged atmosphere of Berlin through his mentor, a scene described half-mockingly by Isherwood in *Christopher and His Kind*:

> Mentor and pupil must have made an arresting pair, as they walked the streets and parks of Berlin together. [...] The Pupil,

Entschluss, »das College zu verlassen, Schriftsteller zu werden und mich auszuleben.« Kein anderer Ort, so schien es, würde sich besser für ein solches Experiment eignen als Berlin, wo laut Isherwood »dem Leben solche Hindernisse und Hemmungen wegoperiert waren«.[13]

*****

Im Jahr 1930 zog Spender von Hamburg nach Berlin. Isherwood, der sich fest in Berlin niedergelassen hatte, nachdem Auden im Juli 1929 für eine Anstellung als Lehrer nach England zurückgekehrt war, hatte maßgeblichen Einfluss auf seine Erlebnisse in der Stadt. Spenders Berichte über seine Berliner Zeit zwischen 1930 und 1933 in *Welt in der Welt* zeugen von einer symbiotischen Beziehung mit seinem älteren Freund, dessen Unabhängigkeit, unkonventionelles ereignisreiches Leben und Abkehr von seinem Heimatland und seiner großbürgerlichen Herkunft Spender faszinierten. Er bezeichnet Isherwood, der Armut und Elend mit fast schon enthusiastischem Eifer hinnahm und sich vollkommen von allen Konventionen oder Standards der institutionellen Anerkennung befreit hatte, als wichtigen Impulsgeber seiner persönlichen und künstlerischen Selbstverwirklichung. Einmal mehr schlüpft Spender hier in die vertraute Rolle des treu ergebenen Jüngers, der sich bereitwillig von seinem Lehrer in die pulsierende, hemmungslose und politisch aufgeladene Atmosphäre des Berliner Lebens einführen lässt. Dieses Verhältnis beschreibt Isherwood in *Christopher und die Seinen* mit leicht spöttischem Unterton:

> Lehrer und Schüler müssen ein auffallendes Gespann gewesen sein, wenn sie durch die Straßen und Grünanlagen von Berlin gingen. [...]

> striding along beside the brisk, large-headed little figure of the Mentor, keeps bending his beautiful scarlet face downward, lest he shall miss a word, laughing in anticipation as he does so. There are four and a half years between their ages and at least seven inches between their heights. The Pupil already has a stoop, as all tall people must who are eager to hear what the rest of the world is saying. And maybe the Mentor, that little tormentor, actually lowers his voice at times, to make the Pupil bend even lower.[14]

The "Pupil" religiously follows his mentor's routines, including his infamous lunches of "horse flesh and lung soup", followed by long walks to Grunewald along the lakeside.[15] In his autobiography he offers colourful glimpses of their life during those early days in Berlin, when Spender would rise early and stroll over from his lodgings in Motzstraße to Isherwood's rooms in Nollendorfstraße. There he would be admitted by Isherwood's landlady, Fräulein Thurau, and find himself amidst the "characters of his as yet unwritten novels".[16]

Here Spender gets to observe the miraculous transformation of the "real [...] [into] the malleable" and study Isherwood's method of scourging life and people for material for his fiction:

> Perhaps Bobbi the bar-tender would shoot fish-like through this central tank and escape into another room, or perhaps Sally Bowles would appear, her

---

> Während dieser Schüler neben der quirligen kleinen Gestalt mit dem großen Kopf, seinem Lehrer, dahinlatscht, reckt er fortwährend sein schönes lila Gesicht nach unten, um ja kein Wort zu verlieren, und lacht dabei vorfreudig. Es liegen viereinhalb Jahr Alters- und etwa zwanzig Zentimeter Größenunterschied zwischen ihnen. Und wie alle langen Menschen, die hören wollen, was der Rest der Welt sagt, hat der Schüler bereits einen leicht gekrümmten Rücken. Kann sogar sein, dass der Lehrer, dieser kleine Sadist, zwischendurch seine Stimme senkt, damit sich der Schüler noch tiefer bücken muss.[14]

Die Beziehung zwischen »Schüler« und Lehrer »entwickelte sich [...] fahrplanmäßig«.[15] Nach einem ihrer berüchtigten Mittagessen in Form von »Pferdefleisch, Lungenhaschee oder ähnliche[m]« unternahmen sie im Grunewald lange Spaziergänge am Seeufer.[16] Spenders Autobiografie bietet eindrucksvolle Einblicke in ihr Leben während dieser frühen Berlin-Phase. Damals stand Spender frühmorgens auf und schlenderte von seinem möblierten Zimmer in der Motzstraße zu Isherwoods Bleibe in der Nollendorfstraße. Dort öffnete ihm Isherwoods Wirtin, Fräulein Thurau, die Tür, und er fand sich »zwischen den Figuren aus einem noch ungeschriebenen Roman Christophers«[17] wieder.

An diesem Ort wurde Spender zum Mitspieler der Verwandlung, »wie sein Kopf die Wirklichkeit umschmiedete« und schaute Isherwood dabei zu, wie er dem Leben und den Menschen den Stoff für seine Prosa entnahm:

> Bobby, der Barmixer, etwa kam wie ein Fisch aus seinem Aquarium herausgeschossen, oder Sally

Places
Nollendorfstraße 17

This building, which has become the object of literary pilgrimage, houses the apartment where Isherwood lodged in the early 1930s. His landlady, a woman named Meta Thurau, became the unforgettable Frl. Schroeder in the Berlin stories. The apartment on Nollendorfstraße is the link between real, imagined, and mythical Berlin in Isherwood's career. In his Berlin novels, he uses it both as a location and as a way to hold together the episodic narratives. The window on Nollendorfstraße offered a vantage point from which he could experience the goings-on in the street as a detached observer. At the same time, the interior worked as a stage where the lives of the characters—Mr Norris, Sally Bowles, Bobby, Frl. Mayr, and of course Chris alias Herr Issyvoo—criss-crossed under the gaze of Frl. Schroeder, the comic anti puppet-master. The typical set-up of the Berlin boarding house, where lodgers lived independently but were forced to interact with one another in shared spaces, features in a number of British memoirs. It provided Isherwood with a clever mechanism to balance detachment and intimacy. Isherwood visited the flat in Nollendorfstraße again on his only postwar visit to Berlin in 1952. His account of the reunion between Herr Issyvoo and Frl. Schroeder, printed in *The Observer*, proved that *his* Berlin had survived the devastation of the Second World War.

Orte
Nollendorfstraße 17

In diesem Gebäude, das mittlerweile ein literarischer Wallfahrtsort geworden ist, wohnte Isherwood in den frühen 1930er Jahren zur Untermiete. Seine Wirtin Meta Thurau diente ihm als Vorbild für das unvergessliche Fräulein Schroeder seiner Berliner Geschichten. In Isherwoods Schriftstellerleben verbindet die Wohnung an der Nollendorfstraße das reale, das erfundene und das mythische Berlin miteinander. Er setzt diesen Ort sowohl als Schauplatz als auch als verknüpfendes Element zwischen den einzelnen Episoden seiner Berliner Geschichten ein. Von seinem Fenster an der Nollendorfstraße konnte er die Ereignisse auf der Straße als unbeteiligter Beobachter gut verfolgen. Gleichzeitig dienten ihm die Räumlichkeiten als Bühne, auf der sich seine Figuren – Mr Norris, Sally Bowles, Bobby, Fräulein Mayr und natürlich Chris alias Herr Issiwu – begegnen konnten. Stets unter den wachsamen Augen der komischen Fräulein Schroeder, die sich verzweifelt darum bemühte, alle Fäden zusammenzuhalten. In dieser typischen Berliner Pension hatten die Mieter*innen ihr eigenes Zimmer und mussten andere Wohnbereiche miteinander teilen. Viele Brit*innen haben in ihren Memoiren von derartigen Erfahrungen berichtet. Für Isherwood bot dieses raffinierte Arrangement den Vorteil eines Rückzugsortes in vertrauter Umgebung. Während seines einzigen Berlin-Besuchs nach dem Krieg kehrte er 1952 noch einmal in die Wohnung zurück. Seinem Bericht über das Wiedersehen zwischen Herrn Issiwu und Fräulein Schroeder, der im *Observer* erschien, ist zu entnehmen, dass *sein* Berlin der Verwüstung durch den Zweiten Weltkrieg standgehalten hatte.

[Fig. 40: A page from Stephen Spender's photo album showing Berlin connections including Christopher Isherwood and Jean Ross. Ross was the 'original' for Isherwood's character of Sally Bowles, unknown photographer, 1930s]

clothes dishevelled, her eyes large onyxes fringed by eyelashes like enamelled wire, in a face of carved ivory. Christopher lived in this apartment surrounded by the models for his creations, like one of those portraits of a writer by a bad painter, in which the writer is depicted meditating in his chair whilst the characters of his novels radiate round him under a glowing cloud of dirty varnish, not unlike the mote-laden lighting of Fräulein Thurau's apartment.[17]

Bowles tauchte auf, schlampig, die Augen gleich großen Onyxen, umrahmt von Wimpern wie lackierter Draht, eingesetzt in ein Gesicht, das aus Elfenbein geschnitzt schien. Christopher lebte hier, umgeben von seinen künftigen Romangestalten, ähnlich wie der Dichter auf den allegorischen Schinken der Gründerjahre konterfeit war: im Lehnstuhl hingegossen, umschwebt von den Geschöpfen seiner Phantasie in schimmerndem Reigen, der an die trüben, mückenumtanzten Lampen in Fräulein Thuraus Wohnung erinnerte.[18]

[Abb. 40: Eine Seite aus Stephen Spenders Fotoalbum mit Berliner Bekannten, mit Christopher Isherwood und Jean Ross. Ross war das Vorbild für Isherwoods Figur der Sally Bowles, unbekannter Fotograf, 1930er]

The routine of the urban *flaneur*, mapped out between cheap cafés and seedy bars, avant-garde theatres, cinemas, and lakeside shores, was occasionally punctuated by holiday trips, such as the one to Sellin, on the island of Rügen, in June 1931, when Spender and Isherwood were joined by Auden. Spender's efforts at documenting their holiday with his camera resulted in the iconic shot of him towering over his two friends on either side, wearing an "expression on his face which suggests an off-duty

Ihre Routinen als Flaneure in der Stadt, die zwischen günstigen Cafés und Spelunken, Avantgarde-Bühnen, Lichtspielhäusern und Seeufern pendelten, wurden immer wieder von kleinen Reisen unterbrochen, die Spender und Isherwood im Juni 1931 auch in Begleitung von Auden nach Sellin auf der Insel Rügen führten. Spender wollte ihren Urlaub mit seiner Fotokamera dokumentieren. Dabei entstand auch die unvergessliche Aufnahme, auf der Spender in der Mitte die beiden Freunde deutlich überragt, »wobei sein Gesichtsausdruck an einen Freizeit-Jesus erinnert, der sich mit den ›Kindlein‹ entspannt«, wie

Stephen Spender schreibt den Berliner Mythos

Jesus relaxing with 'these little ones'", as Isherwood would describe it in his memoir (see figure 8 in the Introduction).¹⁸ The photograph, which encapsulates the ideal of friendship and the possibilities of youth so central to these young English writers' lives in Weimar Germany, was restaged more than fifteen years later on Fire Island, New York, when Auden, Spender, and Isherwood were reunited after the war.

It also captures the myriad shades in which this idea of friendship could be played out, from outright idolisation and

es Isherwood später in seinen Memoiren beschrieb (siehe Abbildung 8 in der Einleitung).¹⁹ Diese Fotografie, die Auden, Spender und Isherwood mehr als fünfzehn Jahre später bei ihrem ersten Wiedersehen nach dem Krieg auf Fire Island im Bundesstaat New York noch einmal nachstellten, steht sinnbildlich für das Ideal der Freundschaft und für die Möglichkeiten der Jugend, die das Leben dieser jungen englischen Schriftsteller im Deutschland der Weimarer Jahre so nachhaltig prägten.

Sie zeigt zudem die unendlichen Formen, die diese Idee der Freundschaft annehmen konnte und die von einer bedingungslosen Verehrung und einsei-

[Fig. 41: W. H. Auden, Stephen Spender, and Christopher Isherwood on Fire Island, New York, photograph by Lincoln Kirstein, 1947]

[Abb. 41: W. H. Auden, Stephen Spender und Christopher Isherwood auf Fire Island, New York, Fotografie von Lincoln Kirstein, 1947]

lop-sided mentorship to homoerotically charged camaraderie, which, as Spender noted in his 1939 *September Journal*, was not "cynical, shame-faced, smart, snobbish or stodgy, as so often in England".[19] From the beginning, Spender sought to counteract his image of bright-eyed pupil by taking on the role of chronicler and myth-maker. His youthful boisterousness is only thinly laced with self-mockery when he writes to Isherwood about the Rügen photograph: "with a masturbatory camera designed for narcissists I took—or it took—the most famous photograph in the history of the world, of US THREE".[20] Often resentful of it at the time, as Isherwood looks back, he acknowledges the impact of Spender's efforts at autobiographically documenting shared experience:

> It was Stephen, not Christopher, who ought to have said, "I am a camera," in those days. Now we survivors can feel nothing but gratitude to him for his tireless clicking. He saved so many bits of our youth for us.[21]

Spender proved to be ideally suited for the task he had set himself. Driven, at least initially, by the disciple's eagerness to absorb, record, and mediate, he would always retain the double inside/outside perspective of the wanderer who moves with ease between the worlds: social, cultural, literary, public, private. While Isherwood—and Auden, later, too, when they both emigrated to the United States in 1939—would readily cut

their ties with their home country, Spender never lost touch with England and always kept one foot within the London literary world. By his own account in *World Within World*, between 1930 and 1933, he spent half of each year in Germany; during the other half, he was busy making use of his high-profile connections in publishing and literary journalism, rubbing shoulders with T.S. Eliot, the Woolfs, the Sitwells, the Lehmanns and other members of the Bloomsbury set to carve out a prominent position for himself in the London literary establishment. Spender was quickly swept up by the social whirlwind of literary life, and would always struggle to negotiate the tension between art and action, between the creative and the public life. The world he encountered he portrays as a splendidly isolated one, whose genteel vision of Europe was limited to the "Salzburg Music festival, French Impressionism, the Lake of Geneva, and of course the museums and art galleries": "Nothing could have been more different from the atmosphere of Berlin than this way of living, which had hardly been shaken by the war or even by the economic crisis".[22] In fact, quite a few members of the London literary circles he frequented were familiar with some of the Berlin worlds in which Spender and his friends moved. Yet, from Spender's retrospective account it becomes clear that he was busy shaping the Berlin Myth and quite determined to exploit it strategically in order to increase his own reputational capital. This led to a temporary falling-out with Isherwood. Trading on the stories of

und später auch Auden, nachdem beide 1939 in die Vereinigten Staaten emigriert waren – den Kontakt zu seinem Heimatland bereitwillig abbrach, gab Spender seine Verbindung zu England niemals auf und stand im ständigen Austausch mit dem Londoner Literaturbetrieb. Wie er in *Welt in der Welt* beschreibt, verbrachte er von 1930 bis 1933 jedes Jahr etwa sechs Monate in Deutschland. In der übrigen Zeit pflegte er seine hochkarätigen Beziehungen zur Londoner Verlagswelt und zum Literaturjournalismus und verkehrte mit T.S. Eliot, den Woolfs, den Sitwells, den Lehmanns und anderen Mitgliedern des Bloomsbury-Sets, um sich eine bedeutende Position im Londoner Literaturbetrieb zu sichern. Schnell geriet Spender in den gesellschaftlichen Strudel des literarischen Lebens. Er befand sich im ständigen Kampf, sein künstlerisches Schaffen und seine gesellschaftlichen Verpflichtungen, sein kreatives und sein öffentliches Leben miteinander in Einklang zu bringen. In London begegnete er nach eigener Beschreibung einer Welt, die vollkommen abseits stand und sich von Europa nur den vornehmen Anblick der »Salzburger Festspiele, der französischen Impressionisten, des Genfer Sees und selbstverständlich der Museen« gestattete: »Es war der denkbar größte Gegensatz zu meinem Leben in Berlin: hier schien alles fast unberührt von Krieg und Wirtschaftskrise«.[23] Tatsächlich waren mehrere Angehörige seiner literarischen Kreise in London mit einigen der Berliner Milieus vertraut, in denen Spender und seine Freunde verkehrten. Doch Spenders rückblickende Beobachtungen machen deutlich, dass ihm vor allem daran gelegen war, den Mythos Berlin fortzuschreiben. Zudem war er fest entschlossen, diesen Mythos strategisch einzusetzen, um seine eigene Reputation zu steigern. Dies führte zum vorübergehenden Bruch mit Isherwood: Als Spender

their life in Berlin, which, in Spender's case, was lived vicariously through Isherwood, Spender not only sparked his "Mentor's" professional jealousy but, more importantly, challenged his ownership over the Berlin narrative and its uses. The storm in a teacup would quickly blow over, but it did prompt Spender to drop the dedication to Isherwood from the first edition of his first published poetry collection, *Poems, 1933*, and offer it to another influential mentor figure, the eminent German literary scholar and critic Ernst Robert Curtius, who had guided Spender's studies in German literature and culture. Curtius declined the honour, and the book's second impression was once more dedicated to Isherwood.

Spender's emancipation from "Berlin disciple into a London literary figure"[23] as well as the increasingly fraught political situation in Germany eventually brought the friends' joint Berlin life to an end, but marked only the beginning of their retrospective myth-making projects. In these projects, the common experience of the twilight years of Weimar Berlin emerges as a central theme that underlies the identity-shaping narrative of a group of young writers who "ganged up and captured the decade", as Evelyn Waugh puts it in his scathing review of *World Within World*.[24] Writing in May 1951, Waugh is violently dismissive of Auden, Isherwood, and Spender and their success in claiming 1930s literature for themselves. He regards their literary fame as largely undeserved and shrewdly recognises that much of it is root-

diese stellvertretend von Isherwood durchlebte Berliner Zeit für seine eigenen Zwecke nutzte, kam es nicht nur zu einem beruflichen Interessenkonflikt mit seinem »Lehrer«. Er stellte damit auch Isherwoods alleinigen Anspruch auf die Schilderung und Verwertung der Berliner Erlebnisse in Frage. Obwohl sich der Sturm im Wasserglas schnell beruhigen sollte, strich Spender im Anschluss die Widmung für Isherwood aus der Erstausgabe seiner ersten veröffentlichten Gedichtsammlung *Poems, 1933*. Er wollte sie stattdessen einem weiteren einflussreichen Mentor widmen, dem angesehenen deutschen Literaturwissenschaftler und Kritiker Ernst Robert Curtius, der Spender bei seinen Studien der deutschen Literatur und Kultur unterstützt hatte. Doch Curtius lehnte diese Auszeichnung ab, und die zweite Auflage des Buchs enthielt wieder eine Widmung für Isherwood.

Spenders Verwandlung vom »Berliner Jünger in einen Londoner Literaten«[24] sowie die zunehmend angespannte politische Lage in Deutschland führten schließlich dazu, dass das gemeinsame Berliner Leben der beiden Freunde ein Ende fand. Doch die retrospektive Mythenbildung stand damit gerade erst an ihrem Anfang. Und die gemeinsamen Erlebnisse in den letzten Jahren der Weimarer Republik bilden das zentrale Thema, auf dem die identitätsstiftenden Erzählungen einer Gruppe junger Schriftsteller beruhen, die »sich zu einer Gang zusammenschlossen und das Jahrzehnt für sich eroberten«, wie Evelyn Waugh in seinem Verriss zu *Welt in der Welt* vom Mai 1951 schreibt.[25] Waugh fällt darin ein vernichtendes Urteil über Auden, Isherwood und Spender und ihren erfolgreichen Anspruch, die Literaturszene der 1930er Jahre maßgeblich bestimmt zu haben. Ihr literarischer Ruhm sei größtenteils unverdient und laut seinem scharfsinnigen Urteil im Wesentlichen auf ihr

ed in their knack for self-promotion and, most importantly, their "chumminess":

> They clung together. They collaborated. It seemed always to take at least two of them to generate any literary work however modest. They praised one another tirelessly and an unfavourable review anywhere raised a babble of protest from the authors' young friends.25

Even as the 'gang' dispersed with the outbreak of war in 1939 and Auden and Isherwood's permanent relocation to the United States, the short-lived but defining experience of Berlin would remain central to their life-long ties of friendship. Both Auden and Spender returned to Germany after the war in official capacities: Auden as a member of the US Strategic Bombing Survey, and Spender in his mission for the Civilian Military Forces of the Allied Control Commission, which had tasked him with investigating the ideological climate among German intellectuals and university teachers. Once more, Spender kept a journal, and his observations, primarily of Bonn and Cologne, formed the basis for his *Rhineland Journal* (first published in *Horizon* in December 1945) and his book *European Witness* (1946). In October 1945, he briefly visited Berlin, complete with a tour of Hitler's bunker, only to find that the city, war-torn and ravaged, was transformed beyond all recognition. And yet, more than 15 years later, on a visit to Berlin in June 1962,

Talent zur Selbstvermarktung und ihre »Geselligkeit« zurückzuführen:

> Sie hielten zusammen wie Pech und Schwefel. Sie kollaborierten miteinander. Es schien, als müssten immer zwei von ihnen zur gleichen Zeit ein literarisches Werk erschaffen, ganz gleich wie unbedeutend. Unablässig lobten sie sich gegenseitig und jedwede negative Kritik hatte ein lautes Protestgeheul ihrer jungen Anhänger zur Folge.26

Selbst nachdem sich die »Gruppe« mit dem Kriegsausbruch im Jahr 1939 und dem dauerhaften Umzug von Auden und Isherwood in die Vereinigten Staaten aufgelöst hatte, sollte ihre kurze, aber prägende Zeit in Berlin einen wichtigen Einfluss auf ihre lebenslange Freundschaft haben. Nach Kriegsende kehrten Auden und Spender in offiziellen Funktionen nach Deutschland zurück: Auden als Mitglied der »US Strategic Bombing Survey« und Spender als Angehöriger der zivilen militärischen Kräfte der Alliierten Kontrollkommission, mit dem Auftrag, das ideologische Klima unter deutschen Intellektuellen und Hochschullehrkräften zu erkunden. Spender führte auch in dieser Zeit Tagebuch. Seine hauptsächlich auf Bonn und Köln bezogenen Beobachtungen bildeten die Grundlage für sein *Rhineland Journal* (das zum ersten Mal im Dezember 1945 in *Horizon* veröffentlicht wurde) und für sein Buch *European Witness* (1946). Im Oktober 1945 besichtigte er während eines kurzen Berlin-Besuchs auch den Führerbunker und stellte bei dieser Gelegenheit fest, dass sich die vom Krieg zerstörte und verwüstete Stadt bis zur Unkenntlichkeit verändert hatte. Nichtsdestotrotz kommt Spender mehr als 15 Jahre später während eines Berlin-Besuchs im Juni 1962 nach einem Abendspa-

following an evening walk down crowded Kurfürstendamm, Spender concludes: "Quite felt I belonged in Berlin again". Rather than on a set of landmarks, it seems that the Berlin Myth most enduringly relies on a feeling—a "feeling of commonality, of belonging to one another", which is rooted in a general sense of "respect for individuality and culture" and which, in turn, binds together those who have experienced it.[26]

ziergang am belebten Kurfürstendamm zu folgendem Schluss: »Fühlte mich doch wieder zu Hause in Berlin«. Es scheint, als beruhe der Berliner Mythos nicht auf einer Reihe von Sehenswürdigkeiten, sondern im Wesentlichen auf einer emotionalen Verbindung mit der Stadt – einem »Gefühl der Gemeinsamkeit, der engen Verbundenheit«, das sich auf eine grundsätzliche »Achtung für Individualität und Kultur« stützt und wiederum all diejenigen miteinander verbindet, die es erleben konnten.[27]

Notes

1 Stephen Spender: Drop Me a Name, in: The Observer, 25 March 1979.
2 Louis MacNeice: The Strings are False. An Unfinished Autobiography, London, Faber & Faber 1965, p. 128.
3 Stephen Spender: World Within World, 1951, London, Faber & Faber 1997, p. 107.
4 Stephen Spender: New Selected Journals 1939–1995, ed. by Lara Feigel and John Sutherland, with Natasha Spender, London, Faber & Faber 2012, p. 736.
5 Ibid., p. 703.
6 Stephen Spender: Life Wasn't a Cabaret, in: The New York Times, 30 October 1977.
7 Spender: World Within World, pp. 127 f.
8 Stephen Spender: Looking Back in 1994, in: World Within World, pp. vii–xviii, here p. ix.
9 Spender: New Selected Journals, p. 742.
10 Stephen Spender: Auden's Funeral, in: London Review of Books 3/10, 4 June 1981.
11 Stephen Spender: To W. H. Auden on His Sixtieth Birthday, in: New Collected Poems, ed. by Michael Brett, London, Faber & Faber 2004, pp. 306 f., here p. 306.
12 Spender: World Within World, p. 63.
13 Ibid., p. 102.
14 Christopher Isherwood: Christopher and His Kind, 1976, London, Vintage 2012, p. 57.

Anmerkungen

1 Stephen Spender: Drop Me a Name, in: The Observer, 25. März 1979.
2 Louis MacNeice: The Strings are False: An Unfinished Autobiography, London, Faber & Faber 1965, S. 128.
3 Stephen Spender: Welt in der Welt, aus dem Englischen von Andreas Sattler, München, R. Piper GmbH & Co. KG 1992, S. 142.
4 Stephen Spender: New Selected Journals 1939–1995, hg. von Lara Feigel und John Sutherland, mit Natasha Spender, London, Faber & Faber 2012, S. 736.
5 Ebd., S. 703.
6 Stephen Spender: Life Wasn't a Cabaret, in: The New York Times, 30. Oktober 1977.
7 Spender: Welt in der Welt, S. 127 f.
8 Stephen Spender: Looking Back in 1994, in: World Within World, London, Faber & Faber 1997, S. vii–xviii, hier S. ix. Das englische Vorwort, aus dem dieses Zitat stammt, ist in der in diesem Katalog zitierten Ausgabe nicht enthalten.
9 Spender: New Selected Journals, S. 742.
10 Stephen Spender: Auden's Funeral, in: London Review of Books 3/10, 4. Juni 1981.
11 Stephen Spender: To W. H. Auden on His Sixtieth Birthday, in: New Collected Poems, hg. von Michael Brett, London, Faber & Faber 2004, S. 306 f., hier S. 306.
12 Spender: Welt in der Welt, S. 94 f.
13 Ebd., S. 138.
14 Christopher Isherwood: Willkommen in Berlin. Christopher und die Seinen, aus dem Englischen von Stefan Troß-

15 Spender: World Within World, p. 119.
16 Ibid., p. 122.
17 Ibid., p. 124, p. 120.
18 Isherwood: Christopher and His Kind, p. 84.
19 Spender: New Selected Journals, p. 8.
20 Quoted in: Isherwood: Christopher and His Kind, p. 84.
21 Ibid., p. 96.
22 Spender: World Within World, pp. 138 f.
23 Ibid.
24 Evelyn Waugh: Two Unquiet Lives, in: The Essays, Articles and Reviews of Evelyn Waugh, ed. by Donat Gallagher, London, Methuen 1983, pp. 394–398, here p. 394.
25 Ibid.
26 Spender: New Selected Journals, pp. 301 f.

bach, 1. Auflage dieser Ausgabe, Berlin, Bruno Gmünder Verlag, 2014, S. 61 f.
15 Spender: Welt in der Welt, S. 157.
16 Ebd., S. 157 ff.
17 Ebd., S. 158.
18 Ebd. S. 162, 158.
19 Isherwood. Christopher und die Seinen, S. 88.
20 Spender: New Selected Journals, S. 8.
21 Zitiert in Isherwood: Christopher und die Seinen, S. 88.
22 Ebd., S. 100.
23 Spender: Welt in der Welt, S. 181 f.
24 Ebd., S. 220.
25 Evelyn Waugh: Two Unquiet Lives, in: The Essays, Articles and Reviews of Evelyn Waugh, hg. von Donat Gallagher, London, Methuen 1983, S. 394–398, hier S. 394.
26 Ebd.
27 Spender: New Selected Journals, S. 301 f.

Sofia Permiakova

From the 1920s to the 2020s: The Myth of Weimar Berlin in Contemporary British Art, Music, and Literature

Von 1920 bis 2020: Der Mythos Berlin in der britischen Kunst, Musik und Literatur der Gegenwart

The *Weimarer Republik* and the Berlin of the 1920s and '30s are cultural landmarks for Germany. What appears increasingly obvious, however, is that the myth of Weimar Berlin is not intended for German consumption only. The centenary of the Weimar Republic in 2019 was also surprisingly relevant for British cultural institutions and British audiences: indeed, in some ways, the occasion was celebrated in the UK with no less resonance and dedication than it was in Germany. 2020s London, finding itself in the liminal space of Brexit limbo, appears to be embracing the myth of 1920s Berlin.

Halfway through the centenary year, Sally Hughes from *The Guardian* noticed that several key British cultural institutions presented programmes inspired by the Weimar Republic and Weimar Berlin. The British Film Institute curated a series entitled *Beyond Your Wildest Dreams: Weimar Cinema 1919–1933*, featuring numerous Fritz Lang films and Berlin classics such as

Die Weimarer Republik und das Berlin der 1920er und 1930er Jahre stehen für eine kulturelle Zeitenwende in der deutschen Geschichte. Doch es zeigt sich auch immer deutlicher, dass der mit dieser Zeit verbundene Mythos nicht nur ein deutsches Phänomen ist. Der 100. Jahrestag der Weimarer Republik im Jahr 2019 hat überraschenderweise auch in Großbritannien das Interesse der Kultureinrichtungen und der Öffentlichkeit geweckt: Die Jubiläumsfeierlichkeiten stießen dort tatsächlich auf eine ähnliche Resonanz und Begeisterung wie in Deutschland. Scheinbar findet das London der 2020er Jahre in der lähmenden Brexit-Übergangsphase Gefallen am Mythos Berlins der 1920er Jahre.

Im Lauf des Jubiläumsjahres bemerkte Sally Hughes vom *Guardian*, dass sich mehrere Kultureinrichtungen in ihrer Programmplanung von der Weimarer Republik und Berlin in dieser Zeit inspirieren ließen. Das British Film Institute kuratierte die Reihe »Beyond Your Wildest Dreams: Weimar Cinema 1919–1933« mit zahlreichen Filmen von Fritz Lang und Berlin-Klassikern wie Walter Ruttmanns *Berlin: Symphonie der Großstadt* (1927). Die einjährige Sonder-

Walter Ruttmann's *Berlin: Symphony of a Great City* (1927). Tate Modern presented the special exhibition *Magic Realism: Art in Weimar Germany 1919–33*, which ran successfully for a full year. The Philharmonia Orchestra and the Southbank Centre curated a series of events focusing on the world of Weimar Berlin in its many assets: concerts, cabaret performances, screenings, and lectures brought together under the title *Weimar Berlin: Bittersweet Metropolis*.[1] The reasons for such a profound interest appear to be, to a certain degree, pragmatic: the myth of Weimar Berlin is highly marketable, and the combination of sensation and tragedy, sexual freedom and modern aesthetics is still effective at attracting young audiences. However, there is also an undertone of didacticism in bringing the German 1920s to 2020s Britain. It is telling that the slogan chosen by the Southbank Centre read "Music, Film and Drama *for* Turbulent Times" rather than "*from* Turbulent Times": in this formulation, the turbulent times in question are clearly today and now, and the relevance of these works—political and inherently modern—to 21st-century Britain is hard to ignore.

In this context, it is not surprising that the series *Babylon Berlin*, portraying the complex and dark (under-)world of Berlin during the Weimar period, was hailed by the *Guardian* as "Germany's first TV blockbuster of the streaming era".[2] With the third season released in 2020, *Babylon Berlin* is one of the few international shows that have 'made it' in a global market that is largely

ausstellung »Magic Realism: Art in Weimar Germany 1919–33« in der Tate Modern war ein Publikumsmagnet. Das Philharmonia Orchestra und das Southbank Centre kuratierten eine Reihe mit Veranstaltungen zu den unterschiedlichen Facetten des kulturellen Lebens im Berlin der Weimarer Zeit: Unter dem Titel »Weimar Berlin: Bittersweet Metropolis« präsentierten sie eine Auswahl von Konzerten, Kabarettaufführungen, Filmvorführungen und Lesungen.[1] Ein solch ausgeprägtes Interesse mag bis zu einem gewissen Punkt auf pragmatischen Beweggründen beruhen: Der Mythos Berlins lässt sich hervorragend vermarkten, und auf ein internationales junges Publikum übt die Mischung aus Sensation und Tragödie, sexueller Freiheit und moderner Ästhetik noch immer eine große Anziehungskraft aus. Doch gleichzeitig hat es auch etwas Belehrendes, wenn das Deutschland der 1920er Jahre einem Publikum im Großbritannien der 2020er Jahre nähergebracht wird. Bezeichnenderweise wählte das Southbank Centre für sein Programm den Slogan »Musik, Film und Drama *für* turbulente Zeiten« (»Music, Film and Drama *for* the Turbulent Times«) und nicht »aus turbulenten Zeiten«. Ohne Zweifel bezieht sich diese Formulierung auf die Turbulenzen im Hier und Jetzt, und die Bedeutung dieser Auswahl von – politischen und zutiefst modernen – Werken für das Großbritannien des 21. Jahrhunderts ist nicht von der Hand zu weisen.

In diesem Zusammenhang überrascht es keineswegs, dass die Serie *Babylon Berlin*, die ein Portrait der komplexen und düsteren (Unter-)Welt Berlins in der Weimarer Zeit zeichnet, vom *Guardian* als »Deutschlands erster TV-Blockbuster der Streaming-Ära« angepriesen wurde.[2] Mit der Ausstrahlung der dritten Staffel im Jahr 2020 gehört *Babylon Berlin* zu den wenigen internationalen Serien, die es auf dem hauptsächlich von englischsprachigen Produktionen

dominated by English-language productions. In his review for the *New Republic*, Adrian Daub comments on the reasons for the TV show's international success:

> As much as Babylon Berlin fits into the long-standing fascination with the Weimar Republic, one gets the feeling it doesn't hold up the 1920s as contemporary Germany's distant mirror, but rather as everyone else's.[3]

Not unlike Weimar Berlin, contemporary Britain often finds itself on "the edge of a volcano" in a lot of public discourse around Brexit. The notion of "Weimar Britain" every now and again appears in both national (*The Guardian*) and international media (*Die Zeit, Aljazeera*). In this media climate, the desire to look back to the Germany of a hundred years ago in search of a warning is a curious strategy, both discursively and politically. With the COVID-19 pandemic happening almost exactly one hundred years after the Spanish Flu pandemic of 1918–1920, the parallels between the 1920s and the 2020s have become increasingly uncanny.

Not all of it is Brexit's fault. Weimar Berlin has not become attractive to Britons just recently: in 1972, the interest in the period increased following the tremendous international success of Bob Fosse's *Cabaret*. In 1976, David Bowie went to Berlin attracted by that image of the vibrant city tragically posed between two world wars which he knew from Christopher Ish-

Places
Ufa Pavillon am Nollendorfplatz

Berlin was a world capital of cinema in the interwar period. It was home to Ufa, the production and distribution company famous for its collaborations with Fritz Lang and F. W. Murnau that inspired many British writers and artists, including, later, David Bowie. For the young Alfred Hitchcock, working with the Berlin film industry was a career-changing experience. Berlin's thriving cinema culture formed part of the everyday life of the city. Many literary accounts of this period note the Berliners' passion for cinema-going and the massive presence of picture-houses throughout the city. The areas around Kurfürstendamm, Nollendorfplatz, and Potsdamerplatz were particularly known for their large glitzy cinemas, such as the Ufa Pavillon am Nollendorfplatz. But there were many smaller cinemas also in the suburbs and working-class districts. Cinema was a great draw for foreign visitors. Some came hoping to make it into the city's burgeoning film industry. Others simply enjoyed the enormous variety that was on offer. Tantalisingly, their memoirs or letters often simply mention that they had visited a cinema, not necessarily which film they had seen. For British visitors, a special attraction of Berlin cinemas was to see Soviet films, which were subject to severe censorship in Britain. Isherwood was an avid cinema-goer and he scattered filmic references throughout his Berlin novels. The English writer Bryher's experiences of Berlin cinema in the 1920s were instrumental to her introducing Eisenstein and Soviet cinema to Britain.

Orte
Ufa Pavillon am Nollendorfplatz

Berlin war in der Zeit zwischen den Weltkriegen die internationale Hauptstadt des Kinos. Hier hatte die Ufa ihren Sitz, die als Produktions- und Vertriebsgesellschaft durch ihre Zusammenarbeit mit Fritz Lang und F. W. Murnau Berühmtheit erlangte. Zahlreiche britische Schriftsteller*innen und Künstler*innen, später auch David Bowie, ließen sich von diesen Regisseuren inspirieren. Den jungen Alfred Hitchcock bewegte die Zusammenarbeit mit der Berliner Filmindustrie dazu, seiner Karriere eine neue Richtung zu geben. Berlins blühende Kinokultur war Teil des urbanen Alltagslebens. Viele Schriftsteller*innen berichten aus dieser Zeit, dass die Berliner*innen leidenschaftliche Kinogänger*innen waren und die Stadt eine riesige Auswahl an Lichtspielhäusern bot. Die Viertel rund um den Kurfürstendamm, den Nollendorfplatz und den Potsdamer Platz waren besonders bekannt für ihre großen glanzvollen Filmpaläste wie den Ufa Pavillon am Nollendorfplatz. Doch es gab auch zahlreiche kleinere Kinos in den Vororten und Arbeiterbezirken. Die Berliner Kinokultur übte eine große Anziehungskraft auf ausländische Besucher*innen aus. Einige von ihnen kamen in der Hoffnung, in der aufstrebenden Filmindustrie der Stadt Fuß zu fassen. Andere wollten einfach nur das umfangreiche Angebot der verschiedenen Kinos nutzen. Es ist bedauerlich, dass sie in ihren Erinnerungen oder Briefen häufig nur einen Kinobesuch erwähnen, selten jedoch, welchen Film sie gesehen haben. Für britische Besucher*innen waren die Berliner Filmtheater ganz besonders attraktiv, weil sie hier sowjetische Filme sehen konnten, die in Großbritannien einer strengen Zensur unterlagen. Isherwood war ein leidenschaftlicher Kinogänger. In seinen Berlin-Romanen werden Filme häufig erwähnt. Die Erlebnisse der englischen Schriftstellerin Bryher in der Berliner Filmwelt trugen maßgeblich dazu bei, dass sie ihre Landsleute mit dem Werk Sergej Eisensteins und dem sowjetischen Kino vertraut machen konnte.

[Fig. 42: Ufa Pavillon cinema on Nollendorfplatz, photograph by Martin Höhlig, 1928]

[Abb. 42: Ufa Pavillon-Kino am Nollendorfplatz, Fotografie von Martin Höhlig, 1928]

erwood's Berlin stories and the works of German Expressionist painters. Bowie corresponded with Isherwood and met him in the States. Isherwood even attended several of Bowie's concerts in the late '70s even though he was, according to his diaries, dreading the experience.[4] Isherwood attending Bowie's concert is a case of the Berlin myth turned on its head: Bowie, drawn to Isherwood's myth, has since become a significant part of the Berlin myth in his own right, attracting tourists, artists, and musicians to the city today. It is a Russian-doll effect, in which older myths of Berlin become essential parts of the more

Christopher Isherwoods Berliner Geschichten und die Werke deutscher Expressionisten bereits vertraut war. Bowie schrieb Isherwood Briefe und traf sich mit ihm in den Vereinigten Staaten. In den späten 1970er Jahren besuchte Isherwood sogar mehrere Bowie-Konzerte, notierte allerdings in seinem Tagebuch, dass ihm vor diesem Erlebnis grauste.[4] Isherwoods Besuche von Bowie-Konzerten sind ein interessantes Beispiel dafür, wie der Berliner Mythos auf den Kopf gestellt wird: Bowie, der sich einst von Isherwoods Mythos angezogen fühlte, hat sich inzwischen selbst zu einem wichtigen Teil des Berliner Mythos entwickelt, der heute Tourist*innen, Künstler*innen und Musiker*innen in die Stadt lockt. Diese Wirkung ist vergleichbar mit einer russischen Matrjoschka: Ältere

recent ones, therefore preserving their cultural significance.

Both Isherwood and Bowie feature as inspiration for the 2020 album of the legendary British pop duo Pet Shop Boys, *Hotspot*. Recorded at the Hansa Studios, a name still synonymous with Bowie's Berlin period, the album creates a space in which Bowie and Isherwood co-exist simultaneously. In the same way, in the song *Wedding in Berlin*, Mendelssohn's famous wedding tune merges with a techno-beat clearly inspired by more contemporary Berlin staples, such as the Love Parade or the Berghain club. The title "Wedding in Berlin" plays with the name of a working-class area in the city's North (Wedding). In an interview with the German magazine *Der Spiegel*, Chris Lowe and Neil Tennant explain how Isherwood inspired the opening song of the album, *Will-o-the-wisp*:

> While writing this song, I thought about Christopher Isherwood. […] Isherwood had a lover here before the start of the Second World War, who became a Nazi. I imagined how Isherwood, returning to the city after the war, sees his former lover again at the opposite side of the U-Bahn platform and wonders if he should even approach him.[5]

The song is steeped in Berlin's geography: the chorus refers to the underground line U1, which connects Charlottenburg with Kreuzberg and Friedrichshain. The U1

Berliner Mythen werden zu wesentlichen Bestandteilen neuerer Mythen und tragen damit zu ihrer kulturellen Bedeutung bei.

Sowohl Isherwood als auch Bowie dienten dem legendären britischen Pop-Duo Pet Shop Boys als Inspiration für ihr Album *Hotspot* aus dem Jahr 2020. Das Album wurde in den Hansa Studios aufgenommen, die auch heute noch in einem Atemzug mit Bowies Berliner Zeit genannt werden. Musikalisch schafft das Album einen Raum, in dem Bowie und Isherwood gleichermaßen präsent sind. So wie im Song »Wedding in Berlin« die berühmten Klänge aus Mendelssohns Hochzeitsmarsch mit einem Techno-Beat verschmelzen, der eindeutig von Berliner Gegenwartserscheinungen wie der Love Parade oder dem Berghain geprägt ist. Der Titel »Wedding in Berlin« ist zudem ein Wortspiel mit dem Namen eines bekannten Arbeiterbezirks im Norden der Stadt (Wedding). In einem Interview mit dem deutschen Magazin *Der Spiegel* erklären Chris Lowe und Neil Tennant, wie sie von Isherwood zum Eröffnungssong des Albums »Will-o-the-wisp« inspiriert wurden:

> Ich dachte dabei an den Schriftsteller Christopher Isherwood […]. Isherwood hatte hier vor dem Zweiten Weltkrieg einen Liebhaber, der Nazi wurde, und kehrte nach dem Krieg zurück in die Stadt. Ich stellte mir vor, wie Isherwood seinen ehemaligen Lover am anderen Ende der U-Bahn wiedersieht und sich fragt, ob er ihn überhaupt ansprechen soll.[5]

Der Song taucht ein in die Geografie Berlins: Im Refrain wird die U-Bahnlinie U1 besungen, die Charlottenburg mit Kreuzberg und Friedrichshain verbindet. Wie auf einer Zeitachse fährt die U1 vom Westen in den Osten der Stadt: Vom luxuriösen Ausgehviertel

goes from West to East almost like a timeline: from the city's most expensive party neighbourhood of the Weimar '20s to the most lively modern area of Berlin, which was—in Isherwood's time—one of its poorest working districts. In the song, the underground train emerges "from below past Nollendorfplatz" which is also an iconic location for the gay Berlin of the 1920s, due to the presence of the most prominent gay and lesbian bars. The protagonist wants to ask his former love interest: "Do you still hang around that old arcade / To see what luck will bring?". The reference to the arcade is not coincidental: in the 1920s, arcades were the centre of Berlin's commercial life and *flânerie* during the day, but they were also famous for cheap male prostitution during the night.[6] As the title of the song suggests, coming back to Berlin the protagonist sees (or perhaps only imagines) the past lover as a "will-o'-the-wisp"—a ghostly light, while the city too has become a ghost of its Weimar past.

Brexit motifs are traceable in this album, too. Two Englishmen recording an album in Berlin in the years following the Brexit vote can hardly ignore this reality, even if they look to Bowie and Isherwood for inspiration. The song *You are the one* starts with the sound of birdsong in a sun-lit Zehlendorf and the proverbial *Kaffee und Kuchen*. A later reference to "A European film we could have seen" then ambiguously points to an actual film the couple missed, while also casting doubt over the idyllic vision portrayed in the song

der Goldenen Zwanziger in ein besonders lebendiges Viertel des heutigen Berlins, das in Isherwoods Zeiten eines der ärmsten Arbeiterviertel war. »From below past Nollendorfplatz«, hinter dem Nollendorfplatz taucht die U-Bahn im Song aus dem Tunnel auf ans Licht. Hier befand sich im schwulen Berlin der 1920er Jahre ein weiteres Kultviertel, das die bekanntesten Schwulen- und Lesbenbars der Stadt beherbergte. Der Protagonist möchte seinen früheren Angebeteten fragen, ob er sein Glück noch immer an den alten Arkaden sucht: »Do you still hang around that old arcade / To see what luck will bring?«. Diese Arkaden werden nicht zufällig erwähnt: In den 1920er Jahren bildeten sie tagsüber das Zentrum des Wirtschaftslebens und luden zum Flanieren ein, in der Nacht waren sie zudem berüchtigte Treffpunkte von Strichern, die hier für wenig Geld ihre Dienste anboten.[6] Wie der Songtitel andeutet, kehrt die Hauptfigur nach Berlin zurück und erblickt (vielleicht auch nur in einem Traum) den ehemaligen Geliebten, der wie ein »Irrlicht« durch die Stadt streift – wie ein gespenstisches Licht in einer Stadt, die ebenfalls zum Geist ihrer Weimarer Vergangenheit geworden ist.

Auch der Brexit wird auf dem Album behandelt. Zwei Engländer, die in Berlin in den Jahren nach dem Brexit-Referendum ein Album aufnehmen, können wohl kaum über diese Realität hinwegsehen, selbst dann nicht, wenn sie sich von Bowie und Isherwood zu ihrer Musik inspirieren ließen. Im Song »You are the one« wird das Ritual von *Kaffee und Kuchen* im sonnigen Zehlendorf von Vogelgezwitscher begleitet. Allerdings enthält der Song etwas später mit der Zeile »A European film we could have seen« (»ein europäischer Film, den wir uns hätten anschauen können«) auch die zweideutige Anspielung auf einen tatsächlichen Film, den das Duo verpasst hat, und das idyllische Bild, das der Song bisher gezeichnet hat,

up until that point. In the song *Dreamland* (and the music video featuring the not-so-dreamy Alexanderplatz underground station), the protagonist who is "tired of [his] homeland" tries to escape reality by travelling to a utopian vision in his dreams. *Dreamland* is the place where "you don't need a visa": a bureaucratic metaphor that is likely to become increasingly meaningful for many Britons travelling to and living in Europe after Brexit. In fact, in light of the threat to freedom of movement posed by Brexit, many British citizens have, in the years following the 2016 referendum, already been actively seeking ways to make Berlin their new home.[7]

Even before Brexit, Berlin had for years, if not decades, been a desirable destination for many Britons. British artists, in particular, were drawn to Berlin by the city's rich history and its reputation as an 'art mecca'. Cases in point are Tacita Dean and Susan Philipsz, both winners of the Turner Prize, who have chosen to live and work in Berlin (Dean moved to Berlin as early as 2000). Both women excavate the Berlin myth and German history in their works. In her sound installations, Susan Philipsz works with narratives of displacement and exile. For instance, the 2014 *Part File Score* focuses on the works of German composer Hanns Eisler who, like many, had to flee from Berlin in the 1930s. Another recurring theme is the dynamic between violence and art in Nazi Germany, explored in *Study for Strings* (also 2014), in which Philipsz de-constructed a 1943 orchestral work by

Pavel Haas, a Czech composer murdered in the Theresienstadt concentration camp. This latter piece was performed in a train station in Kassel, while *Part File Score* was exhibited in the Hamburger Bahnhof, also a train station turned iconic contemporary art museum. Philipsz is particularly interested in train stations as spaces of arrival and departure—often tragic spaces in Nazi history.

Tacita Dean's most famous Berlin works—the films *Fernsehturm* (2001) and *Palast* (2004)—negotiate the heritage of the German Democratic Republic (GDR). Dean has also reflected on Nazi history and its relation to art in her 2005 installation *Die Regimentstochter* (The Daughter of the Regiment), which was exhibited in one of the buildings of the German Bundestag. In this installation Dean displayed thirty-six opera programmes from the 1930s and '40s that she accidentally found in a Berlin flea market, in which previous owners cut out the swastikas printed on the pages, sometimes damaging the text and other visuals by doing so. It is unclear whether the removal of the swastikas was an act of protest or an attempt to forget. This ambiguity and the collage effect, which recalls the famous images of the German artist Max Ernst, make *Die Regimentstochter* an insightful contemplation on German history, memory, and art.

In contemporary British and American novels Berlin also features prominently as a setting. In literature, representations of Weimar Berlin come perhaps only sec-

sie ein Orchesterwerk des im Konzentrationslager Theresienstadt ermordeten Komponisten Pavel Haas aus dem Jahr 1943. Das dabei entstandene Stück wurde in einem Kasseler Bahnhof aufgeführt. Die Ausstellung von *Part File Score* war dagegen im Hamburger Bahnhof zu sehen, der als ehemaliger Bahnhof und symbolträchtiger Ort heute ein Museum für zeitgenössische Kunst beherbergt. Philipsz' besonderes Interesse gilt Bahnhöfen als Orten von Ankunft und Abfahrt, die in der Nazi-Vergangenheit oftmals eine tragische Bedeutung erhielten.

Tacita Dean setzt sich in ihren bekanntesten Berlin-Werken – den Filmen *Fernsehturm* (2001) und *Palast* (2004) – mit dem Erbe der ehemaligen DDR auseinander. In ihrer Installation *Die Regimentstochter*, die 2005 in einem Gebäude des Deutschen Bundestags gezeigt wurde, macht auch sie sich Gedanken über die Geschichte der Nazis und ihr Verhältnis zur Kunst. Die Installation besteht aus 36 Opernprogrammheften der Dreißiger- und Vierzigerjahre, die Tacita Dean zufällig auf einem Berliner Flohmarkt entdeckte. Der oder die Vorbesitzer*in hat die Hakenkreuze aus diesen Heften herausgeschnitten und dabei in einigen Fällen den Text und Abbildungen beschädigt. Ob er oder sie die Hakenkreuze als Akt des Protests oder im Bemühen um Vergessen entfernte, lässt sich nicht mehr nachvollziehen. Die Mehrdeutigkeit und das Collagenhafte dieses Werks erinnern an die berühmten Bilder des deutschen Künstlers Max Ernst und machen *Die Regimentstochter* zu einer einfühlsamen Betrachtung über die deutsche Geschichte, Erinnerungskultur und Kunst.

Berlin ist auch in vielen zeitgenössischen britischen und amerikanischen Romanen ein wichtiger Schauplatz. In der literarischen Verwertung steht das Berlin der 1920er und 30er Jahre vermutlich gleich auf Rang zwei hinter dem geteilten Berlin während

ond to representations of Berlin divided by the Cold War. The Berlin Wall features prominently in Jonathan Franzen's widely acclaimed latest novel *Purity* (2015), in the 2019 Booker-longlisted *The Man Who Saw Everything* by Deborah Levy, and in *An Honest Man* (2019) written by Berlin-based British writer Ben Fergusson. These three novels zoom in on Berlin shortly before the fall of the Berlin Wall, portraying a city inhabited by people making drastic changes in their lives, yet dramatically unaware of much bigger, historical changes just around the corner. In this sense the setting of Weimar Berlin explored by Isherwood, where the Nazi presence is more and more palpable at each turn, and the divided Berlin on the verge of being reunited again have something in common: both are liminal spaces in which the familiar way of life and the old rules are about to be overturned. Both settings allow the authors to intensify their plots by making their protagonists negotiate these new and often extreme circumstances.

There are novels that refer to Weimar Berlin almost in passing, but the memory of this past leaves a strong trace. Such is the case with Jonathan Coe's *Mr Wilder & Me* (2020). The novel is set largely in the 1970s, following the famous Austrian émigré director Billy Wilder on the set of one of his later films, *Fedora*. Wilder struggles to direct in a Hollywood-driven industry which no longer shows interest in his kind of film-making. The novel contains a striking flashback which starts with Wilder as

des Kalten Kriegs. Die Mauer ist ein zentraler Ort in Jonathan Franzens viel beachtetem letzten Roman *Unschuld* (»Purity«, 2015), in *Der Mann, der alles sah* (»The Man Who Saw Everything«) von Deborah Levy, der 2019 auf der Longlist für den Booker-Prize stand, und in *An Honest Man* (2019) des in Berlin lebenden britischen Schriftstellers Ben Fergusson. Im Mittelpunkt dieser drei Romane steht Berlin kurz vor dem Mauerfall. Sie berichten von einer Stadt, deren Bewohner*innen mit einschneidenden Veränderungen in ihrem eigenen Leben beschäftigt sind, während sie gleichzeitig die viel größeren historischen Veränderungen in nächster Nähe auf dramatische Weise an sich vorbeiziehen lassen. In diesem Sinne haben die Kulisse des von Isherwood beschriebenen Berlin der Weimarer Zeit, in dem die Präsenz der Nazis immer spürbarer wird, und die des geteilten Berlin kurz vor der Wiedervereinigung eines gemein: Sie markieren jeweils Übergangsphasen, in denen gewohnte Lebensentwürfe und alte Regelwerke nur noch für kurze Zeit Bestand haben sollen. Beide Szenerien bieten den Schriftsteller*innen Gelegenheit, ihre Handlungen zuzuspitzen, indem sie ihre Protagonist*innen mit diesen neuen und oftmals extremen Umständen konfrontieren.

In einigen Romanen wird Berlin zwar nur am Rande erwähnt, doch die Erinnerung an diese Vergangenheit hat deutliche Spuren hinterlassen. Dies ist der Fall in Jonathan Coes *Mr Wilder & Me* aus dem Jahr 2020. Der Roman spielt hauptsächlich in den 1970er Jahren und folgt den Spuren des emigrierten österreichischen Regisseurs Billy Wilder während der Dreharbeiten zu einem seiner späteren Filme: *Fedora*. Wilder kämpft um sein Ansehen als Regisseur in einer von Hollywood bestimmten Branche, die das Interesse an seiner Form des Filmemachens verloren hat. In einem beeindruckenden Rückblick erzählt

a young man making his first timid successes in the film industry in Berlin (as the novel suggests, "the nerve centre of the whole European film business") shortly before his emigration to France and later to the United States.[8] This is tellingly the most experimental section in an otherwise very traditional novel, as it is written in the form of a screenplay. The use of screenplay in a novel so deeply intertwined with cinema is hardly surprising, yet in the novel it is much more than just an ekphrastic game. It connects film and memory, and represents the process of "watching" one's memories as a cinematic act. But perhaps most importantly it returns the reader to the early 1930s through the medium that, as Laura Marcus explains in her essay, was the most representative of Berlin's modernity and distinctive cultural identity: film.

In the novel, as an older man and a renowned American director, Wilder still longs for the "old" Europe he had known as a young man, and for the culture that he understands as inherently his own. The screenplay flashback opens with a group of friends, most of whom would eventually become famous émigré filmmakers, sitting in the iconic Romanische Café on Kurfürstendamm:

A CAPTION reads: "BERLIN, 1933".

The camera takes in the whole interior of the café—waiters in tuxedos weaving their way between busy tables, old

der Roman die Geschichte des jungen Billy Wilder, der kurz vor seiner Emigration, die ihn zuerst nach Frankreich und später in die USA führte, seine ersten zaghaften Erfolge in der Berliner Filmindustrie feierte (die im Roman als Schaltzentrale der gesamten europäischen Filmbranche, »the nerve centre of the whole European film business«, bezeichnet wird).[8] Innerhalb des ansonsten eher klassisch aufgebauten Romans ist dieser Abschnitt der mit Abstand experimentellste, da er in Form eines Drehbuchs verfasst wurde. Die Verwendung des Drehbuchelements mag angesichts des deutlichen Kinobezugs kaum überraschen. Doch aus inhaltlicher Sicht geht es um weitaus mehr als nur um ein Spiel mit der Figur der Ekphrasis. Das Drehbuchelement verbindet Film und Erinnerung miteinander und stellt den Prozess des »Betrachtens« der eigenen Erinnerung als filmische Handlung dar. Doch vor allem nimmt es die Leser*innen mit auf eine Reise in die frühen 1930er Jahre, und zwar mithilfe eines Mediums, das, wie Laura Marcus in ihrem Essay erläutert, die Modernität und besondere kulturelle Identität Berlins auf ausgesprochen anschauliche Weise repräsentierte: das Medium Film.

Im Roman sehnt sich Wilder als älterer Mann und berühmter amerikanischer Regisseur nach dem »alten« Europa seiner Jugend und nach der Kultur, der er sich aus tiefstem Herzen verbunden fühlt. Der Drehbuch-Rückblick beginnt im symbolträchtigen Romanischen Café am Kurfürstendamm mit einer Gruppe von Freunden, die in der Emigration größtenteils berühmte Filmemacher werden sollten:

Eine BILDUNTERSCHRIFT lautet: »BERLIN, 1933«.

Die Kamera schwenkt über den gesamten Innenraum des Cafés – Kellner im Frack bahnen sich ihren Weg zwischen den vollen Tischen, an

guys playing chess, businessmen reading newspapers, friends exchanging gossip and young couples lost in each other's company—before zooming in on one table near the window, where a boisterous group of young men are engaged in a loud discussion. The air is clouded with cigarette smoke and the steam from innumerable coffee cups.[9]

For the character of Billy Wilder, observing the Berlin of his youth through the cinematic lens is the only possible way of seeing the city. The Romanische Café is portrayed as a nostalgic space representative of free Weimar culture, while the city itself is increasingly coloured by the presence of the Nazis. Coe's screenplay shows how space is gradually closing in on Wilder: it starts with Wilder's scripts no longer being considered by the Ufa Film studios, which now favour Nazi writers; and, at the end, he and his girlfriend turn the corner to see a Jewish man being heavily beaten. The change occurs within two pages, yet it is the act of *seeing* violence at first-hand—the centrality of the director's vision—that makes him flee to Paris. When, at the end of the screenplay, he returns to Berlin looking for the traces of the familiar city after the Second World War, the first thing he notices is that the nostalgic centre of "his" Berlin, the Romanische Café, is gone.

The Romanische Café also features in another recent novel absorbed in the complex and tragic realities of the Weimar Republic, Naomi Wood's *The Hiding Game*

(2019). The novel focuses on a group of six friends during their time at the Bauhaus school. Even as the characters gradually lose their ties with the school, they nevertheless follow its trajectory by moving from Weimar to Dessau to Berlin, as if the geography of their group was in a fatalistic way tied in with the Bauhaus school itself. This is also a movement from happiness and the idyllic "Garden of Eden" represented by Weimar (at the beginning of the novel, Bauhaus reads like a sealed off, utopian, almost magical school) to the conflicted space of political turmoil, personal tragedy, and artistic liberation that is Berlin in the 1930s. In the city, the Nazis occupy increasingly more space—symbolically as well as geographically—and in their final violent act of occupation destroy the Bauhaus school, the point where the novel ends.

Naomi Wood was inspired to write *The Hiding Game* after seeing the images from the famous Metal Ball, one of numerous Bauhaus parties, which the students had to attend in costumes made out of or resembling metal. In fact, the novel itself fully embraces the visual: the text is filled with detailed descriptions of the works of Bauhaus students and masters as well as introspection into the protagonists' creative process. Even the way the protagonist Paul Beckermann describes Kreuzberg, the area that became his home in Berlin, turns it into an avant-garde painting:

> [Kreuzberg] had rats and mice and smell coming off the canal. If you tipped

Game«, 2019) von Naomi Wood. Der Roman folgt einer Gruppe von sechs Freund*innen während ihrer Zeit an der Bauhaus-Schule. Zwar verlieren die Figuren mit der Zeit ihre Verbindung zu dieser Schule, doch sie folgen ihrem Weg von Weimar über Dessau nach Berlin, als wäre der Aufenthaltsort dieser Gruppe auf schicksalhafte Weise an das Bauhaus selbst gebunden. Zu dieser Zeit beginnt auch ihre Reise aus dem Glück und dem idyllischen »Garten Eden«, den Weimar verkörpert (zu Beginn des Romans wird das Bauhaus als in sich geschlossener, gleichsam magischer Ort der Utopie beschrieben), in das Spannungsfeld aus politischen Unruhen, persönlichen Tragödien und künstlerischer Befreiung, die das Berlin der 1930er Jahre prägten. Die Nazis nehmen in der Stadt – sowohl im übertragenen als auch im geografischen Sinne – immer mehr Raum ein und zerstören das Bauhaus in einem letzten gewaltvollen Akt der Besetzung. Damit endet der Roman.

Naomi Wood entwickelte die Idee zu *The Hiding Game*, nachdem sie Fotoaufnahmen eines der zahlreichen Feste der Bauhaus-Student*innen gesehen hatte. Zu diesem berühmten Metallischen Fest mussten die Student*innen in Kostümen aus Metall oder metallähnlichen Materialien erscheinen. Auch der Roman stellt die visuelle Erfahrung in den Vordergrund. Der Text enthält zahlreiche detaillierte Beschreibungen der Werke von Student*innen und Meister*innen und ausführliche Einblicke in die kreativen Prozesse seiner Protagonist*innen. Sogar die Art und Weise, in der die Figur Paul Beckermann seinen neuen Berliner Wohnbezirk Kreuzberg beschreibt, hat etwas von einem Avantgard-Gemälde:

> Hier gab es Ratten und Mäuse und stinkende Kanäle. Auf den Kopf gestellt würde sich ganz Kreuz-

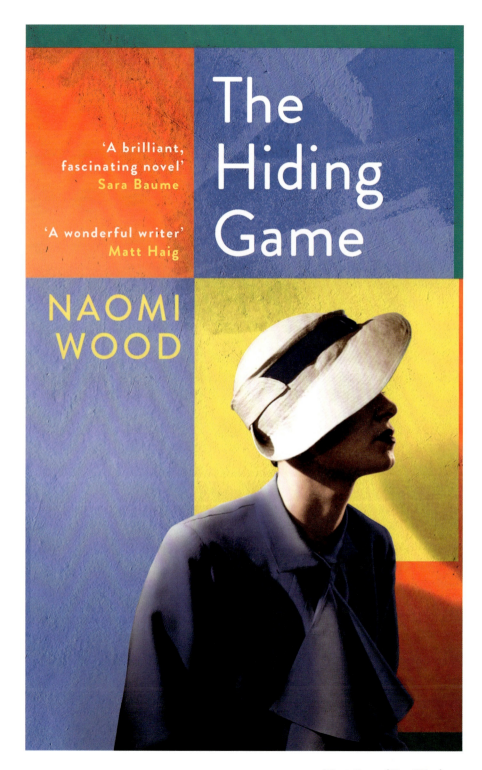

[Fig. 43: Cover of Naomi Wood, *The Hiding Game*, design by Katie Tooke, 2019]

[Abb. 43: Titelbild von Naomi Wood, *The Hiding Game*, Design von Katie Tooke, 2019]

Kreuzberg upside down there'd be tram wires and telegraph cables and washing lines to catch it all in a dirty great net.[10]

At the end of the novel, the central conflict between Bauhaus artists and Nazi opposition is not only ethical but largely aesthetic. Significantly, the villain in the novel is the character who makes money from selling what the "Bauhaus babies" view as very traditional, tasteless, backwards art pieces collectively created in a workshop by "craftsmen", not artists. For Naomi Wood, the world of the Weimar Republic is mediated—and best understood—through its visual art.

It is significant that the visual seems to be the starting point for many contemporary writers who decide to set their novels in the Weimar period. A similar trigger inspired *Delayed Rays of a Star* (2019) by Singaporean-American Amanda Lee Koe. Koe wrote her novel after seeing an image of her teenage hero, Marlene Dietrich, together with the first Chinese-American film star Anna May Wong, and the infamous German director Leni Riefenstahl taken at a party in Berlin in 1928.

This unlikely image could have only been taken in 1920s Berlin, the seat of cosmopolitanism and a capital of a growing film industry, which saw the emergence of the first 'film stars'. In fact, at that time, Berlin embraced Anna May Wong as a star in her own right after she had left Hollywood, annoyed with the conventional roles in which her character inevitably

berg in einem Gewirr aus Straßenbahnoberleitungen, Telegrafenkabeln und Wäscheleinen wie in einem großen schmutzigen Netz verfangen.[10]

Am Ende des Romans stützt sich der zentrale Konflikt zwischen den Bauhaus-Künstler*innen und ihren Nazi-Widersacher*innen nicht nur auf ethische, sondern vor allem auf ästhetische Gesichtspunkte. Die Rolle des Bösewichts übernimmt in diesem Roman bezeichnenderweise eine Figur, die ihr Geld mit dem Verkauf von Kunstwerken verdient. Die »Bauhaus-Babys« betrachten diese Kunstwerke, die Kunstgewerbler*innen – und nicht Künstler*innen – in einer Werkstatt kreiert haben, als traditionsbehaftet, geschmacklos und rückwärtsgewandt. Für Naomi Wood lässt sich die Welt der Weimarer Republik durch die visuelle Kunst dieser Zeit vermitteln – und auch am besten nachvollziehen.

Bemerkenswerterweise hat das Visuelle bei zahlreichen zeitgenössischen Schriftsteller*innen ganz offenbar den Ausschlag dafür gegeben, ihren Roman in der Weimarer Zeit spielen zu lassen. Auch die singapurisch-amerikanische Schriftstellerin Amanda Lee Koe ließ sich aus ähnlichen Motiven zu ihrem Roman *Delayed Rays of a Star* (2019) inspirieren. Auslöser war ein Foto ihrer Heldin aus Teenagerjahren, Marlene Dietrich. Das Bild aus dem Jahr 1928 zeigt die Schauspielerin auf einem Fest in Berlin zusammen mit dem chinesisch-amerikanischen Filmstar Anna May Wong und der berüchtigten deutschen Regisseurin Leni Riefenstahl.

Eine derart ungewöhnliche Begegnung konnte sich nur im Berlin der 1920er Jahre ereignen: In dieser kosmopolitischen Metropole und Hauptstadt einer aufstrebenden Filmwirtschaft, die die ersten »Filmstars« hervorbrachte. Tatsächlich wurde Anna May Wong im Berlin dieser Zeit als Filmstar mit offenen Armen empfangen. Hollywood hatte sie dagegen den Rücken gekehrt, aus Ärger über ihre Festlegung auf kon-

[Fig. 44: Marlene Dietrich, Anna May Wong, and Leni Riefenstahl, photograph by Alfred Eisenstaedt, 1928]

[Abb. 44: Marlene Dietrich, Anna May Wong und Leni Riefenstahl, Fotografie von Alfred Eisenstaedt, 1928]

had to die early on, "because a white hero has to end with a white heroine".[11] In 1928, Berlin was also a place where Dietrich and Riefenstahl could still attend the same party. In a few years' time Dietrich would leave Nazi Germany, unwilling to compromise, while Riefenstahl would become one of the regime's most famed collaborators. This curious intersection of women's lives represented in that photograph becomes the starting point from which Koe unravels the complex fictional storylines of these three women.

ventionelle Rollen, in denen ihre Figuren für das gewünschte Happy End zwischen einem weißen Helden und einer weißen Heldin stets einen frühen Tod sterben mussten.[11] Zudem war es im Berlin des Jahres 1928 noch nicht ausgeschlossen, Dietrich und Riefenstahl auf demselben Fest zu begegnen. Nur wenige Jahre später würde Marlene Dietrich Nazi-Deutschland verlassen, Kompromisse mit den Nazis wollte sie nicht eingehen. Riefenstahl dagegen sollte eine der bekanntesten Kollaborateurinnen des Regimes werden. Dieses Foto einer besonderen Begegnung diente Koe als Vorlage für die komplexen fiktiven Handlungsstränge, die sie in ihrem Roman über das Leben der drei Frauen entwickelt.

Similarly steeped in Weimar artwork is Philip Kerr's latest thriller *Metropolis*, published posthumously in 2019. It is the only novel of the detective Bernie Gunther series set during the time of the Weimar Republic, and in it Kerr pulls out all the stops when it comes to referencing the cultural artifacts of the time. While the novel does not mention Isherwood directly, it constantly winks at him: in the novel it is Bernie who says "Berlin meant boys"—a famous line that comes from Isherwood's retrospective look at Berlin in *Christopher and His Kind* (1976). Bernie's British roommate spends time in the Cosy Corner, a gay bar linked to Isherwood and his crowd, while one of Bernie's sexual interests paints her fingernails bright green like Sally Bowles in the film *Cabaret*. Isherwood 'clues' are playfully placed all across the novel, to be picked up by attentive readers for whom Isherwood is the ultimate voice of Weimar Berlin. While a make-up artist at the Theater am Schiffbauerdamm (today's Berliner Ensemble) turns Bernie into an undercover beggar, the *Threepenny Opera* is being rehearsed next door, which Bernie fails to appreciate because the singers constantly (and, needless to say, purposefully) sound out of tune. Georg Grosz and Otto Dix both make an appearance: the shocking realism of their work is well attuned to the tone of the novel. In fact, the novel is punctuated with Dix's painting *Metropolis*, as each part of the book opens with an image taken from the famous triptych. Central to the plot is the 1931 film *M* by Fritz Lang, to which the novel

Auf ähnliche Weise vom Weimarer Kunstbetrieb geprägt ist auch Philip Kerrs letzter Thriller *Metropolis*, der 2019 posthum veröffentlicht wurde. Als einziger Teil der Reihe um den Privatdetektiv Bernie Gunther spielt er während der Weimarer Republik. Kerr zieht darin alle Register, um Bezüge zu Kulturgütern der damaligen Zeit herzustellen. Zwar wird Isherwood im Roman nicht direkt erwähnt, doch es gibt immer wieder Hinweise auf seine Person: Im Roman ist es Bernie, der mit »Berlin bedeutet Jungs« eine berühmte Zeile aus Isherwoods Berliner Memoiren *Christopher und die Seinen* (1976) zitiert. Bernies britischer Zimmergenosse verbringt seine Zeit im Cosy Corner, einer Schwulenbar, in der auch Isherwood mit seiner Entourage verkehrte. Und die Frau, mit der Bernie gern eine Nacht verbringen würde, hat wie Sally Bowles im Film *Cabaret* grün lackierte Fingernägel. Der gesamte Roman enthält unzählige kleine Isherwood-Andeutungen für all diejenigen aufmerksamen britischen Leser*innen, die den Schriftsteller für einen ausgewiesenen Kenner Berlins in der Weimarer Republik halten. Während Bernie von einer Maskenbildnerin am Theater am Schiffbauerdamm (dem heutigen Berliner Ensemble) für verdeckte Ermittlungen in einen Bettler verwandelt wird, finden im Nebenraum Proben für die *Dreigroschenoper* statt. Bernie zeigt sich alles andere als begeistert, denn die Sänger*innen treffen seiner Meinung nach (und – nebenbei erwähnt – ganz bewusst) keinen einzigen Ton. Auch Georg Grosz und Otto Dix haben einen Auftritt: Der schockierende Realismus ihrer Werke fügt sich hervorragend in die Stimmung des Romans. Dix' Gemälde *Metropolis* gibt dem Buch eine Struktur, indem jeder neue Teil mit einem Bild aus seinem berühmten Triptychon beginnt. Im Mittelpunkt der Handlung steht Fritz Langs Film *M* aus dem Jahr 1931, zu dem der Roman von Anfang an deutliche Parallelen aufweist. So wird

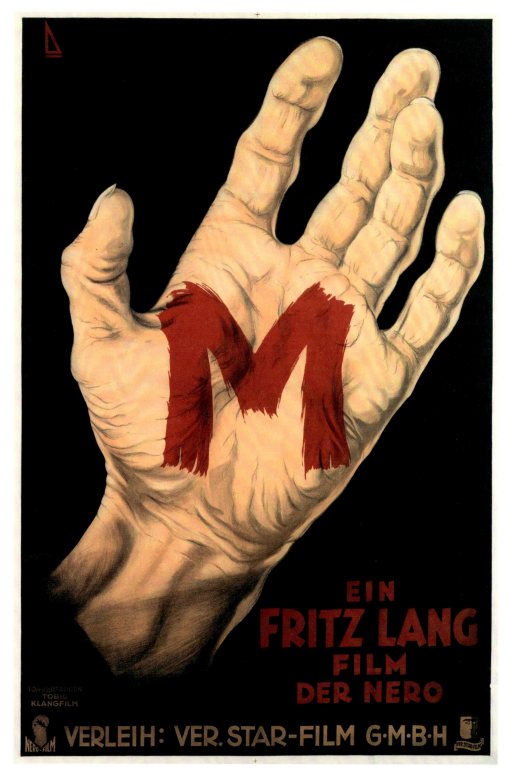

[Fig. 45: Poster for Fritz Lang's film M, 1931]

[Abb. 45: Plakat für Fritz Langs Film M, 1931]

bears a striking resemblance from the very beginning. In fact, it turns out that Lang's wife and co-author Thea von Harbou wants to meet Gunther to receive some pointers for the new script, on which the couple has just started working. In this elegant turn of events, Kerr makes his thriller the primary source for Lang's and von Harbou's masterpiece, and not the other way around. As one reference to 1920s Berlin jumps straight into the next, the novel almost slides into Weimar-inspired fan fiction, however, it also makes it clear how intriguing that era and its culture were to Philip Kerr.

Needless to say, the thriller genre also suits the setting of Weimar Berlin particularly well, and Kerr plays it to his advantage: his other Berlin novels are mostly set in Nazi Germany but, in *Metropolis*, the worst is yet to happen, and that knowledge increases the feeling of suspense manifold. In this liminal space, poverty, violence, and political unrest unfold back-to-back with outstanding works of art: the gruesome murders happen at the same time as the ground-breaking *Threepenny Opera* is rehearsed on stage—for Kerr, the combination of art and violence is the ultimate cocktail of 1920s and '30s Berlin.

Christopher Isherwood is likely to preserve his status as Berlin's most famed British chronicler for the foreseeable future. Nonetheless, his looming presence does not scare off more recent voices. As this chapter has shown, many contemporary British artists, musicians, and writers have turned to the myth of 1920s and '30s Berlin,

beispielsweise Gunther von Fritz Langs Ehefrau und Co-Autorin, Thea von Harbou, um ein Treffen gebeten. Sie ist auf der Suche nach Inspiration, denn das Ehepaar hat soeben mit der Arbeit am Skript zu diesem Film begonnen. Mit dieser eleganten Wendung der Ereignisse macht Kerr seinen eigenen Thriller zur wichtigsten Inspirationsquelle für dieses Meisterwerk, das Lang und von Harbou geschaffen haben, und nicht umgekehrt. Dank einer schnellen Aneinanderreihung von Hinweisen auf das Berlin der 1920er Jahre hätte aus dem Roman beinahe eine Weimar-inspirierte Fan-Fiction werden können. Gleichzeitig wird aber auch die Anziehungskraft deutlich, die für Philipp Kerr von dieser Ära und ihrem Kulturbetrieb ausging.

Und natürlich passt auch das Genre des Thrillers hervorragend in die Kulisse Berlins, was Kerr zu seinem Vorteil zu nutzen weiß: Während seine übrigen Berlin-Romane hauptsächlich zur Zeit der deutschen Nazi-Herrschaft spielen, steht in *Metropolis* das Schlimmste noch bevor, und mit diesem Wissen lässt sich die Spannung ins Unermessliche steigern. Gleichzeitig entstehen in dieser von Armut, Gewalt und politischen Umbrüchen geprägten Übergangszeit auch großartige Kunstwerke: Grausame Morde geschehen, während auf der Bühne die legendäre *Dreigroschenoper* geprobt wird. Bei Kerr vereinen sich Gewalt und Kunst zum ultimativen Cocktail des Berlins der 1920er und 1930er Jahre.

Christopher Isherwood wird seinen Status als bekanntester Berlin-Chronist auf absehbare Zeit verteidigen können. Doch jüngere Stimmen lassen sich von seiner allumfassenden Präsenz nicht abschrecken. Wie dieses Kapitel zeigt, beschäftigen sich zahlreiche britische Künstler*innen, Musiker*innen und Schriftsteller*innen der Gegenwart mit dem Berliner Mythos der 1920er und 1930er Jahre und werfen einen differenzierten und frischen Blick auf diese Ära. Angesichts der

presenting nuanced rewritings of that era. Once the parallels with Brexit Britain come into view, it becomes increasingly hard to ignore the political relevance of that time and place in the context of the twenty-first century, and its relation to the way British artists and writers see themselves. One hundred years on, the culture, politics, and even the topography of interwar Berlin still fascinate writers from all over the world; yet, today, the amount and the intensity of British responses to that era in German history seems surprising. Is it, perhaps, a way to reclaim the troubled past of Europe as part of one's identity? From the nuanced reflections in artworks by Tacita Dean and Susan Philipsz to patchwork visions of the city as imagined by Philip Kerr and the Pet Shop Boys, Berlin is clearly still a place to ask those questions, rather than to have them answered.

Notes

1 On how this and other London-based events relate to the Weimar Myth, see Sarah Hughes: Hedonism, sex and fear—why the Weimar republic is in vogue, in: The Guardian, 25 May 2019, https://www.theguardian.com/culture/2019/may/25/weimar-republic-hedonism-sex-fear-art-culture-celebration.
2 Kate Connolly: Drugs, dancing, cabaret: Babylon Berlin returns for season three, in: The Guardian, 19 Dec 2019, https://www.theguardian.com/world/2019/dec/19/drugs-dancing-cabaret-babylon-berlin-returns-for-season-three.
3 Adrian Daub: What Babylon Berlin Sees in the Weimar Republic, in: The New Republic, 14 Feb 2018, https://newrepublic.com/article/147053/babylon-berlin-sees-weimar-republic.

augenfälligen Parallelen zu Großbritannien in Zeiten des Brexits lässt sich wohl kaum von der Hand weisen, wie groß die politische Bedeutung dieser Epoche und dieses Schauplatzes für das 21. Jahrhundert ist und welchen Einfluss diese Ära auf die Selbstwahrnehmung britischer Künstler*innen und Schriftsteller*innen hat. Auch hundert Jahre später sind Schriftsteller*innen aus aller Welt noch immer fasziniert von der Kultur, der Politik und sogar der Topografie Berlins der Goldenen Zwanziger. Und doch haben die zahlreichen britischen Reaktionen auf diese Phase der deutschen Geschichte in ihrer aktuellen Intensität auch etwas Überraschendes. Womöglich ist es ein Versuch der Rückbesinnung auf die bewegte Vergangenheit Europas als Teil der eigenen Identität? Die Kunstwerke von Tacita Dean und Susan Philipsz mit ihren differenzierten Betrachtungen, aber auch die von Philip Kerr und den Pet Shop Boys entwickelten Patchwork-Ansichten der Stadt machen deutlich, dass Berlin ohne Zweifel noch immer der Ort ist, an dem man diese Fragen stellt, anstatt eine Antwort auf sie zu finden.

Anmerkungen

1 Weitere Erläuterungen, wie diese und andere Veranstaltungen und London mit dem Mythos Weimar in Verbindung stehen, finden sich bei Sarah Hughes: Hedonism, sex and fear – why the Weimar republic is in vogue, in: The Guardian, 25.5.2019, https://www.theguardian.com/culture/2019/may/25/weimar-republic-hedonism-sex-fear-art-culture-celebration.
2 Kate Connolly: Drugs, dancing, cabaret: Babylon Berlin returns for season three, in: The Guardian, 19.12.2019, https://www.theguardian.com/world/2019/dec/19/drugs-dancing-cabaret-babylon-berlin-returns-for-season-three.
3 Adrian Daub: What Babylon Berlin Sees in the Weimar Republic, in: The New Republic, 14.2.2018, https://newrepublic.com/article/147053/babylon-berlin-sees-weimar-republic.
4 Christopher Isherwood: Liberation: Diaries, Vol. 3. 1970 1983, London, HarperCollins 2012, S. 567.

4 Christopher Isherwood: Liberation: Diaries, Vol. 3: 1970–1983, London, HarperCollins 2012, p. 567.
5 Arno Raffeiner: Pet Shop Boys im Interview: Wir setzen uns in der U-Bahn nicht nebeneinander, in: Der Spiegel, 25 Jan 2020, https://www.spiegel.de/kultur/musik/pet-shop-boys-im-interview-wir-setzen-uns-in-der-u-bahn-nicht-nebeneinander-a-b4769795-36d8-47c7-91fe-ca8e23263267 (translation by Sofia Permiakova).
6 Robert Beachy: Gay Berlin: Birthplace of a Modern Identity, London, Vintage Books 2015.
7 According to the Amt für Statistik Berlin-Brandenburg, in 2017 and 2018 over one thousand British citizens living in Berlin applied for naturalisation, compared to only 45 cases in 2015. For the most recent study on British and Irish migration to Berlin, see Melanie Neumann: Recent Irish and British migration to Berlin—a case of lifestyle migration?, Trier, WVT 2020.
8 Jonathan Coe: Mr Wilder & Me, London, Viking 2020, p. 127.
9 Ibid.
10 Naomi Wood: The Hiding Game, London, Picador 2019, pp 296 f.
11 Amanda Lee Koe: Delayed Rays of a Star, London, Bloomsbury 2019.

5 Arno Raffeiner: Pet Shop Boys im Interview: Wir setzen uns in der U-Bahn nicht nebeneinander, in: Der Spiegel, 25.1.2020, https://www.spiegel.de/kultur/musik/pet-shop-boys-im-interview-wir-setzen-uns-in-der-u-bahn-nicht-nebeneinander-a-b4769795-36d8-47c7-91fe-ca8e23263267.
6 Robert Beachy: Gay Berlin: Birthplace of a Modern Identity, London, Vintage Books 2015.
7 Nach Angaben des Amts für Statistik Berlin-Brandenburg haben in den Jahren 2017 und 2018 mehr als 1000 britische Staatsbürger*innen mit Wohnsitz in Berlin die Einbürgerung beantragt, im Jahr 2015 waren es nur 45. Die aktuellste Untersuchung zur Migration aus Großbritannien und Irland stammt von Melanie Neumann, Recent Irish and British Migration to Berlin – A Case of Lifestyle Migration?, Trier, WVT 2020.
8 Jonathan Coe: Mr Wilder & Me, London, Viking 2020, S. 127. [Anm. d. Ü.: Der Roman liegt noch nicht in deutscher Übersetzung vor.]
9 Ebd. [Anm. d. Ü.: Der Roman liegt noch nicht in deutscher Übersetzung vor.]
10 Naomi Wood: The Hiding Game, London, Picador 2019. [Anm. d. Ü.: *Diese goldenen Jahre*, übersetzt aus dem Englischen von Claudia Feldmann, Hamburg, Atlantik Verlag, 2019. Nach Rücksprache mit der Übersetzerin Claudia Feldmann ist die hier zitierte Passage nicht in der deutschen Fassung enthalten und wurde von mir übersetzt.]
11 Amanda Lee Koe: Delayed Rays of a Star, London, Bloomsbury 2019. [Anm. d. Ü.: Der Roman liegt noch nicht in deutscher Übersetzung vor.]

Patricia Duncker

AFTERWORD
Richtung Deutschland!

NACHWORT
Richtung Deutschland!

I first visited Berlin in May 1970. We were a gang of British students, *Gastarbeiter* on temporary permits, raising hell for a year between school and university. We wanted to do three things: march through Checkpoint Charlie, cross the Berlin Wall on foot and go to an amazing production of Goethe's *Faust* in East Germany. We did it all. During that year, I worked in a riding school near Munich, then moved to Hamburg where I learned a great deal about knives as a butcher's apprentice in a supermarket before being taken on as a photographer's assistant. The photographer worked freelance for *Stern*. I was nineteen. And that year in Germany, the country that was my Eldorado, my land of gold, shaped all the years to come.

For of course I was following in the wake of many British literary travellers to Germany, who then became the dramatis personae of my postgraduate studies. Samuel Taylor Coleridge travelled to Germany in 1798 with William Wordsworth and his sister Dorothy. The Wordsworths

Zum ersten Mal besuchte ich Berlin im Mai 1970 mit einer Gruppe britischer Student*innen. Wir waren ›Gastarbeiter‹ mit vorübergehender Aufenthaltserlaubnis und wollten in diesem Jahr zwischen Schule und Universität noch einmal so richtig auf den Putz hauen. Drei Dinge standen auf unserer Liste: durch den Grenzübergang am Checkpoint Charlie marschieren, die Berliner Mauer zu Fuß passieren und eine großartige Inszenierung von Goethes *Faust* in Ostdeutschland besuchen. All dies ist uns gelungen. Im Verlauf dieses Jahres jobbte ich zunächst in einer Reitschule nahe München, bevor ich als Aushilfe an der Fleischtheke eines Hamburger Supermarkts viel über Messer lernte. Anschließend war ich als Assistentin bei einem Fotografen tätig, der freiberuflich für den *Stern* arbeitete. Ich war neunzehn Jahre alt. Und dieses Jahr in Deutschland – dem Land, das mein Eldorado, mein Land des Goldes war – sollte mein weiteres Leben nachhaltig beeinflussen.

Denn natürlich begab ich mich auf die Spuren zahlreicher britischer Literat*innen, die Deutschland besucht hatten, und machte sie später zu den *Dramatis Personae* meines Aufbaustudiums. Samuel Taylor Coleridge reiste 1798 mit William Wordsworth und dessen Schwester Dorothy nach Deutschland. Die Wordsworths ließen sich in Goslar nieder. Coleridge

settled in Goslar, but Coleridge set about educating himself in all things German and enrolled at the University of Göttingen. This time in his life marked the beginning of his lifelong interest in German philosophy and literature. One of my early dramatic encounters with Schiller occurred thanks to Coleridge's translation of *Wallenstein*.

German literature was enormously popular in Britain during the 1790s. Gottfried August Bürger's horror ballad *Lenore* was translated several times in 1796. One version was by Walter Scott and another by M.G. 'Monk' Lewis whose novel *The Monk* (1796) was considered to be shockingly immoral and "in the German taste". Two of the Gothic novels mentioned by Jane Austen in *Northanger Abbey* and praised as delectable, terrifying, and very "horrid" were translations from the German.

Weimar and Berlin were crucial points on the German map for literary travellers. In 1829, the diarist Henry Crabb Robinson visited a jovial and hospitable Goethe in Weimar. The great poet was by then a literary legend, whose *Sorrows of Young Werther* proved so controversial that eight different editions were published between 1779 and 1854. Goethe received Crabb Robinson at the small house in the park, and they enjoyed themselves reading Byron together. George Eliot and her not-quite-husband G.H. Lewes visited Weimar in 1854 and then spent the winter in Berlin. Lewes was doing the research for his famous *Life*

dagegen wollte so viel wie möglich über Deutschland lernen und schrieb sich an der Universität Göttingen ein. In dieser Phase entwickelte er seine lebenslange Begeisterung für deutsche Philosophie und Literatur. Eine meiner ersten dramatischen Begegnungen mit Schiller habe ich Coleridge und seiner Übersetzung des *Wallenstein* zu verdanken.

In den 1790er Jahren erfreute sich die deutsche Literatur in Großbritannien großer Beliebtheit. Gottfried August Bürgers Gruselballade *Lenore* wurde 1796 gleich mehrfach übersetzt. Eine Fassung stammte von Walter Scott und eine weitere von M.G. »Monk« Lewis. Dessen Roman *Der Mönch* (»The Monk«) aus demselben Jahr galt als schrecklich unmoralisch und »ganz nach deutschem Geschmack«. Zwei der Romane, die Jane Austen in *Die Abtei von Northanger* (»Northanger Abbey«) erwähnt und als köstlich, furchteinflößend und »recht gruselig« beschreibt, waren Übersetzungen aus dem Deutschen.

Weimar und Berlin bildeten die Fixpunkte auf der deutschen Landkarte von Literaturreisenden. Im Jahr 1829 notierte Henry Crabb Robinson in seinem Tagebuch, dass Goethe ihn bei seinem Besuch in Weimar freundlich und zuvorkommend empfangen habe. Der große Dichter war zu diesem Zeitpunkt bereits eine literarische Legende. Seine *Leiden des jungen Werther* waren so umstritten, dass in den Jahren zwischen 1779 und 1854 insgesamt acht verschiedene Ausgaben veröffentlicht wurden. Goethe empfing Robinson in seinem Gartenhaus am Rande des Parks. Sie verbrachten die Zeit mit der gemeinsamen Lektüre von Byron. George Eliot und G.H. Lewes, die in wilder Ehe zusammenlebten, statteten Weimar 1854 einen Besuch ab und verbrachten anschließend den Winter in Berlin. Lewes befand sich auf Forschungsreise für sein berühmtes Werk *Goethes Leben* (*Life of Goethe*, 1855). Eliot hatte zu diesem Zeitpunkt noch

of Goethe (1855). Eliot had yet to write a word of fiction, but was already the translator of David Friedrich Strauss's *The Life of Jesus* (1846) and Ludwig Feuerbach's *The Essence of Christianity* (1854). When she returned to Berlin, it was in triumph as a well-known international novelist.

The many British writers and intellectuals who came to Berlin in the 1920s, often as sexual refugees from British laws and social prohibitions against homosexuality, included a group of queer British MPs, mostly Conservative, known as the "Glamour Boys". They became a ferocious, vocal opposition to Hitler in Britain. I want to remember the writers who had to leave Germany, whether because they were Jewish, or opposed to the Nazis, or both. One of our most beloved British writer-illustrators, the creator of many books for children, Judith Kerr, fled from Berlin with her family in 1933—and that experience of exile determined her later life. Her autobiographical novel recounting her experience as a child refugee, *When Hitler Stole Pink Rabbit* (1971), has never been out of print. Her father's books were burned by the Nazis, but are now reprinted. Another writer shaped by the experience of exile was the historian Peter Gay, originally Peter Fröhlich, who escaped from Berlin with his parents in 1939. *My German Question* (1998), his account of growing up in Nazi Berlin, a story that is both unsettling and unforgettable, was a core text on a course I taught—European Writing and the Third Reich. Berlin and German literature

keine Romane zu Papier gebracht, sich dafür aber bereits als Übersetzerin von David Friedrich Strauß' *Das Leben Jesu* (»The Life of Jesus«, 1846) und Ludwig Feuerbachs *Das Wesen des Christentums* (»The Essence of Christianity«, 1854) einen Namen gemacht. Als sie Berlin ein weiteres Mal besuchte, feierte sie bereits Triumphe als international bekannte Romanautorin.

Unter den zahlreichen britischen Schriftsteller*innen und Intellektuellen, die in den 1920er Jahren nach Berlin kamen – hauptsächlich um sich wegen ihrer sexuellen Orientierung der britischen Gesetzgebung und gesellschaftlichen Einschränkungen für Homosexuelle zu entziehen – befand sich auch eine Gruppe queerer britischer Parlamentarier. Diese auch als »Glamour Boys« bekannten Abgeordneten stammten vorwiegend aus den Reihen der Konservativen. In Großbritannien protestierten sie später besonders heftig und lautstark gegen Hitler. An dieser Stelle sei auch an all diejenigen Schriftsteller*innen erinnert, die Deutschland verlassen mussten, weil sie entweder jüdisch waren oder sich den Nazis widersetzten oder beides. Eine der beliebtesten britischen Schriftstellerinnen und Illustratorinnen, die Autorin zahlreicher Kinderbücher, Judith Kerr, floh 1933 mit ihrer Familie aus Berlin. Die Erfahrung des Exils hat ihr späteres Leben nachhaltig geprägt. Ihr autobiografischer Roman *Als Hitler das rosa Kaninchen stahl* (»When Hitler Stole Pink Rabbit«, 1971), in dem sie über ihre Erlebnisse als Flüchtlingskind berichtet, erscheint seit seiner Veröffentlichung immer wieder in neuer Auflage. Die Bücher ihres Vaters, die die Nazis verbrannten, werden heute neu verlegt. Auch den als Peter Fröhlich geborenen Schriftsteller und Historiker Peter Gay hat die Erfahrung des Exils geprägt. Im Jahr 1939 gelang ihm gemeinsam mit seinen Eltern die Flucht aus Berlin. In *Meine deutsche Frage* (»My German Question«, 1998) erzählt er von seiner Berliner Jugend unter den

became part of my life as a professional academic and as a writer. I even played fictional games with George Eliot and her German publisher, Max Duncker, who by a wonderful coincidence shares my name. My novel *Sophie and the Sibyl: A Victorian Romance* (2015), which reimagines their relationship, is set in nineteenth-century Berlin.

There is a particular calendar date which recurs in twentieth-century German history—the 9th November. On that day, 9th November 1918, in Berlin, the German republic was declared and the monarchy was overthrown. Hitler made his first attempt to seize power—the Beer Hall Putsch in Munich—on the 9th November 1923 and the terrifying Nazi attack on Jewish-owned businesses, synagogues, and private homes—the November pogroms known as *Kristallnacht*—took place on 9th November 1938. That date, for both the Putsch and the murderous pogrom, was deliberately chosen.

This uncanny, recurring date, however, now holds an extraordinary, joyous memory for me. In 1989 I was living in South West France and I was visited by two young German writers in search of a warmer climate. On 9th November I turned on the television to watch the news and saw rows of young Germans, standing on the Berlin Wall, singing. I rushed outside, screaming to my German friends. We stood transfixed before the television for hours. And we traversed all the emotions associated with the Wall and the division of Germa-

Nationalsozialisten. Seine verstörende und unvergessliche Geschichte gehörte zu den Hauptthemen einer meiner Lehrveranstaltungen über europäische Schriftsteller*innen und das Dritte Reich. Literatur aus Berlin und Deutschland bestimmten zunehmend mein berufliches Leben als Hochschullehrerin und Schriftstellerin. Ich entwickelte sogar auf spielerische Weise fiktive Wortwechsel zwischen George Eliot und ihrem deutschen Verleger Max Duncker, der wie durch einen wunderbaren Zufall meinen Nachnamen trägt. Mein Roman *Sophie und die Sibylle: Ein viktorianischer Roman* (»Sophie and the Sibyl: A Victorian Romance«, 2015), mit dem ich ihre Beziehung neu in Szene setzte, spielt im Berlin des neunzehnten Jahrhunderts.

Der 9. November ist ein Tag, der in der deutschen Geschichte von mehreren Ereignissen geprägt ist. Am 9. November 1918 wurde in Berlin die Republik ausgerufen und die Monarchie gestürzt. Hitler griff zum ersten Mal am 9. November 1923 mit dem Münchner »Bürgerbräu-Putsch« nach der Macht. Auch die entsetzlichen Angriffe der Nationalsozialisten auf jüdische Geschäfte, Synagogen und Privatwohnungen – die als *Kristallnacht* bekannten Novemberpogrome – fanden am 9. November 1938 statt. Sowohl für den Putsch als auch für die brutalen Pogrome wurde dieses Datum bewusst gewählt.

Ganz persönlich verbinde ich dieses auf unheimliche Weise wiederkehrende Datum heute mit besonders freudigen Erinnerungen. Im Jahr 1989 lebte ich in Südwestfrankreich und erhielt Besuch von zwei deutschen Schriftstellerinnen, die Sehnsucht nach der Wärme des Südens hatten. Als ich am 9. November den Fernseher einschaltete, sah ich in den Nachrichten junge Deutsche singend auf der Berliner Mauer stehen. Unter lauten Rufen eilte ich nach draußen zu meinen deutschen Freundinnen. Anschließend verbrachten wir Stunden wie gebannt vor dem Fern-

ny. Would it all be stopped? Would tanks appear on the streets? How many people would be shot? Is this really happening? Will we all live to see a united Germany? We embraced one another in excitement. Then one of my young friends said: "We must go to Berlin! *Wir fahren morgen früh. Richtung Deutschland*".

seher. Und durchliefen dabei alle mit der Mauer und der deutschen Teilung verbundenen Emotionen. Würde man das Ganze wieder stoppen? Würden Panzer durch die Straßen rollen? Wie viele Menschen würden sie erschießen? Konnten wir unseren Augen wirklich trauen? Würden wir alle ein wiedervereintes Deutschland erleben? Aufgeregt fielen wir uns in die Arme. Dann sagte eine meiner jungen Freundinnen: »Wir müssen nach Berlin! Wir fahren morgen früh. Richtung Deutschland«.

Select Further Reading

Ausgewählte weiterführende Literatur

This bibliography lists the works cited in the essays and those that have informed the project in significant ways. English and German sources, even when they are referred to in both languages in the course of the book, are given only once, in their original version.

Diese Bibliographie umfasst die in den Kapiteln zitierten Werke sowie Texte, die für das Projekt wesentlich waren. Deutschsprachige und englischsprachige Quellen werden hier nur in der jeweiligen Originalsprache angegeben, auch wenn sie im Verlauf des Buches in beiden Sprachen erwähnt werden.

About Berlin | Literatur über Berlin

D'Abernon, Helen: Red Cross and Berlin Embassy 1915–1926, Extracts from the Diaries of Viscountess D'Abernon, London, John Murray 1946.

Auden, W. H.: The English Auden, ed. by Edward Mendelson, London, Faber 1977.

Barnes, Djuna: Nightwood, London, Faber and Faber 1936.

[Bell, Vanessa]: Selected Letters of Vanessa Bell, ed. by Regina Marler, London, Bloomsbury, 1993.

Benjamin, Walter: Berliner Kindheit um neunzehnhundert, Frankfurt a. M., Suhrkamp (1950) 1962.

Blücher, Princess Evelyn: An English Wife in Berlin. A Private Memoir of Events, Politics, and Daily Life in Germany Throughout the War and the Social Revolution of 1918, London, Constable and Co. 1920.

Bowra, C. M.: Memories: 1898–1939, London, Weidenfeld and Nicolson 1966.

Brittain, Vera: Testament of Youth, London, Virago (1933) 2012.

Brooke, Rupert: Collected Poems, London, Sidgwick and Jackson 1918.

Bryher: Film Problems of Soviet Russia, Territet, Switzerland, Pool 1929.

—: The Heart to Artemis. A Writer's Memoirs, London, Collins 1963.

Carter, Huntly: The New Spirit in the Cinema, London, Harold Shayler 1930.

Chancellor, John: How to be Happy in Berlin, London, Arrowsmith 1929.

Coe, Jonathan: Mr Wilder & Me, New York, Viking 2020.

Connolly, Cyril: Conversations in Berlin, in: Life and Letters, ed. by Desmond MacCarthy, IV/22, March 1930, pp. 206–212.

—: The Condemned Playground, London, Routledge 1946.

Dodua-Otoo, Sharon: Sinchronicity, Frankfurt a. M., (2014) 2017.

—: Adas Raum, Frankfurt a. M., S. Fischer Verlag 2020.

Duncan, Isadora: My Life, New York, Boni and Liveright 1927.

Duncker, Patricia: Sophie and the Sibyl. A Victorian Romance, London, Bloomsbury 2015.

Forster, E. M.: The Journals and Diaries of E. M. Forster, ed. by Philip Garner, 3 vols, London, Pickering and Chatto 2011.

Gay, Peter: My German Question. Growing up in Nazi Berlin, New Haven and London, Yale University Press 1998.

Hamilton, Gerald: Mr. Norris and I: An Autobiographical Sketch, London, Wingate 1956.

Hamilton, Cicely: Modern Germanies as seen by an Englishwoman, London, J. Dent 1931.

Hessel, Franz: Spazieren in Berlin, Berlin, Verlag für Berlin-Brandenburg (1929) 2011.

Hulme, T. E.: German Chronicle, in: Poetry and Drama, June 1914, pp. 221–228.

Isherwood, Christopher: Back to Berlin, in: Observer, 28 March 1952.

—: My Berlin Friends—Revisited, in: Vogue, 120, 1 July 1952, pp. 77–78, 109.

—: Prater Violet, Harmondsworth, Penguin (1945) 1961.

—: The Berlin Novels: Mr Norris Changes Trains (1935), and Goodbye to Berlin (1939), London, Vintage 1999.

—: Christopher and His Kind, London, Vintage (1976) 2012.

—: Diaries, ed. by Katherine Bucknell, London, Vintage (1997) 2013.

Kerr, Judith: When Hitler Stole Pink Rabbit, London, HarperCollins Children's Books (1971) 2008.

Kessler, Harry Graf: Tagebücher 1918–1937, ed. by Wolfgang Pfeiffer-Belli, Frankfurt a.M., Insel-Verlag 2017.

Koe, Amanda Lee: Delayed Rays of a Star, London, Bloomsbury 2019.

Koestler, Arthur: Pfeil ins Blaue. Bericht eines Lebens 1905–1931, Vienna, Verlag Kurt Desch 1953.

Lehmann, John: The Whispering Gallery. Autobiography I, London, Longmans 1955.

—: In the Purely Pagan Sense, London, GMP (1976) 1989.

Lewis, Wyndham: Hitler, London, Chatto & Windus 1931.

Levy, Deborah: The Man Who Saw Everything, London, Hamish Hamilton 2019.

Mackay, John Henry: Der Puppenjunge: Die Geschichte einer namenlosen Liebe aus der Friedrichstraße, Berlin, Rosa Winkel (1926) 1999.

McNaughton, Kate: How I Lose you, London, Doubleday 2018.

Mann, Klaus: Der Wendepunkt, Reinbek, Rowohlt (1942) 2006.

Moreck, Curt: Ein Führer durch das lasterhafte Berlin, Berlin, be.bra (1931) 2018.

Mosley, Diana: A Life of Contrasts. The Autobiography, London, Gibson Square (1977) 2009.

Nicolson, Harold: The Charm of Berlin, in: Der Querschnitt, 9/5, May 1929, pp. 345f.

—: The Harold Nicolson Diaries 1907–1964, London, Phoenix 2005.

Nicolson, Nigel (ed.): Vita and Harold: The Letters of Vita Sackville-West and Harold Nicolson 1910–1962, London, Phoenix 1993.

Richter, Fred: Die Weltstadt im Licht. Berliner Nachtfotografien von Martin Höhlig aus den Jahren 1925 bis 1932, Jena, Bussert & Stadeler 2019.

Sackville-West, Edward: Hellmut lies in the Sun, in: The Faber Book of Modern Short Stories, ed. by Elizabeth Bowen, London, Faber & Faber 1937, pp. 446–477.

Sackville-West, Vita: The Letters of Vita Sackville-West to Virginia Woolf, ed. by Louise DeSalvo and Mitchell A. Leaska, New York, Morrow 1985.

Sidgwick, Cecily: Home Life in Germany, London, Methuen 1908.

Siepen, Edith: Peeps at Great Cities: Berlin, London, Black 1911.

Smith, Stevie: Novel on Yellow Paper, London, Virago (1936) 1980.

Spender, Stephen: Life Wasn't a Cabaret, in: The New York Times, 30 October 1977.

—: The Thirties and After: Poetry, Politics, People (1933–75), London and Basingstoke, Palgrave Macmillan 1978.

—: Journals 1939–1983, ed. by John Goldsmith, London and Boston, Faber & Faber 1983.

—: The Temple, London, Faber & Faber 1988.

—: World Within World, London, Faber & Faber (1951) 1997.

—: New Selected Journals 1939–1995, ed. by Lara Feigel and John Sutherland with Natasha Spender, London, Faber & Faber 2012.

Strachey, Alix, and James Strachey: Bloomsbury/Freud: The Letters of James and Alix Strachey, 1924–1925, ed. by Perry Meisel and Walter Kendrick, New York, Basic Books 1985.

Symons, Arthur: Wanderings, London, Dent 1931.

—: Selected Early Poems, ed. by Jane Desmarais and Chris Baldick, Cambridge, Modern Humanities Research Association 2017.

Szatmari, Eugen: Was nicht im Baedeker Steht: Das Buch von Berlin, Munich, Piper 1927.

Van Druten, John: I am a Camera: A Play in three Acts, London, Evans Brothers 1954.

Vizetelly, Henry: Berlin under the New Empire, London, Tinsley Brothers 1879.

Wells, H.G.: The Common Sense of World Peace, London, Hogarth 1929.

Wiskemann, Elizabeth: A Land Fit for Heroes, in: The New Statesman and Nation, 13 July 1935, in: The Europe I Saw, London, Collins 1968, pp. 242–245.

—: The Europe I Saw, London, Collins 1968.

Wood, Naomi: The Hiding Game, London, Picador 2019.

[Virginia Woolf]: The Diary of Virginia Woolf, vol. III: 1925–1930, ed. by Anne Olivier Bell, London 1977.

[Virginia Woolf]: A Reflection of the Other Person. The Letters of Virginia Woolf, vol. IV: 1929–1931, ed. by Nigel Nicolson and Joanne Trautmann, London, The Hogarth Press 1978.

Critical Reading | Forschungsliteratur

Barooah, Niroda K.: Chatto: The Life and Times of an Indian Anti-Imperialist in Europe, Oxford, Oxford University Press 2004.

Bauer, Heike: The Hirschfeld Archives: Violence, Death, and Modern Queer Culture, Philadelphia, Temple University Press 2017.

Beachy, Robert: Gay Berlin: Birthplace of a Modern Identity, London, Vintage Books, 2015.

Bell, Clive: Art and the Cinema: A Prophecy that the Motion Pictures, in Exploiting Imitation Art, will Leave Real Art to the Artist, Vanity Fair November 1922, p. 39.

Bell, Quentin: Virginia Woolf. A Biography, 2 volumes, London, Hogarth Press 1972.

Bridgwater, Patrick: Three English Poets in Expressionist Berlin, in: German Life and Letters, 45/4, 1992, pp. 301–322.

Bryant, Chris: The Glamour Boys: The Secret Story of the Rebels who Fought for Britain to Defeat Hitler, London, Bloomsbury 2020.

Bucknell, Katherine, and Nicholas Jenkins (eds): W. H. Auden: 'The Map of All My Youth': Early Works, Friends, and Influences, Oxford, Clarendon Press 1990.

Clair, René: Reflections on the Cinema, trans. Vera Traill, London, William Kimber 1953.

Cunningham, Valentine: British Writers of the Thirties, Oxford, Oxford University Press 1988.

Davenport-Hines, R. P. T.: W. H. Auden, London, Heinemann 1996.

De-la-Noy, Michael: Eddy—The Life of Edward Sackville-West, London, Arcadia 1999.

Elkin, Lauren: Flâneuse: Women Walk the City in Paris, New York, Tokyo, Venice and London, London, Chatto and Windus 2016.

Emig, Rainer: Transgressive Travels: Homosexuality, Class, Politics and the Lure of Germany in 1930s Writing, in: Critical Survey, 10/3, 1998, pp. 48–55.

Evangelista, Stefano: Literary Cosmopolitanism in the English Fin de Siècle: Citizens of Nowhere, Oxford, Oxford University Press 2021.

Firchow, Peter: Strange Meetings: Anglo-German Literary Encounters from 1910 to 1960, Baltimore, Catholic University of America Press 2011.

Fuechtner, Veronika: Berlin Psychoanalytic: Psychoanalysis and Culture in Weimar Republic Germany and Beyond, Berkeley, California, Oxford University Press 2011.

Gay, Peter: Weimar Culture: The Outsider as Insider, London, Secker & Warburg 1969.

Greatrick, Aydan: 'Goodbye to Berlin': Sexuality, Modernity, and Exile, in: Refugee History, available at http://refugeehistory.org/blog/2017/10/19/goodbye-to-berlin-sexuality-modernity-and-exile.

Hartel, Gaby: »Ein großer Fußgänger«. Samuel Beckett in Berlin 1936/37, Exhibition Literaturhaus Berlin, ed. by Lutz Dittrich, Carola Veit, Ernest Wichner, Texts from the Literaturhaus Berlin, Edition 16, Berlin 2006, pp. 13–27.

Kennedy, Hubert: John Henry Mackay (Sagitta): Anarchist der Liebe, Hamburg, Männerschwarm Verlag 2007.

Kohlmann, Benjamin: Committed Styles: Modernism, Politics, and Left-Wing Literature in the 1930s, Oxford, Oxford University Press 2014.

Kolb, Eberhard, and Dirk Schumann: Die Weimarer Republik, 8th revised edition, Munich, Oldenbourg 2013.

Low, Rachael: The History of the British Film: 1918–1929, London, George Allen and Unwin 1971.

MacNeice, Louis: The Strings are False. An Unfinished Autobiography, London, Faber & Faber 1965.

Marcus, Laura: The European Dimensions of the Hogarth Press, in: The Reception of Virginia Woolf in Europe, ed. by Mary Ann Caws and Nicola Luckhurst, London and New York, Continuum 2002.

—: The Tenth Muse: Writing about Cinema in the Modernist Period, Oxford, Oxford University Press 2007.

—: Dreams of Modernity, New York, Cambridge University Press 2014.

Martin, Alison E.: Bloomsbury in Berlin: Vita Sackville-West's *Seducers in Ecuador* on the German Literary Marketplace, in: Modernist Cultures, 13/1, 2018, pp. 77–95.

Mendelson, Edward: Early Auden, London, Faber & Faber 1981.

Mitchell, Angus: One Bold Deed of Open Treason, County Kildare, Merrion Press 2016.

Montagu, Ivor: The Youngest Son, London, George Allen and Unwin 1971.

Montefiore, Janet: Men and Women Writers of the 1930s: The Dangerous Flood of History, London, Routledge 1996.

Neumann, Melanie: Recent Irish and British Migration to Berlin—a Case of Lifestyle Migration?, Trier, WVT 2020.

Nicolson, Nigel: Portrait of a Marriage, London, Orion (1973) 1992.

Page, Norman: Auden and Isherwood: The Berlin Years, New York, St Martin's Press 1998.

Parker, Peter: Isherwood, London, Picador 2004.

Prickett, David James: 'We will show you Berlin': Space, Leisure, *flânerie* and Sexuality, in: Leisure Studies, 30/2, pp. 157–177.

Schlögel, Karl: Das russische Berlin. Ostbahnhof Europas, Munich, Randhom House 2007.

Schoeps, Julius H. and bpk – Bildagentur für Kunst, Kultur und Geschichte (eds): Berlin, Geschichte einer Stadt, Berlin, be.bra 2012.

Simmel, Georg: Soziologie, Untersuchungen über die Formen der Vergesellschaftung, Berlin, Duncker & Humblot 1908, Kapitel IX: Der Raum und die räumlichen Ordnungen der Gesellschaft, Exkurs über den Fremden, pp. 509–512.

Smith, Camilla: Challenging Baedeker Through the Art of Sexual Science: An Exploration of Gay and Lesbian Subcultures in Curt Moreck's Guide to 'Depraved' Berlin (1931), in: Oxford Art Journal, 36/2, 2013, pp. 231–256.

—: Was Nicht im Baedeker Steht: Exploring Art, Mass Culture, and Antitourism in Weimar Germany, in: New German Critique, 45/1, 2018, pp. 207–245.

Spender, Stephen: Auden's Funeral, in: London Review of Books 3/10, 4 June 1981.

—: New Collected Poems, ed. by Michael Brett, London, Faber & Faber 2004.

Steakley, James D.: Anders als die Anderen: Ein Film und seine Geschichte, Hamburg, Männerschwarm 2007.

Stedman, Gesa: 'A habituée of the Romanische Café'—Alix Strachey's 1920s-Berlin, in: Forum of Modern Language Studies, 3/3, 2017, pp. 338–348.

—: Restoring friendship and confidence as far as possible between the inimical nations—Post-World War I Berlin Through English Eyes, in: Journal for European Studies, Autumn 2021, in press.

Stiftung Stadtmuseum, Chistian Mothes, Dominik Bartmann (eds): Tanz auf dem Vulkan. Das Berlin der Zwanziger Jahre im Spiegel der Künste, Berlin, Verlag M 2015.

Storer, Colin: Weimar Germany as Seen by an Englishwoman: British Women Writers and the Weimar Republic, in: German Studies Review, 32/1, February 2009, pp. 129–147.

—: Britain and the Weimar Republic: The History of a Cultural Relationship, London, I. B. Tauris 2010.

Strachey, Nino: Rooms of their Own, London, Pitkin Publishing 2018.

Sutherland, John: Stephen Spender: The Authorized Biography, London, Penguin 2005.

Symons, Arthur: Selected Letters, 1880–1935, ed. by Karl Beckson and John M. Munro, Basingstoke, Macmillan 1989.

Toffelo, Julia: The Lost Palace. The British Embassy, Leicester, Book Guild Publishing 2017.

Von Ankum, Katharina (ed.): Women in the Metropolis: Gender and Modernity in Weimar Culture, Berkeley, University of California Press 1997.

Ward, Janet: Weimar Surfaces: Urban Visual Culture in 1920s Germany, Berkeley, California, University of California Press 2001.

Waugh, Evelyn: Two Unquiet Lives, in: The Essays, Articles and Reviews of Evelyn Waugh, ed. by Donat Gallagher, London, Methuen 1983, pp. 394–398.

Webber, Andrew: Berlin in the Twentieth Century: A Cultural Topography, Cambridge, Cambridge University Press 2008.

—: The Cambridge Companion to the Literature of Berlin, Cambridge, Cambridge University Press 2017.

Williams, John Alexander (ed.): Weimar Culture Revisited, London, Palgrave Macmillan 2011.

Wünnenberg, Barbara: The 'Weimar Experience' in British Interwar Writing, PhD Thesis, Berlin, Humboldt-Universität zu Berlin, London, King's College 2019.

Zimmermann, Margarete (ed.): ›Ach, wie gût schmeckt mir Berlin‹. Französische Passanten im Berlin der zwanziger und frühen dreißiger Jahre, Berlin, Das Arsenal 2010.

Picture Credits
Bildnachweis

Every reasonable effort has been made to trace copyright holders and gain permission for use of the images in this book. Any queries should be directed to the publisher.

Sollte bei der extensiven Suche nach Rechteinhaber*innen der Bilder und Lizenzgeber*innen jemand übersehen worden sein, bitten wir um Mitteilung an den Verlag.

Fig. 1 The futuristic city: photograph of the model for Fritz Lang's *Metropolis*, 1927. Image source: Murnau-Stiftung, DFF, © Horst von Harbou – Deutsche Kinemathek.

Fig. 2 The radio tower / Der Funkturm. Photograph by Martin Höhliq, 1928. © Fred Richter.

Fig. 3 A View of the Romanische Café, unknown photographer, 1928 © BArch, Bild 183-R68802

Fig. 4 Portrait of Virginia Woolf by Maurice Beck, published in *Der Querschnitt*, 1930 © ullstein photo / Maurice Beck

Fig. 5 George Grosz, Study for *I am a Camera*, c. 1952 (watercolour and ink on paper). Private collection / Bridgeman Images. © Estate of George Grosz, Princeton, N. J. / DACS 2021

Fig. 6 Cover of the *Radio Times* featuring Christopher Isherwood and Liza Minnelli 20 April 1974. Private collection.

Fig. 7 People queuing to swap firewood for potato peelings – a favourite trade on Simeonstraße. Photograph by Carl Weinrother, 1930s © bpk / Carl Weinrother

Fig. 8 W.H. Auden, Stephen Spender, and Christopher Isherwood at Sellin on the island of Rügen, 1931. Photograph by Stephen Spender. Private collection / Bridgeman Images.

Fig. 9 Drawing of the Institute of Sexual Science, in Perles-Titus, *préparation scientifique d'hormone sexuelle. Hormones de rajeunissement d'après la prescription du Dr Magnus Hirschfeld et sous le contrôle médical constant de l'Institut pour la science sexuelle*, Berlin, c. 1930. Collection of Gerard Koskovich (San Francisco).

Fig. 10 Magnus Hirschfeld and Karl Giese in Richard Oswald's film *Anders als die Andern*, 1919. Stiftung Deutsche Kinemathek – Museum für Film und Fernsehen.

Fig. 11 The Mann family with Christopher Isherwood and W.H. Auden (left) 1939, photograph by Carl Mydans / The LIFE Picture Collection via Getty Images

Fig. 12 Café des Westens, Ernst Pauly, Kurfürstendamm 26, postcard, photographer and date unknown. © akg images / Sammlung Evelin Förster, AKG8276907

Fig. 13 Edward ("Eddy") Sackville-West. Photograph by Bassano Ltd, 1930. © National Portrait Gallery, London.

Fig. 14 Film still from G. W. Pabst's film *Kameradschaft*, 1931, Stiftung Deutsche Kinemathek – Museum für Film und Fernsehen.

Fig. 15 Heinz Neddermeyer and four unidentified young men, from Christopher Isherwood's photo album, photographer unknown, 1930s, CI 3113, Christopher Isherwood papers, The Huntington Library, San Marino, California.

Fig. 16 A set of images of a young man, taken in Berlin, from Christopher Isherwood's photo album, photographer unknown, 1930s, CI 3113, Christopher Isherwood papers, The Huntington Library, San Marino, California.

Fig. 17 The Eldorado, 1932, BArch Bild 183-1983-0121-500

Fig. 18 Fancy dress party at the Institute of Sexual Science, unknown photographer, 1920s, Archiv der Magnus-Hirschfeld-Gesellschaft e.V., Berlin.

Fig. 19 Interior of the Institute of Sexual Science, in Magnus Hirschfeld, *Geschlechtskunde*, 4, 1930. Archiv der Magnus-Hirschfeld-Gesellschaft e.V., Berlin.

Fig. 20 Evelyn Blücher. Photographic frontispiece of *An English Wife in Berlin* (1920), based on the portrait by an unknown photographer, c. 1896. Private collection.

Fig. 21 Vita Sackville-West. Photograph by Howard Coster, c. 1927. © National Portrait Gallery, London.

Fig. 22 The British Embassy, 1937, unknown photographer, BArch Bild 183-C11809

Fig. 23 Alix Strachey by Barbara Ker-Seymer, 1930s © Max Ker-Seymer

Fig. 24 Jeanne Mammen, *Sie repräsentiert!* In: *Simplicissimus* 32. Jg. Nr. 47, 1928, Munich, 1928, paper, three colour print, 38,50 cm x 28,00 cm. Inv.-Nr.: SM 2019-00373 © Stiftung Stadtmuseum Berlin, reproduction: Mathias Schormann © VG Bild-Kunst, Bonn 2021

Fig. 25 Luna Park Berlin Halensee – having a good time in the indoor swimming pool, unknown photographer, 1927 © ullstein photo/unknown photographer.

Fig. 26 Elizabeth Wiskemann. Photographer and date unknown. Reprinted by permission of the Secretary to the Delegates of Oxford University Press.

Fig. 27 Cover of Eric Walther White, *Walking Shadows*, 1931. Private collection.

Fig. 28 The Berlin Psychoanalytical Institute, 1930s, on the left-hand side of Potsdamer Straße. Stiftung Deutsche Kinemathek – Museum für Film und Fernsehen/Landesarchiv Berlin, F Rep. 290 (01) Nr. 0214488. Photo: Hans G. Casparius.

Fig. 29 Bryher by Gisèle Freund, 1930s © bpk/Gisèle Freund.

Fig. 30 Cover of the English film journal *Close Up*, 1930. Private collection.

Fig. 31 A homoerotic moment in G. W. Pabst's film *Pandora's Box*, 1929. Film still. Image source: Deutsches Filminstitut & Filmmuseum, Frankfurt am Main.

Fig. 32 A British imperial officer in Vsevolod Pudovkin's film *Storm over Asia*, 1929. Image source: Deutsches Filminstitut & Filmmuseum, Frankfurt am Main.

Fig. 33 A summer evening on the new restaurant terrace of the Adlon Hotel, Berlin, coloured postcard after a watercolour by Karl Lindegreen, c. 1928 © akg-images, AKGINVB45540

Fig. 34 Revolutionaries on Unter den Linden during the November Revolution of 1918, unknown photographer. BArch Bild 146-1970-051-33

Fig. 35 Christopher Isherwood's security file, showing intercepted letters from the early 1930s. The National Archives, ref. KV2/2587.

Fig. 36 Diana Mosley with her sister Unity and Nazi officer friends, 1930s. Unknown photographer. Photograph courtesy of Mary Lovell.

Fig. 37 & 38 Christopher Isherwood, 1930 postcard to Stephen Spender, with the signature of Isherwood's German lover, Walter Wolff. Oxford, Bodleian Libraries, MS. Spender 53.

Fig. 39 Stephen Spender, Berlin account-book. Oxford, Bodleian Libraries, MS. Spender 151.

Fig. 40 A page from Stephen Spender's photo album showing Berlin connections including Christopher Isherwood and Jean Ross. Ross was the 'original' for Isherwood's character of Sally Bowles. Unknown photographer. Oxford, Bodleian Libraries, MS. Photogr.

Fig. 41 W. H. Auden, Stephen Spender, and Christopher Isherwood on Fire Island, New York, 1947. Photograph by Lincoln Kirstein. Private collection/Bridgeman Images.

Fig. 42 Ufa Pavillon cinema on Nollendorfplatz. Photograph by Martin Höhlig, 1928. © Fred Richter.

Fig. 43 Cover of Naomi Wood, *The Hiding Game* (2019). Cover used courtesy of Picador. Cover photograph: © Roger-Viollet/TopFoto. Background photograph: © Alamy. Cover design: Katie Tooke, Picador Art Department. Reproduced with permission of the Licensor through PLSclear.

Fig. 44 Marlene Dietrich, Anna May Wong, and Leni Riefenstahl, photograph by Alfred Eisenstaedt, 1928, via Getty Images.

Fig. 45 Filmposter for Fritz Lang's film *M*, 1931, unknown artist, via Getty Images.

Acknowledgements
Danksagungen

The editors would like to express their thanks to the following institutions and individuals:

Die Herausgeber*innen danken den folgenden Institutionen und Personen:

Institutions | Institutionen

Arts and Humanities Research Council | John Fell Fund | Oxford in Berlin | The Oxford Research Centre in the Humanities | Stiftung Preußische Seehandlung | Bodleian Libraries, University of Oxford | Freundeskreis des Literaturhauses Berlin | Centre for British Studies | Humboldt-Universitäts-Gesellschaft | The Society of Authors | The Strachey Trust | Wylie Ltd.

Individuals | Personen

Heike Bauer, David Bell, Lorenz Böttcher, Alastair Buchan, Katherine Bucknell, Philip Ross Bullock, Andreas Degkwitz, Ralf Dose, Patricia Duncker, Esmé Ellis, Mhairi Gador-Whyte, Sallyanne Gilchrist, Jana Gohrisch, Kathrin Hadeler, Steffen Hofmann, Peter Kamber, Max Ker-Seymer, Mary Lovell, Alasdair MacDonald, Laura Marcus, Sandra Mayer, Martin Maw, Victoria McGuiness, Sarah Meyer, Richard Ovenden, Peter Parker, Sofia Permiakova, Anisia Petcu, Julia Peter, Corinna Radke, Charlotte Ryland, Stefanie Scharnagel, Kira-Lena Scharold, Madeline Slaven, Catherine Smith, Lizzie Spender, Matthew Spender, Monika Stedman, Katharina Tollkühn, Chris Verfuß, Robert Wein, Martina Weinland, Caroline Weinrich, Annabel Williams, Barbara Wünnenberg, Margarete Zimmermann.

We are grateful to all sponsors for their support.
Wir danken allen Förderern für ihre Unterstützung.

HUMBOLDT-UNIVERSITÄT ZU BERLIN

Übersetzungen der englischen Texte (sofern nicht anders vermerkt):
Kathrin Hadeler

Coverdesign, Layout and Setting | Umschlaggestaltung, Layout und Satz:
Caroline Weinrich, Wallstein Verlag

Cover Picture | Umschlagabbildung:
George Grosz, Study for *I am a Camera*, c.1952 (watercolour and ink on paper).
Private collection/Bridgeman Images. © Estate of George Grosz, Princeton, N.J./DACS 2021

Fonts | Schriften: Montserrat, FreightText Pro

Image Editing | Bildbearbeitung: SchwabScantechnik, Göttingen

Printer | Druck: Westermann, Zwickau

Bibliografische Information der Deutschen Nationalbibliothek
Die Deutsche Nationalbibliothek verzeichnet diese Publikation
in der Deutschen Nationalbibliografie; detaillierte bibliografische Daten
sind im Internet über http://dnb.d-nb.de abrufbar.

Wallstein Verlag, Göttingen 2021
www.wallstein-verlag.de
ISBN: 978-3-8353-3987-3